Building An Empire

Building An
Empire

"Big Pants" Harry F. McLean and His Sons of Martha

Teresa Charland

 Riparian House

Merrickville, Ontario

Canada

Building an Empire: "Big Pants" Harry F. McLean and His Sons of Martha

Telephone orders: 613-325-6147
Online orders: http://www.riparianhouse.com

Library and Archives Canada Cataloguing in Publication

Charland, Teresa 1961–
    Building an empire: "Big Pants" Harry F. McLean and his Sons of Martha / Teresa Charland

Includes bibliographical references and index.
ISBN 978-0-9689929-2-0

1. McLean, Harry F. (Harry Falconer), 1883–1961. 2. Contractors - Canada - Bibliography. 3. Businessmen - Canada - Biography. I. Title.

HD9715.C32C44 2007   338.7'690092   C2006-906941-7

Cover and illustrations by Mejan Graphic Design
Copy editing by Jane Broderick
Printed and bound in Canada

For Joseph Justin McNally,
1917–2003

Contents

On Being a Character

McLean is one of that fading group of colorful men who look eternally toward the horizon.

William O. Grenalds[1]

Striking in appearance, he is a giant in stature as well as in deed. He has the nose of a Roman senator and a mass of nearly white hair, profuse and curly. Betraying his Highland ancestry his eyes are misty grey, magnetic and compelling.

Walter Turner[2]

When I am with him, I always feel a deep concern. One never knows what he might do or say.

William Lyon Mackenzie King[3]

I just knew he was Harry McLean. That was the way Harry acted. It never dawned on me he was eccentric. I thought, "That's just Harry acting naturally."

Jack Puddington[4]

He is spontaneous combustion in human form.

Leslie Roberts[5]

My only trouble is balancing my whisky with my carbohydrates.

Harry McLean[6]

I spoke of him as baronial. He is more than that, he is pontifical, not in his talk which lacks dogma though not directness, but in his appearance. The man is magnificent, matching his conquests as men have rarely done since the feudal days when conquerors had to be big enough to wield a battle-axe.

Frederick Griffin[7]

To my mind, Harry McLean was the best railroader that this country ever had, bar none. He was a genius and had all of the courage in the world. Nothing could stop Harry McLean when something had to be done.

Frederick I. Ker[8]

Harry Falconer McLean is one of those rare mortals who is granted the flair for swift decision, who wants to be on the move, who has no aversion to the doing of things with his two hands, but rather proceeds to the doing instinctively.

Leslie Roberts[9]

Railroad men don't talk about things – they build them.

Harry McLean[10]

He lives in a fine old stone house and is the big toad of the ville.

Sir Frederick Banting[11]

I could not but feel if he only had the right sort of wife, with the possessions he has, he could have a beautiful home.

William Lyon Mackenzie King[12]

Women eat too much. They sit around eating cake and sweet things, getting fat and then they rip hell out of men for drinking.

Harry McLean[13]

He is a strange character, kind of heart, but like a child in some ways, yet powerful in others.

William Lyon Mackenzie King[14]

Sitting beside him on a sofa in an engineer's house while he tells stories, and playfully jogs with an elbow like a battering ram, is an experience to remember.

Russell Owen[15]

McLean is the last of the frontier busters, the great pioneers.

Walter Turner[16]

He did a lot of kind things very quietly.

Jack Puddington[17]

No job is too tough for him; if someone else has tried and failed, he is pretty sure to go after it.

William O. Grenalds[18]

Why do they give me all the credit? Do you suppose I could build jobs like this if I didn't have good partners, crackerjack engineers, bosses and men?

Harry McLean[19]

He was a prankster of the worst type...absolutely the worst type.

Joseph J. McNally[20]

I have heard at least a dozen times about that day when he lined up forty-nine Shriners in a row in a Toronto hotel and got them swaying in unison as they helped him out with a chorus of the Song of the Volga Boatmen.

William O. Grenalds[21]

Behind this man of contradictions, there lurked a perpetual sense of the ridiculous.

Leonard H. Newman[22]

Mistaken for a chef – because he was in pyjamas – he entered into the spirit of the thing, proceeded to the kitchen where he whipped up devilish concoctions for the diners – then he dressed himself up as a waiter and served them himself.

Walter Turner[23]

The Number One quality in McLean that is the secret of his ability to get things done on the one hand and of his charm as a person on the other, is the uncomplicated directness of his approach to the world and its ways.

Leslie Roberts[24]

Many people say they don't give a damn. Many people would like not to give a damn. But Harry McLean doesn't give a damn.

Unknown McLean engineer quoted by Walter Turner[25]

He is a generous soul. Makes one feel very sad to think of what a fine powerful influence in the country he might have been had he never known the use of liquor.

William Lyon Mackenzie King[26]

Have anything you want. We've got good Scotch. But you can have either Scotch or milk. They both cost the same.

Harry McLean[27]

BIG PANTS HARRY F. McLEAN

LOVER EXTRAORDINARY

Illustration based on Harry McLean's calling card found in Prime Minister Mackenzie King's "McLean" file.

Replete in plus fours, he had himself piped to the station by a Highlander.

Walter Turner[28]

I understand someone called the piper a son of a bitch. But what I want to know is who called the son of a bitch a piper!

Harry McLean[29]

This man taught me to think in big numbers. He predicted a great future and warned me of the destructive force of money.

Joseph J. McNally[30]

It is the fellows of the McLean breed who are the real Canadians, not the gentlemen in broadcloth who pass out the contracts. As a matter of fact it would have been considerably better for this once up-and-coming young country if we had left the decisions as to what should be done and what should be left undone to the McLeans and their like. Then the railroads wouldn't have been built for reasons political, nor the dams sunk into the riverbeds to satisfy the yearnings of the promoters... As for me, you may give me one McLean and keep all the politicians.

Leslie Roberts[31]

Get the god dam [sic] thing done – never mind asking anyone's permission!

Harry McLean[32]

Introduction

>━┼━◆>━●━<◆>━┼━<

They were strong, muscular, wiry men, the most of them, these railway builders of Canada, well inured to the chance and vicissitudes of the trail. They had followed the builders of railways over the Dominion; they had worked for some of the most famous lines of the United States. There were muckers, and graders and skinners amongst them; men with a weird and mysterious knowledge of donkey [sic] engines and steam-shovels; men who loved the free open spaces, whose lullaby was the coyote scream or the cry of the lone wolf; men who knew the forests and the forest brood; men who only knew the City for a few lurid days in every year, and sought again the wilder, vaster, lonelier places; men who had endured great hardships and who told stirring stories in the glow of the camp-fire in uncouth style, mayhap, – for they were close to the realities – and they spoke strongly and forgetful of the courtesies. Often-times, they slung their heavy packs a-back and fastened on their snow-shoes and explored unknown places – until the railways came. They had worked their lives for the building of railways. They had a passion for the free, hard life of the pioneer.[1]

DECADES AFTER THE last spike of the transcontinental railway had been driven, railway construction in Canada was still flourishing. Canada's wilderness offered formidable challenges to railway builders, with its extremes of topography and climate. Harry Falconer McLean was first and foremost a railway builder, but he adapted to the changing times and branched out to undertake other public works such as hydroelectric development. He became enormously wealthy in the process, prospering in the midst of the Great Depression, although for

McLean the money was inconsequential compared to the challenges of the job.

Driven by a thirst to carve civilization into what was still feral territory, McLean worked gruelling hours, tiring younger associates with his inexhaustible energy. A visionary, he negotiated huge contracts and organized titanic jobs with ease. As soon as one contract was signed, he pursued the next – keeping his men employed was a responsibility he took seriously:

> Any success we've had has been due mostly to the loyalty of the boys. This isn't one-man work. As a matter of fact, all I do is get the boys work. They expect me to keep the organization busy, to go out and get jobs. That's what I try to do. They say there's a depression. All I know is that the outfit's busier than it should be.[2]

McLean did not want to risk losing his experienced workers, many of whom had been with him from the start. He continually downplayed his own efforts, preferring to give the credit to his men. Although McLean would occasionally make derogatory statements about engineers generally, he knew he would be lost without them. He inspired fierce devotion in those who worked for him. So much so that when the childless McLean requested that his employees Charles Switzer and J. B. Humphrey name their infant daughters after him, they did so. Both girls carry the middle name "McLean."[3] He valued his workers and considered them his greatest resource.

When one of his men was injured or killed on the job McLean would ensure that the man's family was taken care of. There are many stories of McLean's paying off a dead worker's mortgage, providing his widow with a pension and financing his children's education. His job sites were models of safety and his workers had the best medical care available.

Weighing in at more than two hundred and fifty pounds and standing six foot four inches tall, McLean was hard to miss. Given his penchant for bursting into song at several decibels above socially acceptable levels and for wrestling unsuspecting acquaintances to the ground, he was impossible to ignore. McLean had many sobriquets: "Big Pants" was a nickname he acquired from the northern Natives, "Little Red God" came from a poem favoured by his friend Berton Puddington, and "H. F." and

"The Boss" were terms often used by his employees – though to his face they always called him "Mr. McLean."

McLean learned the advantages of building strategic alliances from his business associates, North Dakota's political boss, Alexander McKenzie, and the politically savvy Republican supporter Andrew Braid Cook. Like his mentors, McLean had in his pocket a slew of politicians, high rollers and celebrities. It was not just that he knew the right people: he knew how to manipulate them to his advantage.

McLean became a man of influence: either he was exerting it on others or he was under it himself. Liquor was the ink underlying the signatures on many a contract. This hard-working, hard-drinking lifestyle was not unique to McLean, although his capacity for alcohol was legendary. While drinking was a hobby during his working years, it became a full-time occupation after his retirement – just as pyjamas became his preferred attire.

He was enigmatic – neither all good nor all bad, but undeniably a character. Although he travelled much of the time, when he was home in Merrickville, Ontario, he made his presence known. But while he was either revered and reviled in the town, little was remembered about the extent of his achievements. Not forgotten were the outrageous things that McLean did when he was drinking. Hence, on the great balance sheet of life, McLean's inebriated antics obscured his sober accomplishments.

Although he could be extraordinarily generous, for the most part his was a quiet benevolence. He sought no acknowledgement for his good deeds; his charity was strictly on his own terms. He did not take well to requests – or to attempts to trick him out of his money, as one poor chair attendant who tried to take advantage of McLean discovered in Atlantic City. The hoodwink attempt was rewarded by McLean's plucking the attendant off his feet, raising him high in the air and flinging him into the ocean.[4] Although McLean professed to abhor publicity, incidents like this led some to believe otherwise.

A few select pieces of personal information he would share with reporters: he was born of Canadian parents – his father had come from Prince Edward Island, his mother from Glengarry County, Ontario –

and began his working life as a water boy. The practised lines would roll off his tongue like a daily prayer. Then, when asked for other details about his life, he would respond with a cryptic "Railroad men don't talk about things – they build them," and the interview would be abruptly over.

He duped the press and had a good time doing it, knowing that if he kept a straight face they would likely print anything he said. He led a reporter for *American Magazine* to believe that members of the Russian nobility were working for him as labourers. The remark was written up as a statement of fact.[5] Some reporters won his trust, fewer his respect: Leslie Roberts of *Canadian Magazine* was one of the latter group, Ralph Hyman of the *Globe* another. Hyman recalled meeting McLean for the first time in the Vice-Regal Suite of Toronto's Royal York Hotel:

> He turned out to be what I expected – a great big bruiser of a man – shook hands and left three or four of my fingers sort of crushed. He said, "What do you want to know?...you fellas been giving me a bad time in the past... I don't like to be interviewed... If this isn't right...I'll break every bone in your body." So, on that rather inauspicious note we started in. It was an ordinary interview. I came back to the office and wrote it and it appeared – it was about half a column and I forgot about it after that.
>
> Now I got a call from his secretary the following afternoon saying that Mr. McLean wanted to see me and I thought, "Oh Oh! Something's wrong!" I [went] down to the hotel – must've been about eight o'clock in the evening – and went up to the suite. He was dressed in a very vivid dressing gown... Shook my hand again and the fingers he hadn't mashed before he mashed this time. He liked the interview. It was accurate. I said, "Thank you very much."
>
> He said, "Do you smoke?" and I said, "Yes, I smoke." He went away to a corner to a phone and I didn't pay any more attention. I looked out the window and I heard him phoning down to the cigar shop...and he was ordering great quantities of cigarettes and cigars and I thought to myself, "There's something funny here." Anyway, I didn't pay any more attention. We chatted for awhile. About ten minutes later there came a knock at the door. In came two bellboys just burdened down with cartons of cigarettes and boxes of cigars and so I looked at it and looked at McLean. He said, "They're yours," and I said, "What

do you mean, Mr. McLean?" He said, "I asked you if you smoked"…
"There you are." I said, "I can't take these, Mr. McLean. I thought you
were going to give me a cigar or maybe a package of cigarettes. He
said, "These are yours and if you don't take them you are going out
the window. We were…way up on the fifteenth or twentieth floor… I
said, "This is rather unusual. This is enough cigars – well, I don't smoke
cigars." He said, "I didn't ask you if you smoked cigars. I asked you if
you smoked. They're yours!" That was my first experience with Harry
McLean.

The second came at Queen's Park some years later. I bumped into
him in the corridor. Of course he had a phenomenal memory and he
looked at me and said, "Hyman, how did those cigars go?" …I said,
"Fine, Mr. McLean."[6]

To some he was a childish prankster, to others nothing more than a
bully. A simple mistake could be punishable by a near-death experience.
During a luncheon in McLean's seventeenth-floor hotel suite, a waiter
had the misfortune of making an error with his order. Within seconds
McLean was dangling the screaming waiter out of the window by his
belt. After a few minutes McLean pulled the terrified man to safety and
gave him a hundred-dollar tip.[7]

To McLean, weakness was a character trait that was unforgivable,
and one that he would happily exploit. If you showed strength and stood
up to him, you earned his respect. A desk clerk at a Saint John hotel
approached McLean as he stood in the lobby holding a bottle of Scotch
in one hand and a glass in the other. She told him he was forbidden to
drink in public. He wanted to know who was going to stop him. The
clerk said, "I guess I'd have to." McLean went up to his room and sent
his secretary down with a five-hundred-dollar cheque for the clerk. She
kept a hundred in cash and invested the remainder in bonds.[8]

Stories about McLean's unique personal charity abound. Exactly how
much money he gave away will never be known, but he did have plenty
to distribute. By the end of his forty-year career, more than half a century
ago, McLean's impressive résumé boasted construction projects worth
an estimated $400 million. Harry McLean remains Merrickville's most
remarkable resident, a "frontier buster" who changed the face of Canada.

CHAPTER ONE

The Frontier Busters

>———◆———○———◆———<

It is a grand "anvil chorus" that those sturdy sledges are playing across
the plains. It is in a triple time, three strokes to the spike. There are
10 spikes to a rail, 400 rails to a mile, 1,800 miles to San Francisco
— 21,000,000 times are those sledges to be swung; 21,000,000 times
are they to come down with their sharp punctuation before the great
work of modern America is complete.[1]

AT THE RIVER'S edge the railway tracks at Council Bluffs, Iowa, ended
abruptly in anticipation of a bridge soon to be built. Treading gingerly,
the widow Jane "Jennie" Falkner and her children crossed the thawing
Missouri River clutching their belongings. It was early spring 1868. The
train ride from eastern Ontario had been tiring enough without the
unforeseen expedition. However, their arrival was ill-timed. They were
too early for the steamboat ferries and too late to risk the weight of a
loaded wagon on the melting ice. The tracks picked up again on the
other side of the Missouri at Omaha. Although the Falkners could have
taken the train to the latest end-of-track town, arrangements had been
made for them to travel the remainder of their journey by covered wagon
following the well-worn Oregon Trail west.[2]

In the midst of Indian Territory, the safest way to travel was in large
groups, although the ambushes that had plagued the settlers had subsided
after the Treaty of Fort Laramie was signed on April 29, 1868. The
participating chiefs agreed to live on the Great Sioux reservation in

exchange for some concessions from the government.[3] Regardless of the truce, prudent trailblazers kept constant guard as peaceful passage was not assured. A thorough investigation of the slightest sound eased the nerves of the jittery travellers. The lack of bridges ensured that the weary pageant would be regularly drenched on their journey. While fording the swift South Platte River near Julesburg on the Colorado/Nebraska border, young Mary Louise Falkner was certain their "time had come."[4]

Death had claimed Jennie's husband, James Falkner, ten years earlier. The son of William Falkner, a United Empire Loyalist, James[5] fathered six children in his first marriage in 1825 to Annie Hay: Annie, Margaret, Samuel, William M., James and Elizabeth. His wife died in 1838, the year of Elizabeth's birth. Four years later James married sixteen-year-old Jennie McLellan, a niece of his late wife.[6] Jennie and James settled on a fifty-acre farm in the Township of Lochiel in eastern Ontario, adding a further ten Falkners: Jane, Norman, John, Elsie and Christina (twins), Henry, Ellen, Daniel, Mary and another son named William. To differentiate between the two brothers named William, the elder was called Red William and the younger Will or Billy. The Falkners left the farm in Lochiel in February 1857, and in May of that year Mary Louise Falkner was born in Hawkesbury, Ontario. Two years later, in the year of Will's birth, James died.[7]

Jennie somehow managed to keep the family together. In 1867 her eldest son, Norman, took on the responsibility of making a home for the family. Norman left the new confederation of Canada, by train, from Rivière Beaudette, a border town between Quebec and Ontario. He hoped to find work with a construction crew building the Union Pacific Railroad.

Pushing westward from Omaha, the Union Pacific was destined to meet the eastward-bound Central Pacific and become the first transcontinental railroad across the United States. The United States was slowly recuperating from the Civil War and many men were without work. The construction and completion of the railroad were a boon to the postwar economy. Former soldiers from the Union and Confederate armies joined the construction crews in droves, some still wearing their uniforms. Men from the eastern United States and Canada also sought employment with the railroad.[8]

Norman was hired at a railroad work camp located eighty-five miles east of Cheyenne, Wyoming, and owned by the wealthy Edward Creighton.[9] Among Creighton's many diverse and rewarding endeavours were building the Western Union telegraph line from Omaha to the west in 1861 and co-founding the First National Bank of Omaha. Creighton's interests also included large sheep and cattle ranches in southeastern Wyoming.

In February 1868 most of the Falkners left Canada with Jennie to join Norman. These included Red William and the newly wedded Falkner twin, Christina, with her husband, Thomas Gilbert. By that summer the Union Pacific had progressed to the booming town of Laramie, Wyoming, where men and saloons were plentiful but women scarce – and greatly desired.[10] Norman reunited with his family in Laramie and soon the brothers Daniel and Henry were working on the line. The Falkners were scattered along the route, briefly living in the railroad towns of Salt Wells and Red Desert, then packing up and moving as required to follow the progress of construction.[11]

As the track neared Utah to join the Central Pacific, the idea of working with the Chinese labourers was not an appealing prospect to the Falkners. They decided to leave Wyoming and pursue employment opportunities with the Northern Pacific Railroad.[12] During her stay in Wyoming Territory, Jennie met and married Major Richard "Dick" Armstrong, her second husband. All headed east to Dubuque, Iowa, then north by boat on the Mississippi to St. Paul, Minnesota. Around the time of their move to Minnesota, the Falkners changed the spelling of their name to Falconer.[13]

Norman returned to Canada to marry Flora McClennan on December 28, 1869, and then brought his bride to St. Paul. The Falconer men, along with Dick Armstrong and Tom Gilbert, found the work they had hoped for with the Northern Pacific Railroad. They were responsible for cutting ties and clearing the right of way, first at the Northern Pacific junction and then between the newly founded towns of Brainerd and Duluth, Minnesota.[14] The Falconer women and Will remained in St. Paul.

Mary and Will attended the Adams School and Jennie Falconer Armstrong gave birth to her last daughter, Martha "Mattie," on October 26, 1870. The following June the women and children travelled by stagecoach to join the men in Brainerd. The next school year, 1872, Mary and Will were sent by steamer from Duluth to Massena, New York, to attend school. They lived there with their half-sister, Annie McLellan.[15]

>→◆→◦→◇→◁

The Northern Pacific Railroad was chartered on July 2, 1864, near the end of the Civil War, by an act of Congress. The railroad was granted millions of acres of land between Lake Superior and Puget Sound. Construction did not start until July 1870 due to funding difficulties. The banking house that had provided substantial funding to the Union cause during the Civil War, Jay Cooke and Company, took over financing and raised millions of dollars towards the construction of the railroad.[16]

Surveying and building the Northern Pacific Railroad proved just as treacherous as surveying and building the Union Pacific, due to frequent attacks on workers by the Indians. President Andrew Johnson and several bands of the Sioux Indian Nation signed the Treaty of Fort Laramie in an effort to end the frequent skirmishes, but not all Indians had agreed to the Treaty. Among the chiefs of the non-Treaty bands were the legendary Crazy Horse, Sitting Bull and Gall. When the Northern Pacific sent surveying crews into the Yellowstone Valley in the summer of 1872, Treaty and non-Treaty Indians alike were incensed at the intrusion.[17] The Treaty guaranteed that the Great Sioux Reservation, including the Black Hills, would be

> set apart for the absolute and undisturbed use and occupation of the Indians herein named, and for such other friendly tribes or individual Indians as from time to time they may be willing, with the consent of the United States, to admit amongst them; and the United States now solemnly agrees that no persons, except those herein designated and authorized so to do, and except such officers, agents, and employees of the government as may be authorized to enter upon Indian reservations in discharge of duties enjoined by law, shall ever be permitted to pass over, settle upon, or reside in the territory described

in this article, or in such territory as may be added to this reservation for the use of said Indians, and henceforth they will and do hereby relinquish all claims or right in and to any portion of the United States or Territories, except such as is embraced within the limits aforesaid, and except as hereinafter provided.[18]

Continual attacks by the Indians on the work crews effectively ended surveying that summer. The Northern Pacific requested military protection. In response, during the summer of 1872 Companies B and C of the Sixth Infantry built Fort McKeen a short distance from Bismarck on the banks of the Missouri River. They were joined by three companies of the Seventeenth Infantry and six companies of Custer's "Fighting Seventh" Cavalry, come to protect the settlers and railroad workers from Indian ambush. Several months later the fort was renamed Fort Abraham Lincoln.[19]

>─┼─◀▶─○─◀▶─┼─◀

Like the Falconer men, John Angus McLean was attracted to the Midwest by employment opportunities with the Northern Pacific Railroad as well as by the prospect of obtaining inexpensive land. Articulate and determined, the Prince Edward Island native became a contractor shortly after arriving in Brainerd, supplying ties and other construction materials on the line between Duluth and Bismarck. Although Brainerd was a relatively brief stop for John, it was an important one. He became acquainted with Alexander McKenzie, then a foreman on the Northern Pacific. McKenzie became his good friend and a political powerhouse. In Brainerd John also met an attractive young woman who would become his wife, Helen (Ellen) Falconer, known as "Nellie."[20]

Upon learning there was going to be a town where the railroad crossed the Missouri River, many Brainerd residents, including John McLean, moved to Bismarck (then named Edwinton[21]). John arrived on May 27, 1873, intending to open a general store. The Northern Pacific Railroad came into town a week later, on June 5th. Bismarck consisted of little more than tents and a few cottonwood houses and buildings, but opportunities for the ambitious were abundant.[22]

Canadian-born John Angus McLean, merchant and first elected mayor of Bismarck. STATE HISTORICAL SOCIETY OF NORTH DAKOTA A4919

Nellie (Falconer) McLean. Family legend has it that John McLean once ran into a burning building to rescue this photograph. STATE HISTORICAL SOCIETY OF NORTH DAKOTA A3832

The first church service was held on June 15, 1873, in a tent on McLean's property. It was conducted by Reverend Isaac Sloan, a Presbyterian minister and former chaplain who had served in the Civil War.[23] As a church had yet to be built in Bismarck, John returned to Brainerd to marry Nellie. They were wed on September 4, 1873, at the First Methodist Church.[24] John's future partner in the grocery business, Robert Macnider, married Nellie's half-sister, Elizabeth "Eliza" Falconer, also in Brainerd, and Alexander McKenzie married in Brainerd as well. Norman, Daniel and Henry Falconer also lived in the Bismarck area.

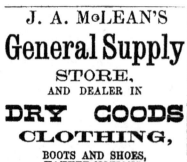

J. A. McLEAN'S

General Supply

STORE,

AND DEALER IN

DRY GOODS

CLOTHING,

BOOTS AND SHOES,
YANKEE NOTIONS,
PROVISIONS,
&c., &c.

GENTS' FURNISHING GOODS,
HATS, CAPS, &c.

Fresh Vegetables,

GROCERIES, FLOUR, FEED,
CANNED and **DRIED**
FRUITS KEPT

Constantly on Hand

Give him a call at his new and nicely fitted up *Store on*

MAIN STREET

BISMARCK, D. T.

Illustration Based on Advertisement in Bismarck Tribune J.A. McLean's General Supply Store

J. A. McLean's General Store at number three hundred and four Main Street in Bismarck opened in the fall of 1873. The upper floor was used as living quarters for the newlyweds, while the ground floor was divided between groceries and dry goods. Eventually display cases filled with decorative items were installed to attract female customers and a long table in the middle of the store, covered with suits, overalls and other apparel, constituted the men's wear section.[25] By all accounts the McLeans were hard-working and respected members of the community.

In contrast to industrious and devout church-going citizens like the McLeans were the iniquitous patrons of the numerous saloons in Bismarck[26] and a few women of "questionable virtue."[27] Among the finer drinking establishments and their slogans were "The Snow Flake Saloon – Keno every night!" and "Concert Saloon and Dance Hall – choice liquors, fine cigars and pleasant associations."[28] Mary Louise Falconer, Nellie's little sister, would later write that associations in the saloons were not always pleasant. In the fall of 1873, after a dispute over a wager turned ugly, a disreputable man named Spotty Whalen shot Thomas King, a soldier, triggering an episode of bloody retribution by the Fort Lincoln soldiers:

> These saloons were the terror of the town as often pitched battles would take place in them, shooting out the lights was the usual signal, at which times someone would be laid out cold in death. In one of these brawls, a soldier from Fort Lincoln was killed – whereupon his comrades threatened to wipe out the town by way of revenge which frightened some of the timid ladies to such an extent that they took refuge in the house of a friend who lived some distance from the scene of the proposed battle. True to their word, they came over reinforced the next night, went to the saloon where their comrade had been slain, and demanded admission. Being refused, they proceeded to riddle the place with bullets. All of a sudden, the door opened and the notorious "Dave Mullen" stood in the doorway, revolver in hand, firing right and left into the crowd of soldiers who returned the fire killing him in his own doorway. This notorious gambler had been the bosom friend of the famous "Squatter Governor," Dannie Hennifin, who said as he gazed at the face of his dead comrade, "There you are, Dave, but you died game to the last."
>
> Seldom was any notice taken of such affairs, only to hear the familiar remark the next day of "another man dying with his boots on." No further notice or explanation was necessary, as these words explained the manner of death they met.[29]

Subsequently Spotty Whalen was apprehended and a suitable spot was found for him in the Fargo jail. Eastern journalists visiting Bismarck wrote of its dangerous and lawless reputation. Reflecting on the reports, Will Falconer disagreed with the characterizations of Bismarck as unruly:

> The stories some writers have given the press about the early days in Bismarck were far from being true. Some of these writers pictured Bismarck as being a very tough town. If we are to believe these stories, there would not be a day go by unless some one died with his boots on. It is true that a few men were killed, but they were the aggressors and probably got what was coming to them.[30]

➤━◆➤━O━◀◆━◀

Main Street, Bismarck, 1873. "Half of the buildings were tents," said John McLean of Bismarck's early days. Main Street was lined with hastily erected cottonwood structures.
STATE HISTORICAL SOCIETY OF NORTH DAKOTA C0529

By the fall of 1873 a downturn in the economy and financial overextension due to the railroad construction pushed the banking firm and financiers of the Northern Pacific Railroad into receivership. The collapse of Jay Cooke and Company exacerbated the loss of confidence in the banking system in the United States (the "Panic of 1873"). Bankers called in loans, panicked investors sold their shares, and the resulting failure of businesses, banks and railroads triggered a severe depression. Work on the Northern Pacific came to a standstill.[31]

Adding to the misery, winter came early that year. A proviso of the Treaty of Fort Laramie was that the Sioux be provided with clothing and rations at designated points along the Missouri River. The terms of the agreement were met until that long winter, when, due to the ice on the river, supplies could not be delivered until spring. The situation was aggravated in the spring as unscrupulous traders made off with the Sioux's supplies by the boatload, assisted by dishonest government officials. Broken promises did nothing to endear the Sioux to the U.S.

government.[32] A growing sentiment of many Americans was echoed in the *Bismarck Tribune* in June 1874:

> The American people need the country the Indians now occupy; many of our people are out of employment; the masses need some new excitement. The war is over, and the era of railroad building has been brought to a termination by the greed of capitalists and the folly of the grangers; and depression prevails on every hand. An Indian war would do no harm, for it must come, sooner or later. A gold excitement, founded as the Black Hills excitement will be, on the report of scientists and officers sent out by the Government, will give the restless spirits of our land something to do, and all something to think of.[33]

In July 1874 the Treaty was violated again by the government. General George Armstrong Custer set off on an expedition, comprising a column of ten companies of the Seventh Cavalry, to the Black Hills, the land "set apart for the absolute and undisturbed use and occupation"[34] of the Sioux. Located in the southern part of Dakota Territory on its border with Wyoming Territory, the Black Hills were considered hallowed by the Sioux. General Philip Sheridan's vague military order directed the expedition to "examine the country"[35] in the Black Hills vicinity. Along with this outwardly harmless purpose, the expedition had a second, unpublicized, agenda. Tagging along with the Seventh were geologists and miners together with reporters and a photographer. The geologists saw nothing of value, but the miners found gold.[36]

Charlie Reynolds, Custer's scout, left the expedition on a dangerous mission with dispatches of the discovery to Fort Laramie. Reynolds rode at night, concealing himself and his fine steed during the day to avoid detection by Indians. He reached Fort Laramie four days later, exhausted, dehydrated and barely able to deliver his message.[37] Talk of a new El Dorado spread quickly through the recession-ridden United States. The Black Hills were soon infested with miners, who demanded the protection of the military.

As something of worth had been found in the Black Hills, prosperity and progress for the white man were the justification for ignoring the terms of the Treaty. Custer made a plea for "the extinguishment of the Indian title at the earliest moment."[38] The government, well aware of the effect that this overt breach would have on the Sioux, sent the military to destroy trainloads of mining supplies and head off mining parties as they entered the area. The Sioux assisted in the destruction of mining parties, albeit in a more permanent fashion. Will Falconer wrote:

> To the credit of our government however, I will say, that it sent troops into the Black Hills, arrested the intruders and drove them out of the Hills and tried to keep them out. But you might as well try and turn back the waters of the mighty Missouri, as to try to keep the miners out of the Black Hills. Gold was there and they knew it.[39]

>┈┼┄◈┄◯┄◈┄┼┈<

That summer a frail Mary Falconer, recuperating from typhoid fever, and her healthy brother Will accompanied their brother-in-law Robert Macnider and moved from Brainerd to Bismarck.[40] Carrying just their clothing and a few personal belongings, they rode the two-coach train, arriving in Bismarck on July 24th. The two-hundred-mile journey from Fargo to Bismarck took eleven hours. A regular contingent of lonesome men met the train, scouring the line of disembarking passengers for potential mates. It was not long before the Falconers learned that watching the train come and the ice go were the two favourite pastimes in Bismarck. Many years would pass before the train ran to Bismarck during the winter months.[41]

Will and Macnider found work in John McLean's store, as clerk and chief clerk, respectively. The Falconers were devout Presbyterians and gave freely of their time to church matters, particularly those that concerned the much-loved Reverend Isaac Sloan:

> The first fair given by the Ladies of the Presbyterian Church, at which time they made over $400.00, was held in the old church in the autumn of '74 which was made memorable by the presence of a noted gambler named Jack White who stepped up to a table of fancy articles at which Miss Mary Falconer was presiding, asking her what she would take for it. She jokingly replied $75.00. He at once handed her the money the sight of which almost took her breath away. She was still more dumbfounded when he afterwards presented the entire table to her and said: "Now go ahead and sell these things all over again." The Ladies, feeling fretful for his literality, asked him if there was not

something which he wished to take as a gift from them. He looked around, saw some geraniums in bloom, and picking out one he said: "I'm very fond of flowers; may I have this?" which of course was gladly given him. Someone asked him afterwards why he had been so liberal in giving such a sum for nothing. He replied: "I just could not help giving it when I saw that dear old man coming down the aisle and taking me by these sinful hands and saying: 'Jack, I'm so glad to see you here tonight'."[42]

Sloan, who "ministered to saints and sinners alike," was known to preach in saloons from time to time and, at collection time, to receive poker chips along with cash.[43] Attempting salvation, Jack White, the wicked whisky purveyor, showed Sloan his treasured and ornate bible, nestled behind some bottles in his bar. "Yes, Jack," Sloan said, "it is a most beautiful Bible, but it is in very bad company."[44]

A blissful occasion in the fall of 1874 turned tragic for the McLeans. In the family quarters above the store, Nellie gave birth to a son, William John, on October 28th. Although she was tended to by Dr. Henry R. Porter, she died six days later of complications resulting from the delivery. "Mrs. McLean leaves an infant son which only a week ago was a well-spring of joy in a happy home," read her obituary in the *Tribune*. "The almost distracted husband and father has the universal sympathy of all in his bereavement."[45] John purchased a burial plot in the Oakland Cemetery in St. Paul, Minnesota, for his wife.[46] Nellie's mother, Jennie, stepped in to help raise William.[47]

Shortly after the loss of Nellie McLean, Bismarck was shaken by the news of another death, this time a murder, compounded by misfortune:

At the close of navigation in the fall of 1874, the Coulson Line of Steamboats were tied up for the winter at the river landing and were left in charge of a young negro called George Washington. He lived in the cabin of one of the boats. On pleasant days the negro would take his shotgun and walk up the river hunting jackrabbits and prairie chickens. A young Swede by the name of John Peterson with his wife lived in a dugout along the river bank about a mile above the river landing, and the negro would stop at Peterson's place on his hunting trips. In the early part of December, the citizens were startled by a report that a man had been found dead in the timber about three miles northwest of Bismarck. Upon investigation it was found that while Peterson was engaged in cutting cordwood on Burnt Creek Bottom he was shot in the back of the head, the body falling forward burying his face in the snow, and he had probably been dead two or three days when the body was found. A Coroner's Jury was empanelled… Subpoenas were issued for about twenty people to appear before the Coroner's Jury. Charles H. McCarthy, the newly elected Sheriff of Burleigh County, and his deputy Clinton M. Miller, drove up the river bottom to serve the subpoenas and, on their return, they drove on the ice on the Missouri river and when about a mile north of the river landing, the team and cutter that they were riding in plunged into an air hole in the river; the team, sleigh, men and everything disappearing; only the cap of one of the men was discovered lying on the ice near the air hole. The water where they went down was about eight feet deep, with a very swift current. Search was made in an effort to find the bodies; grappling hooks were used but without success…

The bodies of these unfortunate men were never discovered, but the team was found about seven months later, lodged against an Island a few miles below old Fort Thomson, having drifted down the river a distance of 500 miles. The team was still fastened together. The negro George Washington later confessed to Capt. D. W. Marratta and others that he killed John Peterson.[48]

The death of Charles McCarthy left a vacancy in the Burleigh County Sheriff's office. John McLean's friend Alexander McKenzie was persuaded to apply for the job. McKenzie had been living in Bismarck for about a year and had been earning a living by manufacturing and selling soft drinks and cronk beer by the wheelbarrow to the local saloons.[49] After his appointment as Sheriff of Burleigh County, on December 24, 1874, by the County Commissioners, his soda-flogging days were over. McKenzie became an influential and infamous "behind the scenes" figure in Dakota Territory politics. Though almost illiterate, McKenzie was viewed as a "natural leader of men,"[50] exerting an "almost hypnotic influence."[51] The Northern Pacific Railroad recognized his strengths and selected McKenzie to represent their interests. John McLean, too, would achieve success on the local political scene.

The City of Bismarck was incorporated on January 14, 1875, with an interim government in place until an election could be held. John McLean entered the first mayoral race that spring and won the election by ninety-four votes.[52] His victory earned a headline in the *Tribune*. Succumbing to the eternal political inclination to condemn the predictably inefficient practices of those who came before, John pledged the oath of the prudent:

Alexander McKenzie. Known as the "political boss" of North Dakota, McKenzie was largely responsible for having the state capitol relocated to Bismarck. Described as "extremely brilliant and resourceful" yet "exceedingly gross and repulsive," he was seen by many as driven solely by self-interest. STATE HISTORICAL SOCIETY OF NORTH DAKOTA A2072

> During the short term of your and my predecessors in office, extending over a period of eight weeks, the debt of the city has, by extravagance and improvidence, reached the enormous sum of Eight Hundred and seventy-five dollars ($875.00). In a large city this amount would be of small consequence, but when we consider our small population, that we can obtain no title to Real Estate, that all our available resources for carrying on a city Government are raised from the taxation of personal property alone, it seems to me that the expenditures of this amount indicates a reckless squandering of means not adequate to our resources. I deem it the duty of all public officials to commit "the greatest good to the greatest number," and I shall, therefore, endeavor to prevent any further wastful [sic] expenditures of the public funds, and to prevent personal agrandizement at the expense of the public interests. I shall use my utmost endeavors to reduce the expenses of the city government; provide safety and protection to all inhabitants of the city; prevent

lawlessness and guard against all unlawful combinations organized to control the patronage and franchises of the City. In fact, it shall be my duty, with the assistance of your Honorable Body, to serve the City with the same fidelity, as though I were serving my own personal interests as one of its inhabitants.[53]

During his first few weeks in office, Mayor McLean energetically set about ratifying laws of every description. Ordinances were passed to address the need for licences to serve liquor, peddle or drive a vehicle, while yet another addressed the problem of stray "dogs, bitches or sluts."[54] Having conquered the wandering canine problem, John's greatest challenge as mayor was to settle the "townsite dispute" among the people of Bismarck, the Puget Sound Land Company, the Northern Pacific Railroad and a multitude of other parties.

The townsite dispute arose when John J. Jackman, an employee of the Northern Pacific, obtained inside information about where the Lake Superior and Puget Sound Land Company intended to locate a proposed new town. The Land Company, a subsidiary of the Northern Pacific, was formed to locate and establish townsites along the railroad. Confidential knowledge in hand, Jackman approached James Jerome Hill, future owner of the Northern Pacific, for financial support to partake in what was commonly known as townsite speculation. Early in the spring of 1872 Jackman and several other men set out to claim the location. When Thomas H. Canfield, George W. Sweet and Chief Engineer General Rosser of the Land Company arrived in the area preparing to stake the site, they discovered Jackman and his associates sitting on the designated land.[55]

Proceeding swiftly to Plan B, Sweet, solicitor for the Land Company, selected an alternative site nearby, had it surveyed and made the plat under his own name. Sweet sold lots in exchange for Quit Claim Deeds along with the promise that title would be cleared up as soon as possible. The settlers, acting in good faith, set about building homes and businesses. Some citizens arbitrarily decided that "they could just as well have the lots occupied by them at ten dollars each as to pay the price the Puget Sound Company would ask,"[56] setting off a grabbing frenzy, with shanties springing up overnight.

While most of the land grab was occurring, there was no land office in Bismarck in which to file plans, as such an office would not be established until early in 1874. Some claims had been filed with the Registrar in Pembina, but an audit revealed that no entries regarding Bismarck had ever been made. The Receiver had supplied unauthorized receipts that were not legally recognized, so the claims were not legally recognized either.[57] Compounding the lack of organization was the fact that squatters and apparently legitimate claimants alike were unaware that the land had already been granted to the Northern Pacific Railroad, by none other than Abraham Lincoln. The settlers began to mistrust the Land Company, as they suspected that Sweet was deceiving them and pocketing their money. Their suspicions were well founded. When questioned about Sweet, the Northern Pacific claimed to know nothing about him. Other land claimants obstinately refused to listen to anything that Northern Pacific officials had to say.[58] When John McLean stepped in as mayor, he opened negotiations with the Northern Pacific in order to resolve the matter:

> The townsite question has long agitated the community, and a variety of opinions as to its proper and final settlement exists among our people, but I desire here to state that so far as any effort of mine is concerned, as head of the City Government, no obstruction shall be placed in the way of a speedy settlement of this long mooted subject. I regard the interests of the people as identical with those of the Railroad Company, and consider that both should work in harmony to secure an amicable adjustment of this difficulty.
>
> Many of us, in fact most of us, have expended money in improving property to which we have thus far been unable to obtain title; toiled for years to obtain that which yet fades before us as the "mist of the morning," and it is a matter of profound regret that because of the personal interests of a few who are not with or of us, that we should be so long, and still continue to be without proper protection in what properly and rightfully belongs to us.[59]

As it turned out, the Northern Pacific wanted to have the people in the town as much as the people wanted to be there – after all, the company stood to profit from selling its land and needed a substantial population to support the railroad. However, the solution was complicated by layers of difficulty:

> On the one hand we have a ring of land-grabbers who refuse to compromise, fighting the Railroad Company, and by any means within their reach, not hesitating to stoop to fraud or means of revenge, aided, indirectly, by a class of citizens whose intentions are no doubt good, but, who seems prejudiced, and whose course is suicidal to the best interests of the town, all opposing with might and main every effort of the Railroad Company to settle the contest.[60]

Mayor McLean worked diligently to settle the townsite question, spending his own money on legal fees.[61] Finally, after the Northern Pacific effectively dismantled the Land Company, and provided assurances to make good on its promises, an agreement was reached to the benefit of the people of Bismarck. During his second term as mayor, McLean successfully registered an eighty-acre tract of land in his name on behalf of the inhabitants of Bismarck at the United States Land Office claiming the land of the Lake Superior and Puget Sound Land Company. At last, the lots were conveyed to the people and McLean's name is listed at the top of every old deed in Bismarck.[62] The *Tribune* commended him on his success:

> The Mayor, John A. McLean, has done more than any other, and to him belongs much honor for the liberality, persistence, shrewdness, and integrity which has been tried, which he has brought to bear in this matter. He never has held to extreme views of notions but always to practical ones, and it was through his negotiations that the Puget Sound people stepped aside and allowed the people to secure title in their own name.[63]

John McLean formed a partnership in the grocery business with his brother-in-law, Robert Macnider, in May 1875.[64] The new business, McLean and Macnider, grew substantially by the fall of that year and would become known far and wide in the Midwest. "The stock they have been able to put in shows pretty conclusively their financial standing; and it shows, too, the estimation in which they hold this country – shows that they have faith in it and seems to indicate that they intend to stay."[65] Their profit was at least fifty percent on every sale. Eggs sold for twenty cents a dozen, potatoes for sixty cents a bushel and butter for thirty-five cents a pound; silk hosiery was three dollars and seventy-five cents a dozen. McLean and Macnider also supplied the steamboats along the Missouri, the sales from those transactions typically being two thousand dollars or more.[66]

Some purchases were traded for skins and gold with the Indians. The squaws were astute traders, asking for separate weighing of staples in small quantities to ensure that they were not being cheated.[67] However, not all of the Indians were interested in amicable trading. An incident in the fall of 1875 would mark the "first real Indian scare"[68] for the people of Bismarck.

CHAPTER TWO

Those Stirring Times

N. P. Clark of St. Cloud, Minn. had the contract to furnish beef at Fort Abraham Lincoln and kept his herd of cattle on Burnt Creek about eight miles north of Bismarck. George F. Lewis and John Wright were the herders and lived in a shack on Burnt Creek. On the day that Wright was in charge of the herd, he failed to show up at night, and Lewis sent in word by a man that was hauling wood to town that Wright was missing. Search was made and the body of Wright found, horribly mutilated. Wright was shot in the back of the head and his head split open by a tomahawk. Near the body a coup stick was planted. The killing of Wright by the Indians created a commotion among the people of Bismarck and Mayor McLean wired to General Custer for troops to come at once. Captain Yates came with his troop of Cavalry, accompanied by the Indian Scout, Bloody Knife, and proceeded to the scene of the murder. A trail was found and followed in the direction of Standing Rock, but after fruitless search the command returned to Fort Lincoln. The Indians were not caught.[1]

WRIGHT'S MURDER LEFT the townspeople shaken and apprehensive. Mayor McLean sent a petition to the Dakota Territory military commander, General Alfred Howe Terry, requesting that "200 stand of arms and ammunition be placed in the hands of the commandant at Camp Hancock" in Bismarck. He felt that in case of Indian attack, the civilians could have weapons at their disposal, to be doled out at the discretion of the camp commander. General Terry responded that he was "unable to comply" with the request but gave his assurances that steps had been taken to ensure the safety of the people of Bismarck and that, if need be, he would send more men.[2]

The inhabitants of Bismarck and the Fort Lincoln soldiers were well acquainted with one another and frequently socialized. Will Falconer recalled the yearly minstrel show hosted by the soldiers and remembered that dances were held both at Fort Lincoln and in Bismarck, particularly during the winter months.[3] Mary Falconer also recalled occasions of merriment with the soldiers:

> Many pretty parties were given in the early days, one of which was made memorable to the presence of general Custer and his wife, his two brothers, Tom and "Boss," also all the other officers from the Fort with their ladies, the gentlemen being in full dress. The party was given by Col. W. M. Thompson, then in the Army, and was held at the farm north of town. Though only a log house, it was entirely decorated with flags and bunting and so brilliantly lighted that one could imagine themselves in a home of splendor. This together with the glittering uniforms of the officers and the handsome gowns of the ladies, together with the strains of the celebrated 7th Cavalry Orchestra, made it indeed an event most memorable.[4]

Visions of grandeur and infinite riches had seized the imaginations of a group of Bismarck men. Veteran gold scout H. N. Ross, who had been on Custer's expedition a year earlier, joined the quest for Black Hills nuggets in December 1875. The men returned in January with two ounces of gold discovered at the placer mines at French Creek. The gold samples found their way into the hands of John McLean and Colonel Clement Augustus Lounsberry.[5] Colonel Lounsberry, a Civil War veteran turned newspaperman, established the *Bismarck Tribune* in 1873. The *Tribune* and its embellished coverage of the Black Hills gold rush held the entire town of Bismarck in its grasp. Will Falconer recalled that even the habitually intoxicated were keyed up with excitement:

> The Hole in the Wall was on Main Street, next to Jack White's saloon, the proprietor, Ed Ware, each evening would give a free lunch, Ed had a bulletin board on the sidewalk in front of his place, and each day, he would have something new printed, setting forth the good qualities of his baked beans, oxtail soup and other dishes.

Louis Aagard, who had a ranch on the east side of the Missouri below Bismarck, known as the Aagard bottoms, was a frequent visitor to Bismarck, especially during the Black Hills excitement, and on each visit he generally would get lit up. Aagard had a habit of getting the cart before the horse. One day, after looking at Ed Ware's bulletin board, he said, "I don't know which make the most excite [sic], the Wall in the Hole, or the Black Hills."[6]

As an established merchant in the town, John McLean profited well from promoting Bismarck as the logical starting point for mining parties. Although Deadwood was the undisputed mining hub, Bismarck was one of four towns where miners could equip themselves. McLean and Macnider expanded their inventory, as well as their operations, to supply mining equipment along with transportation services by ox team to the placer mines.[7] Miners, carrying buckskin bags filled with the magical golden dust, exchanged the contents for twenty dollars an ounce at McLean and Macnider.[8]

The increasing number of miners encroaching on the Black Hills caused further hostility between the military and the Sioux and their allies, the Northern Cheyenne. It was now evident to the Indians that the military was making only a half-hearted attempt at discouraging the miners. For months rumours circulated about reservation Indians joining the non-Treaty Indians led by Sitting Bull and preparing for an attack. After a failed effort by the government to purchase the Black Hills, a new scheme was drawn up to snatch the land away from the Indians. The government

Spring Goods! Spring Goods!

McLEAN &

MACNIDER,

WHOLESALE AND RETAIL DEALERS

---IN---

Groceries and Provisions,
Flour, Feed, Oats,
Pork, Bacon, Fish,
Salt, Lime and Cement.
Canned and Dried Fruits,
East and West India Goods,
HARDWARE, CROCKERY,
BOOTS AND SHOES,
CARPETS AND OIL CLOTHS,
DRY GOODS AND NOTIONS,
LADIES' and GENT'S FURNISHING GOODS,

Spring Styles of Hats and Caps.
Our Clothing Room is Unsurpassed in the City. Elegant and Nobby Suits and
LOW PRICES.
CALL AND SEE FOR YOURSELVES.
We also keep a full Stock of

Miners' Supplies,
GOLD PANS,
SLUICE FORKS,
WASHOE PICKS
AND HANDLES,
GOLD SCALES &
Magnets at Chicago Prices, Freight added.
Also Agents for the
STUDEBAKER WAGON.
McLEAN & MACNIDER.

Illustration Based on Advertisement in Bismarck Tribune
McLean and Macnider

proclaimed that all Indians had to report to a reservation by January 31, 1876, failing which they would be considered "hostile" and forced onto reservations by the military. Once it became apparent that Indians were not flocking to the reservations, the government decided to mount a military expedition against hostile Indians, to forcibly relocate them and keep them under its control. A complicated plan of attack, involving a "three pronged pincer campaign," was to be launched in the spring.[9]

The inhabitants of Bismarck held a meeting with a view to encouraging the government to open a large portion of the Sioux reservation, including the Black Hills, for mining and settlement and, at the same time, promote Bismarck to miners and settlers. They appointed a committee of two, Mayor McLean and Colonel Lounsberry, to lobby on behalf of the town. The two men were to travel to Washington to preach to the (already converted) President Ulysses S. Grant.[10] They left on their mission accompanied by Mary Falconer, making a few strategic stops on the way to Washington. On February 8, 1876, McLean and Lounsberry appeared before the Chamber of Commerce of St. Paul, Minnesota. They hoped to establish regular transportation to Bismarck and the Black Hills by means of stagecoach and rail.[11]

The Chamber adopted several resolutions that day: to open communication and invite travel by the Northern Pacific Railroad via Bismarck and, further, to take whatever measures were necessary to obtain government permits for miners going to the Black Hills.[12] A daily route of stagecoaches from Bismarck to the Black Hills, via the Northwestern Stage and Transportation Company, was instituted. McLean and Lounsberry continued on to the Minnesota legislature, to obtain a "memorial to congress for opening the Black Hills."[13] Then they travelled to Milwaukee and Chicago to try to interest the Chicago, Milwaukee and St. Paul railroads in providing passenger and freight services to the Black Hills through Bismarck. The railroads acted immediately to set freight and passenger rates.

The travellers were buoyed up when they reached Washington, where their welcoming party was both substantial and receptive. McLean and Lounsberry made submissions to President Grant, the Senate and the House of Representatives, as well as to the Secretary of War, William

Worth Belknap. Congress ordered part of the Sioux reservation, including the Black Hills, open to settlement,[14] concurring with Custer's opinion that Indian occupation of the land should be ended without delay.[15] The morning that Mayor McLean, Mary Falconer and Colonel Lounsberry left Washington, a scandal broke over allegations of corruption involving Belknap, his wife and relatives of President Grant's with respect to unlawful sharing of the profits from Indian post traderships.[16]

Upon their arrival in St. Paul, the threesome were prepared to wait, as ordinarily the rail line did not open until April, when the snow and ice could be cleared. However, the Northern Pacific made an exception for its special passengers, General Custer and his wife, Elizabeth, who were returning to Fort Abraham Lincoln from New York City. An enormous train, outfitted with two snow ploughs, three engines and forty railroad employees sent specifically to shovel snow, left St. Paul. Mayor McLean, Mary and Colonel Lounsberry had the apparent good fortune to take the same train as the Custers, along with several Black Hills miners and army recruits.[17]

As they chugged westward, a blizzard swept across Dakota Territory. The train came to an abrupt stop at Crystal Springs, between Fargo and Bismarck, held captive by enormous snow drifts. Despite hours of back-breaking shovelling through layers of snow and ice, no discernable progress was made by the railroad employees working in tandem with the miners. The train was going nowhere and daylight was fading.[18] Mary Falconer remembered this calamity as an adventure. Elizabeth Custer's memories, however, were ones of mere tolerance and grudging compromise for the sake of her husband. The discomfort of the other passengers on the stranded train was the last thing on her mind:

> Night was descending, and my husband, after restlessly going in and out of the next car, showed me that he had some perplexity on his mind. He described to me the discomfort of the officers and Bismarck citizens in the other coach in not having any place to sleep. His meaning penetrated at last, and I said "You are waiting for me to invite them all to room with us?" His "exactly" assured me it was precisely what he intended me to do.[19]

Great care was taken to ensure that Mrs. Custer was snugly tucked in against a far wall in a large bed before any of the Bismarck townspeople were ushered into the Custers' private sleeping quarters. With the lights dimmed and her head under a pillow, Mrs. Custer was unaware of who exactly was rooming with them; she knew only that her husband was beside her. "The audible sleeping in our bed, however, through the long nights that followed," she recalled, "convinced me that the general had assigned those places to the oldest, fattest and ranking civilians." The soundest of sleepers, Mrs. Custer awoke each morning alone, after all of the bedding for her overnight guests had been put away.[20]

As time wore on, and as wood and rations dwindled, Mrs. Custer became increasingly worried: "Everyone made the best of the situation, and my husband was as rollicking as ever. Even though I tried to conceal it, I soon lost heart entirely, and it cost me great effort to join in with the rest in conversation."[21] The men continued to work at freeing the snowbound train, but to no avail:

> The days seemed to stretch on endlessly, the snow was heaped up about us and falling steadily. All we could see was the trackless waste of white on every side. The wind whistled and moaned around the cars, and great gusts rocked our frail little refuge from side to side... I made the best effort I could to be brave and deceived them about my real terrors: I had no other idea than that we must die there.[22]

Fortunately a telegraph was discovered on the train, along with a battery. All passengers were canvassed for their knowledge of telegraphy, and there happened to be a communications expert on board. Some wire splicing was carried out, and a message about their plight got through to Fort Lincoln and the Fargo station. General Custer's brother, Tom, made immediate arrangements and came to the rescue with a sleigh pulled by mules. After her week-long ordeal, Mrs. Custer was carried to the sleigh and deposited in the straw, along with her husband's three hound dogs, for the trip back to the Fort, while John, Mary and Colonel Lounsberry had to wait for the next passing sleigh. The other passengers were not so lucky. Although the Custers sent help and a wagonload of supplies, the soldiers and miners "endured the discomfort" on the snowbound train for a further three weeks.[23]

No sooner had General Custer returned to the safety of Fort Lincoln than he was recalled to Washington by the Senate to testify on the charges of corruption in the War Department. Impeachment was unanimously recommended by Congress as a suitable punishment for Belknap. Hoping to avoid a full public hearing, President Grant had already accepted Belknap's resignation in private, but the inquiry proceeded regardless. Custer's testimony proved embarrassing for Grant, particularly because two of the president's brothers-in-law were also implicated. Grant planned to reprimand Custer by forcing him to remain behind during the upcoming spring campaign. In the end, however, Custer's expertise was needed by General Alfred H. Terry, who had been placed in full command of the expedition in lieu of Custer. Custer was in charge of his own unit only.[24] General Terry soon found himself directly violating the terms of the Treaty whose negotiation he had been party to.

Practical arrangements for the army's spring campaign to control the Indians commenced with officers, soldiers and guides purchasing their supplies from the McLean and Macnider company. John's proposal to equip the latest army expedition to the Yellowstone, Tongue and Little Bighorn rivers with mule teams to carry supplies was accepted by Lieutenant Nowland, post quartermaster at Fort Abraham Lincoln:

> I hereby agree to furnish the United States, for the transportation of military supplies accompanying the Yellowstone expedition en route from Fort Abraham Lincoln, D.T., for fifty (50) days or more, twenty-six (26) two-horse or mule teams, drivers, and wagons, complete and in every respect fit for service required of them in hauling supplies to the said expedition; the teams to be subject to inspection of the proper United States officers before being received; and this for a compensation of ($4.95) four dollars and ninety-five cents per diem for each two horse or mule team so received, the government furnishing such forage for the animals and subsistence for the men as the exigencies of the service will admit while so employed.
>
> I further agree to assume all risk of damage or loss of said teams, except the damage or loss that may occur from hostile Indians.[25]

Days before the Seventh Cavalry departed for the Little Big Horn, Mary Falconer attended a party at Fort Abraham Lincoln. She danced with General Custer and the officers.[26] Will and Mary were among those who watched Custer and the Seventh leave on May 17, 1876.[27] After one final night at camp with her husband, Elizabeth Custer described her last look at the Seventh Cavalry:

> It was a splendid picture. The flags and pennons were flying, the men were waving, and even the horses seemed to be arching themselves to show how fine and fit they were. My husband rode to the top of a promontory and turned around, stood up in his stirrups and waved his hat. Then they all started forward again and in a few seconds they had disappeared, horses, flags, men, and ammunition. And we never saw them again.[28]

A total of two hundred and sixty-one men and officers, including Custer and his brothers, were killed by the Sioux and Northern Cheyenne in the Battle of the Little Big Horn in Montana on June 25, 1876.[29] The inhabitants of Bismarck grieved deeply for the loss of their friends and guardians of the Seventh Cavalry. It would be a long time before life in the town returned to normal.[30]

>-+-+>-+-O-+-<+-+-<

The following spring, when the time came for him to seek re-election as mayor, John McLean declined to enter the race.[31] The boom caused by the gold rush was coming to an end and John sought to diversify his opportunities for prosperity. He travelled frequently to St. Paul, Washington and many other cities to pursue government contracts while at the same time maintaining his thriving wholesale grocery business.[32] He became a director of the newly formed Bismarck, Fort Lincoln and Black Hills Railroad and, later, the Bismarck, Mouse River, Turtle Mountain and Manitoba Railroad.[33] In September 1882 he participated in the Republican county convention.[34]

McLean was co-owner, with Robert Macnider, of the Stark Farm, three miles south of Bismarck. This was a six-hundred-and-forty-acre property where Macnider had his homestead. There they harvested cash crops, namely wheat and oats.[35]

After the closure, on October 6, 1882, of J. W. Raymond and Company, a competitor in the grocery business, the McLean and Macnider company was recognized as the leading wholesale grocer in the

Northwest.[36] If success could be measured by the number of lawsuits launched, then McLean and Macnider was very successful indeed. The company brought actions against several people who had defaulted on mortgages it held, and it seized two of the Peck Steamers over non-payment of account. In addition, John McLean initiated a lawsuit against the United States government over the Yellowstone contract, although this case proved futile.[37]

A respectable amount of time having passed since Nellie's death, on December 3, 1880, John married Mary Louise Falconer, Nellie's younger sister, at the home of Robert and Eliza Macnider.[38] The newlyweds then travelled to St. Paul for a few weeks. John returned to

John McLean family. Standing, left to right: Harry McLean, William McLean, Mattie Falconer, Clarence McLean. Seated: Mary McLean. STATE HISTORICAL SOCIETY OF NORTH DAKOTA D0489

Bismarck on December 30th, leaving Mary in St. Paul, as he feared a blockade.[39] On September 22, 1881, Mary gave birth to James Garfield McLean.[40] Sixteen months later, on January 16, 1883, James died of respiratory diphtheria,[41] a frequent cause of infant and child mortality in the United States at that time. He was buried two days later, alongside Nellie, at the Oakland Cemetery in St. Paul.[42] The following month, on February 18th, Mary gave birth to her second son, Henry[43] (later Harry) Falconer McLean, at their home at 233 First Street in Bismarck. The baby was delivered by Dr. Henry Porter, the only battle surgeon to survive Little Big Horn, and was baptized by Reverend Sloan.[44]

Harry Falconer McLean. STATE HISTORICAL
SOCIETY OF NORTH DAKOTA D0088

Although John McLean had both family and business commitments, he maintained an active involvement in local affairs. A founding member of the local Masonic lodge, he was also a member of the Chamber of Commerce and sat on various committees: Public Improvements, Legislation, Transportation, Finance, Fuel and Fire Protection.[45] In recognition of John's countless contributions to Bismarck and Dakota Territory, he was bestowed with the honour of having McLean County named after him.

The Speaker of the House at Yankton, General E. A. Williams, introduced a bill on March 8, 1883, to create McLean County at the behest of John Satterlund.[46] Like John McLean, Satterlund had diverse interests: he built railroads, operated the Merchants Hotel in Bismarck, ran the first stage line between Bismarck and Washburn, and operated the Black Diamond coal mine at Washburn. "King John," as he was known, acquired land sixteen miles north of Bismarck along the Missouri River. He set out the townsite of Washburn and organized McLean County.[47]

In May 1883 John McLean joined the board of the Dakota Penitentiary and was placed in charge of constructing Penitentiary Number Two.[48] In June he enjoyed a substantial share of over $2 million of real estate transfers in the flourishing city of Bismarck.[49] People were attracted to Bismarck by talk about dividing Dakota Territory and making Bismarck the capitol of the northern part. The *Bismarck Weekly Tribune* noted further evidence of Bismarck's rapidly growing prosperity:

The speed of the average Bismarck nag is only equalled by his beauty. Two years ago a fine horse was seldom seen in the city. Now everyone drives a fast horse whether he does any business or not. The clerk is more likely to possess a fleet-footed steed than his employer.[50]

John decided it was time for a change of vocation. He abandoned the grocery trade in favour of the real estate business, becoming a broker just prior to July 1, 1883, when Bismarck replaced Yankton as the capitol of Dakota Territory.[51] The governor of Dakota Territory, Nehemiah G. Ordway, appointed a commission to choose a new site for the capitol that would be accessible "from all portions of the Territory."[52] Although the commissioners visited many towns, Bismarck was the early favourite, particularly on the part of Commissioner Alexander McKenzie.

Harry and Clarence McLean. Harry graduated from the William Moore School in 1902, Clarence a year later. COURTESY OF JANICE HENSEL

McKenzie played a large part in moving the territorial capitol, a decision seen by many, particularly the residents of Yankton, as illegal. Although a legal challenge by a group of Yankton citizens regarding the validity of the Act concerning capitol relocation went all the way to the United States Supreme Court, and a grand jury indicted some of those involved in the act for bribery and corruption, the challenge was never heard and none of those indicted was ever arrested. The Supreme Court of Dakota Territory approved the relocation of the capitol. Many believed, however, that the decision was ultimately controlled by

McKenzie and Ordway and their connections at the Northern Pacific Railroad, which owned over ten million acres of land in northern Dakota Territory.[53]

By the fall of 1883 John McLean had entered into a partnership with Captain William Harmon, a survivor of the Battle of Gettysburg and a fellow Bismarck pioneer.[54] McLean and Harmon sold property at Prospect Heights in Bismarck. The lots were well situated, with a view of the Missouri River and located not far from the new state capitol buildings then under construction. "Messrs. Harmon & McLean are well and favourably known throughout North Dakota, and recognized as men of sterling worth who have done not a little to place the many advantages of Burleigh county and Bismarck before eastern people."[55]

Family life for the McLeans and Falconers was eventful, with several marriages, births and deaths marking the passage of the 1880s and 1890s. In August 1883 Will Falconer married Emma Bentley at the home of

William Moore School, Bismarck, North Dakota. "*If…any single institution is able to produce a man of destiny, it has done well,*" *boasted the school of one of its graduates, Harry McLean.* DeGraff photo. State Historical Society of North Dakota C0041

Emma's parents, Dr. and Mrs. William A. Bentley.[56] The following summer, on July 21, 1884, Jennie Falconer Armstrong passed away.[57]

Mary McLean had two more sons, Clarence Campbell McLean, born on September 13, 1885, and Walter Scott McLean, born on September 21, 1890.[58]

Another McLean and Falconer union took place on November 29, 1886, when Daniel Falconer, Mary's older brother, married Effie McLean, John's cousin, at John and Mary's home.[59] Mary's half-sister, Mattie, married the photographer John White of Vancouver, British Columbia, in August 1893.[60]

The McLean family had seen many changes since 1872: the formation of the City of Bismarck, the affirmation of Bismarck as the capitol city, and the admittance of North and South Dakota as states.[61] They witnessed Custer riding off to the Battle of the Little Big Horn and lived through the aftermath. They heard of the long-awaited completion of the Northern Pacific Railroad in August 1883. They watched as Fort Abraham Lincoln was abandoned in 1891; Custer's house was dismantled and the salvaged wood used in the construction of many Bismarck homes.[62] The Indians who freely roamed the West now lived within the confines of reservations, their once mighty chiefs successively annihilated.[63] A large fire destroyed much of downtown Bismarck in 1898.[64] The McLeans themselves suffered through hardship due to economic downturns in the late

Harry Falconer McLean. No one, not even Harry himself, could have guessed what he was to accomplish. STATE HISTORICAL SOCIETY OF NORTH DAKOTA D0109

1800s. Unquestionably, the McLeans lived in legendary times. Indeed, an intelligent young man could not help but be influenced by them.

Young Harry Falconer McLean attended primary school at the William Moore School in Bismarck, later recalling that "he once trudged…wearing home-knit mittens so long that they left a tiny furrow in the snow behind him."[65] Although not "particularly noteworthy as a boy," the "gaunt" and "angular" youth grew up with the ideals of the adventurous, believing that "there were no places so interesting…as those beyond the end of steel."[66]

He enjoyed the comfort of belonging to a family viewed by the citizens of Bismarck as esteemed pioneers who had contributed to the city in a substantial way. Harry McLean's pioneering spirit was a gift from the generation that had come before. He too would forge paths through wilderness and give something of himself for the generations to come:

> *Through all those stirring times, either night or day, a respectable woman could walk the streets in safety, and there is not one instance known where a respectable woman was ever insulted or molested, either on or off the streets in the city of Bismarck. There were no thefts or burglaries in those days. A person would leave his ax out on the wood pile and would always find it there in the morning. You could not do that today. People never thought of locking their doors during the night. Those were wonderful days. They are now gone forever.*[67]

CHAPTER THREE

The Spoilers

*Dr. Porter is having a new coat of paint put on his office,
37 Main Street.*[1]

*Billy Thurston and Fred Whittier, take the blue ribbon. They killed
107 mallards and two geese in an hour and a half, Monday.*[2]

*A tape worm eighteen feet long at least came on the scene after my
taking two CASCARETS. This I am sure caused my bad health
for the past three years. I am still taking Cascarets, the only cathartic
worth of notice by sensitive people.*[3]

*To be or not to be, that is the great problem before the people of
Bismarck, and when in future years the self-made men, now struggling
along unnoticed by the outside world, are asked what gave them the
strength and courage to persevere and win, it will be in the early and
constant use of the Belle of Moorhead Flour. For sale by all grocers.*[4]

*Nine-tenths of all of the celery used in the western markets now comes
from Kalamazoo, Michigan.*[5]

WITHIN THE PAGES of the *Bismarck Tribune* one could find
information about practically anything, from the latest news to the biggest
sale. Almost every page sported advertisements for the treatment of a
multitude of ailments – maladies such as constipation, catarrh, itching
piles or nervous prostration. Even insanity, nightly emissions, evil dreams
and lost manhood had a remedy. More often than not, it was the same

chemical potion that would miraculously cure them all. The *Tribune* chronicled the lives of almost everyone in town: who came, who went and where, what their business was, who was over for dinner, who was sick, who was married or dead (or both). Yet not all events made the newspaper. The *Tribune* maintained a discreet silence about the separation of John and Mary McLean.

It is unknown whether it was one incident or several that caused the irreconcilable differences between them, but John left the household for good, and for a time his whereabouts were a mystery to his family. In a letter to his older brother William, Harry McLean mentioned the last communication between their parents: "The last time I heard from him, he wanted to come home and Mother ans[wered] it. (I don't know what she said but we haven't heard a word since)."[6] However, whatever concerns Harry might have had about his father's absence were eclipsed for the moment by his disappointment at William's decision to be elsewhere for Thanksgiving: "Darn it all I thought sure you would be home for Thanksgiving and I went out to Willehelms ranch and got four nice big honkers... Got them all out of one flock with the repeater."[7]

William McLean was a pressman for the *Tribune* when he enlisted with the First North Dakota Volunteer regiment to fight in the Spanish-American War in the Philippines.[8] He found himself in San Francisco, ready to ship out to Manila with a stop at Honolulu. William wrote to the newspaper about his experiences:

> Our stay in San Francisco was a continuous scene of gayety and festivity. Nothing was too good for those who wore the blue and [I] can say with all candor that not a man in our regiment will say that he passed a lonesome hour when fortunate enough to get down town.[9]

Reflecting a longstanding intolerance for any person of Chinese descent, likely a holdover from years of listening to his uncles speak about Chinese labourers on the Union Pacific, William also expressed his thoughts on Chinatown:

> One of the most interesting sights in San Francisco is Chinatown, and it is certainly a sight to behold. About 37,000 of the heathens are quartered there and they are without doubt the filthiest, lowest specimens of humanity that ever existed and the sooner Uncle Sam chases every bloody Chinaman from his domains the better it will be for civilization generally.[10]

After a five-mile-long procession to the ship, the men were whisked aboard amid much cheering, music and cannon blasts. A chant was heard above the thunderous tribute, "We're off to Manila, to hell with Spain, remember the Maine,"[11] a reference to the sinking of the battleship *Maine* by the Spanish in Havana harbour, which triggered the declaration of war by the United States.[12] The festive mood on board dissipated temporarily as rough seas made almost everyone seasick. Once the ship docked in Honolulu, however, the celebratory atmosphere returned and the men were treated to a splendid dinner in a palace courtyard.[13]

The Spanish-American War lasted about six months. As a consequence of losing the war, Spain's overseas empire was dissolved; Cuba was granted independence, Puerto Rico and Guam were relinquished to the United States, and the Philippines were purchased for $20 million. The latter transaction spawned a new conflict. After years of struggling for freedom from Spain, the Filipinos believed that the United States was helping them achieve independence and that its motives were purely altruistic. Instead, the United States shut the Filipinos out of peace talks and ultimately imperialized them. Thus, just as the Spanish-American War was ending, the Philippine-American war commenced.[14]

William McLean applied to stay on and requested that his old employer, the *Tribune*, send a letter of recommendation to the president of the Military Examining Board at the Presidio in San Francisco. William was described as "a young man of exceeding promise, sober, industrious and strictly honorable."[15] His application was accepted.

Back in Bismarck, the McLean family heard through the local grapevine that John McLean was bookkeeping for Alexander McKenzie. By the turn of the decade McKenzie had declared his own war in Alaska, but unlike William McLean he was anything but honourable. As a result of many years in backroom politics, and particularly after his appointment as National Committeeman for the State of North Dakota, McKenzie was acquainted with a number of high-ranking politicians: it was said that he knew "every Republican President from Grant to Harding."[16] Some of the government officials were fine and upstanding, while others, McKenzie among them, were not averse to manipulating situations to their advantage. The latter group included Judge Arthur Noyes of Minneapolis.

In June of 1900 Noyes was dispatched to Nome, North Dakota, ostensibly to bring order to the chaos caused by the gold rush in Alaska. Instead, taking advantage of the state of pandemonium, and under the guise of legality, Noyes teamed up with McKenzie in an audacious plot to take over claims that were rich but disputed because of foreign ownership. Noyes appointed McKenzie as the receiver of several such claims on Anvil Creek. Fortified with heaps of affidavits and orders drafted by underhanded lawyers and churned out by their harried stenographers, McKenzie ousted miners from their claims and, in some cases, confiscated their possessions. He availed himself of as many lackeys and thugs as he could afford so as to continue mining the claims and guard the mines against their owners.[17]

It was not long before their brazen treachery was realized. The miners filed writs to have McKenzie removed as receiver and get their mines back. The problem was that Noyes was still the judge – and the judge refused to hear their appeals, conveniently claiming a lack of jurisdiction. Meanwhile the claims were flourishing under McKenzie's direction, reaping approximately a quarter of a million dollars in gold. The gold dust was supposedly held in a safety deposit box pending settlement of the claims. When the miners brought writs issued by the district court, McKenzie and Noyes still refused to turn over the gold, and when faced with injunctions issued by an even higher court, Noyes simply dissolved them, stating that the matter was out of his hands and that no one was entitled to appeal his initial order appointing the receiver. Even rioting and threats of physical violence did little to dissuade the villainous duo from their pursuit of this golden opportunity. It was only when U.S. marshals arrived to charge them with contempt of court and escort them to San Francisco that their conspiracy was brought to an end.[18]

McKenzie's devotees believed he had become the unwitting victim of "an unscrupulous gang of political pirates."[19] Others disagreed. The court found that McKenzie was not only the instigator but also unquestionably guilty of contempt of court.[20] He was sent to jail for six months in Oakland, California, his supporters proclaiming his sentence

"A Monstrous Wrong."[21] McKenzie's political connections served him well. Although an initial application for his release to the U.S. Supreme Court had been denied in March, McKenzie took his plight to a higher authority and appealed to the Attorney General for executive clemency. In exchange for his release from jail, McKenzie turned over to the Court of Appeals eight thousand dollars in gold dust that had been deposited in the Seattle Mint. He received a full pardon from President William McKinley on May 25, 1901.[22] Despite a period of incarceration, McKenzie continued to serve as North Dakota's Republican National Committeeman until his resignation in 1908.

The immediate outcome of the Noyes trial was a similar travesty. The judges of the Circuit Court of Appeals found that "this conspiracy is outside the charge of contempt, and in view of the fact that Noyes holds a judicial position, I concur in his judgment that the respondent be required to pay a fine of $1,000."[23] In February 1902, however, Noyes was removed from office.

The whole fiasco was immortalized by Rex Beach in a novel, *The Spoilers*, published in 1905. McKenzie was renamed Alec McNamara and Noyes was recast as Judge Arthur Stillman. Despite the addition of a love interest, the story bore a close resemblance to reality. Pages before the passionate moonlit embrace between Helen, the beautiful yet unattainable young woman, and Roy Glenister, the swarthy, heroic miner who saves the day, Roy muses:

> There never was a bolder crime consummated nor one more cruelly unjust. They robbed a realm and pillaged its people, they defiled a court and made Justice a wanton, they jailed good men and sent others to ruin; and for this they are to suffer – how? By a paltry fine or a short imprisonment, perhaps, by an ephemeral disgrace and loss of their stolen goods. Contempt of court is the accusation but you might as well convict a murderer for breach of the peace. We've thrown them off, it's true, and they won't trouble us again, but they'll never have to answer for their real infamy. That will go unpunished while their lawyers quibble over technicalities and rules of court. I guess it's true that there isn't any law of God or man north of Fifty-three.[24]

>━┥◆━○━◆┝━

Harry McLean received business training at the Dakota Business College, although many would assume whe was an engineer. COURTESY OF www.fargo-history.com

William McLean returned to Bismarck from the Philippines just as Harry was preparing to graduate, class of 1902, from the William Moore School. Harry McLean had been industrious during his high school years, working on several ranches in the Bismarck area and as a page in the North Dakota legislature for three sessions.[25] The inhabitants of Bismarck knew Harry for his "prankish activity as well as his periods of sober reflection and study."[26] In his senior year he took first place in an "oratorical contest"[27] and graduated in a class totalling fifteen pupils – thirteen girls and two boys.[28] After high school he found work as a water boy with Winston Brothers Construction of Minneapolis. Then, closer to home and likely highly recommended by Alexander McKenzie, he worked as a timekeeper for Cook and Hinds Construction on the McKenzie to Linton branch of the Northern Pacific Railroad in North Dakota.[29]

Andrew Braid (A. B.) Cook was born in Dundee, Wisconsin, on February 2, 1864, and moved to Montana at the age of nineteen. Like many young men in the West, he found work in railroad construction. Cook gained his experience working with pioneer builders such as Hugh Kirkendall. He broadened his horizons in Missoula, Montana, where he founded a real estate company in partnership with Frank W. McConnell in 1889, followed closely by a term as state auditor. Cook set up his own contracting firm, entering into various partnerships and eventually joining forces with Thomas R. Hinds, a contractor from Butte, Montana.[30]

Returning to Bismarck from Linton in November 1903, Harry McLean caused a sensation, thundering through town cracking the whip behind a large team of mules.[31] With his work finished for the winter, McLean decided he needed business training and entered the Dakota Business College. Located in Fargo, the Dakota Business College was founded by a former tobacco-worm picker, Felix Leland Watkins. The students gained hands-on experience by replicating typical business dealings in class. On the first day they were given two thousand dollars in "Watkins Dough," a faux currency issued by the school, along with ledgers. The students set up their own fictitious businesses and were instructed in the various transactions one might be expected to perform, such as obtaining mortgages, taking on partners and applying for insurance.[32]

Armed with his newfound knowledge of the world of commerce, McLean returned to complete the Linton branch the following spring, then found work in a Bismarck lumberyard.[33] In the summer of 1905 he received a wire from Cook offering him a position in Canada. He accepted the job and, at the age of twenty-two, moved to Canada.[34]

Harry Falconer McLean circa 1905.
PHOTOGRAPH BY FREDERICK LYONDE, 101 KING STREET W., TORONTO, CANADA. A. B. COOK COLLECTION, LOT 2 B6/ 11.08, MONTANA HISTORICAL SOCIETY

Cook, Hinds and two Canadian cousins named George Deeks – George Samuel "Sam" and George Melville "G. M." – formed the Toronto Construction Company Limited on May 27, 1905.[35] Sam Deeks was born in Toronto on September 17, 1859. He taught at the Chatham Grammar School in Kent County, Ontario, prior to becoming a railway contractor. As well as "impressively short of stature," he was described as possessing a "gift for mathematics,"[36] and therefore was in charge of finance for the company – although he also had a knack for concrete work. G. M. Deeks did not take such an active a role with the firm. The head office was located in the Norwich Building, 14 Wellington Street East, in Toronto. Sam Deeks was president, Hinds was secretary and Cook was general manager. All were equal shareholders. Their first contract was with the Canadian Pacific Railway for a section of the Toronto–Sudbury line, which ran through Bolton, Midhurst, Coldwater, MacTier and Parry Sound.

Hinds was the "walking boss," with Harry McLean as his assistant. McLean was quickly promoted to general superintendent.[37] The young timekeeper on the job was James "Jimmie" Therrien, who reported to someone lower in the chain of command. When Therrien's boss was called away, Therrien was instructed to respond to any question that came up by saying, "I don't know." Shortly thereafter, Harry McLean arrived at the timekeeper's office to ask a question and received the prearranged response. Several times that day, Harry went to Therrien's office with different questions, and always got the same answer. Thoroughly irked, McLean went to discuss the seemingly clueless new employee with his boss. "I thought you told me you'd hired a bright kid for the timekeeper's job. Eight times today I've asked him different questions, but every time I get the same answer: 'I don't know!' A bright lad, all right!" "I know," said Jimmie's boss. "That's what I told him to tell you!" Harry chuckled.[38]

On November 20, 1906, Harry McLean gave testimony at a trial heard at the district court in Emmons County. Thomas Burke, a former employee of both Cook and Hinds and Toronto Construction, alleged breach of an employment contract. The trial revealed that there was no contract to breach and, further, that the plaintiff had been borrowing money from Cook, McLean and other employees without repaying it. The judge ordered Burke to pay $170.92, much of which had been borrowed in ten-dollar increments over the course of a year.[39]

After the trial, McLean visited his mother in Bismarck, travelled to Livingston, Montana, and then returned to Toronto[40] to serve as a witness to the marriage of Charles Louis Nelson, his friend and classmate from

Toronto Construction Company, Bolton, Ontario. O. Smithers, Photographer. Lot 2 B6/6.08, A.B. Cook Collection, Montana Historical Society

the Dakota Business College and a fellow railway contractor. On December 24, 1906, Nelson wed Olean Nellie Pilson at Bolton, Ontario, where the CPR line started.[41]

The next year Toronto Construction accepted several CPR contracts: a fifty-mile section of double tracking east of Smiths Falls, Ontario, the Montreal–Toronto line and the Mont Laurier–Normandin line in Quebec. From 1908 to 1910 the company completed the Chipman–Plaster Rock section of the National Transcontinental Railway in New Brunswick. Again, Harry McLean was the construction superintendent.[42] Located in a railway shack at McGivney Junction, McLean's office doubled as his bedroom. A reporter visiting the job site wrote that McLean's "hours for work appear to be from 5 a.m. to 5 a.m."[43] McLean's crew was responsible for constructing the stations and sidings and stringing up the telegraph lines, in addition to laying the track and ballast along the one-hundred-and-seven-mile road. McLean's authority was unquestioned. The Bismarck newspaper proudly reprinted the article, adding the headline "Harry McLean Makes Good."[44]

> Although a young man, he knows the game of railway building and goes about his work with as much coolness as some men display when sitting down to a meal. He is a tireless and systematic worker, a master organizer, and is probably the most popular official on the whole division.[45]

>-+◆-○-◆+-<

Cook and McLean were in constant communication through telegrams and letters, although both men were frequently difficult to track down. In April 1908 Cook married Mary Morgan Pettingell, a blue-blooded divorcée with two children. He divided his time between his domestic obligations and a hectic business schedule, but his pride and joy were the several vast ranches he owned in Montana where he bred Hereford cattle.[46] Cook continued to pursue railroad construction contracts with the Northern Pacific for his St. Paul-based organization, but only for a fair price. He told McLean, "I did not succeed in landing any Dakota work for the N.P. but would much prefer to be idle than work for glory."[47]

Arriving on the New Brunswick job fresh from engineering studies at McGill University was Frederick Innes Ker. Keenly interested in railways, Ker had worked for the Grand Trunk Railway, where he had been selected, along with another employee, to attend McGill. During the summers he worked as a brakeman and as a freight agent.[48] Ker's first encounter with McLean, on August 10, 1909,[49] found the boss dissatisfied with the paltry amount of ballast being brought up the line. McLean asked Ker how many cars of ballast he thought he could manage to bring up each day. Ker replied, "I don't know. I can't tell you that until you give me a profile of the line, with the grades and curvatures and then I can tell you how much I can pull up that grade." McLean said, "Hell, do you need that?" Ker responded, "Certainly, I need that. How else can I tell what stage they're at?"[50]

McLean gave the necessary information to Ker, who set about rating the locomotives and calculated that he could bring up ten trains a day,

Toronto Construction Company using a rail-mounted steam crane to build the National Transcontinental Railway. HARRY FALCONER MCLEAN COLLECTION, ACCESSION 1981-064. PA 212854, LIBRARY AND ARCHIVES CANADA

with one hundred cars each and thirty yards of ballast per car. The ballast foreman, George Armstrong, was sceptical. He had managed to haul only three hundred yards a day and Ker claimed that three thousand could be brought up. But, true to his word, Ker delivered. McLean was impressed and the two men developed a mutual admiration.[51]

Several local subcontractors were employed, including Daniel Hugh Sutherland of River John, Nova Scotia. Like Ker, Sutherland had attended McGill University; however, he did not complete his engineering degree, returning home to help support his family after his brother, Lawrence, was killed in an explosion in Quebec. Sutherland continued to take engineering courses and, along with McLean, was awarded a contract on a section of the National Transcontinental Railway. The lifelong friendship between McLean and Sutherland was launched on that job.[52]

The next contract taken on by the Toronto Construction Company was another for the CPR, the Georgian Bay and Seaboard Railway section running between Coldwater Junction, Bethney Junction, Orillia and Lindsay.[53] McLean was the onsite boss, with Ker as his superintendent,[54] joined by McLean's eldest brother, William, who had moved to Canada from Idaho.[55] Rudyard Kipling's poem "If" was displayed in a large frame on the wall of the field office.[56] McLean admired Kipling and saw him during the poet's visit to Canada in 1907, likely in Montreal at McGill University.[57] Kipling had an enthusiastic following of engineers after publishing his poem "The Sons of Martha," whose biblical references speak of the grave societal responsibilities of the engineer.

The relationship between Cook and his fellow shareholders Deeks and Hinds began to disintegrate. There were some earlier indications of discontentment, on the part of both G. M. and Sam Deeks, with various business arrangements involving Cook. Cook received notice from G. M. Deeks in July 1909 that Deeks and Deeks of St. Paul, Minnesota, a railroad contracting firm in which he had an interest, no longer wished to carry on the partnership with him,[58] and in September 1909 Sam Deeks sold to A. B. Cook his one-fourth interest in the Cook, Deeks and Hinds Grading Company.[59]

Sam Deeks and Thomas Hinds were particularly unhappy with the business arrangement with Cook. They were performing the lion's share of the work and resented having to share profits with an absentee partner who was working on his own projects, apart from the company's interests. Cook was oblivious to the fact that his partners were contemplating severing their business relationship with him. Hinds said, "The fact that a change was impending must have been evident to every one, and nothing but Cook's colossal egoism prevented him from apprehending it."[60]

Late in 1911, with the Georgian Bay job nearing completion, Sam Deeks and Thomas Hinds travelled to Montreal, purportedly on behalf of Toronto Construction, to negotiate a contract with the CPR for a new line, the "Lake Shore" job: Toronto via Peterborough to Montreal. However, Deeks and Hinds had no intention of sharing another contract with the absent A. B. Cook. Once they arrived at the CPR office, the pair set about negotiating for their own new company. The CPR was quite content to give the contract to them without calling for tenders, as their work in Ontario had been exemplary. The fact that Cook would not be included in the new company was explained to the CPR officials but was of no consequence to them. Soon after the contract was secured, Deeks and Hinds called a meeting with Cook to tell him the news. Cook was furious to discover that the name of the Toronto Construction Company was nowhere to be found on the Lake Shore contract.[61]

Harry McLean's youngest brother, Walter Scott McLean, joined Toronto Construction during this tumultuous period, following unswervingly in the footsteps of his big brother. The *Bismarck Tribune* praised Walter for "making good." [62] By all accounts, he was as industrious as Harry and held jobs delivering newspapers and working for the City of Bismarck while attending school [63] A. B. Cook had offered Walter a position in January 1910, but the young McLean declined, opting instead to attend the Dakota Business School.[64]

Sam Deeks and Thomas Hinds formed their new corporation, the Dominion Construction Company, on April 18, 1912.[65] They wanted to wind up the operations of Toronto Construction, and some employees, Walter included, stayed in Toronto with Dominion Construction, while others, like Harry McLean, decided to go to the United States with Cook.[66] Shortly after giving his notice, McLean spoke with Ker about Deeks, Hinds and Dominion Construction:

> Now I'm through. I won't have anything more to do with those fellows and I mean it. They're going to ask you to go down and take my place. Now, it's a good job but you'll have to use your own judgment whether you want to go with them or whether you don't want to go with them.[67]

As McLean had predicted, Deeks contacted Ker and asked him to take over McLean's position. Ker declined the offer and went with Cook and McLean to assist in constructing twenty-two miles of double track for the Chicago/Milwaukee and St. Paul line between Hopkins and Cologne in the Minneapolis vicinity. Jimmie Therrien took over Ker's responsibilities for a while, and then he too followed McLean. Cook, McLean, Ker and Therrien spent some six months constructing forty-five miles of rail for the Great Northern in Montana as well as sixty-eight miles for the Northern Pacific in North Dakota.[68]

The Cook Construction Company, incorporated on July 31, 1912, in Pierre, South Dakota, had its head office at 557 Gilfillan Building in St. Paul, Minnesota. Its inaugural directors were A. B. Cook, the lawyer L. L. Stephens and Alexander McKenzie. The shareholders were Cook with seven hundred and fifty shares, McLean with five hundred shares, McKenzie with five hundred and fifty shares, George Flannery, McKenzie's lawyer, with one hundred shares, and Gilbert W. Haggart, future North Dakotan Senator, with one hundred shares.[69]

Walter McLean received a telegram in July 1912 about the possibility of his working for Cook Construction. Although Walter wished to join the company immediately, he inquired "if there would be any chance of me getting a position in the head office, so that, I can get a line on the books; (not that I care to follow bookkeeping, but I just want to get a general idea of how to keep them, before I take up the outside work…)."[70]

It is unclear whether he was offered the inside job, but in early fall Walter came down with an acute case of typhoid pneumonia.[71] When his condition worsened Harry contacted the rest of the family, who immediately found their way to Toronto. Mary McLean rushed to her son's bedside, dismayed that the treatment he was receiving appeared futile. Clarence McLean had made it as far as Fargo when Walter succumbed to the illness and died, on October 28, 1912, at the age of twenty-two. Harry made arrangements to have his brother's body sent to St. Paul for the funeral service and for burial in the Oakland Cemetery.[72] Walter's obituary in the Bismarck newspaper stated:

> His death removes one who was fairly well started on a successful business career and all his friends regret his removal from the scene of his earthly activity. His accomplishments in the face of difficulties will be a source of inspiration to his friends and associates and his memory will be long cherished by those who knew him.[73]

Mary McLean spent the winter after Walter's death in California, enjoying the comfort of old friends:

> My trip to Catalina Island, Dec. 15th was delightful. I especially enjoyed the maine [sic] gardens and watching the beautifully colored fishes darting hither and yon among the rocks, mosses and beautifully colored

plants beneath the waters of Avalon Bay. A trip to Venice on the Ocean Beach, a summer resort, and a visit to an alligator basin concludes the sight-seeing up to date. If any of the "Hikers" want a fry, I'll send the[m] a baby alligator up.[74]

Mary arrived back in Bismarck in May 1913.

>─┤─◄▷─○─◁►─┤─◄

Cook Construction Company Limited was formed in Sudbury, Ontario, on March 25, 1913, and was awarded a contract on April 1st to build sections of double track on the CPR's Lake Superior division (Azilda-Cartier contract). The shareholders were A. B. Cook with seven hundred and forty-nine shares, Harry McLean with four hundred and ninety-nine shares, Alexander McKenzie with seven hundred and fifty shares, Mary A. Cook with one share and George Flannery with one share.[75] Ker recalled some frosty nights in the nickel belt:

> I was there from the spring of 1913 until the end of 1914 when the war came on. That was hard, tough work. I remember I had a car I slept in…they were converted box cars…the winter of 1913, the temperature got to fifty-eight below zero. The water pail in my car when it was put on the stove late at night to give us some moisture would be frozen stiff to the bottom – we'd turn it upside down – you could do that.[76]

Meanwhile A. B. Cook decided to take legal action against Deeks and Hinds. He contended that in their capacity as directors of Toronto Construction, the pair had no right to sign the Lake Shore contract for their own benefit. Further, Deeks and Hinds had passed a resolution in Cook's absence giving themselves an annual salary from May 1909 to February 1912 totalling $70,461.43, in addition to the substantial dividends they received as directors.[77] The case would remain before the courts for several years, appeal after appeal, as some judges sympathized with Deeks and Hinds and their frustration with Cook while others did not.

In July 1913 Cook Construction was awarded two sizeable contracts. The first was a $2.5-million, three-year contract with the City of Montreal to enlarge its aqueduct near the St. Lawrence River. Specifically, a dam was to be constructed so the work could be carried out in a dry environment, the canal was to be expanded, and the tail-race and forebay were to be deepened and widened.[78]

The second contract, worth $1.5 million, was with the Canadian Ministry of Railways and Canals and it involved the construction of a new railway route at the south end of Halifax and harbour improvement work as part of the updated ocean terminal project. Several contractors were engaged to perform the work. For its contract, Cook Construction formed a partnership with the Wheaton Brothers (Andrew and William) of Moncton, New Brunswick.[79]

Andrew Braid Cook circa 1915. Photographer unidentified. A. B. Cook Collection, Lot 2 B1/2.02, Montana Historical Society

Harry McLean thought highly of Andrew Wheaton and the two men worked well together.

Work started on both projects within weeks of the contracts being signed.

In October 1913 A. B. Cook moved his head office from Sudbury to Montreal. In light of the relocation to Quebec, Cook's Toronto lawyer advised him to immediately take out a business licence in Quebec or face the consequences: "If not, you are sure to get into trouble with the Québec authorities, who are very particular. There are any number of people down there, who have nothing to do but to lay an information against you, which will cost you a lot of money."[80]

But obtaining a business licence was the least of Cook's worries in Quebec. Everything had been proceeding smoothly with the aqueduct job until December 23, 1913, when some confusion over the location of the existing conduit caused Cook Construction to inadvertently sever it.[81] Ker described the misadventure:

> ...they had made offsets in the fence and sketched in the position of it and in the course of time the fence fell down and was broken up for use for firewood..., and when the Cook Construction Company was digging with a very big drag line, I don't know what the dragline's bucket would take, ten or fifteen yards, a huge thing, and it would stretch right out one hundred fifty feet or more, swinging that thing, well that dragged in too close and the conduit pipe broke.[82]

As a consequence Montreal was without water for at least ten days, including Christmas Day and New Year's Day. Montreal city workers and Cook's men scrambled to fix the conduit and restore the water supply, using a substantial amount of unbudgeted money on repairs and on hauling water to the residents. Fires broke out that could not be extinguished due to the lack of water and the City was named in a number of lawsuits.[83]

The Montreal job was not Harry McLean's prime assignment. McLean's efforts were focused on Halifax, a contract in Scranton, Pennsylvania, and the Azilda-Cartier contract in Sudbury, where Fred Ker was overseeing the work.[84] Two Halifax work crews had started at either end of the proposed route, the first at Bedford Basin and the second at the other end of the city near Point Pleasant Park. The upheaval caused by blasting, excavation, and railway and bridge construction was a part of life for Haligonians during the course of the project.[85]

In February 1914 customs officials seized a shipment of Cook Construction equipment destined for Sudbury. It consisted of seven Davenport locomotives, forty-six dump cars, three Jordan spreaders and one Marion steam shovel. The officials alleged "false invoices at undervaluations, thereby evading payment of a part of the duty properly payable thereon."[86] After several futile meetings with customs officials, Cook and McLean provided affidavit evidence of the rapid depreciation in their equipment and board of directors approval for the prices shown on the invoices.

The captive Marion steam shovel was badly needed. The heavy rock work in Halifax was causing problems for the two 100-C Bucyrus shovels,

Davenport locomotives 102 (renumbered 1300) and 107 (renumbered 1435) were seized by Canadian customs officials on the grounds that the company had understated their value to avoid paying duty; Cook Construction claimed that each locomotive was worth three thousand dollars. ANDREW MERRILEES COLLECTION, GROUP D SUB-SERIES VIII, ACCESSION 1980-149. PA 208677, LIBRARY AND ARCHIVES CANADA

HARRY FALCONER MCLEAN COLLECTION, ACCESSION 1981-064. PA 208678, LIBRARY AND ARCHIVES CANADA

which in turn were causing delays and frustrating McLean. The chains on the shovels were breaking at least three times a day, adding to a long list of recurring problems. The Bucyrus representative suggested that his company would be willing to replace the chains and pay for the repairs, but the lack of a timely response prompted McLean to complain to Cook, "The Bucyrus people have certainly given us the worst end of it this time. I think we should cut them out."[87] Several months would pass before customs released the equipment.

Between lawsuits, customs seizures and equipment malfunctions, Cook Construction had its share of aggravation, but such difficulties were commonplace for a construction company: problems arose daily and solving them was part of the job.

Perceptions about what constituted a problem changed drastically that summer. An assassination in Bosnia-Herzegovina on June 28, 1914, set off a chain of events that had worldwide, life-altering consequences:

> *Close to the crowded pavement of a street in Sarajevo, the driver stopped the car. Someone drew a revolver. A policeman on the point of grabbing him was struck in the face by a man in the crowd. Shots rang out. And the Archduke Franz Ferdinand, heir apparent to the Austro-Hungarian empire, lay murdered, killed by a Serb. It was the signal Austria-Hungary had been waiting for...*[88]

CHAPTER FOUR

Triumph and Disaster

*Then, suddenly, in August 1914, the world was plunged into the
maelstrom of war. Many of the railway men leapt to arms when the
call of the Motherland came – joined the Infantry, the Artillery, the
Engineers, – but many waited until the call came in a more intimate
way, in a manner they could not resist, for they were not men who were
trained to understand the niceties and obligations of treaties. Theirs
was a life of open toil, free from all thoughts of International
bickerings, so at first, many of them realized the tremendous issues
involved; but, when the call came for men to build railways over there in
France, they could understand that call and they freely answered it;
and, when they heard that a man whose name was known to all of
them was to take them and lead them to organize them and command
them, then they all came.[1]*

IN THE FIRST few months of World War I the German army astounded
Europe with its manoeuvrability on fronts far and wide. One significant
weapon in Germany's armoury was its railway system. The Germans
had developed a complex network of rail lines, government-owned and
strategically designed by and for the military, surpassing commercial
requirements. So cunning was their battle plan that in the months leading
up to the war the Belgians were persuaded to link to some German lines
at their own cost, unwittingly facilitating the invasion of their own
country.[2] At the onset of the war neither the British nor the French
military deemed the construction of new rail lines a priority, as they

believed that the conflict would be short-lived. Further, they reasoned that, if the first months of the hostilities were any indication, the war would be one of unprecedented mobility over vast territory and thus the rail lines already in place would suffice.[3]

By November 1914 the itinerant armies had turned sedentary and had burrowed into the ground. Frontline battles took place between opposing trenches separated by a strip of earth known as "no man's land." It seemed, then, that the railways were less important when the armies were stagnant. However, it was soon realized that these same forces required gargantuan amounts of supplies, ammunition and reinforcements. The British and French armies came to see that railways would benefit them at the front, considering the portability they afforded.[4]

The absence of Canadian Railway Troops overseas for the first several months of the war was no fault of the railway builders. Many prominent Canadian railway builders persistently advised the Militia that a battalion of skilled railway construction men should be raised in Canada and sent abroad. Starting in September 1914, John William Stewart and Angus McDonnell, both seasoned railway contractors, made continual efforts in this regard. McDonnell went to the War Office in London on Stewart's authority and of his own accord to seek permission to recruit a railway battalion.[5] The British were disinclined to accept help from the Canadians. Colonel Mance, head of the Railway Department, insisted that such skilled railwaymen "would not be possessed of sufficient versatility to undertake any but railway work" and, further, that any railway workers required could be recruited from among "the clay workers [in the] west of England."[6]

Many of Britain's railway workers had enlisted in the early days of the war. As their expertise was not immediately needed, they joined the infantry. Many died, and along with them an untold advantage.[7] In response to a request from the War Office early in 1915, the Canadian government approached Thomas G. Shaughnessy, president of the Canadian Pacific Railway, to recruit and organize experienced men to construct and repair the British railways.[8] Known as the Canadian Overseas Railway Construction Corps (CORCC), five hundred men, most of whom were CPR employees, were placed under the command of Lieutenant Colonel Colin Worthington Pope Ramsey, construction engineer for the Eastern Lines of the CPR. At the age of thirty-two, Ramsey had already spent half his life building railways in Canada and was facing the challenge of directing two companies of skilled railway construction men.[9]

Harry McLean was asked to go over to France as an "advance agent to confer with the authorities and make preliminary arrangements in connection with the Canadian Overseas Railway Construction Corps."[10] Sir Samuel Hughes, the Canadian minister of Militia and Defence, suggested to the British military that McLean investigate the condition of the railway system and then provide an assessment of how it could be improved.[11]

Lieutenant Colonel Colin Worthington Pope Ramsey. ©1915, Canadian Pacific Railway Archives, A4734

McLean arrived in London and found lodging at the Savoy Hotel, then, on April 1, 1915, went on to Paris, making his headquarters at the elegant Edouard VII Hotel, close to the Louvre and the Orsay railway station.[12] Initially, the French general staff were responsible for constructing and maintaining both French and British operation zones in France.[13]

McLean, along with many Canadian railway contractors – particularly after witnessing the conditions at the front – believed that the construction of light rail lines and the deployment of skilled railway workers were critically needed to support the troops. He reported his findings to Major General Sir John S. Cowan at the War Office in London,

Canadian Overseas Railway Construction Corps at Saint John, New Brunswick. (Original copyright D. Smith Reid, Saint John, New Brunswick. ©1915, Canadian Pacific Railway Archives, A 4337)

as well as to General Twiss, the director of rail transport in France.[14] Twiss advised McLean that a couple of Canadian railway workers might be beneficial but that the problem with constructing new lines was the chronic wartime shortage of metal. McLean told Twiss that he could provide him with plenty of metal by tearing out certain lines and sidings in Canada and shipping them overseas. Recalling the meeting decades later, McLean told a reporter:

A brigadier-general told me all he wanted from Canada was a few men with a lieutenant, or at most, a captain. Then he mentioned they could stand some metal plate and a few indigenous tools peculiar to Canadians. Imagine that! I just walked right out of the meeting. When I got back we got about four thousand men together with heavy machinery, cranes, about thirty miles of steel – everything. They'd never seen anything like it before… We walked that track right across France and slapped it over rivers. At least they called them rivers. You could jump across them.[15]

McLean was scheduled to return to North America on the *Lapland,* a ship belonging to the White Star Line, but was delayed.[16] He sailed instead from Liverpool to New York on the Cunard ship the *Lusitania* on its last uneventful voyage – as it was torpedoed and sunk on the return voyage to Liverpool.[17]

He arrived in New York City on April 24th.[18] McLean won accolades for his report and was reimbursed for his expenses. He sent the cash to the newly formed CORCC to start a canteen fund.[19]

A second request for McLean's services in France came in May 1915, shortly after his return to Canada. McLean sent word to A. B. Cook: "The Government have asked me to go to France for them – a special trip for investigation. It will take a month or six weeks. I think it policy – to go."[20]

However, lengthy bouts of illness prevented McLean from returning overseas. In France he had contracted what the doctors suspected was malaria. For several weeks he convalesced at a succession of swanky hotels, including the Greenbrier at White Sulphur Springs, West Virginia. The doctor whom McLean consulted in West Virginia told him that the sulphur in the water would be beneficial and that, in addition to malaria, he was suffering from "nervous shock brought on by too much concentration."[21] McLean warned Cook, "You better take as much outdoor exercise as possible – you would if you got the lecture I did. The little bug will get you if you don't watch out."[22]

His second recovery phase took place at the Park Hotel in Mount Clemens, Michigan. McLean wrote to Cook once again about the diagnosis of malaria, but this time added, "The Doctor says my liver is very bad."[23] Although he liked the surroundings, McLean admitted to Cook that "it *is hard* to get used to the Jews."[24] McLean's last stop on the road to recovery, before returning to Halifax, was the Hotel Pontchartrain in Detroit.[25]

Frederick Innes Ker had enlisted with the CORCC but was called back, at the request of Sir Sam Hughes, to the troubled Montreal aqueduct project, with the proviso that he was still "on call" for the army.[26] Charles W. Switzer, office manager and bookkeeper for Cook Construction, had also enlisted with the CORCC, and was "approved and inspected" by Colonel Ramsey on June 9, 1915.[27] A care package was sent for Ramsey and his men prior to their departure: six hundred and twenty five-cent cigars, two hundred cigarettes and a case of pipe tobacco, courtesy of Ker and Cook Construction.[28] Ramsey had completed recruiting and mobilization for the CORCC within three months, arriving in England on June 25th.[29]

In August 1915 Cook Construction was served with an injunction by the attorney general for Nova Scotia. It was to refrain from blasting in the city of Halifax and, specifically, to immediately desist from shooting "in such manner as to thereby cast upon the houses and buildings or upon any part of the gardens or lawns owned or occupied by the City of Halifax, any stones, pieces of rock, or other missiles or things."[30] McLean advised Cook that "the parties placing the injunction are very presistent [sic] and we are having quite a time with them. We have threatened to stop the work entirely if they insist on the injunction, which will endanger us of contempt of Court."[31] For the next few weeks

Worksite cleared for blasting, April 6, 1915. The empty dynamite boxes indicate that the blast holes are filled and ready for detonation. By August 1915 owners of property adjacent to the site had become infuriated by projectiles flying onto their property. Cook Construction was ordered to refrain from blasting near houses, buildings, gardens or lawns.
HALIFAX OCEAN TERMINAL RAILWAY: COOK CONSTRUCTION CO., LTD. & WHEATON BROS. CONTRACTORS, LOT 2, ALBUM 3, NO 62, PAGE 112, A. B. COOK COLLECTION, MONTANA HISTORICAL SOCIETY

Pile drivers, April 6, 1915. HALIFAX OCEAN TERMINAL RAILWAY: COOK CONSTRUCTION CO., LTD. & WHEATON BROS. CONTRACTORS, LOT. 2, ALBUM 3, NO. 59, PAGE 108 A. B. COOK COLLECTION, MONTANA HISTORICAL SOCIETY

McLean tried unsuccessfully to have the injunction "squashed" by the courts.[32] He continued with the blasting, in order to keep the project moving, but used lighter loads.[33]

One personality associated with Cook Construction was Carlos Warfield, a former mining magnate from Helena, Montana. Warfield became a Canadian citizen in 1911 and settled in Prescott, Ontario.[34] His formal role in the company is not clear, but on many occasions he acted as advisor and mentor to McLean. He regularly reported to Cook on his impressions of progress and of people. No one seemed to mind having him around; he was always welcomed on the job and missed when away from it. "The work at Halifax is going along in fine shape," Warfield reported to Cook. "Harry is working hard and I am doing all I can to help, he seems to want to talk matters over with me and I keep him from having the blurs."[35]

In October 1915 McLean once again fell ill. Warfield stayed with him for three weeks at the Ritz-Carlton Hotel in Montreal, hoping to see some improvement, but McLean was finally admitted to the Royal Victoria Hospital. The doctors were treating him for a bladder inflammation and were puzzled by a recurring high fever. His illness, likely a recurrence of the malaria, continued well into November.[36]

Word later came to McLean from Bismarck that his father's old business partner, Robert Macnider, had died in Salem, Oregon, on December 8, 1915. Funeral services were held at the Presbyterian Church in Bismarck.[37] McLean's uncle, Judge Samuel A. Falconer of Wilton, arrived in Bismarck to attend Macnider's funeral and to visit with Mary McLean. In a bizarre turn of events, the following week, while opening the large doors at the same church, Samuel Falconer suffered a heart attack and died in the vestibule.[38]

Eight days before Christmas 1915, Cook Construction was named the defendant in a lawsuit initiated by the City of Montreal. The dry yuletide season of 1913 had not been forgotten, nor had its perpetrators been forgiven:

> On or about the twenty-fifth of December 1913, in consequence of the gross negligence, the blunder and incapacity of the Defendant Company the said underground Conduit was broken at the place where it crosses the Verdun Asylum property about 12,300 feet from the Aqueduct Pumphouse of the Plaintiff.[39]

The City was forced to buy water from the Montreal Power and Water Company at a dollar and fifteen cents per thousand gallons, spending $25,590.34 in the process. The purchased water had to be transported to the residents by horse and cart. Men were hired to haul the casks of water and drive the horses. The delivery service cost the City another $40,101.26. A new steel underground conduit had to be put in place at a cost of $167,673.88. In addition, what was broken had to be fixed, at a cost of $179,053.67 for material and labour. The City of Montreal claimed a total of $412,481.15 from Cook Construction and jointly and severally from Cook, McLean and McKenzie, who had personally obligated themselves under the contract.[40]

In January 1916 McLean took a break from work and travelled to New York City with a side trip to the Greenbriar Hotel in West Virginia and then Washington, D.C.[41] He had decided to take out Imperial Citizenship papers to become a Canadian citizen.[42] On March 30, 1916, McLean received a telegram from Frederick L. Wanklyn, General Executive Assistant at the CPR and Honorary Lieutenant Colonel of the CORCC, asking him to recommend a commanding officer for No. 2 Construction Corps, Canadian Expeditionary Forces.[43] No. 2 Construction Corps was unique, as it would consist entirely of black soldiers – the only battalion of its kind in Canadian military history.[44]

Narrow-gauge spoil wagons, March 28, 1916. These wagons were used where larger standard-gauge equipment could not be: in confined spaces or at the commencement of work or where the standard-gauge temporary track was not practicable. Narrow-gauge track could be moved quickly and was useful in excavating rock cuts. HALIFAX OCEAN TERMINAL RAILWAY: COOK CONSTRUCTION CO., LTD. & WHEATON BROS. CONTRACTORS, LOT 2, ALBUM 3, NO. 189, PAGE 37, A. B. COOK COLLECTION, MONTANA HISTORICAL SOCIETY

Excavation work, April 17, 1916. HALIFAX OCEAN TERMINAL RAILWAY: COOK CONSTRUCTION CO., LTD. & WHEATON BROS. CONTRACTORS, LOT 2, ALBUM 3, NO. 236, PAGE 63, A. B. COOK COLLECTION, MONTANA HISTORICAL SOCIETY

At the start of World War I many black men answered the call to serve their country only to be emphatically rejected upon arriving at the recruiting stations. The prevailing attitude was that black men would not be accepted in "a white man's war," yet they persisted in their efforts to serve their country. Finally, after years of vacillation and debate between the military and Parliament, No. 2 Construction Battalion was formed as the answer to the importunate question of what to do with black volunteers.[45] Mixing white with black was to be avoided at all costs, as it was "felt that the presence of these coloured troops may cause a certain amount of trouble, especially should they have to be reinforced."[46] The raising of a labour battalion for black recruits was thought to be the ideal solution, as it would avoid the potential difficulties in having to send white reinforcements to a black battalion.[47]

McLean responded to Wanklyn's telegram by offering his assistance in organizing the Construction Corps and recommending his friend Daniel Hugh Sutherland for the position.[48] Thus on July 5, 1916, No. 2 Construction Battalion, CEF, was officially authorized and placed under Sutherland's command.[49] Headquartered at Pictou, Nova Scotia, Sutherland was slow to recruit numbers sufficient to form a battalion. The appeal for black volunteers went out to every province and some black Americans joined No. 2 Construction Battalion as well, but the numbers were still short of a full battalion.[50] Nonetheless, training got under way.

Lieutenant Colonel Daniel Hugh Sutherland, C.O., No. 2 Construction Battalion, CEF.

Courtesy of Mary Beth Sutherland and Reverend Donald Sutherland

In the meantime Angus McDonnell and John W. Stewart were still agitating for the overseas deployment of a Canadian railway construction corps. They were not to be dissuaded, meeting with seemingly every general and colonel in the British army. Authority finally came on May 1, 1916, when Stewart received a cable from Sir Sam Hughes: "Can you raise and take command of railway construction corps. Please wire reply."[51] By the end of the year there were five battalions of railway troops from Canada, in various states of readiness: Stewart's 239th Battalion (which became the Third Battalion CRT), First Construction Battalion (which became the First Battalion CRT) under the command of Lieutenant Colonel Blair Ripley – this was a general construction battalion, comprising many railway builders – and the 127th Infantry Battalion (which became the Second Battalion CRT) commanded by

Lieutenant Colonel F. F. Clarke, as well as two new battalions (Fourth and Fifth Battalions CRT) comprising men from the Canadian Training Divisions in England.[52]

During the summer of 1916 McLean's attention was diverted by the misfortunes of his parents. In June, Mary McLean and a friend, Miss Elizabeth Bayliss, visited Clarence at his home in Mandan, North Dakota, where he was general manager of the Russell-Miller Milling Company. On the drive back to Bismarck on a Sunday afternoon, Clarence drove his car onto the Bull Dog ferry to cross the Missouri River along with another carload of people. In the middle of the river the engine crank failed and the ferry was set adrift. Had the pilot acted immediately to get the ferry to shore, the passengers could have been brought to safety fairly easily. Instead, he decided to try to repair the engine. This lapse of common sense caused several hours of anxiety as the ferry was violently tossed about on the waves. When it seemed that the ferry was about to smash to smithereens, the passengers demanded that the pilot end his futile reparation attempts and that the life boat be cut loose. They made their way to shore safely and the cars were recovered the following afternoon.[53]

Late that July, McLean was in Boston at the bedside of his long-ailing father, John, who had been receiving cancer treatments in Boston and was living with his sister there. He died on July 31, 1916.[54] Alexander McKenzie made the funeral arrangements and served as a pallbearer. John's remains were returned to St. Paul and he was interred in the Oakland Cemetery there on August 5th. Mary McLean attended the service.[55] The obituary in the Bismarck newspaper describes John McLean and others like him as pioneers:

> They toiled; they endured and they suffered that others might enjoy the riches of this Western Empire which their labours and their dreams conceived.[56]

After a tumultuous few months in the upper echelons of the Canadian military, in November 1916 Sir Sam Hughes was replaced by Sir George Halsey Perley as minister of Overseas Military Forces. Hughes had made some highly questionable decisions during his tenure, the most notorious being the selection of the heavy and ever-jamming Ross rifle for use by Canadian soldiers. Managing to offend nearly everyone, from the King to the soldiers in the trenches, with his unflinching arrogance, Hughes was finally undone. He had brazenly overstepped his authority and had become insolent and irrational, leaving Prime Minister Robert Borden little choice but to demand his resignation.[57]

The news of these changes captured headlines and caused a flurry of excitement. McLean's attention, however, was focused – at least fleetingly – on his upcoming nuptials. He took the time to send six hundred boxes of cigarettes to Sutherland's men for Christmas, and in return the men collected money to buy him a wedding gift.[58] McLean married a nurse, Irene Frances Robertson, daughter of Mr. and Mrs. William Stuart Robertson of Montreal, in March 1917.[59] The newlyweds took a cruise aboard the *Bermudian* for their honeymoon, arriving in New York on April 4, 1917.[60] The new Mrs. McLean sent a note of thanks to Andrew Braid Cook and his wife for their wedding present: "I've always wished for a real Grandfather's clock and I am indeed very proud of it. The chimes are so sweet."[61]

Before leaving Canada, a company of soldiers from No. 2 Construction Battalion was called upon by the Canadian Government

Harry Falconer McLean in 1917. Photograph
by Underwood & Underwood Portrait Studios, 417
Fifth Avenue, New York. Lot 2 B5/11.09, A. B. Cook
Collection, Montana Historical Society

Railway to retrieve steel rails in New Brunswick along the Grand Trunk Railway for expedition to France in mid-February. Harsh winter conditions prevailed and progress was sluggish because the rails were buried under snow and ice.[62] On March 13, 1917, Lieutenant Colonel Sutherland appointed McLean as Honorary Lieutenant Colonel of No. 2 Construction Corps.[63] McLean kept in touch with Sutherland, sending cigars and tobacco whenever he could, asking "What is the best thing we can do for your men in the field?"[64] No. 2 Construction Corps boarded SS *Southland* bound for Liverpool, England, on March 28, 1917.[65] There had been some discussion of dividing the battalion into three labour companies to support the Canadian railway troops, but ultimately, in October 1917, Sutherland was ordered to reorganize No. 2 Construction Battalion to join the ranks of the Canadian Forestry Corps, CEF, and thus the Battalion's status was changed to Company.[66]

Building a railway could be arduous at the best of times, but construction in a war zone added a potentially deadly dimension. In addition to their daily work, the troops in the railway construction corps had to dodge bullets and shrapnel. They finally had to resort to working under the cover of darkness to make any discernable progress. Even then, unforeseen circumstances could cause difficulties for the night shift, as witnessed at the outset of the Battle of Messines (Ypres):

> At 9:30 p.m. the shelling ceased and an attempt was made at once to start work but before the party had laid down their equipment and taken up the grading tools, heavy shelling resumed. A farm building

Canadian railway troops grading for light rail, July 1917. Department of National Defence, Accession 1964-114. PA-001808, Library and Archives Canada

close at hand where ammunition was stored was hit and caught fire. The flames illuminated the entire area of the proposed operations: it was impossible to work as the parties were exposed to enemy machine gun fire from the positions overlooking this sector. However, despite all difficulties, 200 feet of grading, 400 feet of fill and a 20 ft. culvert were completed by 2 a.m.[67]

...It must be remembered that our men were worked day and night in the vilest weather; with few, if any, facilities for drying wet clothes; scarcely ever relieved; always under high explosive, shrapnel and gas shell fire on the grade by day and in their camps at night. His fire was well sustained and well directed. Nothing but the greatest physical and moral stamina could endure such hardships and face such conditions for weeks on end without flinching. Even the fighting troops in the line had their regular reliefs but the construction troops at the first had no reliefs.[68]

Canadian railway troops building light railway near firing line, September 1917.
DEPARTMENT OF NATIONAL DEFENCE, ACCESSION 1964-114. PA-001799, LIBRARY AND ARCHIVES CANADA

In July 1917 McLean approached Cook about the possibility of obtaining lucrative contracts with the U.S. government for the construction of camps to house troops: "These contracts are being done on a Force Account basis; the Government paying the Contractor for everything, even rental on his typewriter and his office and travelling expenses. Some of these contracts have amounted to Four Million Dollars. I think we should do everything we can to get one."[69] McLean was also looking into a possible contract in Saint John, New Brunswick, to construct a breakwater, as well as the prospect of stripping coal at Minto, New Brunswick, although neither of these possibilities came to fruition.[70]

On December 6, 1917, McLean was having breakfast with W. A. Duff, chief engineer of Canadian Government Railway, at the Queen Hotel in Halifax.[71] Shortly after nine o'clock they found themselves in the midst of tremendous devastation, caused by the collision of *Mont Blanc*, an explosives-laden French ship, and *Imo*, a Belgian relief vessel – an event now known as the Halifax Explosion. An estimated sixteen hundred people were killed instantly and nine thousand others injured, some wounded by flying fragments of searing metal or blinded by shards of shattered glass. Many, having survived the blast, burned to death as fires from upended woodstoves ravaged the wreckage. Some people believed they were under attack by the Germans.[72]

McLean quickly gathered his wits and put himself and his men to work. Knowing their mother would be beside herself with worry, Harry and William wired a message to Bismarck to say that they were both unharmed.[73] The Montreal *Standard* published an account of McLean's contribution in Halifax: "He set up his headquarters in an old car barn and promptly put his machines to the business of relieving the suffering; but, first on the list was the organizing of communication and

Damage caused by the Halifax Explosion in the North End of the city, near the reservoir, December 6, 1917.

transportation."[74] He took care of traffic into Halifax from Fairview, directing and re-routing as required and ensuring that relief efforts could reach those in need.[75]

Complicating matters, the next day a severe blizzard further crippled the city and hampered relief efforts.[76] Temporary train sheds were erected by McLean's men at the projected location of the new South End Terminals as the North Street Railway Station, once an impressive building, had been destroyed, along with the lines leading to it. Railway crews worked non-stop on the line in order to bring relief trains sufficiently close to the devastated area.[77] When Prime Minister Borden visited Halifax, McLean provided him with transportation, as acknowledged in a note of thanks from Borden dated December 12, 1917:

> Will you permit me to send my very warm thanks for your kindness and attention on my arrival at Halifax during my visit? The car, which you placed at my disposal, was of invaluable service and it enabled me to accomplish a much greater amount of work than would otherwise have been possible.
>
> I hope that the organization of the relief committees is proceeding satisfactorily and that comfort and support are being effectively extended to all those who have suffered from this most disastrous calamity.[78]

McLean rented a hall and bought every cake and cookie he could find to entertain the orphaned children of Halifax at a Christmas party.[79] He worked at a frenetic pace for weeks, then simply collapsed one day and ended up in hospital with a severe case of pneumonia. In March 1918 he went with his wife to New York City for an extended convalescence, where they were joined by Mary McLean for a visit.[80] He recovered in time to win Cook Construction a contract for the rebuilding of the ocean terminals at Halifax.[81]

In December 1917 Cook Construction was served with an interim injunction brought by the Citizens' Association of Montreal, restraining the City of Montreal as defendant and Cook Construction as mise-en-cause from proceeding with the cancellation of the aqueduct contract and with the arbitration of their claims. The grounds for the injunction were that the Montreal Board of Control did not have the power to annul the contract without first consulting City Council and, furthermore, that it was illegal to proceed with the arbitration because no funds had been set aside by City Council and the city comptroller had not sent a certificate to the Board of Control. Finally, the Citizens' Association asserted that Cook Construction was exerting "undue pressure" on the Board of Control for cancellation of the contract and arbitration and that this was "an act of maladministration and detrimental to the best interests of the City and the taxpayers."[82] Cook Construction responded that the first two points were questions of law but that it took exception to the third:

Mary McLean. Courtesy of Ken Pettitt

> For almost five years the Cook Construction Company has been tied down with an undertaking which it contracted to finish in three and could have finished in less than three years, had its work not been inter ferred [sic] with and delayed in every conceivable way... For a large organization and equipment to the value of almost One Million Dollars, cannot have idleness imposed upon it, as ours has, without suffering heavy damages...we must have some rights in the matter, and if after having been held up for nearly five years...we can hardly with fairness be accused of having used undue pressure upon the Board of Control.[83]

Most of the members of the Citizens' Association were unaware that their names were being used by a select few to serve their own agendas. Ker contacted the Association's lawyers and told them he was going to "rent a vacant movie theatre on St. Catherine St...and show pictures of the property owned by some of them which would have to be bought by the city as part of the aqueduct scheme."[84] The injunction was withdrawn.

McLean received several thank you letters from Corporal Hugh Gray, Commander of No. 4 Section, 13 Platoon, of 236 Overseas Battalion, a section for which McLean had received an honorary appointment. It was known thereafter as the Harry F. McLean Section in honour of its generous subscriber, for McLean had sent gifts of money and outfitted the entire platoon in full Scottish regalia. Corporal Gray promised to write McLean as often as he could to keep him apprised of their movements, but warned that "owing to the U. boats we cannot tell what becomes of our mail."[85] Twenty-two days before the end of the war Corporal Gray was killed in action. He lies buried in Auberchicourt British Cemetery in France.[86]

Cook's lawsuit against his former partners Sam Deeks and Thomas Hinds finally came to a conclusion. McLean was called upon to testify and garnered a mention in case law: "Another phase of evidence somewhat pressed during the trial related to the work and remuneration of one McLean, who acted throughout the period in question as a superintendent and commissary man. McLean appears to have been a clever, active and loyal employee of the company."[87] Deeks and Hinds had achieved some success initially, only to have the Privy Council overturn the judgement in Cook's favour: "While entrusted with the conduct of the affairs of the company they deliberately designed to exclude, and used their influence and position to exclude, the company whose interest it was their first duty to protect."[88] This ruling was reaffirmed by the Ontario Supreme Court on March 1, 1918. Deeks and Hinds were ordered to repay the salary they gave themselves, plus court costs.[89] Thomas Hinds had died earlier that year. On November 28, 1918, Cook was paid $112,500 by Deeks and the Hinds estate and the matter was put to rest.[90] The charter of the Toronto Construction Company was surrendered on March 3, 1919.[91]

In stark contrast to the horrors of war and the protracted lawsuits, Mary McLean was bonding nicely with her daughter-in-law. In April 1919 the Bismarck newspaper reported that the "Charming Event of the Week

Irene McLean in an undated photograph.
HARRY FALCONER MCLEAN COLLECTION, ACCESSION 1981-
064. PA 207739, LIBRARY AND ARCHIVES CANADA

Is the Reception Given by Mrs. Mary McLean." The object of the lavish welcome was Harry's wife, Irene. The rooms of Mother McLean's home were awash in pink decorations and carnations for the occasion. The only fissure in the sea of pink was a basket of sweet green peas on the serving table. While the ladies were entertained with music between three and six in the afternoon, tea was poured and "dainty refreshments" served until half-past four.[92] William McLean was also in the neighbourhood that day, but chose instead to visit his brother Clarence in less enchanting surroundings.[93]

By the summer of 1919 a decision had been made to sell the equipment of Cook Construction and to wind down operations in both Canada and the United States. The first sign of growing animosity between Cook and McLean is evident in correspondence after Cook insisted he be consulted on the pricing of machinery. McLean was offended and assured him that the prices had not been adjusted from those Cook had already agreed to, tersely stating, "If you do not refer to the past and refer to the future only, I would like to have a meeting of the Company called at once and this question reopened."[94]

Although much of the legal morass had been straightened up by then, the company did not rebound. The City of Montreal was sued for fire damage that occurred during the conduit incident, and as a result there remained outstanding several warranty cases involving Cook Construction. With the decline of the company assured, Fred Ker tendered his resignation to A. B. Cook in August 1919. Ker had accepted an offer from Sir George Bury, formerly general manager and executive vice-president of the CPR, to manage the Whalen Pulp and Paper Works at Port Alice on Vancouver Island.[95]

> The decision is out and while we have been awarded $308,000 I feel that we have been very badly used. We lost the conduit case and have been assessed some $82,000 in this connection besides about $50,000 on the City's counter claim.
>
> I'm awfully sorry things are turning out the way they are with the Company. I was very proud of it and we could have become very powerful here in Canada. I would like to think that the present pause in its progress would soon be over and that perhaps some day we will resume again even bigger and stronger than we have ever been.[96]

Ker's wish for a resurrected Cook Construction Company was never fulfilled, nor was his desire to work for the railway. Ker married Amy Southam, daughter of F. N. Southam of the newspaper chain.[97] Induced by his father-in-law, Ker became a journalist and eventually editor of the Hamilton *Spectator*.

> *In 1905 I had definitely set my heart on being a railway general manager. Instead I had to become a publisher, editor and President of the Canadian Press. You can never tell. Homme propose, Dieu Dispose.*[98]

CHAPTER FIVE

The Gear Engages

Grenville Crushed Rock Company, Deeks Quarry (1921–1935)

It is their care in all the ages to take the buffet and cushion the shock.
It is their care that the gear engages; it is their care that the switches lock.
It is their care that the wheels run truly; it is their care to embark and entrain,
Tally, transport, and deliver duly the Sons of Mary by land and main.[1]

We build your roads
We build your bridges
We dig your ditches
You Sons of Bitches[2]

FRED KER WAS not the only man considering future career opportunities in the summer of 1919. After three weeks of fishing in Bathurst, New Brunswick, and a side trip to his newly acquired oil property in Texas, Harry McLean met his old boss, Sam Deeks, in September in Toronto. Their happy reunion did not go unnoticed by A. B. Cook or Alexander McKenzie.[3] The decline of Cook Construction was accompanied by the loss of McLean's loyalty to Cook and Cook's tolerance for McLean.

The Toronto Construction Company's successor, the Dominion Construction Company, had prospered during the years when McLean was with Cook Construction. The work done by Dominion Construction consisted largely of railway building for Canadian Pacific in Ontario: the Campbellford, Lake Ontario and Weston line (CLO&W) between Glen Tay and Agincourt, a cut-off between Hamilton and Guelph Junction, and considerable double-track work between Sudbury and Port Arthur. Dominion Construction obtained contracts from the Canadian Northern Railway for track filling during World War I, as well as from the Goodyear Tire and Rubber Company to construct a plant at New Toronto. Dominion incorporated a subsidiary in Niles, Michigan, in 1918 and was awarded several substantial contracts by the Michigan Central Railroad, including one for the construction of a large marshalling yard in Niles.[4]

Railway construction was indeed the foundation of Dominion Construction. Over the subgrade, a railway has three elements: ties, rails and ballast. The ties, typically made of wood, support the steel rails. Beneath the ties is a thick bed of ballast that provides drainage, support for the ties and an even surface for the track. Railway companies in the United States and Canada used a variety of materials for ballast, including brick clay, furnace slag, cinders from coal-fired locomotives, and a combination of earth and sand. This last permutation was the least suitable; the earth frequently washed away when it rained and during the warmer months wafted around in thick clouds of dust as the train passed over it, causing coughing fits among the passengers. After much experimentation, it was determined that crushed rock was the preferred material for ballast.[5]

The CPR embraced the use of crushed rock and opened a few of its own quarries after World War I, intending to exchange the old ballast for crushed rock and carry out much-needed maintenance on lines that had been neglected during wartime. However, the CPR soon decided that it did not wish to be in the rock-crushing business and chose to subcontract the quarrying operations as well as the placement of the ballast.[6]

Colonel Colin W. P. Ramsey returned to Canada after the war, seeking work as a contractor. He approached several railway contractors with a view to forming a partnership, and ultimately selected Sam Deeks and

Dominion Construction. The new partnership was formed in 1920, and Dominion Construction was next awarded a contract for crushed rock ballast by the CPR for its eastern lines. R. C. Huffman, a master organizer and experienced railway contractor, was in charge of getting the work under way.[7] Roughly a hundred acres of land was purchased for the purpose of opening a rock quarry. Known locally as "The Rock Cut," the limestone-laden property is located in the Township of North Grenville near the farming community of Newmanville, not far from Merrickville, Ontario.[8] McLean named the railway flag stop and quarry after Sam Deeks.[9]

Building and equipping a large rock-crushing plant proved to be an expensive undertaking. It took months before the rock plant was operational, leaving a gap before revenue began to flow in. The partners had to pay a considerable amount of money up front. Once it was determined that the rock-crushing equipment would require modification and the further expenditure of capital, Colonel Ramsey decided it was more than he cared to carry. After a year in the business, he sold his interest to McLean. Thus Harry McLean and Sam Deeks were working together once again.[10]

With the change at the helm, a new firm, Grenville Crushed Rock Company Limited, was founded on January 5, 1921, with Dominion Construction and Harry McLean as the principal shareholders. Grenville was the first of several McLean companies.[11] Although it did not usually operate during the winter months, it became a profitable cornerstone for McLean's construction empire as well as a fallback employer for his best men between contracts.[12]

Grenville's head office was established at Smiths Falls, Ontario, with a branch office at 1001 McGill Building in Montreal. Harry McLean was president, Colin Ramsey secretary and Andrew Wheaton treasurer, with the directorship comprising Deeks, McLean, Ramsey, Wheaton and R. C. Huffman. Huffman left the organization shortly after it became operational. J. Paul Bains was the first superintendent of Deeks Quarry, working there from 1921 to 1928.[13]

In the Montreal office, wielding a long cigarette holder and exerting steely control, was Miss L. B. Abbott, the secretary for Grenville Crushed

Deeks flag station, located at Mile 109 of the CPR double line, Winchester subdivision. Harold Bolton, who lived near Deeks all his life, said that originally a station was to be built closer to Burritt's Rapids but that plans changed and a flag station was built at Deeks. "Anyone wanting to board a train was supposed to wave the flag to stop the oncoming train," he said, "but very seldom was the flag ever there so your arm served the purpose." The locals went to Merrickville or Smiths Falls to shop, "up on the noon and back on the five o'clock." Andrew Merrilees Collection, Group D Sub-series VI, Accession 1980-149. PA 211327, Library and Archives Canada. Caption courtesy of Colin Churcher

Rock. Described as a "tiger," Abbott was known for her ability to get things done. She kept a tight rein on McLean, his schedule and the company finances. She was a hardnosed bookkeeper and not the least bit intimidated by her boss. If he wanted a cheque for something she deemed frivolous, "she'd tell him to go to hell, she wouldn't write a cheque for that." McLean told a friend he believed Abbott had no blood in her veins, only ice water.[14]

>─┼─◆〉─●─〈◆─┼─◄

Barely treading water in a sea of bureaucracy, McLean spent much of the summer and fall of 1921 on Parliament Hill in Ottawa on behalf of Cook Construction. The Canadian economy was still in a postwar slump and extracting money from the government for outstanding claims was next to impossible. Settling the Halifax and South River Bridge claims was problematical to begin with, considering the confusion over which department (Railways, Finance or Justice) should handle the claims; then there was the haggling over contract clauses, an impending federal election followed by inevitable changes in the civil service, and the death of a key negotiator. McLean sent Cook many apologetic letters punctuated by excuses:

> I am very sorry we have not made further progress but everybody in this country is on pins and needles and the conditions of the country and all business in it are very bad. I listened to a debate for two days over an expenditure of some $25,000 by the Dominion Government and in the end it was thrown out. Therefore, this is a story without words. But I feel confident that we will get this through some time.[15]

Whenever practical, McLean and Wheaton bought Cook Construction equipment or took over leases to augment their own new business ventures.[16] Efforts to wind up the Canadian and American operations of Cook Construction continued. Relations between McLean and Cook became increasingly strained, as the sorting out of financial matters on both sides of the border was taking longer than either would have liked. Absent throughout the turmoil of wrapping up affairs was the third partner, Alexander McKenzie. He had been out of touch with his partners for the better part of a year and was thought to be somewhere in California.[17]

Concerning the American receivables, McLean implored Cook, "Cannot some effort be made to collect some money on these accounts. Personally I am very short of money and need it very badly at present and there seems to be no reason why these accounts should not be paid. Some of them are long overdue."[18]

Settlement of the largest claim owing to the St. Paul office of Cook Construction was held up because the defendant's two sons had been injured on jobs for the company and a countersuit was threatened.[19] The last of the smaller claims in Canada, the De Santis case, was settled in December 1921. De Santis, a subcontractor, had sued Cook Construction in 1915, claiming over-charge against his account. Several lawyers were of the opinion that the case had no merit. The case was left unsettled for several years due to the fact that McLean believed the plaintiff was undeserving. McLean decided to settle because the procedure of securing witnesses and preparing for trial several times a year had become annoying. The initial claim of $54,669.65 was finally settled for $1,500.[20]

McLean regularly sent Cook dispiriting updates:

> Things are pretty bad at Ottawa. The Government have scarcely a majority and the farmers of the West are causing them a great deal of trouble. The Budget was brought down the other day and they are spending days and days fighting over items of $5000 and $6000... I would not be surprised to see the Government defeated at any time.[21]

The Liberal William Lyon MacKenzie King was prime minister, leading Canada's first-ever minority government after defeating the Conservative Arthur Meighen and the Progressive Thomas Crerar in the 1921 election. McLean continued his weekly forays into the Ottawa bureaucracy: "I have been over to Ottawa so many times that I feel like a Wandering Jew every time I go into the town but I still think our bill will be paid and I have not let up in any way."[22]

While driving around the countryside near Deeks Quarry, McLean passed through the village of Merrickville. A flourishing industrial town in the 1860s, Merrickville was the site of many impressive homes built by prosperous businessmen. However, business there had declined when the neighbouring town of Smiths Falls was chosen as a division point on the CPR's eastern division. Merrickville's historic character was preserved, nonetheless, as there was little money available to modernize it.[23] In 1922 McLean bought a large stone house at the south end of the village,[24] a dwelling built circa 1845 by Aaron Merrick, the son of the community's founder.[25] McLean named his new residence Kinlochaline, after a Scottish castle.[26]

>—⊷—○—⊶—<

After a two-day illness, Alexander McKenzie died on June 22, 1922, in St. Paul. A. B. Cook and Harry McLean were honorary pallbearers at his funeral[27] and the *Bismarck Tribune* commented: "No man was more genial to meet. He understood men and in the game of politics no one knew the moves better and he played it on a grand and not a petty scale."[28] "Alex McKenzie was generosity itself," Mary McLean told the *Tribune*. "While he was a self made man himself, he never forgot the poor people. He pensioned a number of old folks in Bismarck. Alex McKenzie may have had some enemies, but he had a host of loyal friends who will never forget him."[29] The comments of another Bismarck resident were barbed:

Alexander McKenzie standing outside the McKenzie Hotel, Bismarck, North Dakota.

> Alexander McKenzie controlled the politics of Bismarck, Burleigh County and the State of North Dakota. It is a matter of history that he had been instrumental in the location of the Capital at Bismarck, and particularly following the division of the territory into

North and South Dakota – and he never failed to remind us of the fact. He was very difficult to work with, for if he did not generate a project he was indifferent to it, unless somewhere along the line there were contracts to be let, such as the paving of Bismarck streets or building the Memorial Bridge. He was an extremely brilliant and resourceful man, but he used these faculties for the good of North Dakota and Bismarck only when he saw a "pot of gold" available for himself.[30]

But the *Tribune* remained an adamant defender of McKenzie:

The popular conception of Alexander McKenzie was wrong. Those who did not share his confidence pictured him much in the same light as a Tammany boss working on the whims and prejudices of men to gain certain selfish ends... He never sought to secure the passage of laws prejudicial to North Dakota... Nothing but success interested him, but when the political scales went against him at times as they did, he was a good loser and began building his fences for the next battle.[31]

Even after his death, Alexander McKenzie remained a controversial figure. Harry McLean, among many others – including McKenzie's two eldest children – were shocked to learn of McKenzie's second marriage, which did not come to light until his will was read. McKenzie and his first wife had three children, two daughters and a son (the son had predeceased him). Three years after his first marriage ended in divorce, McKenzie married again but kept the union a secret. He and his second wife had three children. The second family resided in New York and McKenzie visited them there at regular intervals, but for all intents and purposes he lived in the Midwest. Just two days before his own death, McKenzie received word, via a telegram, that his second wife had died. The terms of his will and the existence of the second family became known shortly after his passing. McKenzie's will specified that the three children from his second marriage would each receive fifty thousand dollars, while the two children from his first marriage would share the remainder of the estate of more than half a million. Naturally, the second set of children contested the will.[32] Many other claims on the estate followed, including one from McLean for reimbursement of his expenses while pursuing the Halifax claim:

Since you and the McKenzie estate will participate in any award that may be given by the Government, I think it no more than right that I receive a letter from you and the Executor of the McKenzie Estate to the effect that I shall be reimbursed for what money I may spend to fight the case and secure the award.

This is worrying me a good deal at the present time and I shall appreciate an early reply to this letter.[33]

Six weeks later came a terse reply from A. B. Cook:

Regarding the Halifax case you ask for a letter from me that you shall be reimbursed for what money you spend to fight the case & secure the award. You know my attitude & the stand I took the last time You McKenzie & I talked this matter over. I have not changed my mind. I have not felt that you handled this case right – told you in the start – but you could not see it my way.

You then make a deal with an atty [attorney] in Ottawa on a contingent fee – before he has done anything you pay him his fee – when I find out & ask about it you say [if he] doesn't win the case he will return the fee – no I will not agree to pay any expense.[34]

Cook told McLean that he would travel to Canada himself to settle the outstanding claim.[35] The testy exchange between McLean and Cook brought about a meeting of Cook Construction shareholders on January 10, 1923, to close the books and dissolve the company, as well as the partnership of Cook Construction and Wheaton.[36] Regarding the Halifax claim, Cook had confided that "McLean was more than liberal in his settlement with Duff after conceding everything that was asked."[37]

Relations between the two men had soured to the point where they were barely on speaking terms. Charles B. Foster, son-in-law of Alexander McKenzie and General Passenger Traffic Manager for the CPR, and George B. Flannery, McKenzie's lawyer and a former Bismarck resident then living in Minneapolis, served as representatives of McKenzie's estate and also relayed messages between Cook and McLean, thus sparing the two men the unpleasantness of communicating directly with each other.

Adding fuel to the volatile situation was a mystery regarding three purchases of Victory Bonds. Cook could not recall having purchased three bonds for fifty thousand dollars each and grumbled to Foster, "I think if you can get McLean to settle down, he can easily trace this transaction."[38] Two days later the bank manager solved the bond riddle: Cook's share of the bonds (thirty-seven thousand dollars) had been hand-delivered to him at the Ritz-Carlton Hotel in Montreal but the conveyance had slipped his mind.[39]

Frequently, when frustration levels rose over unsettled accounts, either Foster or Flannery would receive gruff letters asking them to intervene: "I think it about time Mr. McLean made a settlement for the amount collected for the Cook Construction Co. Ltd and Wheaton, in settlement of the last claim against the Government. Any suggestions from me seems to anger him."[40]

The one person who might have been able to salvage the relationship between the two men passed away: Carlos Warfield died on February 17, 1923.[41] Then Andrew Wheaton stepped into the role as mediator on McLean's behalf. Gradually the remaining matters regarding Cook Construction were resolved: all claims against the government were settled, bank accounts closed and various assets assigned. The deluge of correspondence dwindled to a trickle and then, by the end of 1924, to nothing.

>─┼─◆>─O─<◆─┼─<

In the postwar years Dominion Construction secured several contracts in the Hamilton area for the Toronto, Hamilton and Buffalo Railway, projects that kept the firm occupied for some time. Much of the work was maintenance: grade separation, pile driving and grading, as well as rearranging the tracks at the Hamilton yard. The company also had the good fortune of a contract extension when Goodyear Rubber decided to further enlarge a plant expansion. The Niles division of the company, Dominion Incorporated, secured a contract in 1923 with Illinois Central for a section known as the Edgewood cut-off through Illinois and Kentucky. This work continued for several years.[42]

In February 1924 McLean and his wife left New York City on board the *Empress of Scotland* bound for Havana, Cuba, on a month-long cruise. They spent several weeks touring the Caribbean, stopping in Jamaica, and then visited one of McLean's old classmates, Dr. William Braithwaite, at the Panama Canal. Braithwaite's father was a steamboat captain. They also paid a visit to McLean's cousin, Harriet Falconer Day, another resident of the Canal Zone.[43] Harry and Irene McLean arrived back in New York City on March 23rd and then returned to Merrickville.[44]

McLean began preparations to re-open Deeks Quarry for another season of rock crushing. He also took over an uncompleted contract on the Nipissing Central Railway between Swastika and Larder Lake in Ontario, where there were several mining areas under development and a need for new rail lines to transport the resulting freight to and from the mines.[45]

Ontario Premier Ernest Charles Drury, head of the United Farmers of Ontario, and George Lee, chairman of the Temiskaming and Northern Ontario Railway (T&NO), announced on April 13, 1923, that tenders would be called for a railway line between Swastika and Kirkland Lake. Management of the railway construction was the responsibility of the government-appointed T&NO Commission. The railway would be built as the Nipissing Central Railway (NCR), as the holder of this federal charter could enter the province of Quebec "and proceed over to the Rouyn region, if further developments warrant it."[46] The T&NO had purchased the NCR in 1911 and integrated the operation under its authority.[47] Some initial findings at Rouyn indicated great potential for mining. Although McLean submitted a bid, he lost out to the Sinclair brothers of Kirkland Lake. The Sinclair Company worked on the line for over a year but lacked sufficient capital to complete the job.[48]

Ontario had a new Conservative premier, Drury having gone down to defeat in the 1923 election. George Howard Ferguson, a native of Kemptville, Ontario, had earned a law degree at the University of Toronto and returned to Kemptville to practise. In 1905 he entered the political arena and was elected as the Member of Provincial Parliament for Grenville County.[49] The Grenville Crushed Rock Company at Deeks Quarry was located in his riding, and McLean, as a constituent, nurtured a friendship with Ferguson that would facilitate his preferential treatment on more than one occasion.[50] A new company, H. F. McLean Limited, incorporated by Harry McLean on May 26, 1924, was called upon, as runner up, to finish the line to Larder Lake.[51]

The subsequent discovery of gold and copper by Noranda Mines in Rouyn Township, and a rumour that the CPR would be extending a line from Angliers, Quebec, to service the mining operations, caused much consternation amongst the T&NO commissioners. Their concern was that ready access to Rouyn by Montreal capitalists would challenge Toronto's mining superiority. In February 1925 Noranda Mines approached the Ferguson government with a proposal: if Ontario would agree to extend the NCR from Larder Lake to Rouyn, Noranda Mines would build a smelter. The proposal quickly evolved from an undertaking by Noranda to one by George Lee, who calculated the potential revenue and was convinced the line would be profitable. Lee furtively contacted McLean, who had just completed the Larder Lake line, with "an interesting proposition."[52] The deal was that McLean would bring all of his supplies and begin his usual preparations for the construction of the eastward line from Larder Lake. Tenders would not be called for immediately, but if the line was completed to Rouyn they might be called for at that juncture. In this way, the commissioners believed, McLean would be in a good position to move quickly and quietly should he win the tender, and should he not be the successful bidder he would be paid for work already done.[53]

It appeared that the planned NCR route through Ontario was the most viable, for three reasons: the Noranda group preferred this route, the plans and the contractor were ready, and ninety percent of the claims in the Rouyn area were Ontario-based. Another railway, the Canadian National (CNR), and the Quebec government had Quebec's interests – and those of its businessmen – in mind and strongly opposed Lee's plan. The president of the CNR, Sir Henry Thornton, countered with alternative plans for a Quebec-based railway to Rouyn from Quebec City, using parts of the National Transcontinental (NTR) and an altogether different location for Noranda's smelter. The Quebec premier, Alexandre Taschereau, supported the CNR, and the battle to reach Rouyn commenced.[54]

In March 1925 Ferguson directed Lee and the T&NO Commission to "resume work in extension of Larder Lake Branch and push construction with all the men and plant necessary to complete work at earliest possible date – Please instruct contractors at once to put on the largest possible number of men that can be economically used to insure expedition."[55] A call for tenders was issued, but McLean, as usual, was already on the job and one step ahead.

In the meantime, the feud between Ontario and Quebec was being fought on many fronts. Relying on its federal charter, the NCR had the right to acquire Crown lands in Ontario and Quebec for the purposes of building the railway. The procedure for obtaining an order-in-council regarding the use of these lands for right-of-way was commenced by the NCR, although Quebec was vehemently against the granting of the land in that province. Ferguson contacted Prime Minister King in an effort to hasten the granting of the order-in-council. King was well aware of the dispute between the provinces but was struggling with a minority government. He wanted desperately to avoid entering the fray for fear of risking support in either Quebec or Ontario and referred the matter to the Supreme Court of Canada.[56]

In June of 1925 the T&NO Commission decided that McLean's crews would grade the line as far as the Quebec border and that his involvement in the project would end there. The remainder of the work, consisting of laying the track and ballast, would be carried out by the T&NO by early September. For the next two and a half years the dispute raged on while the railway sat idle at the Quebec–Ontario border. In the end, the Supreme Court volleyed the matter back to the government. Quebec appealed the decision to the Judicial Committee of the Privy Council in Britain, which in turn upheld the Supreme Court decision and sent the matter back to Ottawa for resolution. While the issues were entangled in the federal bureaucracy, the Quebec government and the CNR built the Rouyn Mines Railway. Eventually the Quebec premier relented on his stance against the NCR, considering that the province had its railway to Rouyn, and allowed the completion of the line from Larder Lake in November 1927.[57]

Closer to home, McLean's Grenville Crushed Rock operations had increased substantially. An abundance of giant, noisy machines – with ropes, pulleys and cranks – clattered and crashed throughout the day. Equipment breakdowns necessitated the fashioning of many onsite repair shops – machine, boiler, welding and forging facilities – to keep things

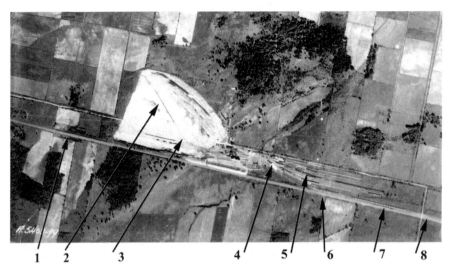

1. CANADIAN PACIFIC RAILWAY, WINCHESTER SUBDIVISION, MAINLINE TOWARDS MERRICKVILLE AND SMITHS FALLS.
2. STONE QUARRY.
3. BALLAST CRUSHING.
4. MACHINE SHOP.
5. STORAGE SIDINGS.
6. DEEKS FLAG STATION.
7. TRAINS OF BALLAST CARS STANDING BY THE MAINLINE WAITING TO BE PICKED UP BY CANADIAN PACIFIC FOR BALLASTING.
8. CPR MAINLINE TOWARDS BEDELL, WINCHESTER AND MONTREAL.

Aerial view of Deeks Quarry, 1936. A5403-99, AT 1:15 SCALE. NATIONAL AIR PHOTO LIBRARY. ANNOTATED BY COLIN CHURCHER.

moving. The 1926 season was the most productive, with 2.7 million tons of crushed rock being processed that year. Many spur lines ran into the quarry, and small locomotives hauled rocks of various sizes to and from the steam-powered plant.[58]

The production of rock ballast was initiated by the resident engineer, who set out a drilling pattern eight feet on centres for the blast holes. The drill operator followed, using a half-ton drill to make blast holes large enough to allow large sticks of dynamite to be slipped through the sandstone. The dynamite was placed in the holes and covered with sand. Embedded in each stick were a wire and a dynamite cap in the explosive. Once approximately thirty holes were filled, the charge would be detonated, the resultant blast shaking the earth for miles around. The largest explosion on record at Deeks Quarry was set off with two tons of dynamite.[59]

Saddletank locomotive No. 44450, built by the American Locomotive Company (Alco).
ANDREW MERRILEES COLLECTION, GROUP D SUB-SERIES VI, ACCESSION 1980-149. PA 208171 LIBRARY AND
ARCHIVES CANADA

The rock was then hauled to the crushing plant for processing. The shovel operators ran steam shovels to load rock onto three cars hauled by a narrow-gauge saddletank locomotive. Fully loaded, the saddletanks could carry about four scoops to the crushing plant. The cars were uncoupled and a dinkey engine picked each of them up separately to take their loads and dump them into the crusher. As each car was emptied, it was hooked up to the locomotive again and the whole process would be repeated until the shift came to an end.[60]

The workers then graded the rocks using vibrating screens to separate the various sizes. The optimum diameter for railway ballast was one and a half inches. The finished product was placed in railway cars and hauled by full-sized locomotives to the interchange siding with the CPR. Each car carried approximately sixty-five tons of rock, which was dumped onto the tracks where required for ballast. The men from Dominion Construction took care of the ballasting part of the operation.[61]

"Rock crushing was a rough operation," according to Earl Sears, a mechanic at the Quarry.[62]

Grenville Crushed Rock air dump car No. 106 was used to carry ballast and fill material from the quarry to the point of use on the railway. The cylinder on the side of the car, between the two trucks (where the number 106 is visible), would then be activated to tip the body of the car to one side or the other for quick unloading. ANDREW MERRILEES COLLECTION, GROUP D SUB-SERIES VI, ACCESSION 1980-149. PA 205862, LIBRARY AND ARCHIVES CANADA

Working around heavy machinery and explosives was undoubtedly dangerous. Injury and death occurred, despite the best efforts to make the job site safe. As a tribute to workers who were injured or killed on the job, McLean directed that a monument be built. Using stone from the quarry, a cairn was constructed and four bronze plates, each bearing stanzas of Rudyard Kipling's poem "The Sons of Martha," were cast in the shop. The largest plaque, with the words "In loving memory of those who worked and died here"[63] was placed on the front of the cairn.

Even though the work could be hazardous, the men were glad to have it. In addition to the job security Grenville Crushed Rock provided to long-time Dominion Construction employees like Charles Switzer, Grenville employed numerous local people. Among the many who had jobs there were Walter Copping, Billy Mews, Zach Bolton, Don Dougall, Earl Sears, Sammy and Willie Dillabough, and several members of the Evans family. The men earned from four dollars and eighty cents to five dollars for a twelve-hour workday starting at seven in the morning.[64]

A long-time local resident, Joe Kelso, recalled going to Deeks as a young boy for food and entertainment:

> They used to have picture shows there twice a week at the quarry. Some used to come from Kemptville and we'd sit on these big benches till ten o'clock at night and fight mosquitoes. Nobody was refused. There were lots of hoboes on the railroad. They always stopped at the quarry for a good meal... You could eat there. If you wanted to eat six pies for dinner you could do it. Fried eggs for breakfast – you could eat whatever you wanted. I can still remember the blueberry pie.[65]

Catching a glimpse of Harry McLean was a memorable event, especially if he was with his wife. Harold Bolton, son of the Grenville Crushed Rock employee Zach Bolton, saw the couple riding down the Scotch Line on horseback and was struck by the sight.[66] At six foot four, McLean usually stood head and shoulders above everyone around him, and when he was in the neighbourhood everyone stopped and took notice:

> [We'd be] milking cows here. It was quiet and you could hear the big Packard come putting along. We'd be milking between five and six in the morning, and he'd go by about three miles an hour. He'd be driving with that big car, just crawling along, and if he saw a coon or a porcupine or something, that made his day. That was the type of man he was. Morning after morning he'd come down the Scotch Line with that big Packard.[67]

CHAPTER SIX

Against Great Odds

Grand Falls (1926–1928)

At one time he had a Packard car. Now, a Packard in those days was really tops, and I can remember driving [in it]... After a while my father said, "Harry, hadn't you better shift gears and get into high? You've been driving in second gear." That was the time with the old gear shift sticks. My father said that Harry [would] often get in a conversation and...shift into second but then [forget] to shift into high.[1]

HIGH ATOP A dramatic rock outcropping, bordered on three sides by the Saint John River, sits the town of Grand Falls, New Brunswick. The site, carved by a deep, plunging gorge, had been known for its geographic suitability for hydroelectric development since the late 1800s. Various companies took over the site, each intending to build power facilities but without success. Lack of expertise, insufficient capital, the outbreak of war or jurisdictional issues over the Saint John River were among the reasons for the failures.[2] Then, in 1925, a subsidiary of the International Paper Company of New York, the Saint John River Power Company, produced a viable plan.[3] Under the direction of A. H. White, vice-president and chief engineer of International Paper, preparations commenced for the building of the largest hydroelectric development in the Maritime provinces.[4]

The newly formed engineering firm of Henry G. Acres, an eighteen-year veteran of the Hydro-Electric Power Commission of Ontario, was selected as consulting engineer and the Dominion Construction Company as general contractor. This was the first of many successful collaborations between Harry McLean and Henry Acres, along with Richard Lankaster Hearn, a highly talented engineer with Acres's firm.[5] Many of McLean's men had gained their first working experience at H. G. Acres and Company. Several joined the ranks of Dominion Construction on the Grand Falls job. One engineer, Arthur McLaren, a graduate of the Queen's University civil engineering program, had just finished working on a hydroelectric project at Lake Temiskaming when he received a telegram from Acres telling him to report immediately to McLean in New Brunswick. Grand Falls was the first hydro project for Dominion Construction. Lacking hydro expertise, McLean made arrangements with Acres to keep McLaren on as resident engineer for Dominion

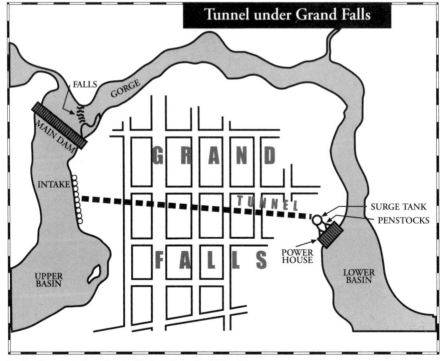

Based on illustration in *Contract Record and Engineering Review*, Oct. 1928, p. 637.

Construction. McLaren was assigned to the power house and shortly afterwards to the intake.[6]

Initially, a firm named Parson and Ed, a subcontractor from Moncton, was hired to construct the intake, but differences between the firm and Dominion Construction resulted in Dominion's taking over the entire job, along with some Parson and Ed employees. Electrical superintendent Charles "Charlie" Hyson was part of that particular deal and would remain a loyal employee of McLean's for two decades.[7] Robert "Bob" Moffatt, "a real old construction man," was initially named main dam superintendent but was sent away on another job. Moffatt's three sons remained behind: Clarence as timekeeper, Dwight as a master mechanic and Earl as a shovel runner. Duncan "Dunc" Taylor, a former Acres employee, took over from Moffatt. Charles "Charlie" Switzer, K. McKay Smith from Smiths Falls and Arthur Bradley (another former Acres man) made up the regular office crew on this job.[8]

>─┼─◆>─◦─<◆┼─<

Harry and Irene McLean were refreshed and relaxed after a summer holiday in New York City and an extended stay at their cottage on Patterson Lake near Perth, Ontario.[9] By the time the Grand Falls project got under way, on August 10, 1926,[10] McLean had renewed his friendship with Berton Armitage Puddington, the town physician and surgeon. Dr. Puddington, a 1903 graduate of McGill University, was for some time the only surgeon in northwestern New Brunswick. McLean had met him during his days building the National Transcontinental.[11]

The Puddington home was a sanctuary for McLean – a comfortable and welcoming escape from the scores of people pestering him for work. McLean once told Puddington: "You and I have been friends for a long time. But you're the only one that I can't do anything for. You've never wanted a job. You've never wanted anything but a pleasant friendship."[12] The Puddingtons' son Jack recalled McLean's weekly ritual:

> The company was the Dominion Construction Company. They of course had a pick-up truck, as we'd call them today. Every Thursday or every Friday that truck came to our house and delivered a case a Scotch. This wasn't all for Harry, but he could sit in the living room

OPENING HYDRO DEVELOPMENT. GRAND FALLS N.B., AUG. 10TH., 1926.

Opening of Grand Falls hydroelectric project, August 10, 1926. Courtesy of Grand Falls Historical Society and Patrick McCooey

talking to my parents, intellectually talking – and culturally, with all the books and things around. And he could easily drink…a bottle of Scotch. He could drink that while they were discussing and get up and walk in to the dining room as sober as a judge. Never fizzed on him at all. But he had it there. If people came to call on him, he'd say, "Let's go over to the Puddingtons'," and he always knew there was plenty of liquor to treat his friends there. But he didn't indulge in that amount that was delivered very much himself… I can remember [my father and mother] saying instead of drinking a whole bottle of Scotch, Harry could have drunk a whole glass of ice water and it wouldn't have affected him [differently]. He'd sit at the table after having consumed [a bottle of Scotch] as quiet and sober, discussing current events and things.[13]

During one of their sessions reading and exchanging books, McLean presented Jack with a copy of Elbert Hubbard's "A Message to Garcia."[14] This short story, written in 1899, described McLean's vision of the ideal employee: a person who can get the job done without asking inane questions. McLean offered Dr. Puddington a similar assessment of his assistant:

The girl who ran [the hospital] and assisted my father in the operating room, Mildred Rogers – I can still remember her name – Harry said to my father one time, "You picked a good one when you got her. She's just ugly enough and contrary enough to be a darned good boss." I guess Mildred met some of his measures for success.[15]

>-+→-O-←+-<

To get the job done at the power facility, an adequate supply of quality aggregate had to be procured. The local sources of gravel were determined by the gravel scientists to be "glacial drift" and unsuitable for use in concrete.[16] A supply of aggregate was located on Sharpe's Island near Woodstock, seventy-five miles south of Grand Falls, and was transported to the site by the Canadian Pacific Railway in gondola cars.[17] The fact that the source was a fair distance from the job site required meticulous planning, to ensure that sufficient quantities would be on hand over the winter months.[18] In order to haul the aggregate, equipment, and supplies to the lower basin and site of the power house construction, a one-and-a-half-mile railway had to be constructed from the main CPR line.[19]

The project was divided into several sections: the main dam located just above the falls, the intake, the tunnel, the surge tank and the power house. Careful scheduling of the various elements of the job was paramount, and was largely dictated by the inevitable flooding in the spring and fall. The decision was made to complete the eastern part of the main dam during the latter half of 1926 and the western part the following summer and fall, after the spring floodwaters had receded.[20] Cofferdams were swiftly constructed at the site of the power house and the main dam, while rock excavation took place simultaneously.[21]

The Saint John River is noted for sudden and extreme fluctuations in water levels caused by comparatively minor changes in the weather – at that time the river level was noted to rise some twenty feet in the spring and fifteen feet in the fall.[22] Precipitous drainage sloping, a rapid increase in the river's depth and the absence of lakes along the river system to naturally regulate the water flow have been cited as reasons for the dramatic changes.[23] In the fall of 1926 heavy rains caused an abrupt increase in the river's flow. Approximately sixty feet of the cofferdam, along with a chunk of the river bank, was swept downstream and water gushed onto the partially concreted work area at the main dam. Small pumps were in place to take care of minor surface leakage, but the torrent taxed the machines beyond their normal capacity. A crane operator sprang to the rescue of the submerged pumps, which were pulled out, and nature was allowed to run its course. Once the water subsided, the pumps were returned to their original locations and the water and mud from the deluge were cleaned up. Although this nasty episode caused some delay, it was regarded as minor and represented the only time the river impeded progress on the job.[24]

Construction of the western half of the main dam started well ahead of schedule. Acres's engineers conferred regularly with Dominion Construction's field engineers in a specially equipped field laboratory to ensure that proper proportions were being used in mixing and to test the strength of the concrete samples. Concreting commenced before the

Construction in Grand Falls, December 15, 1926. COURTESY OF GRAND FALLS HISTORICAL SOCIETY AND PATRICK MCCOOEY

end of July and ended just before the onset of the fall rains in October.[25]
In November 1926 a local newspaper reported:

> Construction operations in connection with the development of the
> hydro power at Grand Falls were reported Friday to be progressing
> rapidly.
>
> Tunnelling into the solid rock for water diversion has been
> advanced to a length of 300 feet. Gangs working in three shifts, are
> projecting the tunnelling at 24 feet per day.
>
> Preparations for the foundation of the power house have been
> completed and it is expected that concrete pouring would be underway
> before the end of this week. Three piers for the main dam are reported
> finished...[26]

A great many men from near and far had been hired, and the
merchants and bankers of Grand Falls revelled in the resultant
prosperity. When the Christmas season rolled around, the main street
in Grand Falls was gaily decorated and a party was held for the children
of the town. The McLeans and Puddingtons watched with delight as
the youngsters were called forward to receive their presents near the
Christmas tree. A quick-thinking Harry McLean was able to avert a
yuletide disaster:

> All of a sudden somebody said, "Great heavens, we've
> underestimated – we're running out of presents for the children!"
> And they were going into the store and they said, "We don't have any
> more money to buy any more presents – we just underestimated."
> Harry said, "Go in and buy everything they've got left in the store for
> Christmas presents and see that no kid is denied a present, that every
> child goes home pleased."[27]

One of the challenges of the job was burrowing a half-mile tunnel
through solid rock some two hundred feet directly under the town. An
elderly subway construction expert, Michael Quinn, and his assistant,
Ford Stokes, were brought in from New York City to supervise the
excavation and construction of Canada's longest pressure tunnel.[28] The
tunnel work schedule was built around that of the intake and penstock
work, to take full advantage of the summer months for pouring concrete.

In January 1927 excavation for the intake was begun on the right
side of the river at the entrance to the tunnel. Designed by H. G. Acres

and Company, the Johnson-Wahlman intake consisted of two horizontal gathering tubes made of reinforced concrete, each equipped with a butterfly valve to control the water. A series of rectangular slots separated by tilting vanes ensured that the water, regardless of the direction of its flow, was taken in at a consistent rate. Steel racks were installed to filter out large refuse and to withstand the spring ice. The gathering tubes joined as a "Y" connection to the horseshoe-shaped tunnel, which in turn led to the surge tank, penstocks and power house.[29] The substructure of the power house, excavated in rock and formed in concrete, was proceeding nicely and was expected to be completed before the spring.[30]

During concreting of the intake on March 23, 1927, the life of Elmo Dumos was claimed in an accident. The Nova Scotia native was smothered by a shroud of concrete from an upended car.[31] Jack Puddington recalled the tragic incident:

> They phoned, knowing Harry was there, and they said, "There's been an accident at the intake." A fellow…was right down at the bottom [with] one of these cars that you see on construction full of concrete

Tunnel excavation in Grand Falls, April 14, 1927. Courtesy of Grand Falls Historical Society and Patrick McCooey

dumped on him, and he was buried down there... Harry went to where the cranes were. He grabbed the shovel and threw it down and reached out and grabbed the wire of the crane. Harry said, "Lower me down there as fast as you can." And he went down there and tried to dig the fellow out, and of course...only a very huge...fellow could do that. And they dug a whole ton of concrete...he couldn't shovel all of that out, so they had to get their regular equipment... I suppose there was workmen's compensation then, but this fellow of course was killed when all that weight hit him. It was rumoured that Harry paid for the funeral and had his body sent [home] and discovered that he had left a widow... I'm not sure about children, but Harry discovered there was a mortgage on the farm and he paid the mortgage off.[32]

Work nonetheless continued at a frenzied pace. Several shifts were put in place to expedite the process of drilling and excavating the tunnel – three eight-hour shifts for drilling and two ten-hour shifts for excavating. Weekly progress was measured in feet: the drilling team was ahead with one hundred and seventy feet, while the excavation team lagged behind with one hundred and forty-four feet. The tunnel, in the shape of a horseshoe, measured twenty-four and a half feet in diameter. In July of 1927 the lining of the tunnel in concrete was started in the hope that the work would be finished by the end of summer. The day shift worked on the concrete, completing a twenty-five-foot section each day. A daily shot fired at half-past five in the afternoon marked the start of the night shift, which was responsible for excavation and moving and resetting the forms.[33] Having worked his men hard and long, McLean recognized the need for enjoyable recreation:

He did throw a party for his staff down in Grand Falls at the end of a three-month or six-month period when they would balance their books and things. There were a bunch of young engineers and young construction people, and everything was free. He had these over at the staff house, and plenty to drink, and some of these young fellows didn't know their capacity – young engineers and things – and Harry would go right on drinking with them, matching them. And the next morning they were hung over. But not Harry. He was right in the office at the starting time, clear in his head as if he hadn't had a drink all the night before and as though he'd had a good, early night's sleep. His physical resources were remarkable.[34]

➤—◆—○—◆—◀

McLean, together with Berton Puddington and Richard Hearn, purchased land on New Brunswick's Tobique River. Whenever the opportunity presented itself, McLean would hire guides and the trio would go salmon fishing:

> He must've had the construction crew build the fishing camp. Cape Cod house, where you had the long roof there and the shorter roof here and bedrooms upstairs, with a balcony where you could be at the fireplace and see all the openings to the doors and people going up to go to bed and all this sort of thing. He really built a wonderful camp.[35]

McLean felt completely comfortable with the Puddington family. Even if no one was around he would make himself at home. Jack recalled his wife's first meeting with McLean:

> We never knew when Harry was going to show up on the doorstep... We drove into the driveway. My wife said, "Great heavens, every light in the house is on. Somebody must have...pressed all the buttons..." I said, "I'll bet it's Harry McLean... There's the plane in the upper basin." So before we could do anything, Harry appeared on the veranda of the house.

Left to right: two fishing guides (left), with Berton Puddington, Harry McLean and Richard Hearn. COURTESY OF JOHN CURLESS PUDDINGTON

So I helped Molly get out of the car and he looked and he just picked her up – she said in one hand [but] surely it must have been two – and here she was, he had her sitting on her bottom in the palm of his hand. And he had guests that he [had] brought with him in his plane, so he walked in to the living room and he said, "Look what I found out on the veranda! I've never seen this before." And he put her on the mantelpiece…and of course

McLean's fishing camp on the Tobique River.
COURTESY OF JOHN CURLESS PUDDINGTON

she couldn't get down. And he kept saying, "I've come here for years, I know this house inside out, but look, I found this right outside on the veranda…" So she never forgot Harry McLean.[36]

McLean was riveted to the radio on September 22, 1927, when the announcer Graham McNamee proclaimed, "Ladies and Gentlemen, ten rounds for the heavyweight championship of the world!! Introducing, from Salt Lake City, Utah, wearing black trunks, weighing 187½ pounds, former heavyweight King – Jack Dempsey!!! His opponent, from New York City, wearing white trunks, weighing 195, Heavyweight Champion of the World – Gene Tunney!!!"[37] McLean was determined to enjoy the match despite a temporary annoyance:

When he and his wife were living in the staff house in Grand Falls, one of the big-time boxing [matches] was on – both outstanding people fighting. And one of the ladies was not very interested in waiting to listen to it…on [the] radio. And in the fireplace the wood was all laid out for a nice, bristling fire… She went over and lit a match, and then in no time, when the fight was coming on, this crickling and crackling of a fireplace fire. Harry just went over and put his arms right underneath the whole thing and threw it out the door. But he never criticized people like that. He just undid what she did in a demonstrative way.[38]

At the end of October 1927 McLean went to visit his mother in Bismarck.[39] He returned to Grand Falls just in time to celebrate the completion of the tunnel excavation on November 10th.[40] The festivities were short-lived, however, for the next day tragedy struck again. A seventeen-year-old resident of Grand Falls, Vern St. Amand, perished on the spot as a bolt, propelled with the force of a bullet from origins unknown, thrust itself into one side of his head, exiting the other.[41] In memory of Vern, Elmo Dumos and another man who died on the job, a Sons of Martha cairn was erected at the intake.[42]

By December of that year some of Dominion Construction's men were leaving Grand Falls and heading west to Manitoba, where McLean had landed a contract to build a railway from The Pas to Flin Flon.[43] There was still work to be completed in Grand Falls, however, making it necessary for McLean to travel regularly between the two jobs.

Several subcontractors were brought in for their specialized services and equipment. Canadian Allis-Chalmers designed, fabricated and

Power house under construction, October 10, 1927. COURTESY OF GRAND FALLS HISTORICAL SOCIETY AND PATRICK McCOOEY

installed the main steel penstock as well as the turbines. The rubber seals for the penstock valves were provided by Dominion Engineering Works. The provision of structural steel was awarded to Vickers and to the Sarnia Bridge Company. The Dominion Bridge Company provided the sluice gates and the Horton Steel Company took care of the draft tube and the plate-steel liners for the tunnel entrance.[44]

Rising ninety-two feet above the centre line of the main penstock, a large Johnson differential surge tank was supported on eighteen steel columns. The tank provided regulation of water surges in the event that a penstock valve should close, thus reducing the possibility of damage to the system. The tank barrel measures seventy-three feet in diameter and sixty feet in height. Erection of the structure began on July 3, 1928, and was completed seven months later, although it proved necessary to use the tank in September before the barrel was finished.[45]

The completed dam is a succession of eleven concrete piers with sluice gates that can be raised or lowered depending on how much water is needed to generate electricity. It spans the river, some five hundred

Completed power house, December 10, 1927. COURTESY OF GRAND FALLS HISTORICAL SOCIETY AND PATRICK MCCOOEY

and ninety-two feet in width. The sluice gates are large: nine of them measure twenty-three by fifty feet, and two smaller gates are controlled remotely from the power house.[46] The main penstock divides into two penstocks and then into four penstocks each measuring fourteen feet in diameter. Every second, thousands of cubic feet of water flow into these penstocks, all of which contain a hydraulic butterfly valve. The penstocks direct the water flow towards the turbines and the Canadian General Electric generators.[47] The velocity and weight of the water turn the massive turbines at high speed, which, in turn, causes the generators to convert the mechanical energy into electricity. Although the power house was designed for 80,000 horsepower, it was originally equipped with three 20,000-horsepower units.[48]

With the work at Grand Falls completed, McLean's attention was diverted to new challenges. He enjoyed supervising the work but always had an eye on the horizon for the next big job. He continued to keep in touch with the Puddingtons and sent them postcards and books during his travels. Now and again the Puddingtons would catch sight of McLean's water plane landing near the upper basin, and within moments of his arrival at their home their friendship would be renewed.[49] Berton Puddington gave McLean a book titled *Songs of Men*,[50] which included a poem called "The Little Red God." As soon as they read it, the Puddingtons thought the poem described McLean perfectly. Thereafter Harry McLean often referred to himself as "Little Red God."

THE LITTLE RED GOD
Anonymous

Here's a little red song to the god of guts,
Who dwells in palaces, brothels, huts;
The little Red God with the craw of grit;
The god who never learned how to quit;
He is neither a fool with a frozen smile,
Or a sad old toad in a cask of bile;
He can dance with a shoe-nail in his heel
And never a sign of his pain reveal;
He can hold a mob with an empty gun
And turn a tragedy into fun;

Kill a man in a flash, a breath,
Or snatch a friend from the claws of death;
Swallow the pill of assured defeat

And plan attack in his slow retreat;
Spin the wheel till the numbers dance,
And bite his thumb at the god of chance;
Drink straight water with whisky-soaks;
Or call for liquor with temperance folks;
Tearless stand at the graven stone,
Yet weep in the silence of night, alone;
Worship a sweet, white virgin's glove,
Or teach a courtesan how to love;
Dare the dulness of fireside bliss,
Or stake the soul for a wanton's kiss;
Blind his soul to a woman's eyes
When she says she loves and he knows she lies;

Shovel dung in the city mart
To earn a crust for his chosen art;
Build where the builders all have failed
And sail the seas that no man has sailed;
Run a tunnel or dam a stream;
Or damn the men who financed the dream;
Tell a pal what his work is worth,
Though he lose his last, best friend on earth;
Lend the critical monkey-elf;
Wear the garments he likes to wear,
Never dreaming that people stare;
Go to church if his conscience wills,
Or find his own – in the far, blue hills.

He is kind and gentle, or harsh and gruff
He is tender as love – or he's rawhide tough;
A rough-necked rider in spurs and chaps,
Or well-groomed son of the town – perhaps;
And this is the little Red God I sing,
Who cares not a wallop for anything
That walks or gallops, that crawls or struts,
No matter how clothed – if it hasn't guts.

CHAPTER SEVEN

The Baloney Road

Flin Flon Railway (1927–1928)

Down, down, down he went into the bottomless lake, leaving behind the
watchers on the shore and a circle of bubbles on the surface of the
water. Soon Flinty could feel his submarine "fish" was being swept
along by a deep current. Ahead he saw a cloud of swirling water
indicating the subterranean river he sought. All at once his fish spun
wildly, hurtling down like a scrap of soap sucked through the drain.
Down, down, down until finally it reached the centre of the earth where
he found a sunless city, laden with worthless gold,
where women ruled...[1]

THE TALE OF a portly grocer and adventurer, Josiah Flintabbattey
Flonatin, captivated a group of prospectors camped near the Churchill
River in Saskatchewan. While portaging between the river and Lac La
Ronge, Tom Creighton, a member of the group, found a weathered copy
of the book *The Sunless City*.[2] Written by Joyce Emerson Preston Muddock,
the science-fiction novel is the story of a man "conspicuous for two
things – the smallness of his stature and the largeness of his perception."[3]
Flintabbattey Flonatin, convinced that there is a river leading to the
middle of the earth, builds an elaborate fish-shaped submarine to travel
there. Night after night, the prospectors read about his voyage to a make-
believe city where gold is so abundant it is considered "rubbish."[4]

Flin Flon Railway

Based on illustration in *Canadian Railway and Marine World*, Nov. 1928, p. 637.

In the summer of 1915, Creighton's group were prospecting near the Saskatchewan–Manitoba border, just northeast of Amisk Lake. They met David Collins, a local Native trapper, who presented samples of sulphide ore he had taken from the shores of a smaller lake. Collins directed the men to the outcrop where he had found the ore. The prospectors set about panning. Substantial amounts of gold fleck led the men to believe that this discovery might prove profitable.[5] Recalling the escape of Flintabbattey Flonatin from the golden land, the prospectors shortened the moniker and christened the lake Flin Flon.[6]

The mineral find at Flin Flon was not Creighton's first. Indeed, he and the other men in his party, Daniel and Jack Mosher and Leon and Isadore Dion, had made various notable mineral discoveries in Manitoba and Saskatchewan, even triggering a gold rush. John Edward "Jack" Hammell, a mining promoter, was told about Flin Flon by Dan Mosher and made arrangements to go there immediately. He sent samples of the find to a custom assay laboratory at Amisk Lake and set out with Mosher to register the claim in The Pas.[7]

Further drilling and testing revealed an enormous body of ore, but it was determined that an equally enormous up-front investment would be needed to exploit the find. The ore was low grade and there was no technology to separate copper and zinc materials from pyrite. The ore would have to be concentrated at a smelter. Hence the first problem: there was no smelter. The second hurdle was transportation; the closest railway line was at The Pas, some eighty-seven miles away. A railway would have to be built. Finally, a smelter would not run without electrical power. A dam and generating station would have to be constructed. Hammell formed a syndicate of prosperous Canadians to raise the capital necessary to start mining at Flin Flon. Unfortunately for Hammell and his syndicate, the cost was prohibitive during the war years.[8]

Other mines, such as the Mandy Mine, operated profitably in the area during World War I. The composition of the Mandy ore was high in copper, a valuable commodity in times of war, although the find was considerably smaller than the one at Flin Flon. The copper made it a lucrative venture, even though the ore had to be hauled out by sleigh or barge.[9] By the end of the war, the rich copper vein at Mandy had been exhausted and the price of copper had fallen dramatically. The Mandy Mine sold most of its equipment to the Flin Flon syndicate.

In 1921 the Mining Corporation of Canada bought a sixty-five-percent interest in Flin Flon that included the claims owned by Hammell, Creighton, the Dions and the Moshers. Various parties conducted further investigations over the next several years. The Mining Corporation of Canada established a subsidiary, the Manitoba Metals Mining Company, which hired a geologist, Paul Armstrong, to analyze the Flin Flon ore and write a definitive report on its "structure, formation and classification."[10] The report and a carefully crafted letter were sent to the wealthy H. P. Whitney of New York City. Harry Payne Whitney was known to have mining interests among his many other lucrative holdings. A Yale graduate, financier and heir to the Standard Oil fortune, Whitney had added considerably to his enormous wealth by marrying a member of another old-money family, Gertrude Vanderbilt, a patron of the arts and founder of the Whitney Museum in New York City. When not consumed with the usual pastimes of the rich, such as polo playing, Whitney was overseeing his vast financial empire.[11]

Whitney sought the advice of the engineers at Complex Ore Recoveries, a company in which he happened to own an interest and whose staff consisted of experts from the Colorado School of Mines. He sent his son, Cornelius, nicknamed "Sonny," to the Toronto offices of the Mining Corporation of Canada to further investigate the situation at Flin Flon. Sonny's report was favourable enough to prompt Whitney to send a group of engineers and scientists from Complex Ore Recoveries to Flin Flon. Their job was to conduct a feasibility study to determine whether a method that they had developed would resolve the difficulties in separating the copper and zinc sulphides in the Flin Flon ore. The process required large quantities of ore and loads of electricity. The required magnitude of ore was established and a potential power source was found at Island Falls on the Churchill River, seventy-two miles away near the Saskatchewan border. Whitney took an option on the Flin Flon land owned by the Mining Corporation of Canada in 1925 and exercised it in November 1927.[12]

The only remaining problem was transportation. Vast amounts of freight would have to be moved in and out of Flin Flon, particularly for construction of the power plant and smelter. The Whitney organization opened discussions with the Manitoba and Dominion governments and the Canadian National Railway (CNR), with a view to extending the railway from The Pas to Flin Flon.[13] An agreement was reached on November 18, 1927,[14] with the Manitoba government pledging one hundred thousand dollars a year for five years towards any operating deficit[15] and Whitney contributing two hundred and fifty thousand dollars towards construction costs.[16] As mining development would reap revenues for both the province and the CNR, the respective parties agreed to cooperate on the construction of the new line. With the signing of the agreement, declared *The Pas Herald and Mining News*, the "future of Northern Manitoba [is] now assured."[17] In addition, the Manitoba government decided that the long-neglected Hudson Bay Railway would be completed from Kettle Rapids to Churchill on Hudson Bay. Major J. G. McLaughlin was the CNR engineer in charge of construction for both this project and the Flin Flon railway.[18]

A construction tender was issued. One of the terms of the agreement was that the line be completed by September 30, 1929, with a bonus of two hundred and fifty thousand dollars if the company could deliver two thousand tons of freight to Flin Flon by December 21, 1928.[19] Dominion Construction partnered with William S. Tomlinson, a

Winnipeg-based construction firm, to submit a bid.[20] Most contractors bid high and believed that the project could not begin before the arrival of warmer weather.

><⠂⠂><⠂O⠂<⠂>⠂⠂<

Harry McLean had visited the area earlier in the winter and had a different vision of the project. Unlike everyone else, he would not start at the beginning and would not wait for warmer weather. McLean's strategy was to use the harsh winter conditions to advantage. Perhaps taking advice from family members who worked on the Northern Pacific and laid tracks across the frozen Missouri River, McLean decided to lay steel over the frozen ground and muskeg. The road bed would be built later.[21] The firm Dominion Construction and Tomlinson was awarded the contract. Upon the signing of the agreement early in December 1927, McLean arrived in The Pas and "immediately commenced to make things hum."[22] Clearing of the right-of-way was started on December 9th.[23]

The Operation of a Railway to the Flin Flon Mines Act enacted an agreement, dated December 17, 1927, between the Manitoba Northern Railway Company (MNR) and the CNR.[24] The verbosely titled legislation was passed to enable the Province to build the line utilizing the newly formed MNR to ensure that the railway was built "in accordance with plans and specifications to be approved by the Minister of Railways for Canada."[25] The CNR would then lease the line from the Province and operate it.[26] That same month, H. P. Whitney established Hudson Bay Mining and Smelting Limited, of which he owned fifty percent.

McLean placed Colonel Kenneth Alan Ramsay in charge of the job. Ramsay, formerly a construction superintendent with the firm of Foley, Welch and Stewart, had served overseas with the Canadian Overseas Railway Construction Corps and been seconded to the Directorate of Light Railways in France as Assistant Director. For his efforts overseas, Ramsay had been awarded the Distinguished Service Order and the Order of the British Empire. He had moved through the ranks, leaving the army (on March 31, 1919) as Lieutenant Colonel.[27] McLean considered Ramsay a key member of his organization. Ramsay's assistant was Charlie Tupper (grandson of Sir Charles Tupper, a former Canadian prime minister).

Charlie Switzer, office manager, had also distinguished himself with the CORCC. He had been awarded the Military Cross for "conspicuous gallantry and devotion to duty. He received an order for the demolition of structures with a time limit, and so was unable to communicate with the railway company. On his own initiative he organized the demolitions and handled quantities of high explosives under heavy shell fire."[28]

Switzer worked with purchasing agent Henry Bancroft and J. G. "Jack" Humphrey, the son of H. Jasper Humphrey, Eastern general manager for the Canadian Pacific Railway. It was McLean's practice to hire young men with influential fathers. His friends from North Dakota, Charlie Johnson and Louis Nelson, were also on the job, along with many other railway-building veterans such as Jack Telford, Dunc Taylor, Jimmy Egan, Inky Pete, Andy Hines, Leo Murphy, Scotty Mackie, Jack Stewart, Gordon Gray, Don McCrae, Bill McKeever, Bill Simpson, Charlie Storey and Frank Mullen.[29]

Dominion's construction equipment was sent to a freight yard in Winnipeg. Office cars and sleeping cars would be moved first. Before Dominion Construction could do anything, the CNR insisted on moving the equipment and cars for the company and later presented McLean with a hefty invoice for doing so. Vexed by this unanticipated expense, McLean would later even the score.[30]

Cranberry Portage, on the shores of Lake Athapapuskow, was selected as the central distribution point. The idea was to get supplies to Cranberry Portage in the winter, and then, with the arrival of spring and summer, have the men take full advantage of the fine weather to complete the final section between Cranberry Portage and Flin Flon. McLean also planned to reach Cranberry Portage by rail before winter's end. This way, both the railway contractors and the mine developers could take full advantage of the open lake to ship supplies via steamboat.[31]

Several groups of workers were sent from The Pas to establish a series of supply camps and to locate gravel pits along the route.[32]

Dominion Construction bought Boarding Coach No. 1223W, a wooden-bodied truss rod car, from the Illinois Central Railroad, Chicago suburban services, circa 1929. It was used in the construction of the line to Flin Flon and was scrapped at Deeks in 1951.
ANDREW MERRILEES COLLECTION, GROUP D SUB-SERIES VI, ACCESSION 1980-149. PA 208174, LIBRARY AND ARCHIVES CANADA

Surviving on heaps of bologna in the camps, the men christened the job "The Baloney Road."[33] The residence of an old Indian agent served as a temporary office,[34] and some existing buildings, part of an ore depot, were purchased by Dominion and refurbished for their new role as a construction camp.[35] The initial group of men travelled by snowmobile to the furthest point of the job, some sixty-five miles, to establish a base camp on Lake Athapapuskow. The remaining men set out with three tractors, dragging behind them four or five sleighs laden with food and supplies. At the halfway point a second crew would take over. The supply relay ran night and day, a round trip taking forty-eight hours.[36] The *Bismarck Tribune* continued to follow McLean's career:

> When he was cautioned that it would be impossible to buck the cold with his construction gangs he replied "There are no 'ifs' about this proposition. We start to lay track tomorrow."[37]

The track laying began on January 3, 1928, "with the mercury so far below zero it was out of sight."[38] Men worked on "clearing gangs" ahead

Track-laying machine. The ties are placed on the prepared ground (left) and the machine, a sort of gantry, is used to position the rails. COURTESY OF FLIN FLON ARCHIVES AND MAUREEN LUNAM

of the steel, blasting rock and cutting through the forest to widen the right-of-way to one hundred feet. The clearing camp received news that the first steel had been laid, and then just days later a warning that the steel crews were threatening to overtake them.[39] A walking boss declared, "Harry McLean will drive her 'till hell freezes."[40] The gangs worked into the frigid nights clad in their undershirts, setting the cut trees ablaze for light and warmth. Undeterred, the track layer approached, "leaving in its wake a network of naked ties and ribbons of steel stretching back over humps and depressions like an endless picket fence laid flat."[41] In spite of furious efforts by the clearing crews to keep ahead, at Mile 16 the steel crew caught up. The clearing crews were directed to focus their efforts on a thirty-foot strip to keep ahead of the track layer and another crew would return later to clear the remaining seventy feet of right-of-way.[42]

"The motto of the contractors seems to be 'Flin Flon within a year or bust'," reported the local newspaper, *The Pas Herald and Mining News*, on January 6, 1928. "Judging from the energy being put into the work they are going to make the grade alright."[43] The newspaper cautioned

Dominion Construction crew on a rail-mounted steam shovel. COURTESY OF F. WILLS, FLIN FLON
ARCHIVES AND MAUREEN LUNAM

potential employees: "Men going into Flin Flon and points along the
right-of-way should be prepared to camp out and should be well equipped
to feed themselves. Some hardships are being experienced by 'green
men'[44] travelling without proper clothing and without food or the utensils
for cooking."[45]

By January 27th fifteen miles of steel had been laid and a thousand
men were at work on the railway. Vast amounts of supplies and freight
were being hauled weekly to points along the right-of-way. "Three
tractors, each hauling four sleighs, leave town four times a week with
120–125 tons of supplies and material. Last week four compressors for
drilling were sent north. A considerable quantity of piling is also being
sent out, some by horse team to Mile 22 and some by tractor to Mile
55."[46] Bridge builders were in demand as wooden trestle bridges would
have to be erected.

The CNR had made a decision in February 1928 to run another line
between Cranberry Portage and the Sherritt-Gordon mining property at
Cold Lake.[47] This forty-mile line would also be built by the firm of

Dominion Construction and Tomlinson, although work on the Sherritt line did not commence until the Flin Flon line was completed.[48] Also that month, it was announced that the nearby Mandy Mine would be re-opened.

McLean took a break from the job to reunite with his wife for a trip to Bismarck, taking time out during his visit to speak to both the Lions and the Rotarians about his work and his youth in Bismarck.[49] Harry and Irene then spirited Mary McLean away for a winter vacation in Los Angeles and other Californian destinations.[50]

Even in his absence, McLean's work crews made great progress. The terrain between The Pas and Cranberry Portage consists mostly of flat limestone, so the ties could be easily laid on the surface. In some softer areas, the men secured the ties in the frozen muskeg by jamming timber underneath.[51] The crew reached Cranberry Portage on March 17, 1928, after managing to lay fifty-one miles of track in fifty-six working days during the frigid winter months.[52]

> The contractors are confident that they have the steel into Flin Flon well within schedule time. Of course, while trains are running over the line, it is not in anything like good shape and fully half the men are employed on this end ballasting, etc. The other half of the men are engaged between the Cranberry Portage and Flin Flon scattered over the last forty miles of the road which will present greater difficulties than the first fifty miles, most of it being rock work.[53]

Dominion Construction began to offer a gas-car service to transport mail and paying customers who wished to go "to the end of the steel."[54] Due to the condition of the rail at that point, the passengers were required to sign a waiver "promising not to sue the company for damages should they happen to get killed or anything like that."[55]

Many problems were encountered along the thirty-four-mile stretch between Cranberry Portage and Flin Flon – some predictable, others not. The muskeg in the area was up to six feet in depth and frost as thick as twenty-eight feet had been found in some sections.[56] When the ground thawed in the spring, work crews began building up the grade from the ballast pits. However, they were frequently frustrated by sinkholes that swallowed large sections of road bed and equipment without warning. Carloads of gravel were alternated with layers of logs in an effort to fill and stabilize the openings. More often than not, the men watched helplessly as the earth opened and absorbed the day's work, leaving only railway ties and rails protruding haphazardly in the air. The worst sinkhole, some two hundred and fifty feet in length, was estimated to have soaked up three hundred and thirty carloads of gravel and added forty-five thousand dollars to construction costs.[57]

This day things had been worse than usual. As fast as material could be offered it had been swallowed without even the usual preliminary hesitation. With the arrival of darkness not the slightest headway was noticeable. Standing in the glare of lights a number of men were discussing the problem and regarding what was literally a bottomless pit. Gazing across the morass, one of the number stared fixedly a moment, then suddenly pointed. Sixty feet from the track where for days the underneath pressure had caused the exudation of tons and tons of slime and muck, one end of a boat was plainly visible.

Open mouthed and silent they stood, as it came slowly into view on top of the quivering slime. A great dug-out, hewn from the trunk

The muskeg and track have caved in, leaving the CNR's engine no. 415 partially submerged in a sinkhole. Courtesy of F. Wills, Flin Flon Archives and Maureen Lunam

of a mighty tree probably hundreds of years before, it lay now in plain sight, an axe-blade deeply imbedded in its prow.

Realizing its historic value the onlookers made every effort to reach it, but over the squirming, treacherous mass it was impossible. For ten minutes it remained there, a link with the past brought again, after many years, before the eyes of man, then, as continued efforts were made to reach the spot, the ground opened up and the great pit leisurely re-devoured its prey.[58]

The men also had to contend with rock slides along the shores of Lake Athapapuskow and Schist Lake. Extensive bridging and heavy rock cutting had to be carried out around both lakes. An entire section of grade disappeared into the depths, taking along with it one of Dominion Construction's locomotives and a caboose. At Mile 73 another slide occurred: "A temporary trestle that for a year had carried trains over an arm of Schist Lake, was being filled. No trouble was anticipated and, on the night of July 12th the foreman reported, 'Trestle Mile 73 filled to base of rail. All O.K.' One hour later a watchman newly from

Although the Mile 73 bridge at Schist Lake supported the weight of a year's worth of trains, a large section of it disappeared under twenty feet of water in just one hour, on July 12, 1928. HARRY FALCONER MCLEAN COLLECTION, ACCESSION 1981-064. PA 212859, LIBRARY AND ARCHIVES CANADA

the Emerald Isle sent in this terse message, 'Trestle fill Mile 73 under twenty feet of water. – Hell!' " Workers were rushed to the scene with timber and supplies. The line had to be set back thirty feet from the shore and the permanent trestle was installed within a few days.[59]

To better service the camps along the edges of the lakes, giant timber rafts bearing supplies were hauled on the water. An entire construction camp floated on rafts in Schist Lake, complete with bunkhouses, offices and kitchens. In this way the camp could easily follow the work.[60] "This railroad is more than two-thirds completed since it started in January 1928. So important are quick results looked for from this enterprise that the management offers the railroad contractors a bonus of $250,000 for the completion of the rails to the mine by December 1st, 1928. So far it looks like they will win in a walk."[61] By this time fourteen hundred men were on the job, along with forty-four teams, seven locomotives, three dinkeys (small steam locomotives) and four steam shovels, although some men were lost when they were beckoned back to their farms by the fall harvest.[62]

Building the Channing Trestle. Courtesy of Flin Flon Archives and Maureen Lunam

In early September 1928 the grade between Cranberry Portage and Flin Flon was ready for track laying. By September 21st the last fourteen miles were being laid to the mines and the railway was "expected to be finished early in October and trains operating from The Pas to the Flin Flon Mines...practically two months before the date specified in the contract. The early completion of this line will permit the mining company to commence bringing in by rail the 28,000 tons of material which will be needed to start the power development facility at Island Falls in the Churchill River."[63]

McLean and Tomlinson collected the quarter-million-dollar bonus – as well as additional sums from the CNR. As the contractors had not relinquished ownership of the railway, they billed the CNR $388,000 in freight charges, thus recovering the money they had been charged some months earlier for freight cartage, and then some.[64] McLean's reputation

Construction of CNR line to Flin Flon, Channing Trestle, Miles 83 to 84, 1928. A series of piles have been driven to provide a solid foundation for laying rails over the muskeg. This would have resulted in a low trestle that may have been filled in later.
PROVINCIAL ARCHIVES OF MANITOBA, STILL IMAGES COLLECTION, N21689

for getting a job done ingeniously was on solid footing. Records had been broken – eighty-six miles of railway in a mere nine months – and Dominion Construction's new track-laying technique was quickly adopted by other railway builders, notably the Hudson Bay Railway.[65] The final task – erecting a Sons of Martha cairn at Sherritt Junction, facing the Flin Flon line – was left to Jack Humphrey.[66]

Upon completion of the Northern Manitoba Railway, the men gathered in a beer parlour to await their final pay. One worker bellowed out the opening words of "The Sons of Martha." The rest of the men joined in to complete the first verse, keeping cadence by pounding on the tables with their fists. Although his men were from a variety of ethnic backgrounds and some struggled with English as a second language, McLean had taught them "The Sons of Martha" in its entirety.[67]

THE SONS OF MARTHA
Rudyard Kipling

The Sons of Mary seldom bother, for they have inherited that good part;
But the Sons of Martha favour their Mother of the careful soul and the troubled heart.
And because she lost her temper once, and because she was rude to the Lord her Guest,
Her Sons must wait upon Mary's Sons, world without end, reprieve, or rest.

It is their care in all the ages to take the buffet and cushion the shock.
It is their care that the gear engages; it is their care that the switches lock.
It is their care that the wheels run truly; it is their care to embark and entrain,
Tally, transport, and deliver duly the Sons of Mary by land and main.

They say to mountains, "Be ye removed" They say to the lesser floods "Be dry."
Under their rods are the rocks reproved – they are not afraid of that which is high.
Then do the hill tops shake to the summit – then is the bed of the deep laid bare,
That the Sons of Mary may overcome it, pleasantly sleeping and unaware.

They finger death at their gloves' end where they piece and repiece the living wires.
He rears against the gates they tend: they feed him hungry behind their fires.
Early at dawn, ere men see clear, they stumble into his terrible stall,
And hale him forth like a haltered steer, and goad and turn him till evenfall.

To these from birth is Belief forbidden; from these till death is Relief afar.
They are concerned with matters hidden – under the earthline their altars are

The secret fountains to follow up, waters withdrawn to restore to the mouth,
And gather the floods as in a cup, and pour them again at a city's drouth.

They do not preach that their God will rouse them a little before the nuts work loose.
They do not teach that His Pity allows them to leave their job when they damn-well choose.
As in the thronged and the lighted ways, so in the dark and the desert they stand,
Wary and watchful all their days that their brethren's days may be long in the land.

Raise ye the stone or cleave the wood to make a path more fair or flat;
Lo, it is black already with blood some Son of Martha spilled for that!
Not as a ladder from earth to Heaven, not as a witness to any creed,
But simple service simply given to his own kind in their common need.

And the Sons of Mary smile and are blessed – they know the angels are on their side.
They know in them is the Grace confessed, and for them are the Mercies multiplied.
They sit at the Feet – they hear the Word – they see how truly the Promise runs.
They have cast their burden upon the Lord, and – the Lord He lays it on Martha's Sons!

>─┤◄►─O─◄►┤─◄

On August 3, 1928, Irene McLean, accompanied by her niece Ina McLaren, visited Mary McLean in hospital at Bismarck.[68] Harry arrived in his hometown shortly thereafter. They stayed in Bismarck for several weeks[69] and then the threesome made their way up to Manitoba to attend the completion ceremony for the Northern Manitoba Railway on September 22, 1928. McLean arranged for a special car to transport a party of notable people from The Pas for the occasion. The train took them as far as Cranberry Portage, and then the group transferred to gas trucks to continue the journey. Among the luminaries were the Honourable John Bracken, premier of Manitoba, and his son George, C. B. Gzowski, chief engineer for the CNR, Senator Vennerstrom of Stockholm, Sweden, and R. A. Talbot of the Hudson's Bay Company, along with local politicians and some employees of Dominion Construction and Hudson Bay Mining and Smelting.[70]

The visitors arrived in Flin Flon at four in the afternoon, in time to watch the track layer place the last ties and ribbon of steel. With the "Last Spike" ceremony about to begin, it was noted that neither Harry McLean nor Colonel Ramsay was present. The pair were riding in the last car in the northern procession and had been sidetracked by "some

126

work on the road"![71] Premier Bracken, with an unflinching Irene McLean as his assistant, drove the ceremonial golden spike at Flin Flon, much to the delight of those assembled.[72] The spike was inscribed, "The last spike in the construction of the Manitoba Northern Railway, opening the mineral district of Northern Manitoba."[73] A round of speeches ensued, each more profound than the one before, extolling the "enterprise and ingenuity"[74] of the contractors and the untold fortunes now within reach. Then the whole party, joined by McLean, travelled southward and back to civilization, stopping only to enjoy an ample meat-and-potatoes supper served on granite plates at a construction camp.[75] The Flin Flon Railway firmly established Harry McLean as a revolutionary contractor who could tackle anything.

Premier John Bracken is assisted by Irene McLean as he drives the golden spike on the CNR line to Flin Flon, September 22, 1928.
PROVINCIAL ARCHIVES OF MANITOBA, STILL IMAGES COLLECTION N21690. ALSO COURTESY OF F. GUYMER, FLIN FLON ARCHIVES AND MAUREEN LUNAM

Mary McLean wrote to her sister Christine "Criss" Gilbert on September 25th that Harry and his wife were in The Pas "comfortably quartered in his private box. They have a good cheff [sic] and nice beds to sleep in – and are enjoying themselves you may depend… You know that Harry will give you and I a trip to Europe if I get so that I will be my old self again. He thinks there are none in the family who can equal us, so be prepared to go if he wants us to. Don't give away the black lace dress or any other nice things in the line of apparel as dress will do a lot of good in the absence of youth."[76] Apparently some members of the Falconer family believed they were descended from royalty.[77] Mary told her sister that she wanted to visit Lancaster, England, where a "vast estat [sic] is situated awaiting all ligitimate [sic] heirs for distribution. If we went before the chancery court all 'fussed' up we could stand a lot better chance than if we come in a less dressy state."[78]

On October 1, 1928, just weeks after the ceremony at Flin Flon, the McLeans attended the grand opening of the Grand Falls power plant.[79] On October 3rd the power was turned on in the town. "Water was let into the tunnel at 1:43 p.m.," reported the local newspaper, "and the first of 4 units generating some 20,000 horsepower was turned on at 3 p.m."[80]

Mary McLean did not have the opportunity to visit Lancaster, dressed in her finest, nor did she ever regain her health. She passed away on October 14, 1928, after a year-long illness. Harry and Irene returned to Bismarck for the funeral service and Mary was interred in the family plot at the Oakland Cemetery in St. Paul. "With the death of Mrs. McLean," read her obituary in the *Bismarck Tribune*, "one of the most colorful personal histories of any pioneer of frontier days in Bismarck is closed."[81]

>─┤◆>─O─<◆┤─<

At the time of Mary McLean's passing, her son's old business partner, A. B. Cook, was in the throes of a serious financial crisis. In a dramatic reversal of fortune, Cook had been forced to sell his prize-winning Herefords, the National Bank of Montana having foreclosed on his loans. Many of Cook's friends and acquaintances were quick to condemn the actions of the bank. These included W. A. Clark Jr., owner of the *Montana Free Press*.[82] In a strongly worded editorial, the newspaper declared that the bank, influenced by the Democratic political interests of the Anaconda Copper Mining Company, had called in Cook's loans as punishment for his politically supporting the Republican Wellington Duncan Rankin, his friend and attorney, in Rankin's bid for the governorship:

> While sympathizing with our old friend, A. B., we rejoice to learn that more than $470,000 was realized from a sale that brought bidders from all over the country and Canada. This result enables Mr. Cook to settle a loan of $235,000 with the copper company's bank at Helena

that put the screws on him and leaves him in the clear with something more than $230,000. But the herd is gone, leaving a gaping wound in the heart of the owner.[83]

The Helena branch of the National Bank of Montana was quick to respond, immediately initiating a libel suit against both Clark and his newspaper.[84] Weeks after the cattle sale, Cook died of a heart attack following an automobile accident in Helena.[85] The lawsuit and controversy, however, lived on for years, much as they had in the case of Cook's business associate, Alexander McKenzie. The bank vehemently denied that its actions had anything to do with Cook's political affiliations, giving evidence that Cook had, for some time, failed to make principal or interest payments to the bank on his outstanding notes and that the timing of the foreclosure and Rankin's nomination (and defeat) was merely coincidental.[86]

At the funeral service, held in Helena, the Unitarian minister delivered the eulogy:

> Mr. Cook was a man of big vision, all his life he was identified with big things. He drew about him men with big enterprising adventure

Fire at Cranberry Portage construction camp, June 1929. HARRY FALCONER McLEAN COLLECTION, ACCESSION 1981-064. PA 212849, LIBRARY AND ARCHIVES CANADA

whose faith in him and themselves was larger than the mustard seed of the gospels. He taught us all the spiritual lesson that not all can do the big things easily, but all can do the little things in a big generous way that gains the loving favor of many.[87]

>⊷⊶⊙⊷⊶⊰

Many of Dominion Construction's workers, including Jack Humphrey, stayed on in Manitoba to work on the Sherritt-Gordon line.[88] The tracks of steel reached Churchill on the Hudson Bay Railway by March 29, 1929, but the road bed remained to be installed the following spring – Major McLaughlin having adopted McLean's ingenious tried-and-true method.[89]

Most of the town of Cranberry Portage was destroyed by a forest fire in June 1929. The inferno almost certainly would have swallowed up the entire construction yard had it not been for the valiant efforts of Dominion Construction's workers and a couple of locomotive pumps.[90]

Humphrey remained on the Sherritt-Gordon job until its completion late in 1929. Then McLean sent him to the Dakota Business College at Fargo, North Dakota – the same college that he, Louis Nelson and Charlie Johnson had attended years before.[91]

Flin Flon's body of ore was finally tapped in 1930 by the Hudson Bay Mining and Smelting Company, which had found a workable solution to the Flin Flon ore problem. The expenditure of some $25 million to build the Island Falls power plant, run the transmission lines to Flin Flon, and establish the mining and metallurgical plants proved worthwhile, as the mine was a profitable venture for sixty-two years.[92]

Canada is no longer a string taut from east to west. It has breadth as well as length. It has a North. The railway in the Flin Flon has shown that.[93]

CHAPTER EIGHT

The End of the Line

The Guysborough Railway, Chapleau and Wolfe's Cove (1929–1931)

Everybody knows that there have been promises made repeatedly, pledges by both parties that railway facilities would be given to Guysboro as soon as possible, and I ask is there to be no morality in politics.[1]

RAILWAYS, BEING A link to development and prosperity, were discussed frequently by the inhabitants of Guysborough County and promised regularly by their political representatives. All agreed that local industries – mining, fisheries and forestry – would benefit from a railway as a means of transporting their products. In comparison to the other counties in Nova Scotia, Guysborough was not blessed with an abundance of track. The entire county possessed a total of seven miles of rail even though it was the third-largest county in the province.[2] This disparity had been pointed out repeatedly since the turn of the century, usually by Liberal politicians seeking votes. Several attempts by the provincial government to construct a railway were derailed due to disagreements about the route, lack of money or death in pursuit of funding.[3]

As Guysborough County residents were decidedly Liberal, Sir Wilfrid Laurier's government made an effort to give them their railway in 1911.

In August of that year, coincidentally just weeks before the federal election, tenders were called for the construction of two branch lines, SunnyBrae to Guysborough and Dartmouth to Dean's Settlement. On September 21st Robert Borden's Conservatives knocked the Liberals out of power after fifteen years. In the last days of Liberal rule the contracts were awarded to the Nova Scotia Construction Company for Guysborough and to M. P. Davis for Dartmouth. The surveys were complete and the plans filed; the next step was expropriation for the right-of-way.[4]

On October 10th Borden was sworn in as prime minister and the railway construction plan changed overnight. As the Member of Parliament from Halifax, Borden had been a proponent of a railway for Guysborough, but as prime minister he cancelled the project – within a day of being sworn in. As a further affront to the good citizens of

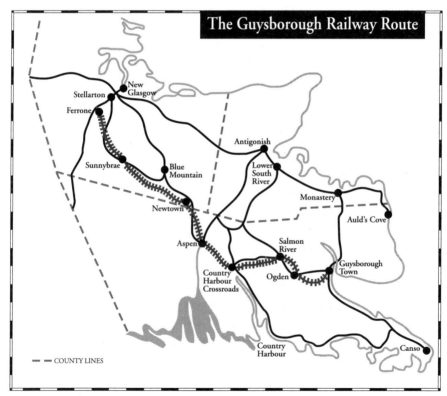

Based on illustration in *The Guysborough Railway,* by Bruce MacDonald, p. 30.

Guysborough, Borden did not cancel the Dartmouth to Dean's Settlement railway. Borden's action caused a furore and spirited debate, as some concluded that the surprise cancellation was a punitive measure for the county's support of the Liberals in the election.[5] James Cranswick Tory, a member of the Nova Scotia Legislative Assembly, concluded a lengthy address by denouncing Borden's decision:

> I regard this transaction as a piece of diabolical political treachery. I regard it as one of the worst acts of political hypocrisy ever perpetrated in this country, and as deliberate robbery of people who could not defend themselves.[6]

The topic of the Guysborough railway was raised by the Liberal Member of Parliament for the county in the House of Commons frequently during Borden's tenure. However, the outbreak of World War I, together with the great cost in men and money to fight it, placed the matter in limbo once again. Even after the war, neither the funds nor the political will to resurrect the project were evident. Yet the people of Guysborough County still clung to the belief that they would have their railway.

The defeat of the Conservative government in 1921 offered fresh hope that the railway project would be revived.[7] Several motions were raised before the House, including a promising one on June 15, 1925, when the following resolution was put forward for the consideration of the members:

> That it is expedient to bring in a measure to provide for the construction or completion prior to the thirty-first day of August, 1928, of a line of railway from Sunnybrae to Guysborough, in the Province of Nova Scotia, by the Canadian National Railway Company...[8]

But the overwhelmingly Conservative Senate refused to pass the resolution. William Lyon Mackenzie King's minority Liberal government was plagued by a Senate that blocked its every effort to construct the Guysborough railway.[9]

The next opportunity to bring up the matter came after a tumultuous period in Canadian politics. King refused to acknowledge his defeat to Arthur Meighen after the general election in the fall of 1925. Disregarding the fact that Meighen had won more seats, King continued to lead the government, using the issue of old-age pensions to win the support of independent and Progressive members. Meanwhile a corruption scandal erupted in the customs department, implicating a Liberal cabinet minister and again causing problems for the struggling prime minister.[10]

Hoping to force an election on the issue of the customs scandal, King appealed to the Governor General, Viscount Byng, to use his power to dissolve Parliament. Byng refused, thus spawning the so-called King-Byng Controversy. Incensed at what he deemed British interference in Canadian domestic politics, King resigned. Byng gave Meighen the opportunity to lead. However, Meighen's rule was short-lived as he failed to win a vote of confidence in the House of Commons. As a result, yet another general election was held, in the fall of 1926, and a still seething Mackenzie King managed to convince the Canadian electorate to vote for him once again, on the basis of their constitutional freedom. Back with a vengeance and a majority government, King began to address the nagging problem of the weighty Conservative Senate.[11]

Finally, in February 1929, Bill 44, "respecting the construction of a Canadian National railway line from Sunny brae to Guysborough, in the province of Nova Scotia," was introduced in the House of Commons by the Honourable C. A. Dunning, minister of Railways and Canals. The bill was read the requisite three times in the House, passed, and sent to the Senate Committee on Railways, Canals and Telegraph Lines for review and approval. King's adjustments to the Senate were enough to carry the bill through.[12]

Surveyors from the Canadian National Railway were sent to the area to re-survey the line for the long-awaited Guysborough railway. The *Eastern Chronicle* reported:

> It is some years since the line was located and the marks have been pretty well obliterated. These engineers will review those marks and have the location plans complete for construction work in a short time… The new railway is to be 67 miles in length… It may be accepted as a surety that the long looked for, much talked of railway, is now to become an established fact. Its construction will call for large expenditure and will mean considerable activity in labor and supply circles in Pictou and Guysborough Counties.[13]

The surveys were completed and a notice of tender appeared in the newspapers in September 1929. Days before the stock market crash, on October 18, 1929, Dominion Construction was awarded the Guysborough railway contract.[14] The *Eastern Chronicle* reported on the awarding of the contract:

> ...a well known railway building concern and has as its head Harry MacLean, a man of decided energy. He recently completed the hundred miles of railway into the Flin Flon mining district. He was given two years to do that job and had it finished six months ahead of time. If the same push is applied to the construction of the Guysboro railway, the sceptics, and strangely there are still some, can buy a ticket for Guysboro within the scheduled time.[15]

By early November some work crews had arrived in Sunny Brae, followed by equipment and then, on the 29th, Harry McLean and his foremen.[16] McLean's brother William was the line supervisor, Charles Tupper the superintendent, Eddie Reade the office manager, and H. McKeen and Louis Nelson the walking bosses. McLean subcontracted smaller sections of the railway and bridge work to his friend Andrew Wheaton.[17]

With winter setting in, the company was deluged with employment applications from local men. The *Eastern Chronicle* noted that

> there is a lot of preliminary work to be done, such as mapping and engineering, before actual construction can be started. It will be the policy to employ local help as far as possible, but they...are not ready to handle a large crew as yet. Men are paying their fares to SunnyBrae to work when there is no chance to take care of them. As soon as there is, the officials say, a call will be made.[18]

In deciding which applications to accept, McLean relied upon the advice of Alexander McGregor, a staunch Conservative. The idea that the "Liberal" railway might be built by Conservatives caused much consternation among the Liberals.[19] McLean was concerned that the job was languishing with an inexperienced crew that seemed "more intent upon its pay than upon its work."[20] Word of McLean's labour problems reached the men in The Pas, Manitoba, who had worked for him on the Flin Flon railway.

The Flin Flon crew, made up of smaller groups of different nationalities, decided to come to McLean's rescue in Nova Scotia, paying the cost of travel themselves. Arriving at the job site, they waited patiently by the tracks, having had no guarantee of employment on the Guysborough job. McLean immediately arranged for extra sleeping and dining cars for his surprise visitors.[21]

The various ethnic groups, among them Polish, Belgian, Italian, Swedish and Norwegian, were sent out as separate crews to work on half-mile or one-mile sections of the railway. There were between fifty and sixty such crews, who were paid by the yard and the money split equally among them. Many of the local men ended up working in the warehouse at Sunny Brae, as they could not keep up with the skilled Flin Flon crews. William McLean supplied the groups with food and supplies, the cost of which was deducted from their earnings. Some workers used their hunting and fishing skills, availing themselves of moose, deer and fish for supper.[22]

Although Dominion Construction owned several steam shovels, the work was inexplicably performed using horse-drawn scrapers and manual labour, supplemented by the occasional stick of dynamite to shake things up.[23] Progress was therefore quite slow, even though the route was far less challenging than that of Flin Flon with its interminable muskeg and landslides. Despite the slower pace, though, accidents did happen. One employee, walking across Guysborough Harbour in the wee hours of February 20, 1930, went through the ice and drowned. Another was killed near Salmon River as a result of a dynamite blast.[24] A Sons of Martha cairn was erected in their memory.

In the spring of 1930 McLean submitted a bid for the construction of a tunnel and a short line for the Canadian Pacific Railway in Quebec City. It would be several weeks before the CPR chose the successful bidder.[25] Returning to Guysborough, Harry and Bill McLean, along with fellow Scotsmen Alex MacGregor and D. J. Chisholm, took a leisurely drive along the route on a Victoria Day outing:

> Since all were of strong Scottish background, Harry insisted that Alex Robertson, the rock-man for the Dominion Construction Company, come along with his pipes. Harry also issued instructions for D. J. to

stop every once in a while; then, Alex would reluctantly step out of the automobile, and walk along the road bed playing the pipes as the car drove along-side. When they reached the Garden of Eden section, where there had been much rock-blasting going on, Harry once again ordered Alex to get out of the car and entertain. After several minutes, Harry permitted the exhausted piper to rest. Noticing a local farmer in a nearby field, Alex walked over and asked him how things were going. The farmer pointed to a number of large gaps and holes in the brush fence around his pasture. When Alex asked him what was the cause of the problem, the farmer stated that the racket in the area had spooked his cattle. The farmer was referring, of course, to the rock-blasting: Alex, however, thought he meant the bagpipes! He therefore stormed over to the car, and tossed the pipes onto Harry's lap, refusing to play another note. Alex then walked all the way back to Sunnybrae Headquarters in a fit of rage all the way.[26]

Richard Hearn recalled another one of McLean's stories from Guysborough:

> There was a post office down there and this chap from the post office [had] been living in the place more or less isolated for a while. One day somebody in his [McLean's] organization had ordered stuff from Montreal and it was sent C.O.D. And when this came into the post office this fellow was terribly concerned. He said, "I have never had anybody ship cod into this post office before."[27]

In the meantime the Dominion was heading towards another general election. The withering economy was wreaking havoc worldwide. Like many, King underestimated the Depression, believing an upswing was just around the corner. The difficult times prompted people to believe that a change in government would make things better. As a result, King lost to the Conservative R. B. Bennett in July 1930.[28] The Dominion government was facing a huge deficit and the Conservatives did not view the Guysborough railway project as a priority. In response to the government belt-tightening and explicit instructions to cease work issued by Dr. Manion, the new minister of Railways and Canals, Dominion Construction laid off men, removed its equipment and sold its draft horses.[29]

In August 1930 Bennett formally cancelled the Guysborough contract. Despite his campaign promise of employment, Bennett put two thousand men out of work when jobs were desperately needed. Over ninety percent of the grading had been completed, culverts and bridge substructures were in place, and twenty-two miles of track had been laid east of Sunny Brae.[30] Dominion Construction was paid $2,852,340.72 and abandoned the job.[31] By April of 1931 government interest in ever completing the line was in doubt:

> Due to the economic situation, the heavy deficit which the Dominion Government faces this year and the shrinkage in revenue, it has evidently been decided that there is no great hurry for the completion of the line on the part of the Ottawa authorities, and it is regarded as one of the public works that can wait.[32]

The Guysborough railway became just another broken political promise. The people of the county were left to wonder what might have been. Although successive Liberal MPs from Antigonish-Guysborough continually raised the matter in the House of Commons, their pleas were ignored. A Liberal MP made one last emotional appeal:

> No sadder picture can be imagined than to drive through that County...and note the political ruins of that enterprise. The grading has been completed and is now growing grass. The right-of-way belongs to the government, having been purchased and paid for. The concrete abutments for bridges are in place. All seems ready for the ties, rails, steel bridges and the station-houses and platforms. As it stands today, it is a travesty upon the viciousness of party politics.[33]

Some employees of Dominion Construction had been engaged in more fruitful labours. A dam and power house were constructed by the company at Chapleau, Ontario, on the north shore of Lake Superior. Again, the work was under contract with H. G. Acres and Company with Arthur McLaren as superintendent. As the job was fairly small, McLaren was in charge of both engineering and construction. The work consisted of constructing a gravity concrete dam, a thousand-foot-long wood stave pipe and a power house, along with a small bridge directly in front of the power house for the highways department. Dominion Construction also obtained a contract from the CPR in Chapleau to build an overhead bridge to connect to the double-track mainline. Once the work was completed, McLaren and his crew were called to work in Quebec at another job for the CPR.[34]

In an effort to attract ocean-bound Americans away from the more popular port of New York City, the CPR commissioned a new luxury vessel from John Brown and Company, veteran shipbuilders of Clydebank, Scotland. With competitors such as the Cunard and White Star lines expanding their fleets, and a sense that the economy was on the upswing, Canadian Pacific thought the new liner could serve transatlantic passengers between spring and fall and embark on world cruises during the winter.[35]

Workers started forming the keel on November 28, 1928, and over the next eighteen months the *Empress of Britain* began to take shape.[36] The *Britain* was launched into the waters of the Clyde River on June 11, 1930, by the Prince of Wales.[37] She was scheduled to undergo a further ten months of outfitting and decorating prior to delivery. As five of England's most prominent artisans were adorning the *Britain*'s public rooms with magnitudes of luxury commensurate with her patrons' wealth,[38] ambitious projects were under way across the Atlantic in preparation for her maiden voyage.

At 42,348 tons, the *Empress of Britain* was the largest ship in Canadian Pacific's fleet.[39] The old docking facilities in Quebec City, located at the convergence of the St. Lawrence and St. Charles rivers, were deemed inadequate for a ship of this size. A site was chosen for a new terminal

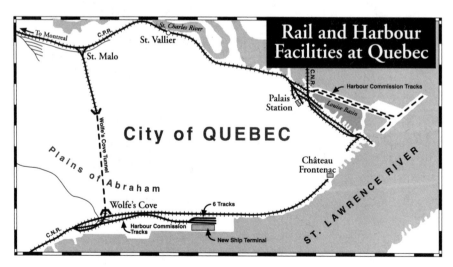

Based on illustration in *Railway Age*, June 1931, p. 1228.

near Wolfe's Cove, the historic landing point for Major General James Wolfe's surprise attack against Lieutenant General Louis-Joseph de Montcalm in the Battle of the Plains of Abraham. Wolfe's Cove offered several benefits. Its main advantages were that the water was sufficiently deep next to the shore to accommodate the enormous vessel, so that little dredging would be necessary, and the area was well sheltered.[40]

Wishing to capitalize on a seamless route to the Orient by linking its Atlantic and Pacific routes to a cross-Canada rail service, the CPR decided that a one-and-a-half-mile single-rail line was required to link the main railway line to the new port facility.[41] The challenge of the short line was that one mile of it had to be run through a sixteen-foot-wide tunnel to the west of the Plains of Abraham in order to avoid altering the historic site.[42] Tenders were issued and, having submitted the lowest bid, Dominion Construction was awarded the contract on July 2, 1930 – although the work was carried out by H. F. McLean Limited. McLean left Guysborough the next day, wasting no time in abandoning that dead-end project.[43]

The terms of the Wolfe's Cove contract dictated that construction of the tunnel be completed in eleven months. Within three days of being notified of the awarding of the contract, McLean had moved a small crew to the site.[44] H. G. Acres was consulting engineer and Arthur McLaren was superintendent of the tunnel work. The six-hundred-man crew was housed in railway cars and fed in dining cars that had been brought to the shores of the St. Lawrence River.[45] Early

South Portal, Wolfe's Cove, August 6, 1930.
HARRY FALCONER McLEAN COLLECTION, ACCESSION 1981-064. PA 212856, LIBRARY AND ARCHIVES CANADA

in August, grading commenced for both the north and south approaches of the tunnel. In the process, some nine thousand cubic yards of material was moved.[46]

Some of the equipment used for the Grand Falls, New Brunswick, job, such as compressors, electric locomotives and motor generators, was resurrected for Wolfe's Cove.[47] Through limestone and shale, the tunnelling work commenced in two shifts starting from each end. The limestone posed few problems, as it was self-supporting, but the shale had to be supported with timbers until the concrete lining could be fitted.[48]

Detonation of several pounds of dynamite marked the start of each twelve-hour shift and the headings advanced about sixteen feet each day. Once sufficient progress had been made, blowers were used for ventilation – to clear the dust and gases resulting from the explosion – and the heaps of muck were sprayed with water so that the workers would not be harmed by the dust. Considerable progress was made with the drilling, blasting and mucking operations, with the muckers racing to load up to twenty muck cars an hour to keep the heading clear for the drillers.[49] The muck at the south end was used as fill at the waterfront.[50] Drilling was completed on February 16, 1930, as the two crews met underground.[51] Progress was described as "satisfactory." The engineers estimated that the entire tunnel would be completed within six weeks.

At the end of March the workers were directed to pick up the pace. The work had to be expedited as the arrival date of the ship was moved forward from the end of June to the beginning. Five concrete-mixing stations were established, one at either end of the tunnel and three inside. Cars delivered concrete to the interior mixing stations, and the sand and rock, in proper proportions for a batch, were shot through well drill holes from one hundred and eighty-five to two hundred and fifteen feet in length from a roadway above, so the delivery of aggregate would not interfere with mucking operations. At each station, the concrete-mixing equipment was supported on wooden towers, each with an upper and a lower platform. Muck trains ran underneath the lower platform, upon which the concrete mixer was located. The upper platform was used to store cement as well as to act as a buttress for a hopper, which passed

Wolfe's Cove. ©1931, CANADIAN PACIFIC RAILWAY ARCHIVES, NS 25977

aggregate through a chute to the mixer below. The concrete placer received set amounts of concrete directly from the mixer.[52]

Where concrete was used to inhibit weathering, a one-foot-thick lining of plain concrete was applied; if there was any concern about potential stresses from any other cause, an extra three inches was added and the concrete was reinforced.[53] Three alcoves were cut into the tunnel so that workers could stand clear of the trains.[54]

Water seepage through the rock was evident in much of the tunnel and was cause for concern during the lining process. Worries that the green concrete would become wet and fail to set properly were allayed through the use of ten thousand square feet of sheet metal, applied to the arch behind the timber to shed the water and allow the concrete to set. The entire tunnel was lined in concrete at the rate of twenty feet at each end on alternate days; it was reinforced with steel in the timbered

Empress of Britain II *at Wolfe's Cove.* ©1935, Canadian Pacific Railway Archives, NS 23521

shale sections.[55] Inevitably, accidents occurred on the Wolfe's Cove project. A Sons of Martha cairn was erected at the site.

The first train, consisting of a locomotive and thirteen carloads of officials, went through the tunnel on May 26, 1931. The track had been completed just days before.[56] The *Britain* sailed from Southampton on the 27th, with the Prince of Wales once again at dockside for the launch.[57] Britain's *Daily Express* reported:

> An event of Imperial moment takes place today. The *Empress of Britain* sails on her maiden voyage from Southampton to Canada. The same vision and faith that flung the railways across Canada from ocean to ocean in superb confidence that settlers and trade would follow have inspired this magnificent vessel. The skill and experience of British shipwrights have built her.

The finest ship on all the seas, she is also a vibrant proof of what Canada and Britain working together can achieve...New York made more accessible from England via Canada than by direct route; the St. Lawrence transformed into one of the greatest of trans-Atlantic and Imperial thoroughfares, such are but a few of the possibilities assured by this commanding stroke of commercial genius.[58]

The ship's first crossing was smooth, taking five days, thirteen hours and twenty-five minutes – a new record for speed. More than one hundred thousand people turned out to see the *Britain* arrive at Quebec City and to participate in three days of gala events and tours of the ship. Many in the crowd hoped to see the Hollywood stars Mary Pickford and Douglas Fairbanks, who were among the ship's passengers. A banquet was held in the opulent dining room on June 2nd. The guests included Prime Minister R. B. Bennett and the former prime minister, Robert Borden, along with a generous portion of high society and representatives from big business.[59]

McLean detested ceremonies and avoided them whenever possible. With the work in Quebec completed and the celebrations under way, he dispatched his men to northern Ontario where two projects were already in progress: the extension of the Temiskaming and Northern Ontario Railway from Fraserdale to Moosonee, and a vast hydroelectric project on the Abitibi River.

CHAPTER NINE

Men Against the Moose

Temiskaming and Northern Ontario Railway, Fraserdale to Coral Rapids to the Moose River to Moosonee

Hudson Bay beckons. The programme of construction entered upon last fall will not cease until tidewater is reached and new sources of provincial wealth made available through the exploitation of the natural resources of the northland. There are great fur and fishery possibilities, which the completion of the road will render accessible to the large consuming centres of Ontario, Québec and the Middle West. There are also timber and pulpwood areas of great extent tributary to the Moose, Abitibi and Mattagami Rivers, and the enormous mineral deposits of the Belcher Islands will provide manufacturing [in] Ontario with a commercial grade of iron ore for the general enrichment of the Province.[1]

In attempting to seek justification for the construction of this extension, I cannot conceive how anyone could have anticipated any profitable traffic to result therefrom.[2]

BUILT IN SECTIONS as could be warranted by potential revenue, the Temiskaming and Northern Ontario Railway (T&NO) was an Ontario government undertaking, intended to attract settlers to the north and gain access to bountiful natural resources. The railway was to be built and managed by a group of "not more than five nor less than

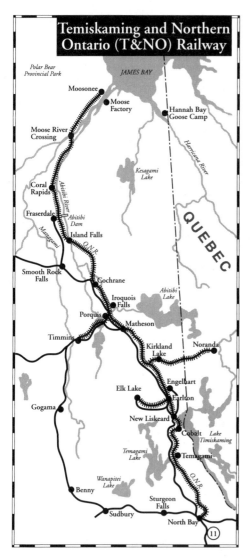

Temiskaming and Northern Ontario (T&NO) Railway

Based on illustration in *Toronto Star Weekly*, Jan. 24, 1932, p. 1.

three persons appointed by the Lieutenant-Governor in Council,"[3] otherwise known as the T&NO Commission. The Act incorporating the Commission, and setting out the rationale for constructing the railway, was passed in 1902:

There are large areas of arable land, well fitted for settlement, and extensive tracts of merchantable pine and other valuable timber and deposits of ores and minerals in the district of Ontario which lies between Lake Nipissing and Lake Abitibi and northwesterly from Lake Temiskaming, which are expected, upon development, to add greatly to the wealth of the province, and that it is in the public interest that the said district should be, at as early a date as possible, brought into communication with existing lines of railway.[4]

Turning the first clump of earth at the sod-turning ceremony for the T&NO on May 10, 1902, was the Honourable Francis R. "Frank" Latchford, minister of Public Works for the Liberal government of Premier George Ross.[5] North Bay, a Canadian Pacific town with a Grand Trunk junction, was selected as the southern terminus.[6] The first section of line, built from North Bay to New Liskeard, was completed in the fall of 1904, coinciding with the discovery of silver and the subsequent boom at Cobalt. With a further extension fully defensible by the increased revenues resulting from the mining industry, the T&NO was extended to Englehart, then to Matheson and finally, in 1908, to Cochrane.[7] Many of the towns along the line are named after politicians or T&NO commissioners.

The progress of the railway was then stalled at Cochrane for fourteen years. Several studies were initiated during those years to determine whether there were sufficient quantities of minerals, petroleum or timber north of Cochrane to warrant further construction. Most of the reports concluded that there were no prospects for development of these resources in the area past Abitibi.[8] The idea of an ocean port for Ontario was appealing to some and dismissed as impractical and imprudent by others. In any case all serious discussion of further expansion to James Bay came to a halt during World War I.[9]

Hydroelectric energy became an increasing source of interest north of Cochrane. The mines and pulp and paper plants drew enormous amounts of power. The owners of these operations told their political representatives and the T&NO commissioners about their grave apprehension that demand would surpass supply. In response to the likely overstated concerns of the plant owners and exaggerated reports of resource potential by George Lee, the T&NO chairman, in January 1922 the Ontario government under Premier E. C. Drury approved the construction of seventy miles of track from Cochrane to the Abitibi River.[10] The railway contract was awarded to two firms: Grant Smith and Company and McDonnell Limited.[11] Another company, Dominion Bridge of Hamilton, was brought in to build the bridge across the Abitibi River.[12]

Delays in construction by Smith and McDonnell led to dissatisfaction on the part of the commissioners. The terms of the contract called for the laying of track to the Abitibi River by December 1922 and to New Post by the end of October 1923, and now it seemed unlikely that either of these deadlines would be met.[13] The T&NO engineers pressured the contractors, who did not respond well to their demands. Disappointed by the slow progress, Lee wrote to Drury:

The present Contractors did not seem to understand what they were going into when they took this contract. I doubt – by the way they are going at it – if they ever had any experience in the matter. However, they claim that they will finish in the specified time and there is not very much action we can take.[14]

To make matters worse, the track arrived at the Abitibi River too late to permit construction before the spring flooding, prompting yet another delay. Lee's reaction to this news was pointed. He told his chief engineer:

If they cannot complete the contract let them say so and get off the Line. No excuses will be taken in connection with this matter.[15]

Both firms withdrew from the contract, taking a loss.[16]

After the summer 1923 election of G. Howard Ferguson as premier of Ontario, it became clear that any further extension of the railway, beyond what the previous government had committed to, was highly doubtful. Ferguson visited the area that year and could find no reason to extend the railway:

There is no immediate prospect of a Temiskaming & Northern Ontario extension to James Bay, and comparatively little likelihood of it within the next decade...

The bulk of the timber is to be found within one hundred miles north of the Transcontinental Railway. Beyond that (Abitibi Canyon) conditions change in a marked degree, and generally speaking, merchantable timber is to be found only on the banks of the rivers. The soil is of low level; a large percentage of it is muskeg and would have to be drained before it could be suitable for agriculture.

As to the feasibility of an ocean port, there is a depth of water in Hudson's Bay [sic], but across the southern end of James Bay and across the mouth of the Moose [River] there are a great many reefs and bars, some of which would have to be dredged to allow even a moderate sized vessel to find dockage in the mouth of the river.[17]

Ultimately the Commission itself took control of the project and sent in C. D. French and Company to complete the work left unfinished by Smith and McDonnell. By December 1924 the work was completed.[18]

After winning another majority government late in 1926, Ferguson reconsidered his stand against building new sections of the line. He had heard the prophecies of the mining and paper industrialists about a pending hydroelectric shortage, as well as rehashed speculation about valuable gypsum deposits along the Moose River. In April 1927 Ferguson agreed to extend the line northward from Mile 68 to Mile 100.[19]

The call for tenders went out and within the month the T&NO Commission was reviewing bids. Although another company had submitted a lower bid, the party line was that some of its prices were found to be questionable by the T&NO chief engineer. Unofficially, Harry McLean was the preferred candidate. The commissioners "unanimously resolved that judging from the past experience and the necessity for the completion of the work this year, as well as the proper performance of the contract, that the tender submitted by H. F. McLean Limited be accepted."[20] The failure of Smith, McDonnell and similar firms to complete projects lingered in their minds, and McLean could be trusted to finish the job. The section was completed by October 18, 1928, with only slight cost and time overruns.[21]

Next on the agenda was a section to the Moose River. In April 1929 the Commission asked its engineers to provide a report on the proposal to extend the line to James Bay. Like the many existing documents on the topic, the report was to outline the prospects for the development of natural resources in the area and the use of Moose Harbour for a significant amount of shipping

Filling in the trestle, T&NO, August 1927.
Harry Falconer McLean Collection, Accession 1981-064. PA 212847, Library and Archives Canada

Workers at T&NO railway camp, November 1927. HARRY FALCONER MCLEAN COLLECTION, ACCESSION 1981-064. PA 212846, LIBRARY AND ARCHIVES CANADA

traffic. The engineers were also to provide conclusions and recommendations. Not surprisingly, the report, issued a month later, was strikingly similar to its predecessors. The only difference was that lignite fields and gypsum deposits had since been found in the area, but whether these could be developed to any extent remained unclear. The main argument of the report was that the area was so vast that it may well have contained quantities of untold resources.[22]

In spite of the speculative conclusions of the report, the Commission prepared the documentation necessary to proceed with the line across the Moose River and submitted it to Premier Ferguson. On January 28, 1930, Ferguson advised Lee to proceed with extending the line as far as the Moose River. The call for tenders went out and three bids were returned. The lowest bidder was H. F. McLean Limited.[23]

In terms of engineering challenges, constructing the line itself was not particularly difficult. The terrain that surrounds James Bay for at least a hundred miles is flat, marshy lowland. Clearing it was not an especially onerous task, as the tree growth in the area was rather stunted. The technique used in building the Flin Flon railway – laying rail over frozen muskeg – served McLean well this time around. The main problem was obtaining ballast: crushed rock had to be shipped in.[24]

In mid-April 1930 negotiations between the T&NO and H. F. McLean Limited commenced for the Moose River Bridge. This time, however, tenders were not issued; on July 3, 1930, the contract was simply let to McLean, at a cost of approximately $1 million.[25] The effects of the Depression caused Ferguson to briefly consider stopping the work altogether; however, in a letter to George Lee dated July 29, 1930, he stated:

> In view of the present unemployment situation I think this work should be continued this year. If we were to stop work now and turn away hundreds of men, it would only aggravate the present difficult labor situation.[26]

On August 19, 1930, two more contracts were awarded to H. F. McLean Limited without tenders

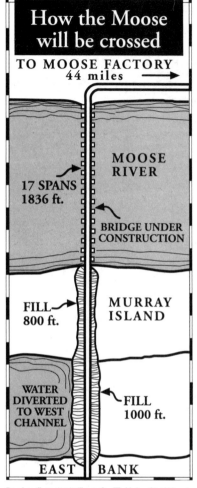

How the Moose will be crossed

TO MOOSE FACTORY
44 miles ➞

MOOSE RIVER

17 SPANS 1836 ft.

BRIDGE UNDER CONSTRUCTION

FILL➞ 800 ft.

MURRAY ISLAND

WATER DIVERTED TO WEST CHANNEL

FILL 1000 ft.

EAST BANK

Based on illustration in *Toronto Star Weekly,* Jan. 24, 1932, p. 1.

being put out. The first was for ballasting between Island Falls and Fraserdale and the second for completing the line from the Moose River Bridge to Revillon's Post near Moose Factory at the mouth of the Moose River.[27]

>-+◆>-◦-<◆+-<

Built circa 1670, Moose Factory is Ontario's oldest settlement. It is located on Factory Island approximately eleven miles inland from the mouth of the Moose River on James Bay. Despite its name, no moose were ever manufactured in Moose Factory. Rather, the name describes the settlement's origins as a trading post. The factor worked as a merchant, buying and selling on commission, and the factory was the merchant company's foreign trading station; the factory sat on the shores of the Moose River – hence Moose Factory. The merchant company in this case was the Hudson's Bay Company and the trade was in furs.[28]

Across the river from Moose Factory, a post was established in 1903 by Revillon Frères, the Hudson's Bay Company's French rival. A site near Revillon's Post was selected as the final destination for the T&NO. "On to the Bay" became the battle cry for a south-to-north railway in Ontario that would extend to tidewater on James Bay.[29] At last, Ontario would have the saltwater port it had long craved. With great optimism, the southern Ontario press pointed out that the benefits were obvious:

> …the Hudson Bay is fed, both on the Ontario and Quebec sides by long rivers. These rivers offer an easy means of transportation into the far northern wilds of the two provinces. The new railhead at Moose Factory will act as a great base of supplies for exploration parties and

H. F. McLean workers riding in a truck converted for rail use. HARRY FALCONER McLEAN COLLECTION, ACCESSION 1981-064. PA 207736, LIBRARY AND ARCHIVES CANADA

Laying the track on the T&NO: The subgrade has been prepared and the ties are placed on top; the rail-mounted track-laying gantry swings the rails into position. The construction train follows behind with the rails, ties and track fastenings. Later, several inches of ballast will be added to reinforce the track – the rails will be raised and the ballast consolidated around the ties. Harry Falconer McLean Collection, Accession 1981-064. PA 212861, Library and Archives Canada

for the shipment of supplies and equipment for the development of discoveries that are almost certain to be made… Moose Factory then will be transformed overnight from a mere name on the map to the key that will open up the wonders of far northern Ontario and Quebec.[30]

Reporters from Toronto visited McLean and his job sites regularly, and their propaganda-laden reports appeared in the big Canadian dailies, waxing about the region's "extensive water power, agricultural and mineral potentialities."[31] One report compared Moose Factory to Calgary because it "lies in about the same latitude"[32] and to southern Ontario because "soil conditions permit the growth of all the vegetables, including potatoes, turnips and lettuce, commonly grown around Toronto."[33] The only new personal information McLean had provided the reporter was that he was fifteen years of age before he knew that a chicken had anything but a neck.[34] The "coupon clippers who sit so softly in the south"[35] were treated to such dramatic gems as this one from the *Toronto Star Weekly:*

> It was a morning of primeval melancholy. Blue-gray fog clouded the dark, snow-patched wilderness that stretched on all sides to infinity. Below lay a land bleak and harsh, winter-gripped and dead. But through it ran the faint line of the ribbon of steel which was the only sign of its new servitude.[36]

McLean was constantly on the move. Between jobs and business meetings, he was known to frequently have breakfast, lunch and dinner in three different places. When he travelled by rail, his private coach, "Renée," served as his office, dining room, living room and bedroom.[37]

When in Ottawa he stayed at the Château Laurier and when in Toronto at the Royal York. He kept suites at both hotels and was well known by the staff, in particular a waiter known as "Frenchie" who

McLean's private car, dubbed "Renée," May 1947. ANDREW MERRILEES COLLECTION, ACCESSION 1980-149. PA 205858, LIBRARY AND ARCHIVES CANADA

Harry McLean with one of his private airplanes. HARRY FALCONER MCLEAN COLLECTION, ACCESSION 1981-064. PA 207738, LIBRARY AND ARCHIVES CANADA

served in the Imperial Room at the Royal York. One day an unsuspecting Frenchie was mobbed by McLean and his business associates. The unflappable waiter endured the manhandling, even when the tails of his formal coat were ripped asunder, leaving his uniform in two pieces. McLean picked up the remnants of the coat and handed them to the still perfectly composed Frenchie, who then escorted McLean and party to his reserved table. Frenchie knew McLean well enough to expect a new coat and a substantial tip the next day.[38]

With his fresh new uniform, Frenchie was hired by McLean to accompany him on a month-long trip to Prince Edward Island, where McLean had a cottage that was always full of guests. Frenchie's main task was to go out and buy beer, and McLean kept him well supplied with hundred-dollar bills for this purpose. At the end of the month McLean remembered that Frenchie had neglected to give him the change. Again, the waiter was wrestled by McLean, ending up completely disrobed and left outside in a vulnerable state. McLean then called the police to have Frenchie picked up and jailed for indecent exposure.[39]

With the distance between projects spanning several provinces, McLean embraced flight as a necessary means of travel. He owned a Stinson and a Beechcraft and employed many pilots over the years, most notably Lew Orton, Dick Preston and Robbie "Doc" Robertson.

> Air travel is essential to the development of the great wild country in Canada. The ordinary methods of travel take days and weeks and months, but with an airplane it becomes a matter of hours. Of course, I've had a few crashes.[40]

During one mishap, McLean and Robertson were forced to land on a northern river. They discovered a cabin on the shore and the trapper's wife invited the men in and gave them dinner. Robertson managed to get the plane going again. Within a week, McLean sent provisions of every description to repay the woman for her kindness and hospitality.[41] Another accident occurred while McLean was en route to Bismarck in early 1930. A fierce snowstorm grounded his party in a wheat field. There were no injuries, but McLean's whereabouts were unknown for some six hours after he had left Grand Forks.[42]

In September 1930 work began on the Moose River Bridge. James Therrien, a long-time McLean employee, had worked his way up in the

T&NO trestle at Moose River. HARRY FALCONER MCLEAN COLLECTION, ACCESSION 1981-064. PA 212848, LIBRARY AND ARCHIVES CANADA

organization and was now a partner in Dominion Construction as well as in Grenville Crushed Rock. Therrien was in charge of the bridge work on the T&NO, as by then McLean was fully engaged at the Abitibi River hydroelectric site. Therrien was smaller in stature than McLean and was described as a quiet man "of costs and figures."[43]

> Where McLean fires on percussion, Therrien lays a time fuse and looks about him before he lights it. Where H. F. would fire snap decisions yes or no, in answer to questions involving million dollar matters – and will be right in his judgment more often than not – Jimmie will sleep on the problem and let you know in the morning.[44]

Murray Island sits in the middle of the shallow Moose River, and its central location was a natural choice for situating the construction camp and concrete-mixing plant. Rather than span the entire width of the river (3,736 feet), a decision was made to dam the east channel, as one channel could easily carry the river flow. To bridge the river, a temporary wooden trestle was built across the east channel and over Murray Island.[45]

By October it was time to fill the channel. Therrien's men started filling it from either side, both to bury the base of the trestle and to hold back the water. The river, however, would not be held back, and it began to sweep the earth away. The men were instructed to fill five thousand sandbags, which in one long day were placed between the wooden trestles. At one point eight trains full of sandbags and earth, stretching about ten miles down the line, were waiting to unload into the river – some 300,000 yards of material in all. The men fought the river for nine gruelling hours.[46]

> The Moose was conquered – and Mr. Therrien told me, with a smile, that two hundred men, away up there in the wilderness, in the light of flares on a winter evening took off their hats and cheered like collegiate boys at a rugby game.[47]

The next task was construction of a 1,836-foot-long bridge over the west channel of the river. It was a race against time, for the work had to be completed before the spring flooding to avoid the risk of having all efforts swept downstream. First, cofferdams were put in place, revealing a loose shale riverbed. Before any concrete could be poured, shale up to twenty feet in depth had to be excavated so that the piers would be anchored in solid rock. McLean's men had gained expertise in pouring concrete in frigid conditions – even temperatures as low as forty below zero – taking care to heat the concrete and shield the forms after pouring. Sixteen concrete bridge piers and two abutments were poured during the winter of 1930 to span the river, using approximately 14,500 yards of concrete.[48]

The relationship between H. F. McLean Limited and the T&NO commissioners was not always smooth. A meeting was scheduled for November 20, 1930, at Ottawa's Château Laurier Hotel between representatives of the T&NO Commission and H. F. McLean Limited to discuss the latter's "great dissatisfaction in the treatment they had received"[49] with respect to ongoing disagreements about grading classification. Grading classification was a sore point with the Commission. Hard-pan excavation was far more expensive, at a dollar per cubic yard, than common excavation, at thirty-six cents per cubic yard. The estimates for hard-pan were low, but, in reality, changes in classification from common to hard-pan cost an additional five hundred and fifty thousand dollars.[50]

Although McLean was in New York that day, an agreement was hashed out between Therrien and the commissioners. Any future misunderstanding between the two parties was to be discussed immediately with the T&NO chief engineer, who was given instructions by the Commission "to deal fairly and as liberally as possible with the contractors, in accordance with the contract."[51]

With the concrete piers securely in place by the spring of 1931, the Dominion Bridge Company of Hamilton was brought in for the third time on the line between Cochrane and James Bay. Its work was exemplary, and the commissioners were impressed with the speed with which the company placed and bolted the steel girders. Dominion Bridge's work on the project was completed within one month.[52]

In June 1931 the commissioners decided that, "in view of all of the circumstances"[53] – namely the Depression – the line would not open that year. The following month McLean escorted a group of prominent businessmen on a tour of the "industrial enterprises of Northern Ontario,"[54] which included two of his projects, the Abitibi hydroelectric development and the T&NO extension as far as the Moose River. Many American financiers were along for the ride, including top executives from the Bank of America and the Guarantee Company of New York. The tour ended in North Bay and all the guests were invited to an informal dinner at the Empire Hotel, where they heard a lengthy speech about the "necessary cooperation between governments, transportation companies and financial institutions with the concerns which were undertaking to develop the great natural resources of Northern Ontario."[55]

Track was laid across the bridge and was ready to carry traffic by the end of August 1931. A Sons of Martha cairn was erected in Moosonee. The remaining line was laid without incident while the bridge was being completed. George Lee sent a telegram to the premier:

> Have pleasure in advising you that steel was laid to Moose Factory at five p.m. on August Thirty First.[56]

The Commission had advised McLean and Therrien to close out the work by the fall of 1931 and to do

> everything that could be done in the way of ballasting, etc., leaving the balance of the work to be undertaken by the commission's forces in the spring.[57]

During the week of September 6 to 12, 1931, McLean played host to a second group of prominent individuals – doctors, lawyers and businessmen – escorting them to Moose Harbour. Praise was heaped upon McLean and the Commission from all those present and the expedition was deemed a success. With a new premier, George S. Henry, installed at Queen's Park, Lee gathered comments from correspondence he received after the event and quoted them in letters to Henry to illustrate the wisdom of extending the line to James Bay. He hoped the comments would convey to the premier "the impression that people get from a visit there. There is no doubt that in the very near future it will be one of the most popular places in Canada."[58] The comments were indeed effusive:

> I distinctly remember some years ago when the various extensions, since completed, were being discussed, the many protests that were made, and the number who said that the traffic results would not

warrant the expenditure. Time, however, has shown the wisdom of the Commissioners on those occasions in going ahead with their plans, and I trust and believe that the extension now about completed to James Bay will prove just as remunerative as those to which I have just referred.[59]

What has been achieved by your Line was certainly a revelation to me and I feel sure that future events will justify the confidence shown by your Commission in completing the Line to James Bay.[60]

We have fired the imagination of all our friends so they are all anxious to make the trip.[61]

The task of naming the northern terminal fell to Lee. Having discovered that the Cree word "Moosoneek" translates as "at the Moose," Lee wrote to Premier Henry in November 1931 to suggest a slightly altered version, Moosonee.[62]

The official opening of the extension to Moosonee took place on July 15, 1932.[63] Invitations had been sent to Prime Minister R. B. Bennett, Premier L. A. Taschereau of Quebec, Sir Henry Thornton, president of the CNR, and E. W. Beatty, president of the CPR, as well as every cabinet minister, politician, businessman and member of the press the

Driving the last spike in the T&NO extension to Moosonee, 1932.
PHOTOGRAPH: www.canadianheritage.ca ID #20039

Last spike ceremony for the T&NO. Foreground, left to right: former Ontario premier E. C. Drury, future premier George S. Henry, and Justice Francis R. Latchford.
F. R. LATCHFORD COLLECTION, ACCESSION 1970-035. PA-213659, LIBRARY AND ARCHIVES CANADA

organizers could think of across the country. Trainloads of men wearing three-piece suits made the day-long journey north.[64] Three "Last Spikes" were driven, the first by Frank Latchford, who had turned the first clump of earth to set the railway in motion thirty years before, the second by E. C. Drury and the third by Premier Henry.[65] Lee was in his glory, having achieved the completion of the line to tidewater.

Not all the invitees viewed the final extension as an achievement. Number Thirty-Eight on the guest list for the grand opening was of the opinion that the line beyond Abitibi Canyon was a waste of time and money. Although at that juncture his opinions were of no particular consequence, a few years later they would influence the entire province of Ontario – and cause utter misery for Harry McLean.

CHAPTER TEN

Powerful White Horses

Abitibi Canyon (1930–1933)

As though Aladdin's lamp had been rubbed and its genie commanded, a hardly believable change occurs. Almost overnight there springs up a virtual town site of over two thousand individuals, who have been marshaled together to cope with the great natural resources of the impressive Abitibi river and canyon, to help harness the powerful white horses which have cavorted in this gorge for aeons.[1]

It had been a mild winter for the North, but now the temperature had dropped to twenty below zero. Wind-whipped clouds raced across a pallid sun. Powdery snow, blown from the drifts, lashed exposed skin like the cut of a sand blast. All this, however, had not interfered one whit with the activities of nearly two thousand heavily clothed men, fighting against time to build a tremendous power dam across the Abitibi River in northern Ontario.[2]

IN THE LATE 1920s the demand for electricity in Ontario increased in parallel with the expansion of industry in the province. Unresolved jurisdictional issues over the Ottawa, St. Lawrence and Niagara rivers increased the probability that the predicted energy shortage would in fact occur. To sate the voracious and escalating appetite for electrical power, the Ontario government and Premier Ferguson entered into contracts with four private power companies: Ottawa Valley;

Beauharnois, Light, Heat and Power; Maclaren-Quebec; and Gatineau. The government also purchased two power companies. The Ontario Power Service Corporation (OPSC), a subsidiary of the Abitibi Power and Paper Company, agreed to sell 100,000 horsepower to Ontario Hydro on an annual basis, on the condition that the government lease the Abitibi Canyon site to it for ten years, rent free.[3]

H. G. Acres and Company had been hired by the Dominion Construction Company to assist in the preparation of a tender to the OPSC for power development on the Abitibi River. Sam Deeks, president of Dominion Construction, had passed away on May 1, 1930. J. Homer Black of the Abitibi Company purchased Deeks's shares and became president of Dominion. The OPSC awarded the contract to Dominion Construction on August 14, 1930.[4]

Dominion Construction wanted H. G. Acres as its supervising engineers, but the OPSC refused its wishes because of past differences with the Acres firm. Instead, Richard Lankaster "Dick" Hearn, a partner at H. G. Acres who had worked on the tender, was given permission to act, in a personal capacity, as consulting engineer and liaison between Dominion and the OPSC.[5] Ever since the project at Grand Falls, New Brunswick, Harry McLean had pursued Hearn to work with him. Although the two men did not always agree, McLean respected Hearn and valued his judgement. An engineering firm from New York City, George F. Hardy, was retained to provide supervision and design services.

>─┼─◄►─┼─O─┼─◄►─┼─◄

Situated some seventy miles north of Cochrane, Abitibi Canyon was accessible only by rail. Large-scale construction jobs were increasingly rare as the Depression wore on, and, despite the remote location of Abitibi Canyon with its infestation of black flies, hundreds of men turned up seeking employment. Many had worked for McLean before and followed him nomadically from job to job.[6] Dominion Construction's core management group was put in place for the project: Gordon Mitchell, general superintendent; Arthur A. McLaren, power house superintendent; H. E. Barnett, project engineer; Charles W. Switzer, office manager;

Colonel Kenneth A. Ramsay, transportation superintendent; and Charles Hyson, foreman of the electrical department.[7]

Hyson arrived at the job site at two in the morning. After a bumpy ride from Cochrane in the company "ambulance" – a steel-wheeled stationwagon equipped with stretchers – he groped around in the dark, found a space in a tent to roll out his sleeping bag, and tried to catch some sleep. Hyson recalled the first day:

> Everybody got up very early and some of the old-timers were there already, doing some road work and also some grading for an extension of the track...early breakfast – and I mean early – there were a couple hundred people in there then, labourers of all types and a few railroaders, and you were assigned your breakfast – number one sitting or number two sitting or number three sitting or whatever it happened to be...you were glad to get something to eat. There was absolutely nothing there. A great gang were clearing and cleaning and burning brush and rubbish and making little access paths and roads here and there to get down to the canyon rim.[8]

The only signs of civilization were a cable bridge spanning the canyon that had been erected by other contractors who had tried – but failed – to land the contract, and a power line brought in by the Abitibi Company.[9]

Dominion Construction established a hiring hall in Cochrane to handle the throngs of potential employees. The hiring manager, Charlie McKay, was "a rough and ready guy" adept at choosing good workers and weeding out bad ones. McKay was known to say, "I have three different gangs, one goin', one workin' and one comin'."[10] Men of every trade were hired. The first job was to build a town.

Given the secluded location and the approach of winter, the prime concern was shelter. Initially the men were housed in tents and eighty railway coaches that Dominion Construction had left over from railway jobs. The company had purchased dozens of old-fashioned wooden coaches from the Illinois Central. With the seats removed and partitions added, the coaches served the management until more permanent accommodations could be built. Each day, dozens of recruits were delivered to Abitibi via the spur line from Fraserdale, Ontario, on the

T&NO. Carpenters were the preferred tradesmen at first, followed by mechanics and general labourers.[11]

Four large bunkhouses with washing facilities and a long dining hall were built to accommodate the hundreds of workers expected to live and work at Abitibi. Warehouses and machine and woodworking shops followed. In anticipation of the large quantity of rock that would be excavated from the site, a crushing plant was constructed as well as a concrete-mixing plant.[12]

More basic requirements like proper sanitation had to be considered. Drinking water was "a bit rough – it was all muskeg and our stomachs weren't accustomed to drinking that kind of slop."[13] Line-ups at the outhouses were commonplace as the workers' distressed bowels revolted. News of the intestinal misfortune of Abitibi employees was a source of amusement for McLean's employees at more civilized job sites. Rolls of toilet paper arrived in the mail addressed to workmates who had moved to Abitibi.[14] The hygiene problem was resolved with the installation of a complete sewer system serving all buildings, and an insulated 25,000-gallon water tank propped up on high timber ensured the little town an ample supply of chlorinated water as well as fire protection.[15]

Maintaining the cleanliness of the bunkhouses was a constant struggle. Groups of men practising varying degrees of hygiene came and went, and some "brought company along in their clothing."[16] Mercifully, blankets were steam cleaned and fumigated on a regular basis.

Alcohol abuse had to be dealt with immediately, as management wanted to avoid having drunken brawls in the bunkhouses. McLean hired a former member of the Royal Canadian Mounted Police, Pat Conway, "a real leatherneck of a man,"[17] to keep the peace. Conway inspected all baggage and confiscated any liquor brought in by new workers. The bottles were sent to the main office, although the eventual destination of the liquor swag remained a mystery to the men.[18]

More than a hundred structures were erected before the winter set in, an average of one building per day. Abitibi became a thriving community with a modern hospital and full-time physician, a post office with postmaster, a store, barber shop, fire hall, offices, stables and construction buildings. Separate houses were erected for management.

Dominion Construction's small, gasoline-powered locomotive no. 3557 was used at Abitibi Canyon. ANDREW MERRILEES COLLECTION, GROUP D SUB-SERIES VI, ACCESSION 1980-149. PA 208177, LIBRARY AND ARCHIVES CANADA

The cooks, mechanics and labourers who lived in the bunkhouses were charged ninety cents a day for board, while the employees who lived in the houses paid a monthly rent.[19]

Hard work produced considerable appetites, keeping the baker and butcher very busy indeed. Each day the bakery turned out six hundred and seventy-five pies, three hundred pounds of cake, and seven hundred and twenty-five loaves of bread. Meat was delivered by the boxcar load and was hung in the walk-in freezer. The butcher dispensed some twenty-six hundred pounds of meat daily. Given the quantities of food to be processed and served, the kitchens were fitted with the latest in refrigeration and with electric ovens, vegetable peelers and dishwashers.[20]

All of the equipment for this colossal undertaking was moved into and around the site by rail, as the management of Dominion Construction was reluctant to see any rubber-tired equipment on the job. There were no trucks of any kind at Abitibi.[21] The purchasing agent, H. D. Bancroft, kept the single phone line to Cochrane occupied buying locomotives, shovels, mixers, and compressors and outfitting the rock-crushing and mixing plants. The list was endless. Reviewing some purchasing requisitions, Hyson would later note:

> The sharpening equipment for drill-sharpening for the drifters and the drills...$34,000. Two Plymouth locomotives, a total of $14,000. A McMarler crane – this was on steel rails, twenty-six-ton capacity – another $8,100. In the crushing plant we had a thirty-inch crusher, an Allis-Chalmers – a new crusher – $23,000, duty not included, I notice here. Revolving screens, another $7,000. Gasoline hoists, four yard cars, two American dinkey locomotives, $8,000. The pan conveyor in the crushing plant, $14,000. Bin gates in the crushing plant, another $5,000. Belt conveyors, Stevens-Adamson, more boilers, more shaft buckets, more skips – twenty skips for handling rock – two-yard capacity each, for a total of $2,500. One hundred horsepower locomotive boilers for heating in the wintertime – we needed those, plenty – and a fifteen-ton Morris crane built by the Herbert Morris Crane Company, $1,500. The quarry cars for handling rock – fifteen of those for a total of $8,000. More derricks, guy derricks – two of those, $10,000.[22]

The favourite piece of machinery on site was, without a doubt, the Shay locomotive, which hauled crushed rock for the concreting operation from a location downstream. A separate spur line was built down to the excavation site at a steep grade that no ordinary steam-driven locomotive could navigate. The Shay whirred as if it were going ninety-five miles an hour uphill when it was actually crawling at ten miles an hour. Instead of the regular horizontal piston type of locomotive, with large wheels on each side cranking around, the Shay had vertical pistons on one side driving a set of gears. What the Shay lacked in speed, it made up for in power. The men relied heavily on this unique locomotive, as it met the demands placed upon it each working day.[23]

Work continued around the clock. The average hourly wage for tradesmen was fifty cents. The men worked ten-hour shifts, six days a week and occasionally Sunday, straight time. The lowest-paid labourers got twenty-seven cents a hour.[24] Each week, a bank teller was sent up from Cochrane to cash paycheques so the men could have some cash on hand or could arrange to send money orders home.[25] Vacation time was non-existent and consequently some families were separated for extended

Shay no. 3298 (built by the Lima Locomotive Works in April 1926) was used by Dominion Construction in 1932, first at Deeks and then at Abitibi Canyon. It can be seen today at Iroquois Falls, Ontario. ANDREW MERRILEES COLLECTION, GROUP D SUB-SERIES VI, ACCESSION 1980-149. PA 208170, LIBRARY AND ARCHIVES CANADA (COLIN CHURCHER)

periods. Arthur McLaren, the power house superintendent, recalled an exchange with McLean regarding Christmas vacation in 1930:

> I had a desk in Mr. McLean's office and he came in – there were two trains that left the canyon each week. The last one before Christmas, Mr. McLean was wondering what I was going to do. Mr. Hyson was on the job, and Mr. Mitchell. Mr. McLean said to me, "What are you going to do for Christmas?" "Well," I said, "Mr. McLean, that's up to you, of course," and he said, "What had you planned?" and I said, "Well, I haven't seen my family since August and I thought it might be nice to go home for Christmas." "Well," he said, "Mac, I'd like to go home and see my wife too, but," he said "you know, we have a job to do here and the spring floods won't wait for us. We've got to have those tunnels built to take care of the flood when it comes in April and we're going to have to work all Christmas, so," he says, "what do you say if we both stay here for Christmas?" Of course, I was working

for Mr. McLean, so I said, "It's whatever you say." So we spent our first Christmas there at the canyon.[26]

Tasks were assigned to ensure that the first Christmas celebration at Abitibi was a success. John Anderson was instructed to cut down a large tree and erect it in the area that would become the skating rink. Anderson was in charge of the barn and eight to ten horses. In addition to more pleasurable tasks in the winter, such as taking care of Christmas trees, Anderson and his horses would fetch ice for the township and plough the local roads in the winter. Hyson assisted Anderson with the tree decorating; a star for the top was fabricated in the machine shop, and the tree was strung with coloured lights.[27] McLean, for his part, acted as the resident Santa Claus and gave every employee a gift:

> He was there himself, shortly before that first Christmas, in the office, and each one was called into a little room and this great big fella would be sitting there with sometimes a piece of paper in his hand. "Well, here, this is for you for Christmas. Now, have a good Christmas. Away you go." That was his way of working.[28]

⤞⬩⟡⬩⤝

The real production was at the job site. Work on the actual power development began shortly after the flurry of town-building activity. Like Grand Falls, Abitibi Canyon was chosen for its geographical attributes, especially water plunging rapidly through a narrow passageway – an essential characteristic for the generation of electricity. Operations were carried out simultaneously on the two sides of the Abitibi. On the opposite side of the river, Frank Mullen, in a camp appropriately named "Mullenville," looked after the excavation for the high-water channel and the clay fill for the wing walls. The crusty Mullen was assisted by Leo Murphy, a railroad man from Kentucky.[29]

Two essential and costly projects were begun, although they would become completely worthless once the dam was completed.[30] The first was the construction of two "unwatering" tunnels along with two cofferdams to divert the river in order to construct the power house and dam in a dry area. The tunnels, nine hundred feet and eleven hundred feet in length and thirty feet in diameter, were excavated by two Bucyrus-

Erie yard shovels through the rock on the west side of the Abitibi River. A smaller, upper cofferdam was built first, to divert the river into the tunnels, followed closely by a substantial structure embedded in the riverbed and standing about eighty feet high.[31] The rock excavated from the tunnels and other areas was crushed in the plant and supplied ninety percent of the dam core.[32]

The second venture was a double-track railway bridge spanning the canyon and a gantry off to the side. A separate contract, the bridge and gantry were built by the Dominion Bridge Company to carry the two twenty-ton cranes used for constructing the dam. The cranes were used for unloading and were placed so they could deliver construction material from the spur track down to the work area below, as well as the heavy generating equipment after the power house was completed.[33] Hyson recalled how ingenuity was used and ultimately rewarded in the final phase of constructing the bridge:

> They jacked up the end of the bridge with powerful hydraulic jacks, and they couldn't use water so they brought in some type of alcohol. And now you can just imagine all the glee they had! They jacked up the bridge and put in the final pieces under it to bring it level with a trestle [that] had been built at the other side of the bridge at that time. We had ways of getting timber across, and the bridge was jacked up level and then all the alcohol drained out, and the boys had a wonderful time. I think it went on for a day and a half or two days with that alcohol. Nobody was poisoned.[34]

The first load on the gantry made the men cringe as the rickety-looking structure shook tremendously under the weight. Some wondered if the load would make it. The Dominion Bridge Company was called back and gave its assurances that although the gantry was shaky it would get the job done.[35]

The power-plant designers from the Hardy company in New York City visited the job site from time to time, although the robust year-round Abitibi residents considered "Hardy" a misnomer for their visitors from the Big Apple. It took some time for the city men to become accustomed to the rustic conditions in the bush, causing more than a few snickers.[36] The Montreal writer Leslie Roberts recalled a misadventure

Dominion Construction Buick at Abitibi Canyon. ANDREW MERRILEES COLLECTION, GROUP D SUB-
SERIES VI, ACCESSION 1980-149. PA 208176, LIBRARY AND ARCHIVES CANADA

travelling to Abitibi on icy rails with McLean, Richard Hearn and George
F. Hardy:

> The driver looked along the drift-hidden right of way and gave her
> the gun. Front tracks hit into snow and jumped. Rear wheels followed.
> There was the jogging crunch of ties under the flanges. Then we began
> to spin and went into a ground loop... Somewhere in the back of this
> head there is the recollection of being tossed here and there, like a cork
> on water and of being wrong side up, or close to it. A sudden jerk, a
> bump and we were at standstill again, but facing in the direction whence
> we had come and on our side. There was a moment of complete
> silence... Forward the engine continued to tick over and more than
> one of us began to think of broken gas lines and flame. Then McLean's
> voice shattered the silence... "Cut your switch!" No answer but the
> ticking of the engine. "Cut that damned switch!" No answer again.
> Then the inexorable ticking of the motor was stilled. McLean had
> contrived to disentangle himself and kill the engine. There are people
> who do things by instinct in emergency, and McLean is of their number.[37]

Preventing accidents and promoting a safe workplace were ongoing
concerns for McLean. Warning signs were posted liberally throughout

171

the site illustrating every imaginable injury. Nets were strung across areas where falling objects could harm unsuspecting workers below. The twenty-four-bed hospital was fully equipped with an X ray laboratory, an operating room and private rooms for patients.[38] "But I get licked in spite of everything," McLean told *American Magazine* reporter William O. Grenalds. "Steel becomes diseased and you can't detect it. Or there's a premature blast, or the human element insists on taking a chance in spite of warnings. You never know when it's going to happen."[39] Hyson remembered the fatalities:

> I can recall the first death. When a locomotive was brought in – and this was a T&NO locomotive which was brought in on rental. This locomotive was sitting on the dead end of a track in the cut which approached the canyon itself and was being steamed up. The fireman and engineer were in the cab. All of a sudden this engine took off. The fireman, who was on the side next to…the sloping side of the cut, got so excited that he decided to jump off, and he rolled down towards the cylinders of the locomotive and was crushed to death. If he had stayed on the locomotive it would have simply run off the track, which would have done him no harm – except to the locomotive itself.
>
> …I can recall another death at the canyon when building the concrete plant. A carpenter was working on the floors of the bins which were over the mixers; this was two layers of boarding with a layer of paper between – felt, tar paper. The carpenters had laid the first layer of bare flooring and had laid out the paper, but they hadn't cut the holes in the paper where the emptying chutes were, and the carpenter, stepping around on this paper, backed up and stepped into one of these holes and fell. Although the distance was only about twenty feet, it killed him.
>
> …Another death was just after the river was diverted into the tunnels. There were some labourers cleaning up the side of the entrance to the portals. There was rock there, and they were shovelling this rock into the water, and this was in early spring and there was a slope of loose rock above these workmen and the sun on the slope was loosening rock. There was one rock became loose and one of the workman saw it coming and he got so excited that in order to escape it, he thought he would have to jump into the running water, which he did, and was swept down through one of tunnels and not found until the river was dried up finally, after the head pond was filled and the river diverted to

the high-water channel, and his body was found at that time wedged between two rocks.[40]

By the spring of 1931 the tunnels were completed and three cofferdams were built: one to divert the river flow through the un-watering tunnels, another to prevent the water from backing up and flooding the area excavated for the power house, and the third to ensure that the water from the high-water channel and lower river would not back up and hinder the tail-race channel excavation.[41] A giant concrete plug had been installed at the bottom of the canyon to reduce the likelihood of leakage under the dam. Construction efforts were in full swing, with approximately twenty-two hundred men employed.[42] With so many workers on the job, opportunities to be idle and undetected were frequent, especially on the night shift. To combat indolent behaviour, McLean and Dick Hearn would make surprise inspections:

Unwatering tunnels, 1931. Harry Falconer McLean Collection, Accession 1981-064. PA 212864, Library and Archives Canada

Harry McLean and I used to wander around on the night shift to see how many people were loafing and who was not loafing but working, and we landed into the sharpening shop where they sharpened the drill, and here the gang were sitting there playing cards. One of the chaps apparently didn't know who Harry McLean was and turned around and said, "Who the hell are you?" – just like that. Harry said, "I'm your conscience, goddammit."[43]

Although McLean pushed his men hard, he had a compassionate side. By the 1st of July 1931, Arthur McLaren could no longer bear being away from his wife and children:

I had to say to Mr. McLean, "I think I've got to go home. You either let me go home or I've got to give up my job. I can't stay here any longer alone." "So," he says, "Mac, I'll tell you what you do. You make up a sketch for three houses…one for yourself and one for Charles Hyson and one for Harold Barnett, and you give them to the property superintendent and you tell him to have yours ready for the 1st of August, and the other two as soon after that as he can." So I went home after being up there a year and spent a month at home and then took my family up there and lived there for the rest of the construction work. Mr. Hyson's family and Mr. Barnett's, they arrived soon after.[44]

Roughly one hundred families moved to Abitibi. Accordingly educational and recreational needs had to be addressed. Two full-time teachers were hired, and for leisure time there were a movie theatre and a recreation hall. The women played cards in the hall, and sometimes dances were held there in the evening. Some of the musically inclined residents would play the piano or the violin while others danced along to the music and then refreshments would be served. People of a more dramatic bent might put on a play, to the delight of the inhabitants of Abitibi.[45] One particular performance by a resident "character" was long remembered:

Mr. McLean had a regular little bat boy up there, a fellow named Scotty Watson. He was a real Scotsman with a burr in his tongue. He was ready for anything. Some of the ladies decided that they would put on an opera [about a] dying swan. Well, it sounded like a real big deal in the bush like that. So they got a bunch of material up and decorated him up to be a dying swan in a real sense of the word. I wasn't privileged to see that famous play at the canyon. I don't know

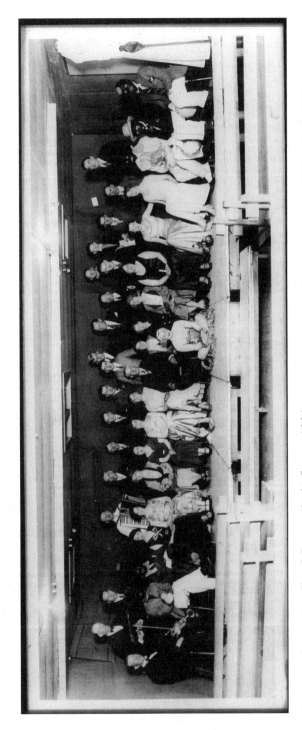

Dominion Construction Choral Group, Abitibi Canyon, 1931. HARRY FALCONER MCLEAN COLLECTION, ACCESSION 1981-064. PA 207735, LIBRARY AND ARCHIVES CANADA

why. Nevertheless I saw pictures of him sitting on the floor dressed up like a little cherub or something and all of the rest of the cast standing behind with big grins on their faces.[46]

In the fall of 1931 the men started pouring concrete for the dam. Built as a conventional gravity-type structure, the dam extended across the width of the gorge and included a parallel section for excess water flow. The power house was built next to the dam in the gorge and eventually housed five generators at a total installed capacity of 330,000 horsepower.[47] In November a concrete placing record was broken at the site – a whopping 93,000 cubic yards was placed.[48] Work continued at a frantic pace, as the dam had to be completed before the spring thaw.

Yuletide was gleefully celebrated to glowing reviews. At Midnight Mass in the dining hall, the priest praised Dominion Construction for taking such good care of its workers. Scotty Watson told McLean that he "almost kissed" the priest for his kind words. Santa delivered presents to all the women by sleigh early on Christmas Day and arrived at the recreation hall at four o'clock to distribute gifts to the children. Nearly everyone received a present. McLean specified that a special one be reserved for the cook of Joe Crombie, the labour boss, marked "To the best looking man in camp."[49] A good time was had by all – "a few were inebriated, but no rowdyism was exhibited."[50]

After Christmas Day the tree was taken down and hockey resumed on the rink. Hyson recalled hockey night in Abitibi:

Looking upstream towards Island Falls, September 23, 1931. HARRY FALCONER MCLEAN COLLECTION, ACCESSION 1981-064. PA 212865, LIBRARY AND ARCHIVES CANADA

Excavating base of power house and main dam, September 30, 1931. Harry Falconer McLean Collection, Accession 1981-064. PA 212862, Library and Archives Canada

I believe the office staff had one hockey team, the train service had a second hockey team, the pipe fitters had a third hockey team and the electricians of course had a fourth hockey team. Some of these games would be played on Sunday afternoon when most people were not working. The odd person would be down on the job doing something special. But sometimes the games would be played at night.

Two chaps that worked for the Dominion Bridge Company out of Lachine, one chap named Charlie Phillips [and] Percy Carpenter – they were construction, one was a foreman, the other an engineer – and they had been hockey referees around the Montreal–Trois-Rivières area, and they would look after the games for us… Each time the electricians played, my wife would put on a spread of food and hot drinks and so forth and both teams would end up in our little house, sitting on every chair and [in] every corner and all over the floor, just to get in out of the zero weather after being half frozen playing hockey outdoors, and filling up with coffee and homemade food – something

Christmas 1931. Skating rink in winter, two double tennis courts in summer.
HARRY FALCONER MCLEAN COLLECTION, ACCESSION 1981-064. PA 212863, LIBRARY AND ARCHIVES CANADA

that they hadn't had for months because they'd been on a diet of the camp food, which got a bit tiresome at times. And some of them would say, "Are we going to play the electricians tonight? Because if we do we're going to get our stomachs full."[51]

After a turkey lunch on Boxing Day, the men played hockey – a one-to-one tie between the electricians and the riggers. The next day it was back to work, placing 1,650 cubic yards of concrete.[52] The work progressed well, despite temperatures of sixty degrees below zero on some days and enormous snowfalls on others. Some men were kept busy simply clearing snow – as much as six feet at a time – off the track into the canyon. Others never adapted to the harsh Canadian winter:

> We had a chap whose name was Wharram, and he came from a nice, warm climate like Georgia, I believe in the second winter of the canyon, and of course he almost froze on the spot. He'd never seen so much cold, and immediately an order was placed by some purchasing

department through a specialty house, I believe in Ottawa, that made him the most elaborate sheepskin-lined coat. It was all leather on the outside, right down to his heels, and great hooded collar and all this sheepskin wool against his inside clothing. He would come to work in the morning all huddled up and take this massive coat off and hang it up on the wall of the office of the machine shop, and it seemed to stretch right down to the floor. This is the way he tried to keep himself warm… If I remember correctly, he stayed for seven or eight months and eventually pulled out and went back south, and we never heard of the gentleman since that time.[53]

A number of workers were bothered less by the weather than by the separation from their loved ones. Lonesome and frustrated, they would quit and leave, only to discover there was no work anywhere else and, inevitably, turn up again in the hiring hall.[54] For a blissful though fleeting moment a few lonely men were finding pleasurable diversions in the local love shack:

> Under the heading of amusements, I mentioned the tennis and hockey and also softball during the various seasons, but one problem that was solved very quickly – we had some ladies of the night move into a trappers' shack, oh, a mile and a half in the bush well buried in the jack pine trees and the muskeg swamps, and these ladies set up business in the oldest profession that man knows. So the boys would trek out there the odd time, and when it became fully known that things were going on, Joe Crombie – he was our labour boss – he had what we called the roustabout gang – all kinds of jobs…would be thrown in with his crew to take care of, and he went out with orders to chase the ladies of the night into the bush, get them back to the railway track to get on the trains and tear down the shack and burn the place out. This was done, and no more trouble from that angle.[55]

Without the distraction of the immoral entrepreneurs, the job progressed smoothly. In June 1932 it was time to put the dam to the test. The unwatering tunnels were to be closed. A plan was drawn up and each man had his role to play. Everyone was provided with written instructions under Hearn's supervision. Two Charlies – Hyson and Drennan – were in charge of closing the gates on the tunnels. They did so one at a time and communicated with a worker stationed at the exit of the tunnel to find out how much leakage was occurring. They raised

High-water spillway running full, June 18, 1932. HARRY FALCONER MCLEAN COLLECTION, ACCESSION 1981-064. PA 212866, LIBRARY AND ARCHIVES CANADA

the first gate once or twice, and then, when it was finally seated, repeated the procedure with the second gate. After the closing of the tunnel gates, four-inch holes were drilled with well drills from the top of the ground, directly in the centre of each unwatering tunnel. Carpenters went into the tunnels to erect a thirty-foot-wide form completely braced on both sides. Once it was determined that the carpenters were accounted for and would not be entombed, concrete was poured into the holes, creating a giant waterproof plug on each tunnel.[56]

With the gates closed, the water gradually crept up, approaching the spillway – so slowly that the men in the office placed wagers on the time of day when the water would start to drip over the spillway into the high-water channel and the numbers of hours it would take. Tickets were sold for a dollar. When the water finally spilled over a party broke out, and after that no one could remember who had won the bet.[57] The celebration was short-lived, however. In the end, the reward for placing an estimated 527,000 yards of concrete, moving 2,660,000 bags of cement, hauling 1,929 tons of reinforcing steel, placing 6,645,956 pounds of structural steel, and excavating 1,240,000 yards of rock and earth was a discharge notice, as the employees of Dominion Construction learned that the financial plug had been pulled on the project.[58]

CHAPTER ELEVEN

A New Broom Sweeps Clean

>─┤◆>─O─<◆├─<

*Our boys were working in the control room and all of a sudden, out of
a clear sky, one afternoon about five [o'clock], the heads of
departments, including myself, were called in and told: "Lay off all of
your men. The job is closing down. There's just no more money to carry
on the project." I had about forty-seven or thereabouts – different
electricians of all types, linemen included, looking after the townsite and
the power house and you name it, everywhere – and we laid off
everybody but two... We had people going out of there with their bags
and baggage. Special trains came from Cochrane and loaded these
people on. They had to be paid and get them out of the way. And then
when they got in Cochrane – that town, back in those years, was kind
of a rough frontier town and there was some wild things going on in
that town...they made sure that the people got out of town on the CN
trains, they didn't want too many people being piled around town there
with a lot of money in their pocket.[1]*

THE NEWLY UNWAGED men were surprised to discover that their
layoff notices were the result of a direct order from Premier George
Stewart Henry. Since early 1932, Harry McLean and Dominion
Construction had been battling the Ontario Power Service Corporation
(OPSC) to get paid for their work on the Abitibi project. By then, serious
financial problems at the parent Abitibi Company and the OPSC were
apparent not only to McLean but also to the Ontario government.[2] The
troubles at Abitibi would become part of a protracted battle between

Premier Henry, McLean and the Liberal leader, Mitch Hepburn – or Number Thirty-Eight on the guest list for the T&NO's grand opening of its extension to Moosonee on July 15, 1932.

The Conservative government's acquisition of auxiliary hydroelectric power had, in more prosperous times, been viewed as prudent, but the effects of the Depression were rapidly changing that perception. During the summer of 1931 allegations of graft and misconduct by Mackenzie King's Liberals with regard to the Beauharnois Power Company prompted a parliamentary investigation. The evidence suggested that Beauharnois had been more than generous with its financial contributions to the federal Liberal campaign, and also that the provincial Conservatives had gained a munificent advantage the day before Premier George Ferguson signed the contract with them.[3] By February 1932 Premier Henry found himself having to deal with a full-blown inquiry into hydro dealings – specifically, the contracts with the Quebec power companies and the guaranteed purchase of 100,000 horsepower from the OPSC.[4]

As of March 1932 the OPSC was making only partial payments on the Abitibi job. The arrears caused a serious predicament for Dominion Construction. Regardless of whether payment was forthcoming, the spring thaw and resulting floods most certainly were. The company had two options: leave the structure at a perilous stage – open to destruction by ice and floodwaters – or continue with the work until the structure was deemed capable of withstanding the rigours of the spring floods. Dominion opted for the latter and sought assurances from the Ontario government that it would be paid.[5]

J. Homer Black and Richard Hearn advised Premier Henry of the critical situation at Abitibi. Henry told them to continue the work until such time as the structure could be deemed secure and promised that they would be "treated fairly." Further, Henry assured the pair that his government did not want to see the men at Abitibi unemployed. On the strength of the premier's word, the work continued and McLean secured financing in the amount of $4 million to complete the project.[6]

Following the death of J. Homer Black, Harry McLean became president of the reconstituted Dominion Construction Corporation. The charter of the Dominion Construction Company was dissolved in August

1932.[7] By July of 1932 payments from the OPSC had stopped altogether, as the Abitibi Power and Paper Company had defaulted on its bond payments the previous month. On July 6th, having been told by Dominion Construction that all was deemed safe at the work site, Premier Henry ordered that all construction cease and that just enough staff be kept on to ensure that the site was protected.[8] Handing out notices was something that McLean always dreaded, but the deal with Henry stipulated that the majority of workers on this job be laid off. The deed was done, and one thousand men were left without work.

Henry's hydro problems abated temporarily as the Hydro inquiry delivered its findings after nine months of investigation. The inquiry commissioners, Justice W. R. Riddell and Judge G. H. Sedgwick, found no evidence of any wrongdoing by the government or Ontario Hydro. Mitch Hepburn remained unconvinced. Certain that something deliciously scandalous had been overlooked, he embarked on an inquiry of his own.[9]

In the meantime, on November 4, 1932, a new contract was signed between the Dominion Construction Corporation and the Montreal Trust Company, the receiver for the bankrupt OPSC.[10] Dominion Construction had been carrying the total expense of protecting the project since the time of the layoffs.[11] On December 17th the Ontario Supreme Court ordered the judicial sale of the assets of the OPSC.[12] The Henry government had been negotiating for months to take over the OPSC, and by March 1933 the transaction was virtually concluded. The Hydro-Electric Power Commission of Ontario was the new owner of the Hydro-electric Generating Station at Abitibi Canyon.[13] The Hydro Commission sent in its workers, who were briefed and assisted by the few remaining Dominion Construction personnel. The first order of business for the new owner was to slash the hourly wage of the employees as a cost-saving measure. The average worker was docked three cents an hour.[14]

The bankruptcy of Abitibi and the OPSC became common knowledge, as did the Conservative government's efforts to rescue the foundering company. However, there was one undisclosed piece of information. Hepburn found the scandal he had been looking for – a juicy conflict of interest involving Premier Henry and the OPSC. In

Downstream face of power house, 1933.
HARRY FALCONER MCLEAN COLLECTION, ACCESSION 1981-064. PA 212867, LIBRARY AND ARCHIVES CANADA

1930 Henry had invested twenty-five thousand dollars in OPSC bonds – bonds that had recovered nicely after the government bailout. Ontario Hydro commissioner Arthur Meighen was also identified by Hepburn for his association, as a director, with companies that had a substantial investment in OPSC bonds. At Queen's Park on April 5, 1933, a squirming Premier Henry acknowledged that he did own the bonds but, with all the activity surrounding OPSC rescue operations, had simply forgotten about them. Fortunately for Henry, more pressing concerns, such as prohibition and taxation rights for Catholic schools, diverted the attention of the public and the Liberal Opposition away from his convenient twenty-five-thousand-dollar memory lapse.[15]

In May of 1933 Harry McLean's relatives in Bismarck attended a viewing of a film he had commissioned during the construction of the Abitibi Canyon. Aptly titled *Abitibi Canyon: The Story of the Conquest of a River*, the film is the first known documentary of a construction project. McLean used it for promotional purposes, as did the Ontario government. McLean's appearance on screen garnered enthusiastic applause from his many friends and relatives in the audience. Afterwards they remembered him fondly "as a boy here in his prankish activity as well as his periods of sober reflection and study."[16]

In the months leading up to the 1934 provincial election, Henry continued to give his assurances to Dominion Construction, pledging that the Ontario government would pay five hundred thousand dollars on account. Four days prior to the resignation of the Conservative government, the cabinet passed an order-in-council authorizing the payment.[17] The Lieutenant Governor, however, refused to sign it, declaring the amount "too large to justify the payment at such a late hour in the life of the government."[18] As election day pressed closer, the growing popularity of the magnetic Hepburn assured his victory. Charming a crowd in Windsor with his witty repartee, Hepburn jibed:

> Honest George they call him, and Charlie McCrea says he hasn't a dishonest hair in his head. That's fair enough because he's bald... Why, [H]onest George is the man who forgot he had 25,000 tucked away in Abitibi bonds. He forgot he was director of a company that had 200,000 in it, and he forgot the Right Honourable Arthur Meighen's companies had 300,000 invested in it... I feel sorry for Honest George. All he has is about a million or so that he made out of Acme Dairy. If any of you farmers water your milk you go to jail. But if you water your stock you get to be Premier of Ontario.[19]

The Liberals swept into power with an unprecedented majority on June 19th. McLean's hopes for payment faded with the swearing in of Hepburn's new government in July. Worse still, weeks after his election Hepburn initiated three commissions of inquiry: one into the affairs of the Niagara Parks Commission, the second into the purchase of hydroelectric power by Ontario Hydro from the Abitibi Canyon dam and the third into the operations of the T&NO. All were designed to elucidate Hepburn's opinion that the Conservatives, during a time of economic depression, had squandered the taxpayers' money on unnecessary projects and that many public servants and utility officials connected to the Conservative party were reaping the benefits of overgenerous paycheques.[20]

The Honourable Frank R. Latchford, the sod-turning, spike-driving former politician, was now the highly respected Chief Justice of the High Court of Ontario. He and the Honourable Robert Smith, former justice of the Supreme Court of Canada, formed the Latchford-Smith Commission to investigate Ontario Hydro's purchase of power from the OPSC. Their mandate was to closely scrutinize and report on any transgressions between the Conservatives and the Abitibi Company. Throughout the summer of 1934 the proceedings of the Latchford-

Smith Commission were well publicized and did much to bolster Hepburn's political crusade.[21]

As a result of Hepburn's zealous investigation of all that was Conservative, not only was McLean's Abitibi payment seriously in doubt, but McLean now had to contend with allegations of impropriety regarding "politics and patronage" on the T&NO.[22] On August 8, 1934, appointed by an order-in-council, the lawyer Armand Racine embarked on a one-man inquiry into the affairs of the T&NO Railway and the Commission.[23] Even before the investigation was complete, Hepburn could not resist expressing his views on the matter. The *North Bay Nugget* was among the newspapers eager to quote him:

> That extension should never have been built. It starts nowhere and ends nowhere. It's just a bill of expense. The extension to Abitibi Canyon might have been justified, but beyond that it was just a contractor's proposition.[24]

⊱•⊰•O•⊱•⊰

Another Dominion Construction job commenced in September 1934, with the Workman's Falls Power Development on Gull River near Minden, Ontario. Designed by J. B. McRae, consulting engineer, the new dam provided extra power for the growing city of Orillia, as the plant on the Severn River was being overtaxed by the increased demand. The management at Abitibi was transferred to Minden; Richard Hearn was chief engineer, Harold Barnett resident engineer and Arthur McLaren superintendent. This project was not as vast as that at Abitibi, but it did provide continued work for a number of Dominion Construction employees through most of 1935.[25] Some Dominion men were sent to pick up equipment at Abitibi and deliver it to the yard at Longbranch.[26]

The Minden project could not accommodate everyone. McLean's chief electrician, Charles Hyson, was dispatched to the McLean home in Merrickville to perform a multitude of tasks. His first job was to rework the inadequate wiring, starting with the transformer on the street. Next was the building of a walk-in refrigerator. Then the well unexpectedly ran dry; Hyson had to find a well driller and lift the roof off the pump house so the driller could reach water under the Merrickville limestone. Occasionally, to remedy the poor acoustics in McLean's stone carriage house, Hyson was asked to hang cloth and velour curtains high on the walls so McLean could screen the Abitibi Canyon promotional film for his guests. Hyson was also instructed to build pens for McLean's pheasants as well as hatching bins for their eggs. Then he was ordered to look after the ducks. In actual fact, the tasks given to Hyson were make-work projects, meant to keep him on the payroll between construction projects. In the fall, Hyson was sent off to a regular job.[27]

<hr />

Racine's investigative report was submitted to the Lieutenant Governor on October 4, 1934. His analysis was divided into three parts: North Bay to Cochrane, Cochrane to Abitibi, and Abitibi to Moosonee – the best to worst sections of railway from a profitability standpoint. The first section was found to be surrounded by land rich in natural resources such as timber and minerals and also agricultural land. The findings on the second section were far less glowing, although prospects for the future were taken into account and for that reason the construction of this section was considered defensible. The third section was judged to be built on marshland dotted with stunted trees and devoid of anything of worth, then or ever, to the province; relying on his own findings and the evidence of various mining experts, Racine determined that the area served by the third section had little to offer in the way of minerals – at least not in quantities sufficient to warrant the investment of time or effort.[28]

Racine also addressed the burning desire of the former regime to have a tidewater port. Establishing a port facility was an expensive proposition, particularly in the north. There were no wharves, and no plans for any. The railway terminus was located at the mouth of the Moose River some fourteen miles from James Bay. Large ocean vessels could not manoeuvre the shallow Moose River, and shifting sandbars meant that dredging would likely become an annual necessity. Finally, James Bay was navigable for only a couple of months a year at best, and floating ice would be both hazardous and destructive.[29]

Also relevant to Racine's investigation of the third section was the tendering process, or – in most cases – the lack thereof and the resultant awarding of contracts to H. F. McLean Limited. With respect to the section between Fraserdale and Coral Rapids, McLean's bid was not the lowest ($710,566, as opposed to $675,866).[30] Racine concluded that the process had been unfair in spite of the questionable pricing found by the T&NO engineer. W. B. Russel, manager and engineer for the losing firm, Construction and Engineering Limited, shared Racine's point of view and had not been aware that his bid was the lowest until Racine's report was made public. Russel declared:

> It is a well established precedent that if there be any doubts about a lower tender, and if all the conditions are complied with by that tender, that he or they be given the privilege of disclosing his or their resources and ability. In this case, that privilege was not extended.[31]

On the tender of the extension between Coral Rapids and Moose River, the hard-pan excavation estimate prepared by McLean's engineer was low. H. F. McLean Limited won the bid and thereafter a reclassification of hard-pan and common excavation material took place. The reclassification resulted in payment to McLean of $384,000 in excess of the tendered amount. A similar instance was found on the first contract, between Fraserdale and Coral Rapids, the end result being additional payment to H. F. McLean Limited. This appeared somewhat suspicious to Racine, and it certainly resulted in a significant amount of extra money paid on the contracts.[32]

Three further contracts, totalling $4,246,281, were awarded to H. F. McLean Limited without tenders being issued: the bridge at Moose River, ballasting between Island Falls and Fraserdale, and construction of the railway line between Moose River Crossing and Revillon's Post. Racine pointed out that while the minutes of the Commission's meetings stated that construction of the James Bay contract would be discontinued "until such time as there is traffic in sight," the reality was that construction was proceeding so that the line could be completed as fast as humanly possible.[33] In the section on contracts in his report, Racine concluded:

> I cannot too strongly condemn the acts of the commissioners in permitting these contracts to be granted to H. F. McLean, Limited, without tenders being called…

I must also come to the conclusion that the engineering department of the commission, headed by Mr. S. B. Clement, was peculiarly lax in preparing the tenders which led to the granting of these two contracts to H. F. McLean, Limited.[34]

Most of Racine's wrath was directed at the commissioners, whose "greatest error" was building the third extension of the railway.[35] Even though "in evidence they threw entire responsibility upon the Government of the day,"[36] Racine believed the commissioners knew full well that the line would not be profitable and should have advised the government against completing the section to Moosonee.

Racine pronounced the commissioners "lax and negligent in the performance of their duties."[37] He also singled out various managers "who had no right or ability to be so entrusted" with the supervision of the line. And he dissected the abilities and performances of staff members: "...showed a deplorable lack of appreciation of the responsibility his position involved"; "...lacks very necessary qualifications – chief amongst these being initiative"; "...totally unfit to hold the position he now holds."[38] Racine recommended that these employees be immediately released from their positions or pensioned off.[39]

His analysis then turned to evidence of extravagant spending, such as on bonuses, huge salaries, passes and private cars. As a result of Racine's second recommendation, George Lee, chairman of the T&NO, resigned with a full pension. H. F. McLean Limited came out of the whole affair relatively unscathed.[40]

The T&NO Commission had chosen H. F. McLean Limited in the first place because Harry McLean had completed jobs where others had failed. Certainly McLean's relationship with Premier Ferguson facilitated his selection as the contractor. With McLean's construction crews and equipment in place after the completion of a section, it seemed sensible to have his company continue building the line, thus avoiding the expense of issuing another tender and having a whole new firm move its equipment in. In truth, the commissioners and the government of the day were determined to complete the line no matter what the cost, and they knew that McLean would get the job done.

The results of the Latchford-Smith Commission were also released in October 1934, and they basically confirmed what everyone already knew: Henry and Meighen had "acted improperly in the matter of the Ontario Power Service Corporation bonds."[41] Meighen was enraged. "This is the most diabolical political inquisition ever held outside of Turkey," he declared.[42]

That same year, armed with an opinion from his wily lawyers, Mitch Hepburn took another swipe at the former government's hydro contracts. It took nine excruciating hours at Queen's Park for Attorney General Arthur Roebuck to finally get to the point, but he concluded his diatribe with the assertion that the agreements with three Quebec hydro companies – Beauharnois, Ottawa Valley and Maclaren's – were "not only outrageous and inequitable but illegal and unenforceable."[43] Roebuck's view was that the matter was out of the authority of the province because the power lines and associated works were interprovincial. Hepburn introduced the "Power Bill," or, in more vulgar terms, "repudiation" on the three contracts. But even members of his own cabinet, notably Harry Nixon, Duncan Marshall and David Croll, concluded that the contracts were legal.[44]

Dominion Construction did not fare much better in its efforts to have the government acknowledge its responsibilities and pay the company for the work done at Abitibi. Hepburn decreed that his government had no legal obligation to reimburse Dominion Construction the five hundred thousand promised by George Henry. Further, whether the company would ever see any of the money owing to it remained at the discretion of cabinet.[45] On Dominion Construction's unwritten agreement and its reliance on promises made by the former premier, Hepburn stated:

> It was a pretty loose method of doing business, this going ahead on the verbal assurance that they would be dealt with fairly…as near as we can gather the company has no legal claims on us, for when the Ontario Power Service Corporation…went into bankruptcy, the necessary steps were not taken by the construction company to protect its account. They just trusted Mr. Henry and let it go at that.[46]

An exasperated Henry implored:

The Dominion Construction Company should be paid the $500,000 and a considerable amount more. I intimated to them when I made the promise that I did not want the work to stop. If it had, the water in the winter time might have washed away all that had been done, involving a tremendous loss of money already spent. They should be paid early. It is only a part of what is owing to them. The project is one [in] which we are very much interested and is of great value to the province. It was essential for the work to go on.[47]

Ultimately, the five-hundred-thousand-dollar payment on account was never made. Dominion's claim was scrutinized by the Hydro-Electric Power Commission, and finally, after years of negotiations, a settlement with the Dominion Construction Corporation was reached on March 20, 1935. Dominion had claimed $3,180,445.50 plus fifty percent of $333,885.20. The Commission's calculation of what was owed to Dominion was, predictably, substantially less – $1,952,537.79 plus costs of $52,018.04 for preparing the claim. Dominion settled for an even $2 million, two years having elapsed since the completion of the work, carrying sizeable debt and interest charges for the project.[48] Henry commended Hepburn on the settlement. Accepting the compliment, Hepburn pointed out that the settlement represented nothing more than Dominion Construction's out-of-pocket expenses.[49]

>─┼─◆>──O──<◆─┼─<

The capital loss was a hardship for McLean and his organization, particularly in the middle of the Depression, but they endured. However, McLean's absence from the home and his hard-living lifestyle took a personal toll. Likely as a result of her husband's long absences and his intoxicated presence, Irene McLean moved out of the house in Merrickville and took an apartment on Oriole Street in Toronto.

Harry and William McLean reconnected with their many relatives in North Dakota and made arrangements to attend the Pioneer Days celebrations in Bismarck in the summer of 1936, staying at the home of Will and Emma Falconer. Harry travelled in his own plane, piloted by Maurice Gauthier. The Falconers had a full house that week. Their daughter, Mrs. Robert Day, was visiting from Spokane, Washington, with her husband and two daughters, Emma and Polly.[50] McLean took Emma to Winnipeg for a few days, then dropped her off at Bemidji, Minnesota, where the Days were heading on vacation.[51] William McLean went to Chicago with Billy Falconer, then continued his journey home.[52]

><·<·>·O·<·>·<

Business continued between the Grenville Crushed Rock Company and the Canadian Pacific Railway. In 1928 the operation expanded to another location, on Hawk Lake near Kenora, Ontario. The Hawk Lake plant was built on property owned by the CPR. The April to September 1929 season was the first full operational one, with 359,407 cubic yards of ballast being crushed. The Hawk Lake quarry was awarded a sizeable contract by the CPR to supply the ballast for the double track between Fort William (Thunder Bay), Ontario, and Winnipeg. Dominion Construction organized rock ballasting camps that were in charge of digging out and removing the old ballast and placing new ballast brought in on CPR trains. The Hawk Lake quarry was put on hiatus after the 1929 season due to the Depression. The 1935 season was the last year of operation at Deeks Quarry. A large stockpile of ballast remained on hand there for future use by the CPR.[53]

Although new railway construction had effectively ended for McLean's companies by 1936, plenty of railway maintenance was required. The CPR determined that extensive ballast work was necessary and the Hawk Lake quarry was re-opened. McLean sent Bob Roberts to head up the operation and Charlie Hyson to dust off the equipment and charge up the power house. The facilities at Hawk Lake consisted of a

Panoramic view of the Hawk Lake quarry. Harry Falconer McLean Collection, Accession 1981-064. PA 212852 - Library and Archives Canada

crushing plant, a power house and machine-shop pump houses for water supplies, as well as houses for management personnel, camp-style housing for all of the workers on the job, and dining facilities. Before the quarry could be made operational again, there was much to be done.[54] Murray Cooke was a freshly hired worker that year:

> …we had to have track laid, shovels moved into position, the drills of course had to drill the rock in preparation for getting it into the drains and into the crusher, so our first job was not actually being brakeman – we laid track under the direction of Billy Mews, the yard boss – he was the gang boss anyways – the track gang – a likeable little fellow, he came from around Smiths Falls, I think Merrickville, someplace near Ottawa. So we carried ties and carried track – sixty-five pounds to the foot, and that was plenty heavy enough. About a dozen men to pick up these lengths – we had to carry the ties, they were CPR culls actually, and they were well tarred so you [would] put that on your shoulder and carry it across the length and breadth of the quarry to where it was needed, drop it down and go back and get another one – a day's work meant a very sore shoulder. Eventually, though, the track was laid, the rock was drilled and the shovel runners got their shovels going and the quarry got rock into the crusher.[55]

After toiling for weeks to get the quarry back up and running, Cooke worked as a brakeman on the quarry trains. These trains consisted of small dinkey engines hauling five or six cars. The cars were built to withstand the rigours of huge rocks being thrown into them and being hit by steam-shovel buckets, on occasion haphazardly run by slapdash operators. Three shovels operated at once; two of the largest were on rails – these were the standard-gauged Marion shovels that had been used on many railway jobs.[56]

> 1936 was the year of the heat. We worked fifteen hours a day from six o'clock in the morning until nine o'clock at night. We had a twenty-minute break for lunch and I forget how long it was for supper but it wasn't very long, maybe twenty minutes or half an hour. The quarry…was measured one day at a hundred and twenty-eight degrees and there wasn't a bit of shade anywhere – naturally in the quarry you don't get shade. Men just shrank. One man I remember in particular, I think his name was Walter Gleeson, he was one of the shovel runners up the top of the hill at the spring switch…he must have gone from

about two hundred and fifty pounds to one hundred and eighty maybe. You could have put two of him inside his regular trousers, that's how much he shrank.

We had a great deal of trouble with the fellows who were inexperienced in the heat and they drank ice water, which gave them cramps and they ended up doubled on the ground. The solution, and they should have followed it, was porridge in the water…that somehow does something to the system and you don't have the cramps, but anyways the men didn't follow the instructions.

One of our little dinkey engines had three different engineers one day. I remember I was standing on the runway of the 317 talking to Percy Drinkwater, the fireman on that shovel, while we were being loaded up on the last car and out from the crusher comes I think it was O'Brien's train, the 3255 – yes, he was heading up the pike…and hanging out the window was the engineer who had passed out, so we frantically waved O'Brien down and he dropped off and picked up the train that went by. Luckily it wasn't going too fast and he was able to hang on and put the brakes on the thing. Actually, they had to put the old 3255 on the sideline. Every valve and every connection in her was

Rail-mounted crane no. 3235 is attached to saddletank locomotive no. 1. Built by Davenport in January 1925 for Dominion Construction, this locomotive first appeared at the Flin Flon project and eventually made its way to Hawk Lake. Harry Falconer McLean Collection, Accession 1981-064. PA 212851 - Library and Archives Canada

leaking steam, and it was bad enough in the heat without that happening, with steam blowing around, and moisture. Nobody could stand it – they just caved in and passed out. Two of them passed out and the third one said, "I've had it, I'm not doing that any more." So all in all we had a wonderful summer, you might say, in the heat. At thirty-five cents an hour, it was quite a job. Of all the years I was at Hawk Lake, I guess 1936 had the biggest impression on me. It was the heat, for one thing. You wake up in the morning and go up to the quarry – not too far off on the horizon at six o'clock in the morning was the sun. I read and heard about balls of fire, but that was the biggest ball of fire you would ever want to look at.[57]

The "all round quarry boss" was Frank Mullen, sent by McLean to work at the Hawk Lake quarry and keep things in order:

He had three fingers – "Three Finger Mullen," they called him – and a very distinctive man he was...very, very distinctive, the only man in the whole camp whose voice could be heard above the roar of the crusher. He could stand beside a shovel when it was fully blasting and give you an idea just what he thought of you, your antecedents and also your children coming up. A very volatile man when he got mad, and one thing that did make him mad was carelessness. He was continually "firing people" – that should be in quotations – I don't know if he ever fired anybody but he was threatening to all of the time, and carelessness was one thing that could perhaps make him fire a man. [H]owever, he had 5,000 yards a day of rock to get out of that quarry and then into ballast for the CPR, and he made mighty sure we did it.[58]

In the 1936 season, from May to August, 312,052 yards of ballast was crushed.[59] McLean was usually engaged elsewhere, but his presence at Hawk Lake one day made an indelible memory for Cooke:

He didn't impress me the first time I saw him... I was on the 317 loading up the cars of rock to take in to the quarry when over on the top of the quarry edge – I forget how far it would be, a couple yards or more away – this huge figure appeared, and he was up against the horizon – you could see him. To everybody's astonishment...this figure dropped his trousers and proceeded to go to the toilet, and then very calmly finished and away he went. Now, he would be in complete view of the camp and of the quarry boys. Percy Drinkwater...the fireman on the 317, said, "Well, that's old H. F. himself and he just doesn't care."[60]

Eleven well drills with long cables were used to drill the rock, nine electric and two gasoline-driven. A large bit, four inches in diameter, was used to drill the rock face, which was in some places thirty feet high. The powder men followed, loading the blast holes and clearing the area. The jackhammer operators worked to break the rock again so it would fit in a Bucyrus bucket or Marion shovel to load into steel dump cars. The smaller locomotives, the Porters or the Davenports, would take the rock down to the crushing plant to be tipped into the Allis-Chalmers crusher. The rock went through several contraptions: the pan conveyors, the fine reduction crusher, more rubber conveyor belts, a screen house and more gyratory crushers. Eventually the rock found its way down to the wooden bins located at the bottom of the crushing plant. The rock at Hawk Lake was a very hard type of granite or granite equivalent with a very high silica content.[61] Hawk Lake was the scene of several catastrophic accidents:

> There was one particularly tragic day when one of the men who were jackhammering one of the large rocks and were preparing to blow them into smaller pieces for the shovel to pick up, and there were two of the men there behind the old 317 – the rock they were standing on was doing fine but the one behind them started to move, and I don't know exactly how large that rock was – I imagine it would be about ten feet by ten feet, a plain big hunk of rock. They jumped down but one man caught his foot in the rock and he fell and the thing rolled over on top of him. It happened midway through the afternoon and nothing could be done. I remember Percy Drinkwater on the 317 – they shut the shovel down and he just refused to have anything to do because there was the man – they left him lying under the rock, his hat was on top of the rock, there was a blanket thrown over what was showing from under the rock, and he had to stay there until the coroner came out, and that wasn't until well after quitting time. It wasn't very pleasant. You had to ride by this scene every time you had to go by the shovels on the way to the crusher. That was one of the rather bad things that happened.[62]

Another day one of the younger employees was standing on top of the crusher, drilling rock. His lack of judgement resulted in tragedy as the rock split in two and the young man headed into the jaws of the crusher. He was not wearing a safety belt.[63] While working at the quarry,

Murray Cooke had a life-altering accident, losing his leg below the knee. What caused his mishap is unknown, and McLean did not hear about it for many years. Rye whisky was the best medicine available at the time:

> Bill Bicker found a bottle of rye. I'll never forget it. He poured half a glass into me, which I never even tasted. And he said, "Boy, I need a drink too," and he wheeled another half a glass into himself. That was my first, you might say, transfusion. I lay down on the floor of the office.[64]

In 1936 McLean spent a quiet Christmas in Merrickville with his brother William. They stayed close to Kinlochaline, as severe winter conditions were causing many drivers to veer into ditches.[65]

As a matter of its own survival, Dominion Construction adapted to the times – steam to diesel and gasoline, steel to rubber, railways to highways. In the latter part of the 1930s, Dominion was working on a multitude of dock installations: the Island Ferry dock at Wood Island,

Grenville Crushed Rock locomotives: Porter locomotive no. 5430 was built in 1913, purchased by Grenville in 1933, and scrapped between 1950 and 1952. No. 2029 was a Davenport 0-4-0 saddletank built in January 1925 for Dominion Construction in Winnipeg. Andrew Merrilees Collection, Group D Sub-series VI, Accession 1980-149. PA 208172, Library and Archives Canada

Prince Edward Island, jobs at Rimouski and Augliers, Quebec, for the Department of Public Works, a dock at Cherry Street in Toronto for the Toronto Harbour Commission. The site for the airport at Dartmouth, Nova Scotia, was cleared and graded by Dominion. Two hydro projects were undertaken: one on the Madawaska River at Barry's Bay (Bark Lake), Ontario, and the other a power plant at Liverpool, under contract from the Nova Scotia Power Commission. A total of 294,075 cubic yards of ballast was crushed at Hawk Lake in 1937. McLean also secured a number of jobs grading highways in Ontario: the Trans Canada Highway near Hearst, sections of highway around Green Valley and Sharbot Lake, and Highway 11 near North Bay, as well as grading and paving the highway at Mount Bridge and the Queen Elizabeth Way for the Ontario Highways Department.[66]

On the Queen Elizabeth Way job in 1937, a lanky Irish carpenter by the name of Joseph Justin McNally caught McLean's attention. McNally was young, hard-working and confident. McLean took the lad under his wing as his protégé. McNally found himself quickly rising above the

Underpass at Highway 27 and Queen Elizabeth Way in 1938. Note the concrete plant and hoist. COURTESY OF JOSEPH J. MCNALLY

Early cab design: L.O.AC. bulldozer with Baker blade. Courtesy of Joseph McNally

rank and file. Unknown to McNally at the time, he also met an unwritten requirement for bosses at McLean work sites – no one could run one of Harry McLean's jobs unless he stood at least six feet tall. McNally had that prerequisite beaten by four inches.[67]

That same year, under the supervision of consulting engineers H.G.Acres Limited and Gore and Storrie Limited, Dominion Construction began work on what is arguably the most resplendent water-filtration plant ever built. Named for Rowland Caldwell Harris, a former Commissioner of Works for the City of Toronto, the R. C. Harris Water Filtration Plant is located in the Beaches neighbourhood of Toronto. McLean put Colonel Kenneth Ramsay in charge of the project, with Richard Hearn as chief engineer. Harold (Barney) Barnett was the office engineer and Arthur Bradley and Doug Reid ran the office. The project was in able hands and was completed to the great satisfaction of the City of Toronto.[68]

With all under control at his job sites, McLean was pursuing the next big opportunity. With the slowly recovering economy, discussions on the construction of an aqueduct in New York City that had been postponed due to the Depression were now resumed. Millions of dollars would be up for grabs to the lowest bidder in the Big Apple, and Harry McLean wanted a bite.

CHAPTER TWELVE

Ruthless, Grasping Thieves

The Delaware Aqueduct

*Labor is not on trial here...These men are business partners in crime,
and the business of the partnership is extortion...they are shakedown
artists – ruthless, grasping thieves who have lined their pockets at the
expense of the laboring man they represent.[1]*

THE NILES, MICHIGAN, division of Dominion Construction, located
at Alexandria Bay, submitted bids to the New York City Board of Water
Supply early in 1937 for the construction of sections of the world's
longest continuous tunnel – the Delaware Aqueduct.[2] This chain of
dams, reservoirs and tunnels was designed to connect unquenchably
thirsty New York City with an estimated five hundred and forty million
gallons of water daily from the Delaware-Catskill watershed.[3]

The price tag for the aqueduct was about $300 million, although the
sacrifice made by people living in its path was incalculable.[4] Entire towns,
along with the livelihoods they supported, would disappear underneath
manmade reservoirs as the aqueduct pushed through. Expropriated
property owners were typically paid half the assessed value of their
land. Nonetheless, the work proceeded, the welfare of the people in the
colossal city outweighing that of the relative few who were displaced.[5]

Due to the size of the project, the Board solicited proposals from
numerous contracting and engineering firms all over North America.[6]

Inexplicably, all initial submissions were tossed out by the Board and some months later the whole process was begun again.[7] By the time the new tenders were called, Harry McLean and Louis Perini of the Massachusetts-based construction company B. Perini and Sons had founded the Seaboard Construction Corporation in Delaware, on March 23, 1937.

McLean's management personnel, including Arthur Bradley, H. D. Bancroft and Charles Hyson, were moved to an apartment building in Westchester County. Hyson and Bancroft took care of the electrical end of things, from the design to the purchase of all electrical supplies. George Thompson, who had worked on some of the East River tunnels in New York City, was the electrical superintendent. Arthur McLaren, superintendent of the tunnel, moved down to Katonah, New York. McLean rented a magnificent dwelling in the village of Armonk, large enough to both house the design team from Chicago and allow him to entertain his fellow shareholders.[8]

McLean's business associates, J. P. (John Paris) Bickell and Bernard E. "Sell 'em Ben" Smith, had attributes similar to his own: they were distinctive, powerful and occasionally notorious. As a young man, Bickell had started his own brokerage firm, becoming a millionaire by the age of thirty – while also earning the dubious distinction of being the defendant in three cases before the Supreme Court of Canada. His next challenge was running McIntyre-Porcupine Gold Mines in Ontario, which prospered under his presidency. Bickell's endeavours were diverse – from providing the financial backing for the building of Maple Leaf Gardens (home of the Toronto Maple Leafs hockey team) and acting as its first president, to serving the war effort with Britain's Ministry of Aircraft Production under William Maxwell Aitken, better known as Lord Beaverbrook.[9]

The other Seaboard shareholder, Bernard E. Smith, was one of the infamous stock speculators of the 1929 crash and Bickell's pal. After losing a sizeable sum in the bull markets of the 1920s, Smith earned his renown by shifting his bullish trading philosophy to that of a bear speculator. He engaged in the risky practice of "short selling" as the stock market was entering its steep decline in 1929. As a short seller,

Smith would borrow stock from a broker and sell it in the hope that it would go down. Then, if all went according to plan, he would buy the stock back for less than he sold it for, return the stock to the broker, and keep the difference.[10]

Smith acquired his nickname during the stock market crash as a result of hollering into the crowded board room of a brokerage house, "Sell 'em all! They're not worth anything!"[11] He became enormously wealthy as the downturn of the stock market worked to his advantage. Some found it deplorable that Smith was reaping huge profits at the expense of others. The American press pounced on him, vilifying him for his part in hastening the decline of the stock market.[12] Time served as Smith's best ally, as harsh characterizations in the press such as "traitor" and "opportunist" were softened to "character" and "daring." Harry McLean admired Smith's business savvy, referring to him as "Ten Percent Ben."[13]

In April 1938 Seaboard was awarded two contracts for sections of the twenty-three-mile-long West Branch-Kensico tunnel in Westchester County.[14] The first, Contract 323, included the construction of a 5.8-mile concrete-lined pressure tunnel and two shafts near Mount Kisco, one of which was a drainage chamber that would be equipped to un-water twenty miles of tunnel. Work on this contract commenced on May 19, 1938.[15] The second contract was offered by McLean to his friend Stephen Healy of the S. A. Healy Construction Company of Chicago. Healy happily accepted after his own bid had failed. McLean made arrangements with the Board to transfer the contract.[16]

The ink on the $9.3-million contract was barely dry when the local union made its presence known to McLean.[17] Union representatives strongly suggested that McLean purchase his sand and gravel from their designated suppliers at wildly inflated prices. McLean told them to "drop dead" and, like several other Delaware Aqueduct contractors, set up his own sand and rock-crushing plants.[18] Undaunted by the obstinate McLean, the union sent a higher-ranking menace to Seaboard's head office. While McLean was away on other business, James Bove, international vice-president and Eastern representative of the Hod Carriers, Building and Common Laborers Union, reacquainted himself with Louis Perini at a New York City hotel.[19]

A year prior, B. Perini and Sons, a non-union employer, had been awarded a contract to construct approaches to the Lincoln Tunnel at Union City, New Jersey. Since the project was conveniently located in his jurisdiction, Bove made Perini an offer: he would write the labour contract and iron out any difficulties that might arise for a mere fifty grand. A reluctant Perini paid the money in seven instalments.[20] Bove reminded Perini of the potential consequences on the aqueduct project for non-compliant contractors: the labour supply could be stopped as easily as turning off a tap, job sites would be plagued by strikes, and equipment might be mysteriously destroyed. As luck would have it, Bove explained, all such enmity could be avoided in exchange for just one hundred and twenty-five thousand dollars from Seaboard and fifty thousand from B. Perini and Sons for the smaller aqueduct contract.[21] A magnanimous Bove declared:

> We are going to give you some very good men up there. We are going to see that you are not going to have any labor difficulties or labor disputes and we are going to see that this job goes along very smoothly.[22]

Having left his bulging wallet at home, Perini told Bove he would pass along the generous offer to McLean. Perini managed to negotiate his own company's share down to twenty-five thousand, arguing that fifty thousand was disproportionate to the amount of his contract.[23] Upon hearing about Bove's demands, an infuriated McLean invaded a meeting of the Union of Operating Engineers as they were organizing the job. McLean bolted to the podium, shouting, "Who is the head of this outfit?" One member answered, "I'm the local President." McLean roared, "I don't want the god-damned local President, I want the boss of this union! I only talk to the bosses! Bring him to me!"[24] McLean's wish was granted.

The Boss was Joseph "Big Joey" Fay, who had begun his union career as a business agent for Local 805 in Newark, New Jersey.[25] His main function was, ostensibly, to vigorously defend the rights of the union members. In reality, his motivations were less than noble. Typically, business agents were not well paid, but they had the authority to call strikes – a power that was considered by less-than-scrupulous individuals like Fay to be enticingly lucrative. A well-placed payment with a business agent would ensure the absence of labour problems, the ability to hire capable men and a job completed on time. Fay had coerced his way to the top position in the union, counting as his closest allies several members of the New Jersey political mob, including Frank Hague, the corrupt mayor of Jersey City.[26]

In addition to being a part-time tyrant, Fay was vice-president and Eastern representative of the Union of Operating Engineers. Described as both gruff and convivial, Fay had the looks of a stern, heavy-jawed high school principal. Known for his excessive drinking and hair-trigger temper, he was not averse to using brass knuckles on occasion. Fay lived a well-heeled lifestyle courtesy of the generosity, albeit oblivious, of his union members and incessant extracting of money from non-union workers and contractors. A mansion in Newark and a Cadillac were simply perks of the job, along with a liberal supply of spending money to support his ample vices.[27] He and his ghoulish sidekick, James Bove, controlled eighty-five percent of the labour for the aqueduct project.[28]

As insisted by McLean, the union boss met with him, but despite McLean's best intimidation tactics Fay would not be out-bullied. Both men knew that any labour-related complications on the job could be costly; at a minimum, all bidders on the aqueduct project were required to post a surety bond indemnifying the City of New York in the event that the work fell behind schedule. The conditions of the bond provided for payment of five hundred dollars to the City for each day the job was not completed, plus reimbursement of any out-of-pocket expenses.[29] McLean knew he had no alternative but to accept Fay's instalment plan. Seaboard's job proceeded as promised – with no labour problems.[30]

To McLean this expenditure was, rightly or wrongly, the cost of doing business in graft-laden New York City. In fact many large contracting firms were known to include a bribery allowance when preparing their bids.[31] McLean was concerned not only for his own well-being but also for the safety of his men. Many of the unions were outright rackets, remnants of Al Capone's mob racket in Chicago.[32] There were scores of reports of violence on job sites that were not under Fay and

Bove's "protection," involving beatings with tire irons and other such devices.[33] And there were allegations that Fay had been involved in something far more sinister. Together with Samuel Rufus "Subway Sam" Rosoff, a colourful New York contractor, he was suspected of plotting the 1937 mob-style murder of Norman Redwood.[34]

Redwood, business agent for Union 102, the Compressed Air, Tunnel and Subway Workers (the "Sandhogs"), had directed a strike at Rosoff's jobs at the Sixth Avenue subway and sewer construction under the East River in New York City. Rosoff was irate and allegedly said he would kill Redwood "stone dead."[35] Redwood was also a source of aggravation for Fay: he refused to join Fay and Bove's merged union and continually resisted Fay's efforts to intimidate or bribe him.[36] In the days leading up to his demise, Redwood argued with Fay and Rosoff, who both demanded that Redwood get his workers back on the job and obtained a court injunction to force him to do so. Despite the injunction, Redwood refused to call off the strike, stating prophetically that his men would not work "with a gun stuck in their backs."[37] The next evening when Redwood arrived home, he was welcomed by six bullets from an unknown assailant. He was found slumped in the front seat of his car, minus the left side of his face and some grey matter.[38] Fay was questioned twice by the Bergen County prosecutor in connection with Redwood's death but his culpability could not be proven.[39] The question of Fay and Rosoff's guilt lingered and the murder remained unsolved.[40]

⊱┤◆⟩•○•⟨◆├⊰

Not one to be kept down for long, McLean managed temporarily to put Fay, Bove and the other union thugs out of his mind and amused himself in the Big Apple:

> There were times in Mount Kisco when he'd be in the city of New York on a trip of some kind...raising hell, and he'd take a complete orchestra from some night spot and pack them in taxicabs and take them all the way to Armonk village and get in that big living room of that home that he leased and say, "Now you so and so's, you play for me anything I say, and you play until the sun comes up, or else." He'd sit there with a great big bathrobe on – the McLean Tartan – and call

the shots, and if those fellows made a move to head for the door, they were in trouble. The next day, it was back to business.[41]

Ben Smith and Jack Bickell were close friends with Mitch Hepburn and the trio socialized constantly. McLean flew Ben Smith to Hepburn's forty-second birthday party at Hepburn's Bannockburn Farms on August 12, 1938.[42] A hearty pat on the back and the bottom of a glass later, their past misunderstandings had been put aside, as it was not good business for McLean to hold a grudge against Hepburn. After all, the two men found that they had something in common – they both enjoyed a drink. Many other powerful figures of the day were in attendance: the premier of Quebec, Maurice Duplessis; the head of Algoma Steel, Sir James Dunn; and the best guy to invite to a party, Larry McGuinness, the distiller.[43] A conciliatory Hepburn conceded to McLean, on the matter of his Hydro and T&NO crusade, "I shouldn't have done that to you, Harry."[44]

Bernard E. "Sell 'em Ben" Smith (left) and Harry McLean (right) are greeted by Premier Mitch Hepburn as they arrive at Bannockburn Farms for Hepburn's birthday party, August 12, 1938. Accession 1963-023 E003895010, Canadian Broadcasting Corporation/ Library and Archives Canada

A few days later, on August 18th, McLean attended the opening of the Thousand Islands Bridge between Collings Landing, New York, and Ivy Lea, Ontario. The Right Honourable W. L. Mackenzie King and President Franklin D. Roosevelt were on hand to deliver speeches. The Dominion Construction Corporation of Niles, Michigan, had built the substructure on the American span.[45]

The Hawk Lake quarry had been dormant during the summer of 1938 after word had come through that the Canadian Pacific Railway

Mitch Hepburn's birthday gathering, August 12, 1938. Front row, left to right: Judge Duncan Ross of St. Thomas, Ontario; Larry McGuinness, president of McGuinness Distillery; Maurice Duplessis, premier of Quebec; airplane pilot. Middle row, left to right: Hepburn's mother, Maggie, wife, Eva, and son Peter; Hepburn and his daughter Patricia; Harry McLean; William Tapsell, manager of Bannockburn Farms. Back row, left to right: Harry Johnson, secretary of the Ontario Liberal Association; Ben Smith; Colin Campbell, Ontario minister of Public Works; L. J. Dingman, publisher, St. Thomas Times-Journal; *L. B. Birdsall, reporter,* St. Thomas Times-Journal.

President Roosevelt and Prime Minister King at dedication ceremony for the Thousand Islands Bridge, Ivy Lea, Ontario, August 18, 1938. Laurier House Collection, Accession 1986-204 C-090217, Library and Archives Canada

would not be requiring crushed rock.[46] The 1939 season was the second-last year of operations.[47]

McLean made plans to fly around the world that year, accompanied by his nurse, Inez Atkinson.[48] Gearing up for the monumental flight from Montreal on February 2, 1939, McLean's plane was the first to land at the new airport on Toronto Island.[49] The centrally located airport provided an easy escape route for McLean after one of his outrageous practical jokes at the Royal York Hotel:

> Mr. McLean took a policeman's horse up the service elevator to his suite, called the desk clerk and said, "There's a horse in my room, come and remove it right away." Then he left with his pilot, Dick Preston, and flew out of the Toronto Island airport to Ottawa. When Ottawa police questioned him, he said he didn't know anything about

it. Several of his friends stated Mr. McLean had been in Ottawa and couldn't have taken the horse!!![50]

McLean departed Ottawa, then Canada, leaving his business interests in the care of his best men. Frank Mullen was again in charge of the workers at Hawk Lake. According to Murray Cooke, who was rehired for the new season, Mullen grew more cantankerous with each passing year:

> There are so many things to talk about – little incidents – the 1939 episode where I was fired, actually, and fifteen minutes later re-hired... [Mullen's] son was the shovel runner on the 100B. He loaded a rock on the car on my train... I told him he couldn't do it because it wouldn't go into the crusher – it was just too long and it would stick and pull and it wouldn't go, that's all. So, he being the boss's son, he was very definite, so I took it down. I didn't care, it didn't matter to me. Anyway, I forget the fellow's name on the crusher, he said no way, so back around it goes again and I took it back. The son, he turns around and gets a bunch of small rocks piled on top of it. Back down to the crusher we go, and immediately the fellow in the hook looked around and he says, "I've seen that thing before"... so back around I go again, and I had a big fight with Moon Mullen that time and almost came to

Bucyrus Erie steam shovel no. 100B, Hawk Lake quarry. Harry Falconer McLean Collection, Accession 1981-064. PA 212850 - Library and Archives Canada

fisticuffs…to get him to take that thing out of there and to break it up, but he shifted it around and piled more gravel on top of it and down we went. This time they put the hook on it and up she went, and the rock caught on the corner of the car and pulled the car into the top of the crusher. Well, that was that. Naturally, everything stopped.

It wasn't very long before Mullen appeared on the scene – that's the man himself. He took off up one side of me and down the other, and I told him what I thought of him and his son too, so he waved a few fingers in my face and told me to pack up my kit and get out of town. So I stood around watching for a while, and Mr. Roberts, who was the superintendent, appeared. Three Finger Mullen went over and shook his finger in his face, and he was yelling and screaming his head off, and they were trying to get this car and the rock out of the top of the crusher. So finally Roberts came over and talked to me and I told him what I thought of the whole business and I was re-hired. He just told me to forget about it. Anyway, the crusher was down about three hours that time, and actually I was thanked very much by the boys because by this time they were kind of fed up anyway – it was that time of the day when they needed to rest.[51]

Alcohol abuse became a major problem at the Hawk Lake quarry that year. Steps were taken to ban all alcohol in the camp after a couple of incidents came to light. Not all of the alcohol stashes were found, though, as Cooke would discover at the end of the season:

I remember going out in 1939 to see the boys away. I don't know who the fellow was but I guess he wasn't the only one who had a suitcase, and he said, "Come on, we'll go in the men's room." He may have had two shirts and a couple of pairs of socks. The rest was a solid line-up of whisky, and he was taking off and heading back home. I wondered if he ever got there or not. There was quite a few of the boys that did that – drank their way in and drank their way out again.[52]

><+>·0·<+·<

In the early morning hours of September 1, 1939, German forces attacked Poland, marking the start of World War II. By September 3rd all diplomatic efforts and ultimatums by Britain and France to secure a voluntary withdrawal had failed and war was declared.[53] Canada declared war against Germany on September 10th.

Unlike World War I, this conflict had no immediate effect on McLean's operations. In fact by the next fall Seaboard's contract in New York was seven months ahead of schedule and more than half finished. All excavation had been completed for the shafts and tunnels and the concrete lining was being installed.[54] Predictably, McLean would show up on the job site at unpredictable times:

> Mr. McLean was in the city somewhere…at a party with some people, and very late at night or early in the morning came out to Shaft 14, and of course we always had a watchman at the gate. The area had to be fenced in. This was Westchester County and you had to fence it in and paint the fencing all green to match up with the trees and all of the trimmings around that were natural. Mr. McLean attempted to bust into the place by walking through the gate, and this watchman had no idea who this big guy was and he threatened to throw him out… Mr. McLean told him who he was and he said, "It makes no difference who you are. I've been told by Mr. McLaren that nobody is to get in this place unless they can show me a pass, and that means everybody that comes to this gate. Now you'd better move on." So this tickled the boss and the next day…orders came to the office: "Get up there with a box of cigars and give it to that guy…what we need is more people like that fellow around us."[55]

Delaware Aqueduct. View of tunnel at Mount Kisco, New York, 1939. HARRY FALCONER McLEAN COLLECTION, ACCESSION 1981-064. PA 212855 – LIBRARY AND ARCHIVES CANADA

The Unions held a "colossal souse party" for the Delaware

Aqueduct workers in November 1940. In a newspaper article, part of a series on union racketeering that won him the Pulitzer Prize in 1942, Westbrook Pegler reported:

> I met a sandhog in a tavern at Beford [Bedford] Village with a bundle of tickets which had been handed to him by some foreman. He said his contractor had bought them by the pound… They were floating all over the counties like autumn leaves. If even half of them turn up in White Plains on Saturday night there would be hell to pay. One promoter in [S]eaboard [C]onstruction said sure it was a racket but 500 tickets at $5.50 was a small item in the price of precious union cooperation on a multi-million-dollar contract.[56]

As expected, the hall was filled beyond capacity. The service was slow and the food was cold. The union representatives had sold three times as many tickets as there were plates and pocketed the extra money. At a nearby tavern, the workers who were turned away at the door got progressively drunker and angrier until "bottles and chairs began to fly."[57] The local police managed to keep the disorderly men at bay. What could have been a fiery story about corrupt union officials in the next day's newspaper was effectively neutered and the incident was reported as a minor skirmish.

"What the hell ails the Boss?" asked a reporter visiting the construction office in Armonk. "We had a tough day today," was the reply. "One of the muckers went and got himself killed in the shaft."[58] McLean had been on site when a load of drill steel suddenly shifted, crushing a worker. This fatality was one of fifty-eight on the Delaware Aqueduct project in 1941, with the majority of work finished.[59] McLean carried the corpse to the ambulance and travelled to the deceased's home in a nearby town. He handed five hundred dollars to the grieving widow and left without uttering a word.[60]

This unfortunate event was to be followed by some expected and less tragic but no less onerous occurrences. Although the aqueduct project was nearing completion, McLean's spending habits and creative bookkeeping were the source of much consternation amongst Seaboard's other shareholders, particularly Bickell and Smith. McLean was pushed out of the company and sold his shares in Seaboard Construction to

Smith.[61] Due to the continued threats from Fay and Bove and his expulsion from Seaboard, McLean vowed never to set foot in New York State again, hiring a bodyguard for added protection.[62]

In February 1942, Frank Smithwick Hogan, the highly ethical and incorruptible district attorney for Manhattan, commenced an inquiry into labour practices on the Delaware Aqueduct project. The thrust of the investigation was to find evidence that Fay and Bove were using their positions as union representatives for personal gain.[63] The Fay-Bove case would prove to be one of the most arduous of Hogan's lengthy career.[64] It was also the first and last case he would argue alone.[65] Hogan, known as "Mr. Integrity," would go on, during his five-decade-long career, to prosecute in such high-profile cases as those involving the television quiz show *Twenty One*, the gangster Frank Costello and New York basketball rigging.

Hogan's fourteen-month-long search focused on contractors that were without labour problems, such as Seaboard Construction. Hogan suspected that McLean had made substantial payments to Fay and Bove, as did an assistant district attorney who was pummelled by McLean in Toronto after discovering unexplained withdrawals in Seaboard's books.[66] Hogan and his assistants faced many difficulties building their case, as the contractors were for the most part uncooperative.[67]

On the subject of Hogan's obtaining the testimony of the contractors, Fay told him: "They won't testify at the trial. I'll see to that."[68] When approached in Canada by an assistant district attorney to

Frank Smithwick Hogan, district attorney for Manhattan, 1941–1973. COURTESY OF MRS. IDA VAN LINDT, OFFICE OF THE DISTRICT ATTORNEY, COUNTY OF NEW YORK

testify, McLean refused, as Fay had predicted, saying he would go to New York City "only with a ring in my nose and my feet shackled."[69] McLean later told Joseph McNally, his protégé, "I'd be awful careful crossing the border because if they ever get me on the stand I've got to tell the truth."[70]

Other contractors approached by Hogan also declined to testify. These included Stephen Healy, who also refused to enter New York State. Healy could not be legally compelled because there was no law in the State of Illinois forcing a potential witness to testify at a criminal trial in another state.[71] Some time later while in Florida, Healy was grabbed by the authorities but jumped bail and returned to his home state. Hogan's office reported that a year and a half later Healy met with them in New York only to tell a "fanciful tale of having indeed received threats, but from a contractor since dead, and having indeed paid money, but to an associate of Al Capone."[72]

An assistant district attorney tracked McLean down at the Battle Creek Sanitarium in Michigan and tried to secure his testimony, but McLean leapt out of a window in the middle of the night and slipped out of the United States and back to Canada.[73] This action did nothing to endear McLean to Hogan, who had no use for people who shirked their civic and moral duty. To Hogan, the paying contractors were as blameworthy as the extortionists.[74] Pegler, the investigative reporter, agreed:

> …it is definitely known that some other contractors have been just as crooked as Fay and Bove. Theirs has become, if it has not always been, a dirty, corrupt business in which cynical men submit to some exactions without a struggle knowing that they can pass the burden to the clients, who hire them for big construction, whether the clients be taxpayers in public works or the stockholders in private projects.[75]

Morality aside, graft in New York City did not begin with the Delaware Aqueduct project, nor would one trial put an end to it. Corruption ran far and deep, from politicians to the police. The union tentacles stretched an awfully long way. McLean and the other contractors had an understandable reluctance to take a bullet between the eyes or elsewhere. Fay and Bove had proven their means and ability to make good on their threats.

With Fay and Bove otherwise occupied in court, the job was completed to the satisfaction of the Board of Water Supply, and on March 3, 1943, the West Branch–Kensico tunnel became operational.[76] Bernard Smith, as chairman of Seaboard, was busy in his new capacity as construction magnate submitting bids for projects in Central and South America. Believing that all was forgiven after duping McLean, Smith contacted him with a new job opportunity:

> Ten Percent Ben phones and says he's got a hot deal in Mexico, would McLean take part in it? Harry is saying, "Oh yeah, sure." They had a fight, but this is something else, this is a whole new job. Anyways, he says, "Go ahead and pick it up. We'll go. I'll send you a man down right away." So he sent Chum Therrien down.[77] Chum Therrien ends up in Mexico. Chum was in Mexico two years. "The first thing they did," Chum said, "they took my passport away from me." I forget what his job was. Chum used to talk about the banditos in payroll. Honestly, I was sitting in McLean's living room in 1943. McLean is laughing like hell. He said, "I sent Chum down. That's all he's going to get out of me. Now the son of a bitch is stuck with that contract. He suckered me," he said. "I suckered him really good this time."[78]

Finally, in May 1943, the Grand Jury concluded the indictment of Fay and Bove. With respect to Seaboard, the indictment stated:

> The said defendants, in the County of New York, from on or about April 1, 1938 to on or about July 1, 1942, wrongfully, wilfully and extorsively obtained the sum of $125,000…from Harry F. McLean and Louis R. Perini, officers and agents of said corporation, with their consent by the wrongful use of force and fear induced by threats of said defendants to Harry F. McLean and Louis R. Perini…to do an unlawful injury to the property of said corporation; by unlawfully and corruptly placing picket lines in front of and near the places of business of said corporation, by unlawfully and corruptly using their power to prevent said corporation from entering into contracts with the International Union of Operating Engineers and the International Hod Carriers, Building and Common Laborers' Union of America and other labor unions; by unlawfully and corruptly using their power to prevent said corporation from employing members of said labor

unions; by unlawfully and corruptly using their power to prevent said corporation from employing members of said labor unions at prevailing and reasonable rates of wages; by unlawfully and corruptly using their power to prevent said corporation from hiring and employing efficient, skilled and competent workers; and by otherwise unlawfully and corruptly hindering, impeding and interfering with the conduct of the business of the said corporation.[79]

Back at the district attorney's office, Hogan was having a difficult time finding jurors for the trial. At least fifty potential jury members filed excuses for not serving, fearing retribution from Fay and Bove.[80] Eventually the jury was selected and housed at the only hotel in New York City that could accommodate them all – the Waldorf Astoria.[81] Fay and Bove's criminal trial commenced on February 26, 1945, after years of legal manoeuvring and delaying tactics by their herd of lawyers.[82]

Among the more novel defences attempted during the trial was that payments had indeed been received but these were actually voluntary and constituted an effort by the contractors to obtain "the legitimate aid, assistance and cooperation of Fay and Bove."[83] This feeble defence prompted the assistant district attorney to state, "To say, under such circumstances, that the money was 'voluntarily' paid to the defendants for 'legitimate' purposes is to defy every consideration of reality and common sense."[84] Of the amounts that were reported, Fay and Bove benefited to the tune of at least $368,000, but Hogan suspected that the total was "closer to $1,000,000."[85] In the end, the jury rejected their arguments and convicted the pair, on March 15, 1945, of conspiracy and extortion.[86]

On March 26, 1945, a shipment arrived at Hogan's Manhattan office courtesy of Harry McLean. It was a barrel of oysters, sent at McLean's instructions by Émile Paturel, a fish merchant in Shediac, New Brunswick. Hogan promptly returned the oysters to Paturel, stating that as a public official he could not accept such a gift and adding a curt message:

When next you see Mr. McLean, will you kindly tell him that the District Attorney of New York County spurns his good wishes and his compliments. He is a notorious flouter of the law. If he were less of a coward and more of a good citizen, Mr. McLean would come into

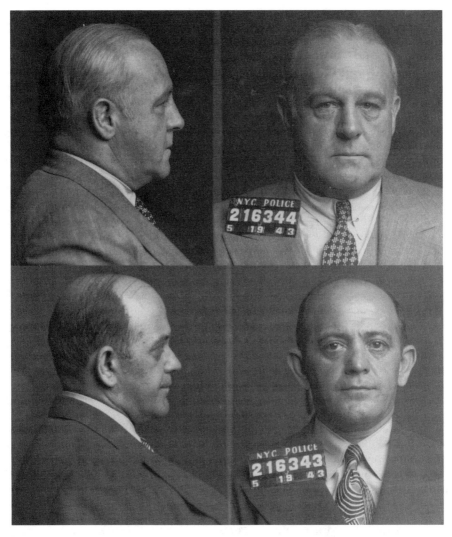

Mug shots of Joseph Fay (above) and James Bove. D.A. CASE #905-1943. PHOTOGRAPHS COURTESY OF NYC MUNICIPAL ARCHIVES

this jurisdiction. Then I would take him before a New York County Grand Jury, where he could give testimony in aid of honest law enforcement.[87]

He went on to express his regret for any inconvenience caused to Paturel by Hogan's "distaste for Mr. McLean and his ilk."[88]

At the sentencing hearing before Justice William Munson on April 5, 1945, Hogan publicly denounced McLean for his refusal to testify, describing him as a "dipsomaniac."[89] (Pegler concurred with Hogan's assessment, calling McLean "a spectacular drunkard."[90]) Hogan epitomized Fay and Bove as "ruthless and grasping thieves"[91] and asked the jury to show no leniency, adding:

> They undeniably had the power to ruin the business of these contractors and if the money were not paid the business of these contractors would be ruined by labor trouble. That is no different than putting a gun to the head of a man and demanding money. I have more respect for a man who uses a gun – he takes more chances.[92]

On the count of conspiracy to commit extortion, a misdemeanour, the men were sentenced to one year in the New York County Penitentiary and for the count of extortion, a felony, a consecutive sentence of seven to fifteen years in the New York State Prison.[93] In spite of the finding of guilty and the subsequent sentencing, Fay maintained a loyal following of business and church leaders and labour union officials, who showered the court with letters begging for clemency for Fay.[94] Hogan summarized his thoughts on this outpouring of pleas for mercy:

> Isn't it discouraging that this man is indicted in 1943, the jury returns a conviction and there is no move to drive the crook from the ranks of labor! Not even a word of censure! It is the most discouraging thing to think that no responsible labor leader would have the courage, the Americanism, to say, "The jury has spoken, and he has no place in our ranks." It is the most discouraging thing for any true friend of labor that the workingman has to be saddled with such inept and cowardly leaders that they won't denounce such crooks as these persons who disgraced labor for twenty-six years.[95]

Although Fay managed to avoid jail for over two years pending the results of several appeals, Bove, his "No. 1 Dough Boy,"[96] was not so fortunate. In Westchester County on May 25, 1945, Bove was found guilty on seventy-four counts of grand larceny and forgery relating to the funds of his union and was immediately sent to the New York State Prison.[97] Charges of income tax evasion were also in store for both Fay and Bove, and again Bove would draw the short straw, receiving a further five-year sentence.[98] After a final appeal failed to sway the United States

Supreme Court, Fay's conviction was affirmed on June 23, 1947, and he was sent to Sing Sing to serve his sentence.[99]

Even with Fay and Bove locked up, however, Harry McLean was true to his word. He never returned to New York City.

CHAPTER THIRTEEN

Stand To Tiger Moth[1]

*"Can you run that job, McNally?" "If you've got the money, Mr. McLean,
I've got the time." "And you've got the nerve too, you s.o.b."*[2]

DURING THE FIRST months of World War II, the Honourable Clarence
Decatur (C. D.) Howe was diligently working to assemble his own army:
a brigade of Canada's top businessmen from a wide array of industries
to assist him with supply and procurement for the war. By order-in-
council under the *War Measures Act*, Howe was freed from the bureaucracy
usually associated with government procurement. Howe believed that
businessmen from the commercial sector would have greater freedom
than their civil service counterparts to get things done quickly. Without
remuneration, Howe's executive recruits assumed positions of great
responsibility and made an invaluable contribution to the war effort.[3]

On April 9, 1940, after Mackenzie King and his Liberal party were
returned to power in a late-March election, the Department of Munitions
and Supply formally came into being under Howe's direction as minister.
The next month, $700 million was reserved for the war effort and Howe
was responsible for spending the lion's share of it on the Canadian
industrial war program. Howe put businessmen in charge of specific
activities at Munitions and Supply – for example, controlling Canada's
oil supply. He understood the importance of delegating tasks; further,
once entrusted with their assignments, these men were given full authority

to make decisions. As a businessman, Howe also knew that men accustomed to being in command would not take well to continual meddling. After the responsibility was assigned, Howe would turn his attention elsewhere, confident that matters were in good hands. Scores of younger specialists were seconded from Canadian businesses to Munitions and Supply, at no cost to the government.[4]

Howe also established a number of government-owned companies to oversee the rapidly expanding war production efforts in Canada, and to expedite urgent requirements and ease some of the burden on Munitions and Supply.[5] One of the first such companies was Allied War Supplies Corporation (AWSC). Its mandate was to create and manage an "entire new industrial production capacity"[6] for explosives, chemicals and ammunition, as the British government had expressed a keen interest in manufacturing explosives and chemicals in Canada.[7] The company was set up and presided over by Harold Crabtree, president of the Canadian Manufacturers' Association. Within months, the AWSC assumed responsibility for administering, supervising and directing a number of large projects across Canada; most of its ventures were initiated by virtue of a "go ahead" letter, as time did not permit the development of a full contract at the outset.[8]

Many Canadian companies reorganized their operations to assist with the war effort. Canadian Industries Limited (CIL) established a subsidiary, Defence Industries Limited (DIL), to take on contracts from Munitions and Supply.[9] In May 1940, as Winston Churchill was settling into his role as British prime minister, representatives of the British government and of Munitions and Supply in Canada discussed the need for a substantial supply of propellants, well above the supply from DIL plants at Beloeil, Quebec, and Nobel, Ontario.[10] DIL received a "go ahead" letter from the deputy minister of Munitions and Supply on May 31, 1940, to construct the plant on de Salaberry Island near Valleyfield, Quebec.[11] Several months later the project was transferred to the AWSC to complete negotiations and administer the contracts. The entire undertaking was paid for by the British government.[12]

The fall of France in June and the subsequent evacuation of British armed forces without their army equipment at Dunkirk forced all construction plans for war-related factories in Canada to be expedited and extended.[13] The original plans for de Salaberry called for the construction of a manufacturing plant for twelve thousand tons each of nitrocellulose cannon powder and trinitrotoluol (TNT) per year. These were expanded to include facilities to manufacture dinitrotoluol (DNT), rifle cordite and tetryl.[14]

Six general contractors submitted proposals to DIL. On June 26, 1940, H. F. McLean Limited was selected to provide general contracting services at cost plus a fixed rate of forty-five thousand dollars and a plant rental fee of two and a half percent per month.[15] DIL was responsible for paying the up-front cost of the construction, including material and labour expenses. Common labourers were paid thirty-five cents an hour for a forty-eight-hour work week.[16] The TNT plant was to be completed and in production by January 1, 1941, and other plants by May 1, 1941.[17]

⊱┈◈┈●┈◈┈⊰

C. D. Howe and Harry McLean had been acquainted since Howe's pre-politics days as a civil engineer and construction man. Their paths had crossed while Howe was supervising the construction of grain elevators for the Board of Grain Commissioners, then again as Howe entered politics in 1935 as minister of Railways and Marine.[18] Described as a "fascist, but a nice fascist,"[19] Howe brandished an enormous amount of power and was accused of running his department and Canadian industry like a dictatorship. Howe believed his methods were required in order to respond expeditiously to requests from both the Canadian and British armies for materiel and munitions. On June 17, 1940, he spoke before the House of Commons:

> We have used the powers indicated in this Bill to dictate the prices at which people shall undertake work. We have gone into a plant and said, "We want this article. The price is so much. You must manufacture this article. If you are not satisfied with the price you can take your case to the Exchequer Court." As the need grows more urgent, we will use this power very extensively. We are getting to the point where, if a manufacturer has a thing which the Government needs, we pre-empt it; we pay him what we think is a fair price, and if he does not think so

he has, as I have said, an appeal to the courts. In many instances we have imposed our price.[20]

On July 2, 1940, Colonel Kenneth Ramsay arrived at the Valleyfield job site as field superintendent, assisted by Joseph McNally on this project, which was dubbed the "Nitro." Rapid progress was made and by the end of the month construction of the various buildings – bunkhouses, contractor's house, hospital, and foundations for the power house and TNT plant – were well under way. On July 12th a hundred and fifty men were on the job; fourteen days later the number had increased to five hundred and forty-nine.[21] Barney Barnett was project engineer, Charles Hyson electrical superintendent and Richard Hearn chief engineer. Substantial and successive changes in the plan at the onset caused delays and flared tempers. McNally recalled a heated exchange he had with Hearn:

I'm over in the office in Valleyfield one day and Dick says, "Come in here, McNally." So, I go in. "We're behind schedule here, behind schedule there, behind schedule on this"…as if I was responsible for all of this, so I said, "Mr. Hearn, you may know how to build a dam, you may know how to do a hell of a lot of things, but you don't know bugger all about building. If you want the goddamned job on schedule, give me some lumber." He said, "You want lumber?" I said, "Yeah." "How much do you want?" So I told him. Man, he packed lumber in there every day like you wouldn't believe – six or ten carloads every day. Just piled it in there.

So about three months later I come back to my office and Hearn is sitting at my desk with his feet up, smoking his pipe. "Sit down, McNally," he said. "You knew what was wrong with this job all the time, didn't you?" I said, "Yes." He said, "Why didn't you come and tell me?" "Well," I said, "you're chief engineer; I didn't think it was my business to tell you what to do." He said, "Joe, my door is always open. I can help you. I'm chief engineer. I can do a lot of things. Together we can do a lot more things. Let's try and cooperate with one another." From that day forward, Dick Hearn and I were on a first-name basis.[22]

H. F. McLean Limited "did everything of every nature" on the project, including plumbing, electrical, roads, sewers, water and heating. Hyson's department alone employed a hundred and seventy men. TNT manufacturing called for "buildings of the queerest construction of all designs and styles."[23] Some two hundred and fifty buildings were built in all, mostly out of wood, with "a planned minimum life of five years."[24] Special structures were erected to house acid concentrators, ammonia oxidation and nitric acid production. Indoor rifle ranges for testing ballistics of all kinds were constructed. Steam for process and power generation as well as heating was used extensively throughout the plant. This required continual delivery and stockpiling of coal. In case of explosion, giant baffle walls were built around the facility and filled with sand.[25]

Certain areas of the plant were restricted. Security was put in place to combat potential sabotage: men armed with shotguns paced between a lookout and little cabins, all within sight of one another. They guarded the whole facility continually, twenty-four hours a day, seven days a week. No one was allowed to carry matches or anything that might be combustible, except for McNally, who did carry matches.[26] McNally recalled a "security breach":

> I'm in charge. We're commissioning the plant, and the commission of a place like this – this is an explosive plant…things happen, they blow, and so you have to set yourself up [so] that you can handle anything. And we decided we should get a carload of coke [coal]. We used to use coke in those days for salamanders… A salamander is between eighteen and twenty-four inches in diameter, steel piece of pipe with some holes in the end that you can put a rod through and two men can carry it. It's got a grate in the bottom of it, and you can put some wood and some coke in there and start a fire. Now you've got a coke fire. You put tarps up and break the wind, you put the salamander there, and now a man can lay bricks. So if you're laying brick in twenty-below weather…it's a fire. Anyways, I ordered a ton of coke.
>
> One of the buildings blew up in the early fall. It was cold, so of course we started using coke – that's what I got it for. And I think the second day the truck driver says to me, "You know, that's the last load of coke, Joe." "What? It can't be." He says, "It's all gone." So, I say, "Okay." This plant… I had the privilege of ordering anything I wanted. I had special numbers. I could phone a local supplier and give him a number and he'd supply me with a keg of nails or a ton of coke. I'd give him a number and that's it. No purchasing agent. If something

happened, we'd need it now... I called the local agent and sent a truck down and we got a load of coke from him. So three or four weeks later I've got a friend of mine in the hotel in Montreal and he's in the booze pretty good and he says, "When are you going to order some more coke, Joe?" The wheels are going. I know where my coke went. That guy was in charge of security and what he had done was he'd pirated that coke for their homes...he and a bunch of his friends were using my coke in their homes. I was very meticulous about a lot of things – lead in one pile and iron in one pile – just don't touch what is there... About six months after that I had them up in court for looting company property... Unbelievable. That was a real nightmare.[27]

>—!—◆>—O—<◆—!—<

The *Empress of Britain*, the ship McLean's men had worked so hard to accommodate at Wolfe's Cove, had been called into wartime duty for troop transport, along with many other passenger liners. Although her white hull had been painted a dingy grey, she retained her elegant interior. The troops who sailed on the *Britain* were treated to the same sumptuous meals and spectacular service that had been enjoyed by the paying first-class passengers during her world cruises. On October 26, 1940, the *Britain* suffered several direct hits from bombs dropped by a German warplane. Forty-nine people died as a result of the attack and the remaining five hundred and ninety-eight people on board were rescued and taken to Ireland. The ship did not immediately sink and an attempt was made to tow her to port, but the commander of the German submarine *U-32* had other ideas. On October 28th two torpedoes were fired at the *Britain*, the second of which caused her to capsize in less than ten minutes. The nine-year-old liner was the largest passenger ship sunk at sea during World War II.[28]

The de Salaberry project was falling behind schedule. Between the siphoning of men to fight the war and increased construction at home, skilled labourers were in short supply.[29] McLean's men worked through the holidays, Christmas Day and New Year's Day, in ten-hour shifts during a work week of up to sixty hours in sub-zero weather. By the end of February the first units were delivered and communications systems became a critical item. McNally was in charge of expediting the communications installation:

> With an explosive plant, the communication has to be buried. You can't put it up on the aerial – you'll lose it… So you've got snow so deep, cold. Ramsay says, "Hire some men, McNally." "Yes, sir." The next week he says, "How many men do you have on communications, McNally?" I said, "About two hundred and fifty, sir." He said, "McNally, can you not think as high as one thousand, or don't zeroes mean anything to you?" By the next week I've got a thousand men. Have you ever seen this many men? All lined up with a pick and shovel. And they never leave anybody behind – they all help one another. In three weeks I end up getting the whole thing wired. Unbelievable how quick.
>
> The job was winding down and we were sitting in the lobby at the hotel there one night. The Colonel says, "You learned anything, McNally?" I said, "Yes, I've learned an awful lot. This job has been a real education for me." "Now," he said, "do you remember you went to the gate and hired everybody and gave them a pick and shovel?" This is early March; the weather is cold. I said, "Yes, sir, that was a lesson to me how quickly it all went together." He said, "The important thing, Joe, the job is finished. All we've got to take back to the yard is picks and shovels, consumables. We've got no overhaul, we've got no rebuild, just picks and shovels – they'll all be used up. More important than that, you went to the gate and hired everybody – the young, the old, the lame, anybody. You gave them all jobs. They all went home to their wives, their children and their lovers. They all had money. They think the company is fine in town. We've given them a few weeks' pay in the middle of winter. You left a lot of good will in the county, and always keep that in mind." These people were very conscious of their position.[30]

Although the changes in the initial plans and the need to obtain skilled labour caused some difficulty, the plants were completed with only a slight delay. By the summer of 1941 production of explosives and propellants was under way to satisfy the requirements both for export to Britain and for ammunition filling plants in Canada. H. F. McLean Limited stayed to clean up odds and ends while the training of personnel in all of the various stages of the manufacture of smokeless powder got under way. McLean sent in mechanics from other jobs, including some old railwaymen to install seven miles of narrow-gauge track between certain points on the grounds of the facility to serve as a process conveying system, along with eight miles of standard-gauge track. The plant site was connected to the Coteau–Valleyfield branch of the CNR by a two-mile-long spur line.[31]

Remarkably, the actual cost of building the entire facility was $4 million under budget. However, not all of the savings were attributed to the efficiency of H. F. McLean Limited. Based on estimates hurriedly obtained from the United States, costs had been over-estimated to begin with, and some components of the work were never carried out.[32] Howe reported to the House of Commons in March 1944 that the government's commitments for the expansion of industrial capacity due to the war were approximately $857 million, $158 million of which was directed to "Chemicals, Explosives and Pyrotechnics."[33]

Wartime Housing decided to build a small townsite near the plant to house the various personnel in prefabricated homes, and H. F. McLean Limited was awarded the contract to build three hundred houses. Bunkhouses, dining rooms, office buildings and laboratories were also constructed, to accommodate scientists so numerous that Hyson declared, "We had them coming out of our ears."[34] A carpentry superintendent was brought on and McNally looked after the structural end of the job. Sewers, roads, waterlines and everything else imaginable were installed by H. F. McLean Limited.

⊱—◆◇—○—◇◆—◆⊰

On November 6, 1941, Dominion Construction was awarded the contract by Munitions and Supply to build the Point Edward Naval Base at Sydney, Nova Scotia.

Point Edward was to be an operational base for the Royal Canadian Navy to accommodate, service, and supply corvettes and various other types of naval vessel. The original estimated price to build the base was $1,490,500, plus a monthly fee of $37,500.[35] Colonel Ramsay was in charge, Charlie Tupper was Ramsay's assistant and H. O. Thomas was the office manager.[36]

Time was of the essence with a wartime contract; the facilities were required urgently, but as an added incentive for McLean's men to work quickly, a "Cessation of Hostilities" clause allowed the minister to terminate the contract "as regards all or any part or parts of the work or works not theretofore completed" if the war should end.[37] Renewed optimism about an early end to the war came in December 1941 with the surprise raid on Pearl Harbor by the Japanese and subsequent declarations of war by the United States against Japan and Germany against the United States. With the Americans now part of the worldwide struggle, victory seemed certain. This turning point in the war was all the more reason to complete the contract at the earliest opportunity.

By early 1942 Ramsay was having to deal with a largely uncooperative workforce at the Sydney job. McLean's chief engineer and one of his most treasured assets, Richard Hearn, had resigned from Dominion Construction. Hearn had returned to work for the Hydro-Electric Power Commission of Ontario, where he had started out back in 1913. He was to serve as executive assistant to the chairman, T. Hogg. Ontario Hydro subsequently loaned him out to participate in the war effort as chief construction engineer for the Polymer Corporation's synthetic rubber plant.[38] Although Hearn and McLean had had their differences from time to time, Hearn's expertise would be sorely missed. Ramsay recognized the need for a project engineer and called for McNally, who was still at Valleyfield:

> "Joe, get a berth to Sydney." I said, "Colonel, I'm locked in here for the war; he won't let me out of here." "Joe," he said, "you'll be sprung in three days. You'll get a call from Ottawa in three days. Get a berth. It's a lot easier travelling down to Sydney in a berth than it is sitting up all of the time." "Okay, sir." So I get a berth. I get a call to be on the first train going east.
>
> When I was sent down to Sydney, my instructions from the Colonel were to "clean that job up and get it on stream – now." So I'm there about five days, and the Colonel said, "What do you want to do, Joe?" "I'm going to fire half these men; they don't understand that they've got a new boss." He said, "When are you going to do that?" I said, "This afternoon, after dinner." The Colonel said, "Yeah, you'll do better on a full belly."

There were five hundred men on the job, so that afternoon, bang, there were two hundred and fifty… I didn't realize at the time but I think McLean thought, "Jeez, that McNally's a bugger."[39]

Among the first tasks to be done were clearing, grubbing, surface drainage, and constructing two and a half miles of road and a water and sewage system. Then came the construction of living quarters for the officers, barracks, dining halls, training classrooms, training workshops, and a large hospital and dental clinic, along with inflammable and minesweeper stores and a torpedo depot.[40] Ramsay and McNally turned the job around in short order. Common labourers were paid the least, at forty cents an hour, while truck drivers using their own trucks were paid the most, at a dollar and forty-five cents an hour. The asbestos insulation workers were paid sixty cents a hour.[41] With everything running smoothly, McNally decided it was time to serve his country and enlisted:

I was sent down to Sydney to get that job back on track, and I got it going pretty good… We were up to about seven hundred and fifty men and everything was on schedule…and I decided to join the army… So I told Colonel Ramsay goodbye. He said, "You young guys are all the same." …I'm young, I don't care. I got on the train and I got as far as east of Sackville. The army came through the train asking, "What's your name? Where's your bag?" I'm on the train back to Halifax right away. The army said, "You get the hell back where you came from and don't show your face up here again." I get to Sydney and the Colonel is waiting for me. He said, "We knew where you were every hour. It took us a little while to get the paperwork done."[42]

The construction of the wharf was completed under a separate contract with another contractor. Days after the wharf was finished and as the Navy started to settle in, a blow torch ignited the highly flammable creosoted timber. The wooden structure piling of the wharf was quickly engulfed in flames. Hyson recalled that the blaze was

about a thousand feet long, the weirdest fire I've ever seen. The whole end of Nova Scotia was lighted up. Good thing submarines weren't lurking by, because you could see it for miles and miles. We had every fire department that could travel the roads there trying to pour water, but the fire was so intense. We even fought it from the harbour side, the water side, with tugs from Dominion Steel and Coal, but without avail. The black smoke – you couldn't see – miles of smoke.[43]

Dominion Construction was awarded the contract to demolish and rebuild the main wharf.

Among Ramsay's and McNally's regular duties was bailing McLean out of jail. After a drunken fight for reasons unknown in a hotel lobby in Sydney, McLean was detained and spent the night in a cell. The next day he asked his office manager to prepare a five-thousand-dollar cheque with a note for the police chief to clean up his jail. He told a reporter about his incarceration, stating that the holding facility was the "dirtiest jail I ever saw. Sat up all night counting rats."[44] A year later McLean invited the local press to see how his investment had been spent:

> "Come and see how they've improved the jail." He went back to the jail and said, "Hell, that bed is wired up to the wall. And look at all the graffiti, look at all the junk around you. You've done nothing. Where has my money gone?" Then he came back laughing like hell. He said, "That fellow will never put me in jail again, nor any of you fellows." This was part of his image. The men thought, this guy is just a little different... He had a lot of men working for him and, by God, he was going to show them he was as good and tough as they were and he was part of the gang.[45]

>─┤◆├─O─┤◆├─<

In March 1942 Dominion Construction was completing the final concrete placement for the dam at Bark Lake, Ontario, on the Madawaska River. A long section of Highway 60 and the village of Madawaska were flooded due to the change in water levels; the highway was realigned and the village was relocated.[46]

The Battle of the Atlantic had spread to Canada as ships in the St. Lawrence River were falling victim to attacks by German U-boats. The infiltration of the St. Lawrence occurred during the summer and fall of 1942: five convoys were attacked and seventeen merchantmen sunk, as well as a full troop ship and two warships.[47] The influx of servicemen to Halifax since the start of the war had caused a severe housing shortage, transportation difficulties and line-ups for just about everything. The population had increased by forty thousand between 1939 and 1941 and the city was feeling the strain.[48] The Navy determined

The German submarine U-190 *at Sydney, September 5, 1945. The crew of* U-190 *sank the last Canadian warship to be lost during the war, HMCS* Esquimalt, *near the entrance to Halifax harbour. After the crew surrendered, in May 1945,* U-190 *was commissioned by the Royal Canadian Navy. The infiltration of the St. Lawrence by U-boats led to the closure of the port of Montreal. This, and the overburdened infrastructure of Halifax due to the steady influx of military personnel, served to hasten the construction of the Cornwallis base.* COLLECTION CANADA. DEPT. OF NATIONAL DEFENCE ACCESSION 1967-052. PA-134173 D.J. THORNDICK/LIBRARY AND ARCHIVES CANADA

that moving the recruit training centre HMCS *Cornwallis* out of Halifax would help to relieve the pressure.

McLean and McNally were called to negotiate with the Navy. The proposal was to build a base that would accommodate ten thousand people. Two sites in Nova Scotia were considered: Shelburne and Deep Brook. McNally travelled with McLean to the favoured Shelburne site and immediately voiced his concerns:

> I said, "Mr. McLean, do not take that contract. That's a political minefield. We can't win. You can't get freight through Halifax – through the troop movements and materiel moving the freight line. We're stuck for materiel all the time getting to Sydney – it's killing us; we can't keep any schedule. And furthermore this place is rocky as hell. Don't touch it."[49]

Within days, McLean had arranged to change the location of the new base to Deep Brook. For compelling reasons, McNally made a further demand:

> "I do not want to work on any more jobs where the design is done in Ottawa, because the bunch of asses in Ottawa – they send us drawings for buildings we haven't built, and we get buildings framed and waiting for drawings and we can't get them… And the bungled drawings every day. Revisions – I spend more time throwing out revisions than I do getting any work done. Now, I want the design on site."

> Three days later we had a vice-president of CPR East, Mr. Collins. Very fine gentleman. He and I turned out to be very good friends. About a week later he said, "I think we can get the design on site too, Joe." We settled on that property…in Annapolis Basin. We used CP from Montreal to Saint John, then the ferry over to Digby and then the Dominion Atlantic railroad that ran into Halifax. So we got good communication…we had a nice little operation. CPR thought I was a king. They entertained me for a long time.

> Within the week, McLean had arranged that. He knew who to contact. This man, his tentacles reached a long way… We all had a lot of admiration for him because of the depths of his thinking. And his capacity to touch the people you needed to do something… Can you imagine the federal government agreeing to send the design people all to a job? It was never done before. We had architects, we had engineers, we had the design people – all of the engineering – all right in that one

office. They went across the country and they picked up Gerry Dineen, [an] engineer from Hamilton. No municipal work [was] being done at this time and these fellows were literally sitting there on their hands. So the government sent out the word and down they came. Very competent and able men. And they were all there to get something done. Wonderful.[50]

By early summer McNally was in Digby with Ramsay awaiting the arrival of Major Lyons, the land buyer from Toronto, to negotiate the purchase of the property where the base would be located so that work could get under way:

On this property was a very large home, beautiful home…that was not finished inside – just the framework up and the studs inside and the garage was finished – a four-car garage with service quarters over it all done in beautiful oak…which we used for an office. Beautiful building. The land buyer went up to Clementsport… This was the Morse estate. Mrs. Morse was still alive and she was living in Clementsport. We went up to Clementsport to make a deal with her. I'll never forget. I'm at the hotel. Major Lyons came back. He said, "We got the property. You got a deal, Joe." I said, "Wonderful, we'll go to work tomorrow." "Yes," he said. I said, "Okay." Then he

Little more than a shell at the time, the Morse house was converted to an officers' mess.
COURTESY OF JOSEPH J. McNALLY

The first day on the Cornwallis job, Joseph McNally posed for a photograph with Laurie Ellis (right), president of Dominion Atlantic Railway. McNally was very well treated by the railway executive. COURTESY OF JOSEPH J. MCNALLY

proceeded to get drunk. I never saw a man get so drunk. I never saw a man so upset and so embarrassed. I'm serious – this guy was crying. He said he hammered this widow down to twelve thousand bucks. A hell of a big farm, building and all – twelve thousand. She signed the deal and then she said to him, "Now, Major, since the Government of Canada is in such bad shape, I'll give you a cheque for the twelve thousand." He was devastated.[51]

Major Lyons was not aware of the widow's background. Edward Phinley Morse, her deceased husband and the owner of the property, was raised in the Deep Brook area. Some years later he moved to the United States and he eventually founded United Shipyards in Brooklyn, New York. After making his fortune and living a life of affluence in the Hamptons, he retired in 1929 and bought the property at Deep Brook. He started building a large home but died before it was finished. His widow was left a very wealthy woman indeed.[52]

Within days of completion of the deal with Mrs. Morse, McLean and McNally were on the site preparing for the groundbreaking.

While in Digby, McLean received word that his estranged wife, Irene, had died in a fire in her apartment at 60 Oriole Gardens in Toronto. At approximately one o'clock on the morning of July 10, 1942, the building superintendent, J. W. Burch, had been alerted by one of the other tenants about smoke coming from Mrs. McLean's apartment. Burch tried to get

Left to right: Joseph McNally, Charles Hyson and construction superintendent Percy Cunningham. COURTESY OF JOSEPH J. MCNALLY

into the apartment but had to resort to breaking down the door. He found Mrs. McLean lying on her bed and thought she was unconscious. It was only after dragging her into the hall that he realized she was dead. Burch called the fire department and the police, and the police contacted McLean's Toronto office. Charles Switzer took control of matters and made the funeral and burial arrangements.[53]

The Office of the Fire Marshal concluded that Irene McLean had died accidentally of burns and smoke inhalation caused by her cigarette igniting her bedcovers after she had fallen asleep.[54] Prime Minister Mackenzie King sent McLean a telegram expressing his sympathy.[55] Irene McLean was buried in Mount Royal Cemetery in Montreal. She was survived by one sister, Hope Traversey of Montreal.[56]

McLean remained stoic and appeared unaffected by the tragedy. "When he was in his cups he'd talk about her," recalled his chauffeur. "He loved her dearly, but something came between them over the years."[57] Life went on, and so did the work.

With the Navy contract signed on July 28, 1942, McLean moved men from various other jobs to Deep Brook: McNally was the project engineer and Hyson was on the job to take care of the electrical end of things. Patrick J. McNally, Joseph's brother, took over as project engineer at Sydney.[58] McLean's old friend Colonel Sutherland was given a job operating the crusher.[59] McLean kept records on his employees and their work abilities. Whenever a new job commenced, he would refer to these cards and the men would be contacted.[60] For the most part, the men followed McLean:

Erecting the trusses for the drill hall at Cornwallis, at that time the largest naval training establishment in the British Commonwealth. COURTESY OF HERBERT S. FAIRN/ JOSEPH J. MCNALLY

> In Digby, I'm in the office one day and somebody says, "There's a big man down there walking around talking to the labourers." "Oh, oh, big man? That's the boss." He'd walk right on the job. He wouldn't come in the office – he'd go out on the job and start talking to the labourers. He said to me one day, "If you want to find out what's wrong with a job, Joe, go and talk to the labourers. The labourers know every mistake the engineers made. They'll tell you whether his levels are right, or whether the grade is right, or if he moved something twice and made an error. The labourers know all of the

Skating rink. COURTESY OF HERBERT S. FAIRN/JOSEPH J. MCNALLY

> errors. They never forget the errors. Go and talk to your labourers. They'll tell you what's wrong with the job."[61]

Both McNally and Hyson regularly made the trip from one end of Nova Scotia to the other, between Digby and Sydney, to check on the two sites:

> I'm out on the job one day and I've just got my leather jacket on… I'm walking down the road. A car pulls up. "Get in, Joe." So I get in. It's McLean, came down to Saint John, bought a car, put it on the boat, and now he's picking me up – a forty-ounce bottle of rum on the seat. He said, "We're going to Kentville." I said, "Okay." We end up in Kentville, and he's sucking on this rum the whole time. We end up at the Cornwallis Inn – that was a big hotel there. We get a couple of rooms there. I'm tired – it's six-thirty or seven. McLean says, "We're going to have a meeting tonight," still sucking on his rum. So I go

down to the dining room and get something to eat and go back upstairs. "Now, Joe," he said, "You're here for one reason. I want to know everything that is said in this room tonight."

Physical Training (PT) building. Courtesy of Herbert S. Fairn/Joseph J. McNally

We were in a strike position in Sydney and the labour situation...was very dicey. The coal mines and the steel mines and the federal government set the rates. We couldn't set the rates – the federal government did that. At this time, there were about two thousand men on the job. This is a pretty important job – that this base be continued without interruption – and a couple of men came down, Charlie Tupper...three or four men from Halifax, Department of Labour, provincial and federal, and me and McLean; we were all in the room. They were talking about how they were going to handle things. They were going to do this and they were going to do that. And the meeting breaks up and they go their way.

Preparing to build the gunnery school. Courtesy of Herbert S. Fairn/Joseph J. McNally

Next morning I get a call about seven-thirty... "Get down." I get down to his room and he's sitting on the edge of his bed. His eyes are hanging out, dirty old robe on him. "Stop me when I'm wrong." He repeated, "He said this, he said that, he said something else, he said something else – this is what we're going to do, Joe." He put on this act that he was stoned, half crazy...it's funny how men will talk when they think the other fellow is loaded. You get a little careless with your chatter. But that man knew everything that was said.[62]

Like all of the other wartime jobs, the Cornwallis base involved the construction of an entire community, with all the conveniences and services that would be found in a small town. Timber was hauled in by

Recruits with fixed bayonets, HMCS Cornwallis, *Deep Brook, June 1943.* ACCESSION 1967-052 NPC. GILBERT ALEXANDER MILNE/CANADA DEPT. OF NATIONAL DEFENCE. PA-128091, LIBRARY AND ARCHIVES CANADA

the carload for the multitude of structures that would be swiftly erected: ratings', wrens' and officers' quarters, barracks, food warehouses, administration buildings. The Morse home was converted to an officers' mess. A 650,000-gallon-capacity swimming pool was the centrepiece of the recreation facility. Training quarters for asdic, gunnery and seamanship were also built. A large hospital and a dental facility were constructed on site, while the religious concerns of the residents were addressed by the inclusion of several chapels of various denominations. The largest drill hall in Canada was built at Cornwallis, its truss raised in twenty-seven working hours.[63] With all of the many jobs that McNally was expected to oversee, he was called upon yet again to bail out his boss:

> We were at the Beatty Hotel in Saint John. We were going to stay in the hotel and get the boat [to Digby] first thing in the morning. …McLean goes out to get some air in front of the hotel and there's a woman there with three children. She's struggling with her bags to put them in

The Cornwallis base looking towards Digby. COURTESY OF HERBERT S. FAIRN/JOSEPH J. MCNALLY

the cab. The doorman is standing there and he says to the doorman, "Get over there and help the woman!" The doorman says, "Who do you think you're talking to?" McLean says, "You!" POW! So he ends up in jail again. So I get a call about ten o'clock at night…to get him out of jail. I've got to make arrangements and call one of the suppliers: "The boss is in jail again."[64]

With McNally's arrangements not proceeding as quickly as "the boss" would have liked, McLean called Berton Puddington in Grand Falls. McLean implored his friend, "For heaven's sake, identify me! Let these fellows know I'm responsible and respectable. They're all for putting me in jail." Puddington assured the authorities of McLean's virtue and he was released.[65]

By March 15, 1943, the Point Edward Naval Base was opened. The contract price had been increased on five occasions: the final price was $7,677,165.60, with a monthly payment of $143,000.[66] On April 14, 1943, HMCS *Cornwallis* was officially transferred to Deep Brook. The final cost of constructing the base was $9 million.[67]

McLean always liked to leave something of worth behind:

McLean says, "Go to the Catholic church. Find out how many parishioners they have." "Yes, sir." He says, "Give them five thousand dollars. If he has five hundred parishioners, that's ten dollars apiece."

McLean signed this photograph for his old friend Colonel Daniel Sutherland, "With my best wishes to the Colonel, Harry McLean, 1944 – 60 years young." Courtesy of Reverend Donald Sutherland and Mary Beth Sutherland

Then he says, "Go to the Anglican church, the Baptist church, and give them the same percentage per person for the membership as you gave the RC church." He said, "You know, when we've left here, Joe, they'll still be busy for a long time afterwards."[68]

As a lasting gesture of good will, he donated ten thousand dollars towards the construction of a twenty-room nurses' residence in Digby. The prominent architects C. N. Blankstein and J. H. G. Russell of Winnipeg designed the building. McLean told McNally, "We'll leave a mark here long after we're gone. They need it."[69] When Harry McLean was remembered, it was not always for his munificence.

CHAPTER FOURTEEN

Forward and Onward

*No trail too rugged, no obstacle too large, no mountain too high to stop
the sturdy frontiersman, with sureness of purpose, with daring
adventure, and from generation to generation the pioneering spirit moves
always forward and onward to greater goals.*[1]

WHEN THE EXCESSES of their lifestyles left them feeling particularly
wretched, the Battle Creek Sanitarium in Michigan was the destination
of choice for men like Harry McLean and his friend Gerald Grattan
McGeer. A lawyer turned politician, McGeer held several high-ranking
offices during his career, serving as mayor of Vancouver, a Member of
both the British Columbia legislature and the Canadian Parliament, and
finally a Senator. McGeer, like McLean, was colourful, fearless,
outspoken, hard-working and hard-drinking.[2] The latter two qualities
necessitated regular visits to Battle Creek for bouts of abstinence,
something that McLean's employees referred to as the "Gold Cure."[3]

The "San," with its long and colourful history, was the creation of
Dr. John Harvey Kellogg. Kellogg, of health-food, peanut butter and
nasal-inhaler fame, promoted well-being and fitness among the wealthy
through unusual methods at his luxurious facility. A sparkling-clean bowel
was the focal point of his therapy, in addition to a strict vegetarian diet,
rigorous exercise and sexual abstinence. Nurses at the San, well versed
in the exacting science of the enema, would see to it that the bowels of
the patrons were flushed with alarming frequency using combinations

of water and yogurt. If the incessant flushing was not quite doing the trick, Kellogg, a skilled and prolific surgeon, would perform abdominal surgery. The San bottomed out after the stock market crash but managed to limp along throughout the 1930s. In the 1940s Kellogg scaled back considerably, moving the whole outfit into a smaller building.[4] Regardless of the change in venue, McLean and McGeer devotedly undertook the journey to Battle Creek.[5]

While McGeer was having what remained of an overworked kidney removed at a traditional hospital, in March 1942,[6] McLean was convalescing at the San. Away from the demands of work and the mind-altering effects of whisky, McLean could enjoy other pursuits and catch up on his reading. McLean and McGeer were both avid readers and great admirers of Abraham Lincoln, devouring book after book about the revered U.S. president. McLean recalled a conversation with McGeer about meeting the renowned sculptor Avard Tennyson Fairbanks, who showed McGeer photographs of his most recent work – a monument to their hero titled *Lincoln the Frontiersman.* McGeer told McLean that he was so impressed by Fairbanks's work he had commissioned the Michigan-based artist to do a bust of himself.[7] Inspired, McLean decided he too would commission a monument, but, not being one to immortalize himself, he would pay tribute to the pioneer families of North Dakota. McLean telephoned Fairbanks at the University of Michigan in Ann Arbor to discuss the idea.[8]

Fairbanks was born in Provo, Utah, in 1897, the second youngest in a family of eleven. He left home at thirteen to study at the Art Students League in New York City. For a

Gerald Grattan McGeer. CVA 677-738, CITY OF VANCOUVER ARCHIVES

creamery exhibition at the Utah State Fair, Fairbanks carved a lion out of butter, winning accolades, recognition and sufficient funds to continue his studies for three years in Paris. He earned numerous academic degrees – a bachelor of fine arts from Yale, a master of fine arts from the University of Washington and a doctorate in anatomy from the University of Michigan. He served as Artist in Residence at the University of Michigan, succeeding the poet Robert Frost, and also designed various hood ornaments for the Chrysler motor company, most notably the "Ram," which made its debut on the 1932 Dodge. Somehow, while accomplishing all of this Fairbanks also found the time to father eight sons and adopt two daughters.[9]

Clay in hand, Fairbanks arrived at the Battle Creek Sanitarium. McLean described his concept to the artist. Over the next couple of days the design for *The Pioneer Family* came to life in the form of an eighteen-inch-high model that would be cast in bronze in "heroic size 3/2 life." A section of the statue was inspired by McLean and a young boy at a ball game that he and Fairbanks had attended. The boy, part of the local "knot hole gang," had taken up residence in the reserved seating. Sensing that the lad might be thrown out of the ball park, McLean came

New addition to the Battle Creek Sanitarium in Michigan, 1935. Reprinted with the permission of Willard Library, Battle Creek, Michigan

to his rescue and assumed the role of father, taking him by the hand. Fairbanks remembered the touching scene and joined the father and son together at the hands.[10] McLean was pleased with the design and told Fairbanks to start work immediately. Negotiations about price were unnecessary, as McLean's lawyer arrived with a contract at the price Fairbanks had requested. McLean did not contact Fairbanks for progress reports or changes during the entire execution of the work.[11]

Fairbanks's sons Virgil and Jonathan posed as the pioneer father and son. Fairbanks spent thirty months on the statue, working mostly in the evenings, as he still had daytime responsibilities as a faculty member at the University of Michigan. The abandoned auditorium of University Hall served as his studio. Once the sculpture was created in clay, Fairbanks made plaster casts, which were cut into sectional moulds and sent to the Bedi Rassi foundry owned by the Gargonni family in Brooklyn, New York. Owing to the unavailability of bronze for civilian use due to World War II, casting of the statue had to wait.[12]

The Pioneer Family was the first major work to be undertaken in the United States after World War II. However, the process did not run smoothly, the sculpture taking, in fact, a further two years to cast. With the dedication date set and the deadline looming, Fairbanks was dismayed to discover that the Gargonni family was working on other projects, after having received most of the money in advance. To make matters worse, the statue itself required several moulds due to its complexity. Another Fairbanks son, Elliot, went to the foundry to do what he could to compel the Gargonnis to finish the work. At last, the figures were completed and welded together.[13]

The next challenge was to move the statue from New York to its permanent location on the lawn in front of the state capitol building in Bismarck, North Dakota. Fairbanks had assumed that he would be using the rail system, but owing to severe time constraints and the lack of guarantees by the railroads as to the delivery date, he had to resort to transporting the sculpture by truck. He decided to buy a vehicle, as this would cost the same as moving the statue by train. To make the purchase, he enlisted the help of Elliot, who was joined in Brooklyn by yet another Fairbanks brother, Justin, and a cousin, Ortho. They pulled their new

Dodge truck up to the foundry, loaded the statue into it, and set off for Bismarck.[14]

But difficulties with the statue did not end when it left the foundry. Fairbanks arrived in Bismarck a few days before the dedication date, just in time to oversee the completion, by the granite artisans, of the installation of the granite base. A portable bridge crane had been used to lower the base, and the same crane was employed to lift the statue from the truck onto the base. Much to the dismay of everyone concerned, the statue was leaning distinctly to one side.[15] The granite artisans were quick to point out that the problem was not the granite base but, rather, the bottom of the statue itself. By then it was late afternoon and the situation called for swift action.

Fairbanks sent Justin to the hardware store to buy hacksaws and blades, then determined where the base should be cut to resolve the problem He drew a line around it and then he, his sons and a couple of volunteers commenced sawing. They sawed well into the night and were up again sawing at five the next morning. Despite soreness and blisters, the exhausted crew managed, with the help of the crane and some well-placed caulking, to fit the statue perfectly onto the base.[16]

The dedication ceremony took place on September 20, 1947.[17] Gerry McGeer did not live to see the monument for which he was indirectly responsible, having passed away a month earlier, on August 11th.[18] McLean was predictably absent and asked for "no honorable mention for himself or his family."[19] A fatigued Fairbanks was present, along with the local high school band

The Pioneer Family *statue, state capitol grounds, Bismarck, North Dakota.* PHOTOGRAPH BY AUTHOR

with its obligatory and cacophonous accompaniment.[20] Amongst the usual smattering of local dignitaries was McLean's cousin, Judge W. B. Falconer, who spoke on the benefactor's behalf:

> There are pioneers in numerous fields of endeavor but we are gathered here today to pay tribute to the pioneer who on foot, on horse-back, and with their covered wagons, broke the boundaries of a civilization and blazed the trails into the great expanses of land lying westward to the Pacific Ocean. Lands where the waters of many bridgeless streams hurried on to the sea. Lands where hostile Indians were resisting the advances of civilization. It was a hard land with no comforts and many hazards. In blazing the pioneer trails, it has been truthfully stated that, only the strong started and the weakest of these perished along the way.
>
> On behalf of Mr. McLean, I give this monument, *The Pioneer Family*, to his native state of North Dakota. It is his wish that it be dedicated to the Pioneer of the West and that it be an ever-lasting monument to the memory of the few who gave homes to so many.[21]

The podium was turned over to Nels G. Johnson, attorney general for the state of North Dakota. Johnson spoke of McLean's father, regarded as one of the pioneers of the state, then continued:

> Through a pioneer who left his energy and his qualities of progress to an able son, and the son's vision, and the art of a famous sculptor, there now resides in our midst a pioneer family, who here sturdily stand silently expressing the lessons to be learned by us from the pioneers, which it will impart to all those who come to gaze upon it and reflect upon what they have seen.
>
> The State of North Dakota accepts from you, Harry F. McLean, this beautiful work of art and its fine portrayal which you, the son of a pioneer of this state, have so unselfishly and with magnitude of heart and mind donated to the State of North Dakota.[22]

Concluding the ceremony was a rare acknowledgement, by Judge Alexander G. Burr of the Supreme Court of North Dakota, of the contribution of the pioneer woman, "who suffered the most":

> Many of the women were so hemmed in that a year would pass without their seeing the face of a stranger, unless the itinerant minister looked in or a new settler passed by. No doctors, no nurses, little

society. The educated woman and the peasant woman were on an equality. Each had her longings, her desires, her frustrated ambitions. She toiled side by side with her husband, uncomplainingly doing her part. She reared the children, she taught them correct things. She endured the pangs incident to her sex, she struggled, she fought her way, she was the unsung heroine.

Think not that the tar-papered shack or the sod house had no expressions of culture. The little flower in the half window, the cheap but clean curtain, sometimes an old-fashioned musical instrument, a book here or there showed the touch of the feminine hand. Within that log house there was a hospitality unknown today, a companionable friendliness, a genuine interest and curiosity, a charity, nobleness and sympathy born of travail and experience, an unexpressed but clearly evident natural gracefulness of life and kindness of heart... Without her steadfast courage the pioneer father could not have succeeded.[23]

Following the protracted ceremony, Fairbanks provided the local press with statistics on the raw materials that had gone into the creation of the monument: three tons of bronze and fifteen tons of granite sitting on a twenty-ton concrete base. "I don't think we have to worry about it blowing over," he said.[24] Fairbanks went on to discuss the significance of various aspects of the monument: "The wheel symbolizes progress and the young boy who is holding it goes forward into the world, the hand with which he is holding his father's hand symbolizes the holding of the ideals of the pioneers. The mother and child are symbols of motherhood and they complete the pioneer family."[25] As with all of his works, Fairbanks had researched the subject meticulously, even down to how the wheels were affixed to the pioneer wagons (with pins slipped through a hole in the axle, as opposed to nuts and bolts).[26]

After the crowd had dispersed, an additional problem with the statue was detected. The Gargonnis had used iron nails, rather than bronze, to separate the mould from the core. The difficulty was that the remnants of the ground-off nails had started to rust and, if the problem was left unchecked, after a few good rainstorms the statue would be dotted with holes. Before returning home, Fairbanks had to drill out all the iron nails and replace them with bronze – a time-consuming yet vital task.[27]

The pioneer may be and is now a vanishing race. The age that produced him has passed away. The qualities which he developed have been modified to a large extent. A new generation has followed, and new time and new conditions have produced a new type. Have we improved what we received? [28]

CHAPTER FIFTEEN

A Perfect Fool

>─┼─◀▶─◆─○─◆─◀▶─┼─◁

*Harry McLean had come out to call. A strange character, kindly and
generous in nature, but a perfect fool. I had never been able to place him
before. Evidently, he just wanted to pay his respects and to be able to
say he knew me personally. He spoke of a speech I had made in
St. John in 1908 which he remembered and had followed my career
from that time. I showed him over the house.[1]*

HARRY MCLEAN'S IMPULSIVE visit to Prime Minister William Lyon
Mackenzie King spawned a relationship akin to a courtship that would
flourish for years. Both King's mind and his waistline expanded as a
continuous flow of newly released books and epicurean delights such as
oysters, fresh salmon and Virginia ham arrived at Laurier House,
compliments of McLean. Aware of the prime minister's fondness for
roses, McLean dispatched dozens on every possible occasion. McLean's
overwhelming generosity prompted Norman Scrim, an Ottawa florist,
to say that he could not possibly fill all of his orders but had "difficulty
in explaining this to Mr. McLean." One particular request by McLean
was that an orchid be sent with the message "You are doing a damned
good job Mackenzie."[2] As decorum dictated, King acknowledged all of
these gifts promptly and courteously, although he was wary of McLean's
intentions.

It took six years of persistent, obsessive wooing on McLean's part
to get from "Dear Mr. McLean" to "My Dear Harry," but in spite of

King's initial misgivings, the two men became friends and remained so until King's death in 1951. While King disapproved of his friend's drinking habits, McLean was steadfast in his admiration for the prime minister. All things considered, King could overlook the drunken binges as long as McLean continued to stroke his ego.

McLean visited King on September 4, 1942. "As usual, he had been drinking," King wrote, making note of McLean's state of insobriety in his diary. Even though McLean was inebriated, he managed to pique the prime minister's interest by offering his Merrickville residence as a summer home "to the State as a sort of Chequers."[3] King made no comment on the offer, but later reflected on the visit:

> He was ready to turn it over at once, anxious I should come out soon and see it. He had spoken before of its fine library – says it is "perfectly run" – He is a strange character, kind of heart, but like a child in some ways, yet powerful in others. I rec'd him cordially, but gave him tea instead of whiskey and was not deceived by his motive. Indeed rather complimented by his line of approach – liking to do things for public service, – my interest in books… "Chequers" a natural appeal etc.[4]

McLean, Gerry McGeer and their mutual old friend, Ian Alistair Mackenzie, then serving as the minister of Pensions and National Health, approached Avard Fairbanks about a commission to sculpt a bust of King. They asked that Fairbanks speak with the prime minister directly to discuss the idea. On January 29, 1943, Fairbanks met with King and

Ian A. Mackenzie, 1890–1949. Jules Alexandre Castonguay Collection, Accession 1965-057. C-036646, Library and Archives Canada

told him he wished to sculpt a bust of King "as among the men outstanding in the new world movement today."[5] Although he was flattered, King told Fairbanks he could not afford to pay a commission. Fairbanks said he would be willing to pay his own way for the opportunity. King explained that he was busy but would mull it over. Though he did not let on to Fairbanks, the prime minister was intrigued by the idea, noting, "It was rather interesting to have a man with a photo of his statue of Lincoln on his lap suggesting that he should like to make a bust of oneself in time of world change such as the present."[6]

King was another aficionado of Lincoln. At Easter 1943 McLean sent him the book *Lincoln Talks*.[7] In his thank you note, King wrote: "Like you and Lincoln, I experience moments when it seems the bottom has about gone out of the tub. The fact that men like Lincoln and yourself have survived experiences of the kind gives me fresh hope."[8] King also remarked on a lynx-paw rug that McLean had sent for presentation to the British foreign secretary, Anthony Eden. "It was very like you to wish to give to one who is playing the part in world affairs which the Rt. Hon. Anthony Eden is playing, some memorial which would be a lasting reminder of his visit to the Dominion of Canada."[9]

Some months later the prime minister was again approached about sitting for Fairbanks, this time by Gerry McGeer and Ian Mackenzie, to mark King's twenty-fifth anniversary as Liberal leader. King briefly entertained the idea but concluded that for the party to undertake something so personal might be inappropriate given the "war and all."[10] In discussing the matter further with Mackenzie, King remarked that the Liberals would not necessarily be the governing party by the time the bust was completed. Mackenzie replied that no matter which party was in power, the milestone should be recognized. On July 7, 1943, King met with McGeer and Fairbanks, capitulating to the unrelenting demands of the artistic badgers. Sculpting sessions at Kingsmere were arranged for October, with McGeer and "others" taking responsibility for the project.[11] It was decided that a bronze bust of King would be created, for presentation to the National Liberal Federation, along with a sterling silver statuette of King with his beloved late dog, the first of three named Pat.

Fairbanks arrived in Ottawa on Thanksgiving 1943. The library at Kingsmere was chosen as the makeshift studio. King had spent most of the day prior to the artist's arrival deeply engrossed in biblical study of Balaam and his ass, interrupted by the occasional holy apparition. Unbeknownst to Fairbanks, King experienced a divine hallucination upon viewing the set-up:

> To my amazement – here from the centre of the board rose like bits of electric wiring the whole looking exactly like a serpent coiling itself round the top of the pole – It was exactly like the picture in the bible of Moses raising up the brass serpent in the wilderness – to save the people – those who looked to it being delivered of the poison of the serpent that had bitten them – the forerunner of symbol of the later crucifixion of Christ "I, if I be lifted up, shall draw all the men unto me." The sacrifice on the cross saving the sins of the world. – It seemed to me to be the strangest & most significant thing in the way of "psychic phenomena" I have known – The rock – the rods – the pole – the serpent – etc. etc.[12]

Wisely, perhaps, the prime minister kept his visions to himself. The two men found they had much in common. They took walks in the country, engaging in long conversations about "Religion & Art & Politics,"[13] with Pat Number Two in tow. But most of the time the sculptor was hard at work, and making good progress. King was overjoyed with Fairbanks's work, as he believed that no photograph had ever done him justice. After one of their walks, he noted in his diary:

> On the way, I let Joan & Fairbanks go on ahead & knelt down and thanked God for the portrait given me or rather to the world as a record. I have suffered so greatly from bad pictures in the press, on the radio, etc that I have become so that I can hardly stop or bear to look at any pictures of myself. I felt here at least, at last, is something that does not lie – something that is true to what I am. I wondered if Michel Angelo had not helped to guide the hand of the Sculptor – he had been in much of our thoughts & conversations.[14]

By Friday of that week Fairbanks was wearing out his welcome. King's day began with a waking dream of his father being drunk and King being disgusted with him, to the point of wanting to strike him. Initially he thought the dream was a "warning against eating late at night before going to bed,"[15] but, as with many of King's visions, the rich symbolism would indubitably crystallize as the day progressed. That same morning, Fairbanks told King about his "weird idea"[16] of having his sons join them in order to transport the sculptures. The prime minister responded with an emphatic no, for a variety of reasons: the risk of publicity, his lack of time to entertain Fairbanks's sons, his wish to have a quiet Sunday. Fairbanks dared not pursue the idea further. Nonetheless, King was piqued by Fairbanks's disclosure of his acquaintance with "Big Pants" McLean and, moreover, of McLean's helping to finance the sculptures.[17] The meaning of his vision earlier that day suddenly became clear to him:

> It meant first that "his success had gone to his head" – meaning Fairbanks, a natural elation over joy in completion of his work, and my evident feeling towards himself, he was finding a way to have his sons meet the P.M. enjoy a brief stay in Ottawa, etc… The other thing is the association of Big Pants McLean with the project. He quite looses [sic] his head & his heart when he drinks, does all kinds of extreme things. – My feeling of resentment was a precognition of what I felt in a way at Fairbanks suggestion, which would have put a quite impossible burden on me at this time.[18]

King spent most of Saturday nitpicking the sculpture of Pat, determined to ensure that Fairbanks captured the dog's true "benevolence."[19] Then, when it became obvious that Fairbanks would not have time to both cast the moulds and catch the eleven o'clock train, he bitterly mourned the loss of his precious Sunday. Barely managing to contain his disappointment, King amused himself while his bust was being "plastered" by Fairbanks, thinking how he might have looked had his life "been one of self-indulgence, over eating, over drinking, disippation [sic], etc."[20] He went on to ponder "how noble in appearance Churchill might have been, with his great intellect, & gifts, had he disciplined himself from youth… The marvel is he has preserved the Soul & Spirit he has, in the body he carries about."[21]

Pressured by the increasingly petulant King to finish the job, Fairbanks worked slavishly past midnight and well into the next day. After an uncomfortably silent dinner on Sunday with King, the prime minister being "too tired to say much & rather put out at the 'overstaying' of time so long," Fairbanks packed up.[22] King watched his bust being loaded into the back of the "station car" and mused that "it was like watching one's own funeral out of the window." He was thankful to see the taillights of the car that night, but likely not half as thankful as Fairbanks was to be in the car and leaving Kingsmere. After reflecting on Fairbanks and the events of the week, King wrote, "He is a fine character, sound in heart & soul, but just lacking in 'understanding' of some things, but it has been an event in my life to have had him with me for an entire week & these records made."[23]

After a few more modifications, particularly to the silver Pat, the bust and statuette were completed to King's satisfaction. The prime minister wasted no time in sending a letter of thanks to McGeer:

> I think the work is excellent. The more so in that I am far from having the cast of countenance which lends itself to high accomplishment in art. For better or for worse, he has, I believe portrayed me as I am. At least, that is the way I feel about it, and I cannot say how profoundly grateful I am that somewhere, also for better [or] for worse, there will be a record which can be regarded as true... Please let this letter bring to you my warmest thanks for your thought and interest in this matter which is one so personal to myself... I cannot say how truly grateful I am to you.[24]

McLean found himself in court on July 5, 1944, in Lévis, Quebec, charged with drunkenness and assaulting a provincial police detective. On his way back to his camp during a fishing trip on the Little Cascapedia River, McLean had entered a Lévis restaurant with his secretary and grabbed Detective Joseph Cote by the front of his shirt. A melee ensued, with bystanders joining in, and McLean was arrested. Chief Guay of the Lévis police announced that at the police station McLean had seventy-five cents in his possession. McLean was fined twenty-five dollars plus two hundred dollars in costs, of which the detective was awarded half.[25] Unruffled by the experience, McLean resumed his fishing expedition, sending the prime minister an eighteen-pound salmon.[26]

On August 7, 1944, the bronze bust was presented to the National Liberal Federation at a ceremony at the Château Laurier Hotel in Ottawa.[27] A crowd of about one thousand rose to applaud King as he was piped into the great ballroom. Speaker after speaker cited the leader's countless merits.[28] McGeer took his turn at the podium, explaining that

Statuette of Mackenzie King and his dog, Pat; bust of King. COURTESY OF EUGENE FAIRBANKS

his friendship with the sculptor had come about "through an incident of our common belief that Abraham Lincoln still lives as the greatest humanitarian statesman and the wisest political economist that modern Liberalism has yet produced"[29] but that King was the second-greatest humanitarian statesman. Although not always complimentary towards King, on this occasion McGeer was bountiful in his praise for the man, proclaiming that King possessed "an intellect bordering on genius; an unrelenting loyalty to any ideal; a prodigious capacity for work; courage based on the conviction of reasoned thought, and the tolerant humility of natural kindliness."[30] He concluded by commending Fairbanks: "I know you will all join me in congratulating the sculptor on the success he has achieved in preserving the memory of that soul and personality which has endeared Mackenzie King to all who have been associated with him in maintaining Liberalism as a great progressive force in the life of Canada and her people."[31] The festivities were a complete success. King wrote:

> The evening proceedings passed off in splendid fashion. There were no delays. All of the speeches were exceptionally fine. As tributes nothing could have surpassed them. All had been prepared with evident care.[32]

Since he had not had time to prepare a speech, King improvised, using the list of speakers as a reference to say a few things about each – and adding yet another story about Lincoln. Although he was scheduled to speak for only fifteen minutes, his discourse of gratitude lasted over an hour. It was "the little replica of Pat in silver" that pleased King the most. His delight seemed to eclipse any resentment he had harboured about Harry McLean's "association" with the sculpture project.[33]

In the privacy of his diary, however, King expressed a different view. Some months later he wrote rancorously about the "little circle" of men, including McGeer, McLean and Mackenzie, "who think they are going to win my favour by touching on family relationships being things that they feel kindliest about, also gifts of flowers, small attentions and all that kind of thing – that went with the bust at the 25th anniversary, etc. – they are a lot of children. A terrible lot to handle affairs of government."[34]

➤◦━◦━O━◦◦━◦◦

In September 1944 the prime minister hosted the second Quebec summit, attended by two of the "Big Three." Winston Churchill and Franklin D. Roosevelt were in Canada to discuss plans for postwar Germany. Lacking Roosevelt's dog-toting status, King left Pat Number Two in Ottawa.[35] He returned home on the evening of September 17th and, prompted by the gift of a box of roses from McLean, made a visit to Merrickville. Arriving at the dinner hour, King and his chauffeur, Robert Lay, were met by Colonel Kenneth Ramsay and escorted to McLean's cottage on Corktown Road, just outside Merrickville on the Rideau River. McLean occasionally sought refuge at the cottage, a short drive from Kinlochaline, from the many visitors to the private zoo he kept in his backyard. King found McLean in fine form and was "struck with how clear his memory was of the different times he had communicated with me or sent me fish or flowers or books."[36] They toured the property, then went into the main house and climbed the dramatic freestanding three-storey spiral staircase to the rooms upstairs.

When showing King the bedroom of his late wife, McLean commented that he had "left it just as it was."[37] McLean's own bedroom was filled with eclectic furnishings and expensive rugs, reminding King of "Sir Thomas Lipton through having so many things that had been picked up and collected, all jammed together."[38] As they stood there admiring the view, McLean told the prime minister of his "great admiration" for him, saying that men like him were "scarce," that "the country needs you" and that he wished to help out in any way he could. King "appreciated his readiness to help." He thought the house was "a fine specimen of the best of old stone built houses; wonderful masonry." Again, McLean offered to bequeath it to the prime minister as "a Chequers for Canada." King declined the offer, saying that it was the responsibility of the government to provide a residence for the prime minister.[39] Ramsay joined them for dinner. McLean's most prized art works were two large Krieghoff paintings, and parts of the house were liberally decorated with the results of his hunting expeditions – mounted, stuffed big game heads. McLean explained that he had bought certain items to help people out and that "the press had exaggerated what he had given away." Mary McLean's portrait hung over the fireplace. McLean spoke affectionately of his

Harry McLean with a resident of his private zoo in Merrickville. Harry Falconer McLean Collection, Accession 1981-064. PA 207740, Library and Archives Canada

Harry McLean's home in Merrickville, Ontario. PHOTOGRAPH BY THE AUTHOR

mother, saying that "any good he had he felt he owed to her." After they watched some slides of World War I, King decided it was time to leave.[40]

On parting, neither man was left empty-handed; King gave McLean an autographed picture and received in return a couple of melons from McLean's garden. McLean also offered the prime minister tickets to see Lily Pons, the singing sensation from the Metropolitan Opera, as he had purchased hundreds to give away to servicemen. King declined the offer and drove away.[41]

But the night was not over. Five miles outside Merrickville the prime minister's car overheated. Clearly more politician than automobile mechanic, King assessed the problem: "the belt of the wheel that cools the boiler had broken." After a call from Lay, McLean and Ramsay came to the rescue. McLean insisted on driving King himself, leaving Lay and Ramsay to fend for themselves. As they drove, King listened to McLean talk about his hopes and dreams for the future, particularly his wish to help the prime minister and to "do something worth while before he died." To this end, McLean suggested he spruce up Kingsmere. King turned down the offer, saying that after the war he would like to do this himself.[42]

At around eleven o'clock McLean pulled up to Laurier House. King's driver arrived minutes later without Ramsay. King sensed that McLean was uneasy about driving at night alone, but McLean bravely made the journey home. King was ambivalent about the evening, describing it as "an experience that made one both happy and sad."[43]

⮞⬦⬥◦⬥⬦⬥⮜

A short time later McLean moved his operations closer to home. The directors of Dominion Construction met in Merrickville on October 12, 1944, to officially change the company's head office from Toronto to Merrickville.[44] In 1943, in anticipation of the move, McLean had paid five thousand dollars for a large stone three-storey structure on the main street. Erected in 1861, it had once been a department store. McLean completely renovated the building, installing apartments upstairs and an impressive private gymnasium.[45] McLean also owned a farm near Burritt's Rapids where he kept Scottish cattle.

Deeks Quarry had been resurrected as an army supply depot during World War II. Although it had started out as a quarry, producing crushed rock ballast for the Grenville Crushed Rock Company, Deeks was transformed by the addition of a machine shop for carrying out repairs to the steam locomotives, passenger and freight cars, and equipment used on the various Dominion Construction projects (including Flin Flon, Moosonee and Abitibi Canyon). When the projects were completed, the locomotives and equipment were returned to Deeks for repair and storage until their next assignment. Records are not precise, but some thirty locomotives are believed to have been kept at Deeks at various times. In addition, twelve baggage cars and thirty-two passenger cars, purchased from the Illinois Central Chicago Suburban services in 1929, were stored at Deeks in 1946. An additional nine baggage and nine passenger cars were stored at Hawk Lake.[46]

With the cessation of Dominion Construction operations, Deeks became a graveyard for locomotives and cars seeking new owners. Very few were disposed of, and the railway equipment at Deeks was scrapped in 1951 and that at Hawk Lake in 1952.[47]

Fourteen spur lines ran through the old quarry property, where millions of dollars worth of trucks, gun carriers and war materiel were stored. Most of the forty-acre property was filled. Approximately thirty-five men were employed to crate and load the equipment on Halifax-bound trains.[48] One of these men was Harold Bolton, and he recalled a visit from McLean one evening when the men were working overtime to load a shipment. McLean and several of his office employees walked in and were greeted by Harold Finnerty, the reeve of Kemptville, who was among those working in the quarry:

> "Goodnight, Mr. McLean. How are you?" McLean never said a word. He just hit him a slap and knocked him end over end and walked on. Harold wouldn't come back to work. He had a black eye.[49]

The Hawk Lake operation had been dormant for several years. In 1944 Lieutenant Colonel F. N. Timchenko, Commercial Attaché to the Legation of the USSR, made inquiries to the Canadian government about obtaining quarry equipment. Timchenko was referred to McLean, as the government was aware that the Hawk Lake Quarry had been idle. The Russians were interested in the entire crushing plant from floor to ceiling, locomotives to pressure gauges, and wanted the whole operation bundled up and sent to the Soviet Union via Vancouver.[50]

McLean sent for Charlie Hyson in Sydney to take care of this special assignment. Hyson's job was to meet and accommodate two Russian engineers who were coming to inspect the plant. Hyson flew to Winnipeg and took the train to Hawk Lake, arriving well ahead of time to prepare for his guests. He enlisted the help of two women in Kenora, asking them to set up a couple of houses and make arrangements for food while he dusted off the machinery.[51]

The engineers arrived with Russian/English dictionaries in hand. For the next ten days Hyson provided his guests with every record he could possibly find. The three men communicated with each other by making charade-like gestures. After the engineers went back to the Soviet Union, Hyson set about obtaining estimates from bridge companies to dismantle and carefully mark the steel for re-erection in the Soviet Union.[52]

Machinery at Hawk Lake: four diesel electrical units, each 360 hp. Harry Falconer
McLean Collection, Accession 1981-064. PA 212857, Library and Archives Canada

The weight of equipment had to be estimated as well, and W. J. Knox Limited, a Toronto-based large-equipment company, was hired to assist with preparing a proposal for this colossal undertaking. All equipment was separately identified as to packing requirements; some would have to be disassembled, and everything would have to be sealed to avoid saltwater damage during the long ocean voyage. The plant would have to be re-opened and re-staffed at a substantial additional cost. Winter was another factor: if the Russians wished to have the plant shipped in winter, a twenty-five-percent premium would be added to the price. An estimated sixty-five railway cars would be required for the shipment. Organizing the proposal was a costly venture, entailing days of travel time and months of work.[53]

In November 1944 Harry McLean was at the Battle Creek Sanitarium in Michigan. He sent a barrel of oysters to Laurier House for Mackenzie King.[54] While relishing his oysters, the prime minister was likely contemplating the greatest political crisis of his career: the issue of overseas conscription. King did not favour conscription, believing it would divide the country, but many members of his cabinet did not agree. Sensing conspiracy everywhere, particularly in the camp of his minister of National Defence, Colonel James Ralston, the prime minister surprised the cabinet, and especially Ralston, by accepting the minister's resignation – on the strength of a letter Ralston had written in 1942. By the end of the month, after his new minister of National Defence, Colonel Andrew McNaughton, failed to attract sufficient numbers of army volunteers, King was forced to order conscription.[55]

The issue to be decided by McLean during that month of November 1944 was not nearly so momentous. McLean reviewed the Soviet proposal to buy the Hawk Lake facility one more time: if successful, the plan would net Dominion Construction about $330,000 without the cars and locomotives. A few days later the Russians declared that they were no longer interested in the whole package but might possibly wish to purchase the primary crusher. "Tell them to go to hell," was McLean's response from the comfort of his room in Battle Creek.[56]

CHAPTER SIXTEEN

The Mysterious Mr. X

Sometimes it was awful. People nearly pestered me to death.[1]

IN EARLY NOVEMBER 1943, even though World War II was raging, the soldiers convalescing at the Christie Street Hospital in Toronto had something to smile about. They were the lucky beneficiaries of the generosity of a mysterious philanthropist. A woolly haired, cigar-chomping leviathan was handing out hundred-dollar bills in the hospital wards. And when the contents of his huge pockets were emptied of cash, he wrote out cheques. "It's not the first time he's been here," said the hospital chaplain. "Every time he comes, the men are so cheerful."[2] The identity of the philanthropist had been known by reporters for years, but he had sworn them all to secrecy. The man with the quirky benevolence was to be known only as "Mr. X."

Halifax was the next destination of the cash-flinging Mr. X. Bellhops and switchboard and elevator operators were among the many recipients of his unconventional philanthropy. Inevitably, Mr. X's identity was revealed. The news spread quickly that it was none other than the business tycoon Harry McLean. The Halifax press disregarded the oath of silence by reporting that McLean's signature graced a two-thousand-dollar cheque for the education fund of Kenneth Whalen, the five-month-old son of a taxi driver, Roy Whalen.[3]

Whalen estimated that McLean gave away ten thousand dollars to servicemen during their drive through Halifax. "He took me and a soldier to a restaurant," said Whalen, "and boy, did he eat! He polished off three dozen raw oysters, then a dozen breaded oysters. He didn't have any money and asked me to pay, also to give the waitress a five dollar tip. As we left the restaurant there was a soldier standing there and he asked me to give him five dollars too."[4]

The reporters who had managed to respect McLean's wish for anonymity all those years lambasted their Maritime colleagues for violating "journalism's unwritten law" and wondered if McLean would

Dante the Magician. Reprinted with the permission of Betty Davenport

ever give away another cent. They did not have to wonder for long.[5]

In typical "Big Pants" style, McLean purchased a short-term contract with the renowned illusionist Dante the Magician.[6] Dante, a.k.a. Harry A. Jensen, toured the world many times during the course of his long career. His magic revue, "Sim Sala Bim," featured an ornate set with hand-painted backdrops and scores of elaborate props. Mind-boggling illusions were performed by the master, with the assistance of the lovely, exquisitely turned-out Moi-Yo Miller. Indeed the conjurer's assistant would float, vanish, reappear or feign dismemberment, to the delight of the rapt audience. With his silver hair, natty upturned moustache and goatee, Dante looked every bit the classic mystical magician.[7] McLean was enchanted by Dante's performance after attending his show in Toronto. When he returned to the Christie Street Hospital on November 16, 1943, McLean brought along the magician and a supply of hundred-dollar bills.[8]

The two men burst into one of the hospital wards with McLean bellowing, "Are we winning the war?" The soldiers answered with a resounding "Yes!!" McLean made his way around the room to introduce Dante, and the pair distributed some thirty-three hundred dollars in cash. Dante was touched by the experience, later admitting, "The scene brought tears to my eyes." McLean told a patient, "Some dirty so-and-so went and used my name in the newspapers in Halifax a week or so ago. Ever since then all sorts of people have written me – some of them crazy women who want to marry me. I'm not interested in crackpots, but I do want to do something for you fellows. I'm crazy about you guys." After handing out all of his cash,

The words "Sim Sala Bim," taken from a Danish nursery rhyme, signified it was time for applause. Reprinted with the permission of Betty Davenport

McLean said, "That's all boys. I've only got eleven cents left." One patient later commented, "The guy with the little goatee didn't make any bills disappear."[9] At Christmas, McLean sent the hospital a shipment of turkey in sufficient quantities to feed all of the patients.

McLean took Dante on a side trip to Grand Falls, New Brunswick, to visit his old friend Berton Puddington. Puddington's son, Jack, recalled the event:

He arrived in Grand Falls and stayed at our house and had this fellow who was the magician over at the hotel. He said to my father, "When you finish doing your rounds, I want to take this fellow up to the hospital and have him put on some of his tricks to entertain the patients." So my father said, "Oh, sure, if you want to." He knew that anything Harry did would be reasonable. And when they came back my father said, "Harry, where in the devil did you get that guy?" Harry said, "I don't know. I think I drank too much at this floor show and they told me that I had bought his contract. I've got the contract in my pocket but how in the devil...I bought him or what?" So here was this fellow travelling around the country with him. Harry said, "I don't know what to do with him. Occasionally, I [can] use him, like here to take him up to the hospital to entertain people. I guess I'm stuck with him" – for however long it was, I guess two or three months or something. A lot of things like that he did were really remarkable.[10]

McLean gave three mink and three beaver coats to Dante's "girls" as a gift. However, when the entourage was re-entering the United States at Buffalo, New York, customs officers seized the coats. In order to keep the coats, the girls had to pay duty of fifty percent of the assessed value, and in the end only one girl could afford to pay the thousand dollars.[11]

On March 29, 1944, McLean went on another spree, throwing five thousand out of the window of his room at the Prince Edward Hotel in Windsor, Ontario. Motorists and pedestrians alike scrambled gracelessly about the sidewalk, frantically clutching all the money they could hold. To the reporters gathered in his room at the time, McLean said, "I like to see people happy. This is the way I spread joy among mankind."[12]

McLean proceeded to the Windsor police station, where he gave Sergeant Emerson Mitchell a thousand dollars "to help you out with your rose garden" and Inspector Willis Brumpton five thousand for the policemen's burial fund. "I always liked policemen," said McLean, "in fact, I like them so well that I am willing to contribute a bit to help bury them."[13] The *Zanesville Signal* of Zanesville, Ohio, editorialized that the policemen thought McLean was crazy, "but it was only Mr. McLean's solvency and not the sincerity of his generous impulse that made the chief reverse the insanity verdict."[14]

After stopping at the bank, McLean distributed more cash at the Norton-Palmer Hotel. Irene Hooper, a telephone operator, was given two thousand quarters, a maid one hundred dollars in cash and an elevator girl a cheque for five thousand. By the time the extravaganza was over, McLean had showered an estimated fifty thousand dollars in cash and cheques on the people of Windsor.[15]

The police provided protection for McLean as throngs gathered to help relieve him of the money he was apparently so eager to get rid of. "I just wanted to start something and I did," said McLean of the unprecedented giveaway. "Financially I'm cut off now, but look out for me again."[16] The banks were not so generous with McLean's money. Most of the cheques he distributed in Windsor were returned by the Bank of Toronto inscribed with the words "Not arranged. Refer to drawer."[17]

Many people had opinions about what McLean should do with his money instead of pitching it out of a window for just anyone to pick up. An editorial in the Toronto *Globe* suggested that rather than create a public nuisance and have people "grovelling in the gutter," McLean might consider donating his money to the Hospital for Sick Children, build a new hospital or, at the very least, purchase some equipment "which will help heal the bodies of little children."[18] The editorial in the *Zanesville Signal* interpreted McLean's antics more sanctimoniously: "It's a shame that we consider a man eccentric when he is only trying to follow the scriptural directions for a rich man to enter the Kingdom of Heaven. Here's hoping he makes it."[19]

Another consequence of the disclosure of McLean's identity was the inundation by the Merrickville post office of requests for money addressed to him. Though "deeply touched" by the letters, some of which included discharge papers or certificates of rejection from military service, McLean said that even if he possessed "the wealth of the national mint" he would be unable to help everyone.[20] Recounting the experience to a reporter in 1956, he said: "At one time I got about 1,000 letters a day and they started crawling around the lawn here on their hands and knees. Mostly women. They wanted to marry me. Imagine that! Marry me!"[21]

With all of the news stories about McLean tossing money around, Avard Fairbanks thought it might be wise to collect the final payment on his statue, *The Pioneer Family*. Fairbanks travelled to Ottawa to meet with McLean at his hotel, the Château Laurier. When Fairbanks arrived, McLean's banker asked for confirmation of the amount owing. Once Fairbanks verified that it was ten thousand, the banker handed him a shoe box full of one-hundred-dollar bills. "I don't know what to do with all of this cash," declared a flustered Fairbanks. "I'll show you what to do with it," replied McLean. At this, Fairbanks tightened his grip on the box and asked if the banker could deposit it for him. Although it was late, the deposit was made that evening and transferred to Fairbanks's bank in Ann Arbor, Michigan.[22]

For McLean, charity began at home in Merrickville. Religious affiliation meant nothing to him: he provided a new organ for the Anglican church, contributed to the rebuilding of the Catholic manse after a fire and paid for the wife of the United Church minister to have an operation. Children were given ponies; adults were given cars. McLean's benevolence around Merrickville was boundless, whether it was paying off a mortgage, covering the cost of a funeral or sending a youth to college. St. Francis Hospital in nearby Smiths Falls also benefited from his generosity: its Mother Superior kindly took care of McLean when he sought help with this alcohol addiction; in return, he donated thousands of dollars.[23]

During a visit to Bismarck, McLean became embroiled in a religious argument. Although the hour was late, he telephoned the rectory of St. Mary's Catholic Church. "Send a priest down to the Patterson Hotel, please," he demanded. "We have urgent need for him and would like to see him right away." When Father Thomas Tracy obediently went to McLean's hotel and settled the dispute, he was rewarded with a cheque for five hundred dollars. Father Tracy used the money for a trip to his native Ireland.[24]

McLean practised conventional philanthropy as well, his favourite charity being the Canadian Red Cross. Driving down the street in Merrickville one day, Dr. Leonard Newman was stopped by McLean. McLean took off his enormous fur coat and shoved it through the window of Dr. Newman's car, telling him, "Give this to the Red Cross." (The next day, however, McLean dispatched one of his employees to retrieve the coat.)[25] He made donations to the King George V Silver Jubilee Cancer Fund for Canada, the Canadian Legion and the Smithsonian Institution's Scientific Series Program.[26] Estimates of McLean's charitable spending run as high as $3 million, although his associates have placed his contributions in the hundreds of thousands.

During a visit to Toronto's Royal York Hotel, and after more than a few drinks, McLean and some acquaintances were peering over a balcony into the lobby below. Proclaiming that the people in the lobby were rich, and obviously idle, McLean decided to stir things up. He flung all of his change – mostly pennies and dimes – over the railing and watched as the people wrestled each other for the few meagre coins. He hollered, "Look at those lazy s.o.b.'s fighting for pennies," and turned away disgusted.[27]

><+><+>+O++<+>+<+>

With all of this money being casually flung about, one of McLean's business partners, James Therrien – no doubt wondering why *he* did not have piles of cash to throw away – launched a lawsuit against McLean, Dominion Construction and Grenville Crushed Rock, alleging "illegal disbursement of company money."[28] Therrien claimed that McLean had "caused large sums of money, the property of the said Dominion Construction Corporation Limited, to be wrongfully, illegally and improperly disbursed to himself and to other persons"[29] and demanded repayment of any such illicit funds. On August 3, 1944, Therrien's application for the production of a more detailed affidavit by McLean was refused until he could prove his right to relief in his Statement of Claim. Therrien appealed the August decision and brought a motion in the Ontario High Court on September 20, 1944, before Judge Barlow. Therrien could not actually prove anything until he had the opportunity to examine the company's books, and he sought the court's assistance in forcing McLean to produce them.[30]

Therrien had further hurdles to overcome. The first was proving that fraud had occurred, since he had no tangible proof. The second stumbling block was that Therrien, as a shareholder, had approved an audited balance sheet at the last annual meeting of Dominion Construction. McLean's lawyers argued that they were under no obligation to produce anything because Therrien had failed to prove his case. The outcome of the motion was that the court favoured Therrien, stating that, as a shareholder, he had every right to scrutinize the books in order to prove his allegations. In addition, the fact that Therrien had approved the balance sheet did not serve to deprive him of the right to view the books, but "merely throws upon him the burden of proving his allegations of fraud."[31] The case was not reported on further in case law. It is likely that the case was settled out of court before reaching trial.

The lawsuit severed the relationship between McLean and Therrien, leaving McLean feeling bitter and betrayed. He had known Therrien for decades. Therrien had worked for Cook Construction under Frederick Ker from 1912 to 1916 and was discharged by Ker. Subsequently, McLean hired Therrien on in Halifax. Therrien stayed with McLean's companies, eventually becoming a partner. McLean acknowledged to Ker, "You were so right in firing Therrien and I was so wrong in taking him on at Halifax."[32] Despite this parting of the ways, Therrien remained a favourite with Dominion Construction employees, many of whom went to work for him after Dominion ceased operations.[33]

Seldom thereafter would McLean resume his Mr. X persona. On August 9, 1945, the day the atomic bomb was dropped on Nagasaki, McLean was showering servicemen with money at Ottawa's Union Station. If McLean saw evidence of overseas service, his overstuffed wallet would emerge from his pocket and the person would be richer by fifty or a hundred dollars.[34] At the Christie Street Hospital in Toronto on February 7, 1946, he and three bellboys from the Royal York were handing out orchids, roses and snapdragons. After nearly depleting the inventory of the hotel's flower shop, McLean asked an airman who was in the shop buying two roses for his wife if he would rather have an orchid. The man replied, "You must be drunk." But then someone told him who McLean was and the airman accepted. His wife was delighted.[35]

In the end, the well-publicized escapades of Mr. X caused McLean more grief than pleasure: the lawsuit with Therrien, and a loss of credibility and respect among his political allies, most notably the powerful "Minister of Everything," C. D. Howe.

CHAPTER SEVENTEEN

Power-Drunk Political Tin Gods

I will close my office and board up my house and be finished with this
whole outfit, for I refuse to be further badgered, bullied and bludgeoned
by a gang of power-drunk political tin gods.[1]

JAMES THERRIEN'S LAWSUIT marked the start of a troublesome
theme associated with Harry McLean's money-squandering reputation.
For the next couple of years McLean would be inundated with problems
relating to money in one way or another. By late 1944 the time had
come for him to settle with the government on construction claims for
Cornwallis, Point Edward and some smaller projects. Joseph McNally
had been staying at McLean's home to help him with the negotiations in
Ottawa. The two men attended meeting after meeting to collect amounts
owing, but they were having little success squeezing money out of the
bureaucrats on Parliament Hill.[2] McNally remembered the events of
one snowy night in Ottawa:

> One night we were at the Château Laurier and it started snowing around
> eight. We're in the car. He says, "Turn this way, Joe. Turn there…stop
> here, stop, stop, stop. Come on in." So we go in this apartment house
> and [he] bangs on the door – there we go, it's C. D. Howe. So the two
> of them get in the booze – these are old buddies… I didn't drink
> much. It was about twelve thirty. We've got to get back to Merrickville.
> It's snowing and there was no ploughs there, pretty minimal. "Let's get
> on the road." We're standing at the door. I'll never forget. McLean is

standing there and I'm saying, "C'mon, Mr. McLean, it's time we went now." C. D. Howe is about this big and doesn't have very much hair and McLean is circling his hand over Howe's head. McLean is saying, "Clarence, think money, Clarence, think money. My business runs on money, Clarence. Think money, money." The second most powerful man in Canada: "Think money."[3]

By the summer of 1944 there were 1,838,000 Canadians engaged in the war and its related industries. That autumn Howe was assigned to the newly created Ministry of Reconstruction, responsible for ensuring a smooth transition to a postwar economy. Even before the war ended, Howe was terminating war contracts and settling with contractors.[4] However, McLean's unrestrained spending habits and drunken antics had branded him as "political dynamite,"[5] and Howe was reluctant to hand over money to a contractor who threw it away. McNally recalled the negotiations with the government: "They became very chary in advancing or making settlements with him that were fair or anywhere near fair."[6] The government negotiators refused to pay some of McLean's claims, as they were unwilling to concede that all were legitimate. For

McLean's "political tin gods," Mackenzie King and his cabinet, June 19, 1945. Front row, left to right: Louis St. Laurent, J. A. MacKinnon, C. D. Howe, Ian Mackenzie, King, J. L. Ilsley, J. G. Gardiner, C. W. G. Gibson, Humphrey Mitchell. Back row, left to right: J. J. McCann, Paul Martin, Joseph Jean, J. A. Glen, Brooke Claxton, Alphonse Fournier, Ernest Bertrand, A. G. L. McNaughton, Lionel Chevrier, D. C. Abbott, D. L. MacLaren. C-026988, LIBRARY AND ARCHIVES CANADA

example, McLean had ordered the construction of a nurses' residence in Digby as a lasting gesture of good will in the community, but the government was not willing to pay for McLean's benevolence. Ultimately, Howe's position was that McLean would not get "another damned cent."[7]

While the government was busy taking with one hand, it was also taking with the other. McLean became painfully familiar with the provisions of the *Excess Profits Tax Act* of 1940. Corporations were taxed on profits exceeding $116^2/_3$ percent of their standard profits. The standard was calculated based on a corporation's top three earning years between 1936 and 1939. The tax rate was one hundred percent on the excess and no corporation was permitted, after tax, to retain profits equal to more than seventy percent of its standard of excess business profits made during the war.[8] As a result, wartime jobs meant a meagre profit or even a slight loss.

The war had effectively gutted McLean's operations. Some of McLean's workers had gone off to join the war effort, others had been recruited by the government, and still others were, like his antiquated equipment, approaching retirement age. "He lost a lot of his key men, and that of course is why I very rapidly became in the position I was in."[9] McNally vividly recalled the scene in the library when McLean announced his plans to retire. Nursing a glass of Scotch, McLean turned to him and said, "They've taken all of my men from me, my equipment. We've had four or five years of tough going. I'm sixty years of age. I'm too old to start again, Joe."[10] Embittered and defeated, McLean decided to wind down his operations.

⊱—┼—◆—●—◆—┼—⊰

Even with his troubles, McLean did not forget the children of Merrickville. He went ahead with the annual Christmas tree gathering at his home. Pupils at Merrickville Public School were "asked to name a Christmas gift they would like, and to their surprise and delight, each pupil received their choice of gift at Mr. McLean's tree on Christmas morning."[11] And every household received a turkey appropriate for its size.

Some years McLean would invite the whole town to a Christmas party. He would hire an orchestra and provide plenty of food and drink.

At some point during the evening McLean himself would appear at the festivities, piped in by a local musician.[12] Years later Glen Burchell, a resident of Merrickville, would recount his childhood Christmas memories for a reporter:

> Harry was everything. He was a king living in a mansion – Santa Claus, every day of the year, handing out presents – and the world's greatest clown, who was funnier than the great Emmett Kelly. Growing up in the village with Harry was like living in the land of make-believe. Harry supplied apples and milk to the school, for the children to have at recess.[13]

Dell Bower had similar boyhood memories of McLean:

> ...H. F. was so wealthy he just made purchases of all types and description at the blink of an eye. ...each time [a] kid would say something like "Jeez my dad is going to buy me a new bike," everyone else would say, "Who does he think he is? Millionaire McLean?" Even simple things like one kid buying another a soft drink would...get a response like, "Who do you think you are? Millionaire McLean?"

>━◆>━O━<◆━◄

Deeks Quarry was closed and the buildings for the most part torn down. The sawmill was moved, and the machine shop was rebuilt by one of McLean's employees, Don Dougall, and moved to Merrickville.[15] Some Dominion Construction workers had found work with Therrien's new organization after McLean's job well had all but dried up, but some long-time employees were kept on to wrap up operations. Charlie Hyson was put to work arranging to have electricity brought to McLean's other cottage – at Patterson Lake, near Perth – and doing odd jobs at Hawk Lake, such as building a cairn.[16] Charles Switzer and Miss Abbott, the secretary, were also kept on the payroll.

McLean managed to resist last-ditch efforts by the New York district attorney, Frank Hogan, to have him testify at the Fay and Bove trial in Manhattan. In his leisure time he read voraciously and telephoned the World War I flying ace Billy Bishop to order a thousand copies of his book, *Winged Peace*.[17] To Prime Minister Mackenzie King he sent gifts of books and epicurean delicacies, as well as a message of condolence following the death of President Roosevelt on April 12, 1945.[18] A few weeks later, on May 8th, Canadians listened as King addressed the nation at the end of the war in Europe – VE day.[19] The following month King was re-elected, an achievement that not even Winston Churchill could manage in that end-of-war climate.

McLean continued to visit the prime minister – sometimes in a sober state, sometimes not. Mike Murphy, a local writer, recounted a story told to him by McLean's chauffeur about a visit McLean made to King while under the influence: "As they drove in, Harry saluted King's two RCMP guards with the words, 'Why don't you fellows get lost.' King, hearing him come to the door, said, 'I see you're drunk again Harry; the same as yesterday when you sent me a truckload of roses. What do you propose I do with all those flowers?' 'Send them to your girl friends in Hull,' was Harry's reply as the two entered King's residence."[20]

On October 17, 1945, McLean responded to what was likely a form letter signed by the Honourable James Lorimer Ilsley, minister of National Revenue, urging him to buy Victory Bonds. The government conducted several Victory Loan campaigns in order to raise funds against the enormous costs of fighting World War II. McLean's reply read as follows:

In reply to your request for the next Victory Loan;

I hope some of it may be used to locate Tax-Dodging International Jews, who may live on small rocks in the West Indies. They may have some difficulty to hang on to the rocks, but none whatsoever to hang on to their money.

Referring again to the New Loan:-

My present bank account makes it almost impossible for me to do much.

My shattered financial condition is due to the Federal Laws, Provincial Laws, County Laws, City Laws, Corporation Laws, Liquor Laws, Mother-in-laws, Brother-in-laws, Sister-in-laws and Out-laws.

Through these laws I am compelled to pay a business tax, amusement tax, head tax, school tax, light tax, gas tax, sales tax, carpet tax, furniture tax and excise tax. Even my brain is taxed.

I am required to get a fishing license, car license, truck license, hunting and fishing license, not to mention a marriage license, dog license and radio license.

I am also required to contribute to every society and organization which the genius of man is capable of bringing to life; the women's relief, the unemployment relief and the gold digger's relief; to almost every hospital and charitable institution in the city including the Red Cross, the Black Cross, the Purple Cross and the Doubel [sic] Cross.

For my safety I am required to carry life insurance, property insurance, liability insurance, burglary insurance, accident insurance, business insurance, earthquake insurance, tornado insurance, unemployment insurance, old age and fire insurance.

My business is so governed that it is no easy matter for me to find out who owns it. I am inspected, expected, suspected, dis-respected, rejected, dejected, examined, informed, required, summoned, fined, commanded and compelled, until I supply an inexhaustable [sic] supply of money for every known need of the human race.

Simply because I refuse to donate to something or other, I am boycotted, talked about, lied about, held up and robbed, until I am almost ruined. I can tell you that except for the miracle that almost happened, I could not enclose this cheque.

The wolf that comes to my door now-a-days just had pups in my kitchen. I sold them, and the proceeds will be used to buy Victory Bonds.[21]

In November 1945 McLean was pulled off a Windsor-bound train by three police officers at the behest of Graham Ford Towers, Governor of the Bank of Canada. It was in his capacity as head of the Foreign Exchange Control Board (FECB) that Towers had ordered the detention of McLean, undoubtedly as a result of the publicity surrounding McLean's alter ego, the money-tossing Mr. X. The mandate of the FECB, established at the start of World War II, was to ensure foreign exchange stability and support the value of the Canadian dollar. The Board introduced many regulations – for example, permits were needed to buy foreign currency or securities and for travellers to export funds, and eventually Canadians were required to sell all of the foreign currency they owned to the FECB. After McLean produced the whopping sum of ten dollars from his wallet, the police let him go. He was incensed at being treated like a "major criminal."[22]

As if police detention were not bad enough, next came a tax bill, in the amount of $30,931.25, from the Department of National Revenue dated December 8, 1945, for arrears, penalties and interest spanning an eight-year period.[23] On December 28th an enraged McLean dictated scores of letters to his frantically typing assistant. His missives were addressed to various government officials:

> I beg to inform you that I do not consider I am indebted for taxes in the amount mentioned and do not agree with the items of taxation on which this amount is arrived at. The treatment accorded to me by your particular office over a number of years has been of a very prejudicial nature, even down to the least of your employees whose names I think you will be quite familiar with. So far as I am concerned, you are at liberty to take legal proceedings as I have no intention of being bludgeoned into paying money that I do not owe.[24]

Next, he challenged the Department of National Revenue to a legal showdown, reaffirming his opposition to government controls by vowing to "fight them with all the resistance I have in my Scotch disposition."[25] (A few days later, however, he would suggest a compromise by offering to pay any "differences" to the Red Cross, his favourite charity.) McLean further pointed out that he had carried out "five hundred and fifty million dollars worth"[26] of work in Canada – which, incidentally, was $155 million more than he had ever stated previously.

That late-December day he sent eight letters to Mackenzie King alone. McLean would almost certainly win the prize for most letters sent to the prime minister by any one person on a single day.

> Government controls throughout all the departments have meant the throttling of private enterprise, ambition, initiative and incentive. A bureaucracy with arbitrary power over the whole country has built up a monopolistic state, headed by a small group of officials who will hold to their acquired powers with whatever strength they possess – while the nation as a whole is tied hand and foot in a mile of red tape, hampered and held down under a mountain of forms in duplicate, triplicate and quadruplicate, in pink, blue, green and yellow; and left to

wander through a maze of regulations, restrictions, rules with appendices, codicils, amendments and sub-amendments.

Freedom has not been won with the end of the fighting in the field. There can be no freedom while such controls and restrictions emanate from the "ivory tower" of Ottawa officialdom and penetrate into every phase and aspect of daily living.

Since it is no longer possible to run a business with any semblance of accomplishment conditions have reached a point where my patience, hope and tolerance are at an end, and while such insidious and ubiquitous controls remain like a great spider's web over the country and its industries, I will take no further part in trying to make it a country worth living in. What I have done and tried to do is to-day being undermined and destroyed. The final touch comes when the Department of National Revenue should start resurrecting its records of thirty years ago, sending out new assessments to collect payments of taxes paid fairly at the proper time.[27]

In addition to his endless battles with the bureaucrats, McLean had to contend with the loss of influence that accompanied his retirement. In a letter to King he lamented the loss of his considerable clout: "I could borrow money in those days – but now…"[28]

Efforts to surrender the charter of H. F. McLean Limited were stymied by questions about amounts owing for tax arrears on profits for the years 1941, 1942 and 1944. The problem appeared to be minor – a payment misallocated to a different tax year – but it held up the issuance of the clearance certificate for several years.[29]

His letter-writing marathon to King ended with a light-hearted quote from an Alexander Woollcott sketch about Brigham Young, who had sired many children, most of whom were present at his death in Utah; according to Woollcott, some of Young's fellow Mormons decided to erect a memorial to him at his Vermont birthplace bearing the words "On this spot Brigham Young was born in 1801, a man of great courage and superb equipment."[30]

McLean's old friend Fred Ker asked him why he was so free with his money and did such strange things with it: "People will think you're a little off your head." McLean replied, "…there are a lot of very poor people in the streets. In the back of my mind, the government had dealt so rotten with me on some things, that I am determined to give them as little in succession duties as I can give them."[31]

➤━◄➤━○━◄➤━◄

On a happier note that winter, McLean built a fifty-foot tower and tobogganing chute for the children of Merrickville, along with ski runs and a shed filled with skis, poles, boots and toboggans. On an average winter weekend more than five hundred people clambered to the top of the chute and flung themselves down, attaining speeds of fifty miles an hour on days when conditions were particularly slippery. He installed a hockey rink as well, and provided the children with skates, sticks and hockey gloves. To further entertain the youngsters, McLean flew in a team of huskies – Kegsted, Ruben, Volk, Bill, Lynx, Tsar, Fox, Stefan and Matt – and a sled from St. Jovite, Quebec.[32]

In the summer McLean had a section of the Rideau River at Merrickville dredged for swimming and had a wharf built. His tennis court was at the disposal of anyone who wished to use it.[33] He regularly contributed to the Merrickville Agricultural Society. One year, after hearing that McLean was ill, the Society decided not to bother him about his annual donation. But Dr. Leonard Newman, a long-time member of the Society, received a call from McLean asking, "What happened you didn't call me this year?" and within thirty minutes a "very fine and a very acceptable cheque was sent."[34] Sometimes McLean arrived at the Merrickville Fair riding a donkey.[35] The Boy Scouts in town were outfitted in new uniforms for the town parade courtesy of McLean, though their female counterparts, the Girl Guides, were overlooked and had to make do with their tatty old uniforms with hand-dyed sashes.[36]

Not all of McLean's activities spread joy and good will amongst the inhabitants of Merrickville. He did not handle his leisure time well and his binges became more frequent. Although his housekeeper and secretary (and later wife), Margaret "Reta" Fitzpatrick, attempted to restrict his alcohol intake by watering down his liquor and serving it to him in amber-coloured glasses, her ploys were soon discovered.[37]

Once in a while McLean would call upon certain townspeople and invite them to dinner. Two such people were Mr. and Mrs. Arthur Heroux of Merrickville. Mrs. Heroux's friend (Babs, a striking, raven-haired beauty) was arriving by train from Montreal, and she was invited along. Dinner was served, although McLean was not present at the table. Then the guests, perhaps eight in all, retired to another room where a projector and screen had been set up. The lights were dimmed and the film begun, with McLean still absent from the group. About halfway through the screening the projector was abruptly stopped and the lights turned up. McLean was standing in the doorway of the room with a police officer in tow. "Someone here stole my watch," he said, "and no one is leaving until we find it, even if it means searching everyone." All the guests were aghast, except for Arthur Heroux, who knew of McLean's fondness for practical jokes. The house was searched and the watch was found under McLean's bed in his slipper.[38]

For the average Merrickville resident, catching a glimpse of McLean was rare and speaking with him rarer still. Although Harold Bolton worked for McLean, he had but one short exchange with him: "He stopped up on the hill on our field. He yelled at me, 'How do you get back to Merrickville, you little so and so.' I said, 'However in hell you like.' He said, 'You so and so.' That was the only conversation I ever had with the Honourable McLean."[39] Occasionally an intoxicated McLean would saunter into town wearing his bathrobe and slippers. Joseph Kelso, a long-time resident of Highway 43, remembered an encounter with McLean while visiting his wife-to-be at her Merrickville home:

Mary's mother's house was the stone house right on the corner next to the hotel. It was close to twelve o'clock and there was a bang on the front window. She said, "Oh, my God, what's that?" It was McLean going down the street with a cane, and he broke all the windows from there to the bank. When he got to the...window at the bank he had to hit it four times before he could break it. It was this oval glass that went round the corner... Next day all the windows were replaced.[40]

One steamy June day, Kelso and a friend were driving near McLean's home when their car stalled. A bear-like McLean bounded out of the ditch wearing a fur coat in the sweltering heat. "He must've weighed two hundred and seventy-five and never combed his hair," recalled Kelso.

McLean called his housemaid to escort the two men into his house for a drink. "What will you have?" he asked. "Nelson's Blood, Black & White, beer or buttermilk?" The drunken McLean knew that if he hosted guests he would get to drink too.[41]

A Merrickville resident told a reporter, "Short while back, Harry had a couple of mountain lions – cougar, he called them. Kept them back of the house. Every now and then he'd take one into town on a leash. Scared [the] hell out of us."[42] For many years McLean kept a private zoo in his backyard, which served as a tourist attraction.[43] Children were instructed to stay away from McLean's foul-mouthed parrot,[44] but otherwise people were free to walk about the grounds to view deer, pheasants, a fox, a raccoon, a pair of crocodiles and a bull elk.[45] The elk grew mean, as some of the visitors teased, poked and prodded it with their fingers. One day it charged McLean, who then went upstairs, grabbed his rifle from a gun rack and shot the animal from a third-floor window.[46]

Kelso accompanied McLean on a few local hunting trips, knowing that anyone who went hunting with him would get a new rifle. Even if there was no wild game, the hunters would manage to shoot something. McLean said to Kelso, "C'mon, I want you to go with me, we'll go hunting." Kelso told him there was nothing to hunt. "No matter," said McLean, "if we don't find anything we'll shoot the cattle."[47]

McLean re-established his friendship with the former hockey player Frank "The Shawville Express" Finnigan, who had purchased the Louis Hotel, a drinking establishment in Merrickville. During his days as a right-winger in the National Hockey League, Finnigan played for the Ottawa Senators and then the Toronto Maple Leafs. McLean attended hockey games as the guest of J. P. Bickell in Toronto and, as usual, stayed at the Royal York. Members of the hockey team, such as King Clancy and Finnigan, stayed at the same hotel. In the middle of the night McLean would come banging at their door. Finnigan remembered McLean standing in the hall, barefoot, in his pyjamas saying, "Come on up, you bastards, I'm having a party."[48] Clancy and Finnigan knew it was futile to resist. Back in McLean's room in the wee hours of the morning would be a drowsy chef with a portable stove preparing oysters for McLean and his guests, perhaps accompanied by members of the hotel's orchestra. Finnigan wistfully recalled, "Oh, there have been times when I've played some great games on Harry McLean's oysters."[49]

McLean would frequently knock on Finnigan's door at the Louis Hotel hours before opening time. While at the bar, he would fling the occasional bottle and become belligerent.[50] Everyone was his friend if he needed a drinking companion. On one occasion he sent his bar mates home in a hearse from the local funeral parlour.[51] When he was feeling generous, McLean would buy rounds. Finnigan would keep track of how much liquor was consumed and have the bill presented the next day to Reta Fitzpatrick. McLean rarely carried cash.[52]

The lack of meaningful relationships was another cost of McLean's fast-paced lifestyle. During his career he was rarely home long enough to form any lasting friendships, and thus had a limited social life. Before retiring he had little contact with people in the Merrickville area. His acquaintances were for the most part formed strictly for business purposes; once the work was over, so was the connection.

For over forty years McLean had thrived on the constant movement and pressures of the construction business. He could work anywhere: he had the men and the organization to do it. Work was his life. Then suddenly he was out of business, and ill prepared for the glut of time. McLean was bitter and resentful about the treatment he had received from the government. He had provided employment all through the Depression, at a loss to his business, and the government repaid him by hitting him with an excess-profits tax and stripping him of his best men. It was not until he retired himself that McNally fully understood what McLean had experienced:

> Twenty-five years ago I couldn't tell you this – I didn't know it – but suddenly here is a man…it's hard for me to describe. He's on the train, he's here, he's there, he's looking after a lot of work all over the country. The war is over, they've taken all his men and now he's sitting in Merrickville. Nobody wants to see him any more. The government doesn't want to give him any money because politically he's been a little careless with it, in the government's view – politically he's kind of a minefield.[53]

McLean struggled with the abrupt change of pace and his diminished power. All challenges seemingly behind him, he floundered. But not for long.

CHAPTER EIGHTEEN

The Evening of Our Lives

> ❯—i—◆❯—◯—❮◆—i—❮

...Last scene of all,
That ends this strange eventful history,
Is second childishness, and mere oblivion.[1]

BY 1947 HARRY MCLEAN was settling reluctantly into retirement. He spent the early summer at one of the cottages at Hawk Lake. At first he was content to pass the time fishing, but, not one to remain inert, he grew restless and decided he was in need of some adventure.

Consequently, at the age of sixty-four, he hired several guides to take him from Sioux Lookout via the Albany River by canoe to James Bay, a trek spanning the better part of northern Ontario. Arriving in Fort Albany, he re-acquainted himself with many people from his days working in the north. He spent a pleasurable day At Fort Albany with Father Jules Le Guerrier, who would later become Bishop of Moosonee.[2]

After returning from his northern excursion, McLean visited Mackenzie King on July 29th. King's offer of tea was met by a request by McLean for whisky, but the prime minister told him he "was too good a friend to give him any."[3]

> [McLean] was very nice in the way he talked. Combination of interest and mind of a child with some keen observations based on the rugged life he has lived. He kept repeating how great his affection was for me and of how kindly other people felt towards me. He wondered if

looking as well as I do, I might not be prepared to take on another campaign. I told him on no condition would I do that.[4]

As usual, McLean had not arrived empty-handed. He presented King with a letter from General Jan Christian Smuts, the South African statesman, soldier and philosopher. Apparently McLean's relationship with the Canadian prime minister had garnered him visitation rights and he had dropped in on Smuts while in the neighbourhood. The second offering was a letter from the mayor of Perth, Ontario, mentioning a one-thousand-dollar donation that McLean had made to the town for flood relief. The third was a cougar skin, which may have been from an animal he had felled himself.

Harry McLean. Harry Falconer McLean Collection, Accession 1981-064. PA 207741, Library and Archives Canada

McLean told King that while in Africa he had killed only to feed the Bushmen, who lived solely on raw meat, but intended to request permission to kill some animals to donate to a museum in Ottawa.[5] The prime minister wrote:

> I quite enjoyed his little visit. When I am with him, I always feel a deep concern. One never knows what he might do or say. He has aged so much that I should not be surprised if he were to be taken away almost at any time.[6]

King's concern for McLean's health was part of his obsession with the health of those around him. King thought that many people looked as though they were about to expire on the spot. He had made similar observations about Mitch Hepburn:

Hepburn, himself, seemed to me to be in bad shape physically. He has bronchial trouble, and I think will break up completely before very long... The truth of the matter is he does not know his own mind and really is not able to control himself. The group by which he is surrounded is the worst possible for a man of his temperament, and I should not be surprised at a collapse at any moment.[7]

His assessment of McLean's poor health was greatly exaggerated. At least McLean's appetite was showing no sign of waning, and he continued to send the prime minister generous quantities of freshly raked oysters, salmon, turkey and Virginia ham. All but one of his countless gifts to King was courteously accepted. On August 21, 1947, ten days after the death of King's second beloved dog, a kilted McLean appeared unannounced at the prime minister's door with a replacement Pat:

I was nearly beside myself at the time as I was trying to get the two speeches into final shape with no end of conversations over the phone. I was sorry to be abrupt and asked him to excuse me and not to press the little dog on me at this time. I let him see that I felt it would not be fair to my little Pat. I told him I would be grateful if he would wait for another year.[8]

McLean had underestimated King's affection for his dog and the intensity of his loss. His gaffe was soon forgiven, treated as yet another example of his unpredictable nature. But his generous gifts ending up causing the prime minister a great deal of anxiety:

The pleasure and progress of the day was upset by the indifference of servants & their unpardonable neglect.– Yesterday a box of oysters in shell arrived at L. H. from Harry McLean. Another today. It was by merest chance...that I found out nothing had been done about them... There was no barrel or pail into which to put them, they were left upstairs... Mrs. Gooch seemed to know little of how they were to be kept and cared less. It is this sort of worry which holds me back both physically & mentally.[9]

Communication between the two men was far more frequent now that McLean had retired. The tone of their letters was relaxed, characteristic of people who are comfortable with one another. Every week brought an exchange of correspondence, some amusing and some obviously written when McLean was intoxicated. Just before Christmas 1947, McLean wrote:

> My brother wired me today that he made up a box of lemons and limes, the lemons as large as grapefruit, which he raised in his own little garden at Laguna Beach, California, and took it down to send to me express prepaid – no Canadian dollars involved as it was coming in as a gift – but they refused shipment because of the embargo. I quote from a poet incognito:-
>
>> I'm sending this card to tell you
>> That the government has taken away
>> The things that I really needed
>> My workshop, my reindeer, my sleigh.
>> Now I'm making my rounds on a donkey,
>> He's old and crippled and slow,
>> So you'll know if I miss you at Christmas
>> That I'm out on my ass in the snow.[10]

William, Harry and Clarence McLean. Both brothers were involved in Harry's companies: William worked most of his life with Harry in Canada and retired to Chapleau, Ontario; Clarence moved to California but was a director of H. F. McLean Limited. STATE HISTORICAL SOCIETY OF NORTH DAKOTA A4939

That same day brought McLean's driver to the prime minister's residence with a young girl from Glengarry, Ontario, whom McLean had dispatched to Laurier House bearing a live gift for King – a cocker spaniel puppy. Since McLean believed that King had rejected his previous gift because it was not purebred, this one came with a six-generation pedigree. King wrote in his diary that the puppy was a "beautiful creature that attached itself to me in a moment in a most affectionate way."[11] Like the last dog McLean had sent, this one too was rejected.

During his more lucid moments, McLean read the classics and struggled through "translating Cicero's orations" and "interpreting Horace's poems."[12] He also spent a great deal of time studying the Bible. Since King shared his love of literature, McLean kept the prime minister apprised of the book du jour.

> I have been more or less of a biblical student all my life and always knew Rebecca was at the well, however when I called up about twenty-two clergymen for more information on the subject they one and all replied "just wait a minute. I haven't read my scriptures just lately, but I will look it up and call you back." I must confess that after reading thirteen thousand years of Chinese history I still don't know whether the capital is "Meepongpoo" or "Poopongmee" but I did recall the story of Rebecca. So much for our clergy.[13]

On January 16, 1948, Ian Mackenzie, then the minister of Veterans' Affairs, called on McLean in Merrickville. The purpose of the visit was to offer McLean a Senate appointment. McLean told Mackenzie he had been previously approached by the Honourable James Malcolm, the minister of Trade and Commerce, to fill a vacancy in the Senate. McLean declined both offers. All he wanted was a personal letter from King "testifying to the extent of his construction and building projects on Canada's behalf." Mackenzie wrote to King the following day outlining his conversation with McLean. He requested that King write a testimonial letter, adding that McLean "has always been a real friend of our methods of thinking in Canada."[14]

King was facing the prospect of the end of his political career. He delivered a speech in January 1948 announcing his retirement after a

Liberal leadership convention scheduled for August that same year. McLean commented on King's address[15]:

> I listened very attentively, and under considerable strain to your farewell address to the Canadian people. In common fairness, and in common candour, my prejudices and predilections have always been listed on the side of Canadian liberalism. Because of my great affection for you, I greatly feared that at some time during the course of your address you might make a serious error, but I personally can say that it was SPLENDID! SPLENDID! SPLENDID!
>
> If ever human feet stumble, as human feet are prone to do, God and the Canadian people can never gainsay the purpose with which you guided them.[16]

"A little bird" named Ian Mackenzie reminded King of McLean's sixty-fifth birthday, on February 18, 1948. McLean received the words of recognition he longed for from the prime minister, for his support of the Liberal party and his public works:

> For a long time past, I have meant, as Leader of the Liberal Party of Canada, to say to you how much I have appreciated the support you have given the Party over many years. I do not know that a more appropriate occasion is likely to present itself for me to express this word than on a birthday anniversary. There is a further word I should like to express, and that is a word of appreciation of the services you have rendered Canada itself in the work of construction which you have carried on in different parts of the Dominion and this on a scale that must have been a surprise even to yourself with the vision you have in matters of the kind. I know you have never been interested in recognition in the way of honours or position. I feel, however, that some word of acknowledgment of your services to our country in construction projects cannot be unwelcome, and it affords me a special measure of pleasure to make this acknowledgment on the eve of your birthday anniversary.[17]

McLean responded the next day:

> The dawn of my sixty-fifth birthday brought with it your very warm and generous greetings which helped to make the day one of the happiest of my life.
>
> We are both fast approaching the evening of our lives, and it is good to have a friend express themselves as you so kindly did in your

birthday letter to me. I think we both have tried to serve this great Dominion of ours to the best of our ability – you in your big way and I in a very small way – and if my small achievements have aided in any way the future generations of young Canadians I feel amply rewarded.[18]

＞–＋◆＞–Ｏ–＜◆＋–＜

Many of McLean's relatives had passed away during the 1940s. His Uncle Will (William A. Falconer) died in Bismarck on June 5, 1943. A well-respected resident of the town, Falconer had held various positions with the City of Bismarck, retiring as the city assessor in 1930.[19] His wife, Emma Falconer, passed away on June 21, 1948, of bronchial pneumonia.[20] McLean's younger brother, Clarence Campbell (C. C.) McLean, died at Laguna Beach, California, in early September 1948.[21]

On July 26, 1949, McLean purchased property in the Township of New Richmond, Quebec, on the Little Cascapedia River.[22] His friend D. H. MacDougall, president of Dominion Steel and Coal and a mining consultant on the Delaware Aqueduct job, was a regular guest, as was McLean's old friend Berton Puddington, as recalled by Jack Puddington:

> The Little Cascapedia is the crème de la crème of salmon rivers, and Harry wound up with a camp on the Little Cascapedia. Right away he contacted my father and said, "Now, you have been a salmon fisherman for a long time – you must come over and spend time here on the Little Cascapedia." So for three or four years my father was over there...as Harry's guest, and I can't remember the name of some fellow [who] was famous for his wealth...he seemed to be the king of the platinum industry in the United States, and he had a wonderful place over there – he sure had a substantial stretch of river on the Little Cascapedia.[23]

＞–＋◆＞–Ｏ–＜◆＋–＜

In the fall of 1949 McLean accompanied John Ashwin on two lengthy recruitment drives/safaris. Great White Hunter extraordinaire, Ashwin worked for the Native Labour Association in Southern Rhodesia (now Zimbabwe) procuring labour for diamond-mining companies.[24] He lived on a sprawling estate on the shores of the Zambezi River at Katima

Mulilo, about one hundred miles from Victoria Falls. Ashwin ensured that McLean, his friend, had every possible comfort, having at his disposal "first class trucks and several hundred natives."[25] According to McLean, Ashwin's moniker among the Natives was "Zakany angaro," meaning "leaves nothing undone," while his own was "Kafut amaruli," meaning "he shoots straight."[26] Owing to the lack of rain, the trucks would repeatedly get bogged down in the sand. A contingent of weary Natives would heave until the vehicles were freed. McLean enjoyed camping under the stars along the banks of the Zambezi while listening to elephants munching a late-night snack, and he took the time to write about the experience.

> It is simply beautiful out on the desert at night. Night lies still on the land and the skies are a blaze of stars. The cough of a leopard prowling in the shadows breaks the silence, a lion grunts and the hyenas laugh in mocking echo; animal eyes are gleaming in the dark; animals are prowling in the shadows, crouching at the water pools, standing motionless, listening by the trees...
>
> To see nature at its best, to watch a play, which is God's not man's, with its decoy the bush and the forest and the mountains, with its lighting, the moonlight and the starlight – dawn, sunset and dark – and for actors all the wild animals, all the game that still abounds and for me, danger, excitement and sweet rest and peace.[27]

On one outing McLean's hunting party blasted "three lions, one hyena, one leopard, four sasabi [sic], one roan, two reed bucks"[28] and other animals too numerous for him to remember. McLean's single written reference to anything remotely erotic relates to this trip:

> And speaking of the wild life of Africa – and quite untamed they are – are the female of the species. At one village we camped for the night and I found myself beating a tom-tom on a large sized drum. The native women went into their dance, – hopping about and weaving their shiny black bodies in a perfect rythm [sic], – with nothing to impede their movements except a sort of "centre-piece" – which impeded nothing at all![29]

McLean took along a film crew to document the safari. With stilted narration describing his every movement, he appears well rested in his pristine hunting garb. The film shows that the trip was not in the least arduous for McLean – there was no need for him to pick up or carry anything heavier than his gun. The trucks, laden with animal carcasses of numerous species, resemble Noah's Ark after a plague. Scores of Natives scurry about, breaking into spontaneous dance. McLean responds in kind, performing a spirited and unwieldy jig to the delight of all.[30] McLean loved Africa, in particular the people, and vowed to return on a yearly basis: "The people of Africa have hearts as big as their great big country, and their homes and their fortunes, whether large or small – are yours."[31]

The early 1950s marked the end for a number of McLean's friends and acquaintances. Jan Smuts died on September 11, 1950, J. P. Bickell passed away on August 22, 1951 (in New York City) and Mitch Hepburn died in his sleep on January 5, 1953. Mackenzie King succumbed to pneumonia at Kingsmere on July 22, 1950. The last of his diary entries that mention McLean states:

> I have been amazed at the greetings that have come in there are dozens of telegrams I have not yet had a chance to read & hundreds of other messages. It is overwhelming. Harry McLean sent 75 roses tonight. It breaks my heart not to be able to distribute these gifts immediately. I am so helpless alone.[32]

McLean and Reta Fitzpatrick arrived in Livingstone, Northern Rhodesia, by air from London on October 22, 1951,[33] after making unscheduled stops at Tripoli and in the Belgian Congo due to mechanical trouble. Charles Switzer received a telephone call from Africa in the middle of the night: "The Pope just married Reta and me."[34] Reta, who was twenty years younger than McLean, had lived in his house as his housekeeper and personal secretary for many years. It was said that he made a promise to take care of her if she took care of him and the marriage was the promise fulfilled.

McLean left his bride in the safety of the Ashwin home and flew off to Katima Mulilo for a safari with Ashwin. Accompanied by eleven Natives and plenty of water and equipment, the two hunters set forth once again to eradicate African wildlife.

The first casualty of this trip was an ornery water buffalo that had been wounded by a lion. Responding to the persistent requests of an elderly Native, Ashwin and McLean tracked the animal into a thicket.

McLean described the excitement as the buffalo charged at their hunting party:

> He came out fast, about forty yards distant, and broadside. The first shot knocked him down, – the 470 has a tremendous striking power, – but he was up in a second. Another shot knocked him down again, and he came up once more. I was pulling the trigger when he dropped back, and the bullet went over the top and through an 18 inch hardwood tree. (Some gun!) He lay quiet finally.[35]

Six shots and a decapitation later, the water buffalo was unquestionably lifeless. Ashwin had told McLean that the only way to be sure a water buffalo was dead was to slash its throat. McLean wrote of the grateful tribesmen: "The Chief Headman of the village made me a speech: 'Tu meze mulera, Ku-Rya, ye noti ya masire kun enghirt'." McLean's translation: "I thank you, Sir, for shooting this very dangerous buffalo."[36] He claimed that the Natives were grateful to the big game hunters for providing them with meat, which otherwise they would have to do without.[37]

Some days later McLean became re-acquainted with Mitch Spencer and his wife. Spencer was the brother of McLean's former pilot, Edward "Ted" Spencer, who was killed in a fiery plane crash on January 25, 1947. Ted had just acquired a Douglas C-47 for his company, Spencer Airways, and was carrying twenty-three passengers and crew to Salisbury, Rhodesia, from Surrey, England. Shortly after take-off the plane rolled right, then left, at a forty-degree angle at low altitude. Just as the aircraft appeared to be level again, it suddenly veered to the right and smashed into a Douglas DC-3. Twelve passengers managed to flee the wreckage. Attempts were made to rescue the remaining eleven people but the flames and extreme heat made this impossible.[38] Although McLean maintained that Spencer, as a highly experienced pilot, could not have been at fault, the crash investigators reached the opposite conclusion. The experts claimed that Spencer lost control of his semi-stalled, heavy aircraft and, given the poor visibility, crashed into the other plane.[39]

McLean accompanied Mitch Spencer on a daytime hunting expedition. He would learn that, unlike Ashwin, Spencer was an inexperienced hunter:

Mitch and his wife and I, accompanied by three "trackers" started out on a hunt which could very well have ended in tragedy. I had already sent back the 470 gun with Ashwin, and had nothing but the Manlicker. Mitch had an army 303. We left Mrs. Mitch in the truck, and proceeded toward a water hole some distance away. As we came closer, we saw five lions drinking there, and realized we were in a hazardous spot. We were not prepared to deal with this situation, so we remained quiet, hoping the animals would not get our scent. Afterwards, Mrs. Mitch reported that these five lions passed close by the truck in which she was waiting, – but took no notice. That was the first narrow escape of this expedition! I was to realize later that my companion knew practically nothing about big game hunting, although he pretended otherwise.[40]

Not in the least deterred by the near miss of "Mrs. Mitch," McLean, Spencer and three trackers continued their hunt. The men became separated. McLean spotted a water buffalo and shot him from a distance of two hundred yards. The bull fell, then rose and was shot again. As Ashwin had warned, a water buffalo with his throat intact could not be trusted to die. The bull retreated into the underbrush and McLean rejoined the hunting party. Spencer advised that he too had blasted a buffalo but the animal had retreated into the bush. Chaos reigned as the men tried to ascertain the animal's location by the blood splatters on the ground. Finally it was determined, much to McLean's dismay, that there were likely three buffalo – all very perturbed after being shot several times and now surrounding the hunting party. McLean wrote:

These animals have a fighting method more deadly than other animals in Africa. As soon as they know you are on their spoor, they match wits quickly. They will select a bush, make a short circle around, and within a few yards of their spoor. They will let you pass, and then charge from the rear.[41]

Spencer led and McLean followed, mostly walking backwards in case of a charge. Hours passed while the great hunters plotted the demise of the "vicious, wounded animals." Ultimately the six guns prevailed over the three water buffalo. After the party returned to safety McLean was rebuked by his friend Ashwin:

"Why did you stay in the picture, – after all I have told you when we hunted together." One false move and we could have been gored to death. Of course I had to protect Mitch. It was a close call, and he was altogether too reckless. We got the three buffalo and distributed the meat among the natives. I heaved a sigh of relief. Never again. It was not for some days that I realized that this careless jaunt could have been the end of years of experienced hunting. ...this was the first time, and the last, believe me, – that I was left practically helpless and at the mercy of these jungle creatures.[42]

After McLean's brush with death, he and his bride left Ashwin's home and took a pleasurable detour on the way back to Canada. The newlyweds landed in Nairobi just prior to the visit of Princess Elizabeth and Prince Philip, then flew to Rome and spent two weeks touring the Coliseum, the Catacombs and various museums, art galleries and churches. McLean wrote:

> No other place on earth holds such a wealth of priceless treasures, – the works of Da Vinci and Michel-angelo and other sculptors and artists of long ago. Thousands of people have dedicated their lives to care for and preserve all this beauty and magnificence, for the joy and inspiration of past, present and future generations. As for me, I felt humble and insignificant, in this environment of Rome, – a city which is described as "Eternally beautiful."[43]

The zenith of their stay in Rome was a private audience with Pope Pius XII:

> In his presence, one seems to glimpse an ethereal being, so appealing, that one believes that, – here in this hallowed place, is the very root of Christianity which shall endure forever. After this visit to Rome, more than ever I find it difficult to understand why any Christian organization or any country, should it feel unwise or inappropriate to have close diplomatic relationship with the Vatican. No other source on earth has a comparable knowledge of human and international affairs, and I think it foolish not to take full advantage of this.[44]

From Rome they travelled to the Riviera, remaining in France for two weeks in order to retrace some of McLean's steps while in France during World War I. They took day trips to Mal Maison, Fontainebleau, Vimy Ridge and the site of the signing of the Armistice in 1918:

> To pause there and reflect upon that Day, – in the light of what has transpired in the world since, was a sobering moment. At the tomb of Napoleon, again one is prone to meditate, and try to decide which

leaders of today fall into the same category of Hitler, Napoleon, or Mussolini. It is for God alone to judge men, and only history which will be written in the far distant future will tell the real story of many who are today considered traitorous, and others who are considered heroic.[45]

Finally, they stopped in England for a couple of days and "were impressed, as always, with the valiant spirit of these people who are still living more or less under war-time austerity."[46] The couple arrived home in Merrickville on March 1, 1952.

⊱┈◈┈◯┈◈┈⊰

On the home front McLean's drunken outings became fewer but no less spectacular or bizarre. In the town of Smiths Falls he kicked in a plate-glass window at the Rideau Hotel and some time later, during the Old Home Week parade, brought traffic to a standstill by stopping in the middle of Beckwith Street wearing his usual summer attire of coonskin coat and derby. On both occasions he wound up at the police station.[47]

In August 1953 and June 1954 McLean stayed in one of the cottages at Hawk Lake. He wrote a series of incoherent letters to Charles Switzer, his train of thought running at full throttle. Switzer was then vice-president of Dominion Construction, preparing balance sheets, looking into the status of leases and handling unusual requests from McLean:

> #1- when Bickle [sic] & I were at Parry Sound – for we were lost in the snow – you sent me some Toilet Paper – every color in the Rain Bow – with verses that shocked & amused everybody – Could you procure me some more – not too many.[48]

Slipping between the present and the past in his writings, McLean commented on the condition of the road, then, in the next sentence, "I did find that everything said and all charges had no foundation. Old Jas was handling the truth recklessly. I am sorry we had anything to do with him." In one note, McLean spoke of the tourists who paid more than the usual price for fish at the packing plant and then commented, "I cannot understand why we crushed so much rock that nobody wanted – It looks like a mistake by some jack ass official who resented us coming on western lines."[49]

298

Some old quarry employees at Hawk Lake still lived in the area. Murray Cooke, who had lost his leg in a quarry accident, saw his boss for only the second time while McLean was spending the summer at the quarry:

> I met Blackie Wagner, who used to guide for Mr. McLean down at Hawk Lake. They were sitting in Blackie's truck. …I was on my way to work and he called me over and said, "Mr. McLean, this is Cooke. He used to work for you." So he says, "Hello," and two minutes later he says, "Where did you lose your leg?" I said, "I lost it working for you." He came back with this: "You're a goddamned liar." I said, "Okay, that's fine," and Blackie said, "No, you did." …we talked again about Hawk Lake and hunting and fishing and so on and so forth. And about 10 or 15 minutes later he said, "Where did you lose your leg." I said, "I told you, I lost it working for you at Hawk Lake." "You're a goddamned liar," he says. It happened a third time and I said, "I don't care whether you believe me or not. Goodbye." I went on my way and went to work. Poor Blackie was still trying to explain but I guess he didn't have any more luck than I did. And that was my last look and my closest look at H. F. McLean.[50]

McLean contacted his relatives in Bismarck regularly to catch up on their news, to reminisce or to get clarification on something he was trying to remember. He would frequently call his cousin, William B. Falconer, a member of the North Dakota legislature. McLean was still held in esteem in his hometown as a man of success. The Midwestern author Erling Nicholai Ralfsrud published a number of books about North Dakota and noteworthy North Dakotans, and McLean was to be included in his next book, *Arsenic and Biscuits*. Ralfsrud approached Falconer to ask for some clarification and for his permission, on behalf of McLean. He received this reply from Falconer:

> I sent your first draft of Arsenic and Biscuits to H. F. McLean and received a reply. However his own comment was that in the building of the west that Arsenic and Biscuits were among the chief causes of death and that he hoped that your new book would not have the same effect on the subjects therein dealt with.[51]

McLean's brother William died on February 10, 1960, in Chapleau, Ontario.[52] Harry was now the only one left in his immediate family. He

Harry McLean. Courtesy of Joseph J. McNally

had plenty of time for introspection, as his final years were spent in obscurity and solitude. Describing McLean as "a man, very much alive, though many believe him dead,"[53] *Toronto Telegram* staff reporter John MacLean visited him at his home in 1956 for what would be McLean's last interview. When the reporter stopped at a local hotel to ask for directions, a long-time Merrickville resident responded, "Harry McLean? Sure, he lives here. We don't see much of him anymore. I guess I haven't spoken to him now for over a year. But he'll be glad to see you. I think he's a pretty lonely man these days. He's 73 now and not many people go up to see him."[54]

At McLean's home the reporter was met by Reta, who showed him to the study. He noted the "wonderful aroma," describing it as "equal part mixture of cigar smoke, fine Scotch whisky and coffee, with just a trace of furniture polish."[55] It was not long before McLean made his entrance, extending his large hand and evaluating the reporter from head to toe. For the next two days MacLean was enraptured with stories of McLean's feats and escapades.

Although the resulting story in the *Telegram* focused on Harry McLean's days as Mr. X, a gentler and reflective McLean was revealed. Towards the end of the interview he pointed to a large willow tree in his yard. "They told me it was crippled and twisted and I should just throw it away," he said. "It was just a little fellow. I planted it. Look at it now. Couldn't find a better shade tree." The same tree held a bird's nest. "Orioles did that," he said. "They build a long nest and hang onto it while they're building it. Must be damn hard work. Don't think I could do that myself."[56]

A Good Life

*Well there isn't any money left now. It's just about all gone. But I've
had a good life and I don't regret very much. It's pretty good when you
don't have regrets, isn't it?*[1]

*He just sort of dwindled out and petered away. It's hard to think of
such a domineering personality just petering out and dwindling
away…and no family. It was a sad way for him.*[2]

*The men of Harry McLean's stature and outlook are few, and each
one of them is unique in himself. But they are the real doers of this
earth. Without them this would be a dismal place. So long as our
country can produce a Harry McLean now and then, there will be
hope for us. Hail and farewell!*[3]

HARRY MCLEAN DIED in his sleep at his home on April 30, 1961,
reportedly of a heart attack.[4] Reta called a couple of local men to help
dismantle an enclosed porch so that her husband's large body could be
removed from the home.[5] A Requiem High Mass was held at St. Ann's
Catholic Church in Merrickville – confirming the belief that he had
converted to Catholicism in his later years. He was buried at Notre-
Dame-des-Neiges Cemetery in Montreal.

Reta was named sole beneficiary in McLean's will. His beloved Kinlochaline was sold and Reta moved to Montreal to live with her sister. She died there in 1978.[6]

McLean left behind a fraction of the millions he had made in his lifetime: a total of $108,058 – "$38,605 in stocks, $12,417 in securities, $26,200 in real estate and $30,760 in household goods" – plus $75.62 in cash in his wallet.[7] Along with the cash was a short verse written on a well-worn piece of paper by a poet unknown:

> *And Martha's sons will be there*
> *Just as natural as earth*
> *Building a bridge to Heaven,*
> *For the Boss that knew their worth.*[8]

APPENDIX 1

The Franks Flying Suit

> ⊱┈⟡┈◯┈⟡┈⊰

*This war more than any other will be a fight of brains and science
and creative ideas.*[1]

AT THE OUTBREAK of World War II Sir Frederick Grant Banting
and his fellow scientists in the Banting and Best Department of Medical
Research at the University of Toronto were already hard at work for the
war effort. Believing war to be inevitable, a proactive Banting had offered
the research assistance of his staff to National Defence several months
prior.[2] He re-enlisted in the Royal Canadian Army Medical Corps. In
discussions with Major A. A. James of the RCAMC about possible
research projects, Banting learned of a potentially lethal phenomenon
experienced by fighter pilots. Coupled with the inherent danger of flying
in a war zone and evading bullets in aerial dogfights, pilots were "blacking
out" when making fast turns or pulling out of diving manoeuvres.[3] The
predicament was described in the University of Toronto's *Varsity
Magazine*:

> The centrifugal force created in pulling out of a fast dive could amount
> to several times the pull of gravity. At a force of seven Gs – seven
> times gravity, a 150-pound pilot weighs more than half a ton. His
> blood, heavy as iron, pools in the elastic vessels of his legs and
> abdomen, and his heart is not strong enough to pump it up again.
> Starved of blood and oxygen in the brain, the flier first loses vision,
> then hearing, [and] finally falls unconscious.[4]

Dr. Wilbur Rounding Franks, another scientist at the University of Toronto, became interested in solving the problem. Prior to World War II, Franks's work had centred on cancer research. Uncertain that he could make any discernible contribution to the blackout problem, Franks remembered experiencing difficulties when using a centrifuge in his laboratory. The force required during the vaccine-purification process was so great that his glass test tubes continually shattered. To resolve the problem, Franks floated the glass tubes in water inside larger, stronger tubes. With the support of the water, the centrifugal force was neutralized and the breakage problem did not recur.[5]

Dr. Frederick Banting during World War II.
ARCHIVES OF ONTARIO, F 9-3-4-1, 10005400

Franks thought this solution could be applied to the problems the pilots were experiencing with centrifugal force – if only the pilots could be encased in water. Franks tested his hypothesis on mice wearing nothing but two-layer rubber and water suits made from condoms. In spite of enduring phenomenal G-forces, the dizzy rodents were unscathed by the experience. Inspired by this success, Franks designed a rubber suit that could encase a layer of water around a full-grown man. He discussed his findings with Banting. The next step was monetary.[6]

An unpleasant task for research scientists is raising sufficient funds to continue their work. Although as a co-recipient of the 1923 Nobel Prize for the discovery of insulin as a treatment for diabetes Banting could attract capital, he was not exempted from this chore. His initial efforts at securing funding for Franks's research were unsuccessful. Then, on October 10, 1939 – one month after Canada had declared war against

Germany – he contacted Harry McLean: "Tonight I phoned Harry MacLean, the eminent Canadian Engineer, at Merrickville, 40 miles from Ottawa, concerning Franks' desire to do further research on 'Blacking Out'."[7]

The result of the conversation was an invitation to visit McLean in Merrickville. Late in the evening of October 13th Banting and Franks boarded an Ottawa-bound train in Toronto. Arriving in Ottawa at six o'clock in the morning, the bleary-eyed scientists were met at the station by McLean's chauffeur. Upon their arrival at McLean's home, they were brought to the kitchen where they sat enjoying a large open-grate fire.[8] Some thirty minutes had passed when the pair were startled by someone shouting. Banting later wrote in his diary:

> It was McLean. He was tight. He had been telephoning off and on all night & had fired one of the helpers and had not been to bed. He insisted that we have a John Collins. We then had breakfast. I was all for getting out. However after breakfast he assumed a business like manner & wanted to know what we wanted. When Franks was about half through with his description McLean said – ["]How much will it cost. – $5000." "I [will] give it to you."[9]

Nothing more was said that day about Franks's research or McLean's funding of it. McLean entertained his visitors with his travel stories: "He told us of the Holy Bulls in the Bank in Calcutta & the Holy Cow that blocked traffic."[10] The scientists observed "a blonde visitor in the morning" as well as other "people coming and going all day."[11] That evening Banting and Franks rode in McLean's Packard, "at about 85 miles per hour," to the Château Laurier in Ottawa, where a party was in full swing in McLean's suite.[12] The scientists managed to extricate themselves from the festivities, having secured McLean's promise of financial support.[13]

Two weeks later, on October 30th, McLean and Jack Bickell paid a visit to Banting, along with "two pheasants & two nurses."[14] Entertaining though the visit may have been, no money was forthcoming. Banting had the clever idea of sending a note to McLean thanking him for his generous pledge. Sure enough, McLean made good on his word.

On November 8th Banting wrote, "McLean's representative phoned to say he was sending $5000 to the Bursar."[15]

McLean's contribution allowed Franks's research to continue, and it led to the invention of the Franks Flying Suit. Completed in 1940, the first suit covered the entire body from neck to toe and, in the prototype stage, also served as a quick weight-loss device as there was no escape for perspiration.[16] Franks himself put the suit to the test at Camp Borden. He recalled the first trial:

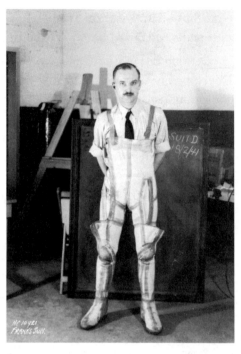

Wilbur Franks and his flying suit, February 18, 1941. "G" Suit, ver. D. RCAF Series, Canadian Department of National Defence Collection. PA-063923, Library and Archives Canada

It had been cut to fit me perfectly standing up. In the airplane, I was sitting down, and when the pressure hit, I thought it was going to cut me in two. The idea became practical only when we realized that great areas of the body could be left outside the fluid system. We also learned that if the blood could be kept from pooling below heart level, the heart had the strength to pump it up to the brain even under several Gs.[17]

However, Franks's invention was not widely used during World War II. Out of fear that the suit would be copied by the enemy if Allied pilots were shot down prior to the invasion of Europe, it was kept out of service. The suit was later tested by a squadron of British pilots. They complained of discomfort while wearing it during long flights. Upon hearing this, American pilots were also reluctant to wear it. Due to the secret nature of the project, Franks's contribution was not made public and patent protection for the invention was not pursued until after the war. Nonetheless the technology of the suit itself was a fundamental contribution to aviation medicine: the G-suits used by jet pilots and astronauts today are based on the principles of Franks's invention.[18]

Banting became actively involved in the War Technical and Scientific Development Committee, whose mandate was to distribute the monetary contributions of Canadian industrialists among various wartime research projects.[19] Projects that received grants of from twelve hundred to three hundred and fifty thousand dollars ranged from field testing in chemical warfare and effects of war gases on the lungs to a prototype refrigeration unit for transporting smoked bacon to England. Donors included the Canadian Pacific Railway, the T. Eaton Company and International Nickel.[20]

Although involved in many projects, Banting remained a stalwart promoter of the Franks Flying Suit. He and Franks planned a trip to England to convince the British Army to hasten research on the suit and investigate suitable manufacturing facilities.[21] They were to fly together, but Banting managed to get an earlier flight, on February 20, 1941, on board a Lockheed Hudson bomber. About an hour after take-off from Gander, Newfoundland, the plane's left engine stalled, then the right. Although the pilot managed to avoid plunging into the depths of the Atlantic, he crash landed on an icy pond and clipped a tree with the left wing. Two crew members perished immediately and Banting succumbed a day later to injuries sustained in the crash. The pilot survived.[22]

The War Technical and Scientific Development Committee met four days later:

> Dean Mackenzie referred to the untimely death of Sir Frederick Banting, a member of the committee, while en route to England in connection with war research activities in which he had taken such a prominent part. He stated that there was nothing he could say which would adequately express the extent of the loss which Canada has suffered, particularly in relation to war research, through the death of Sir Frederick. He expressed the opinion that when the time arrives to make known the details of Canada's war activities it will be realized that Sir Frederick's work on insulin, as great as it was, has been surpassed by the work which he has done, since the outbreak of hostilities, in furthering Canada's war activities.[23]

APPENDIX 2

The Iron Ring Ceremony and the Sons of Martha Cairns

❧ ⊹ ❧ ⊹ ❂ ⊹ ❧ ⊹ ❧

THE RITUAL AMONG Canadian engineers known as the Iron Ring Ceremony was the inspiration of Professor Herbert Edward Terrick Haultain, Professor of Mining Engineering at the University of Toronto.

An unidentified couple in front of the Deeks Quarry cairn. HARRY FALCONER MCLEAN COLLECTION, ACCESSION 1981-064. PA 207734, LIBRARY AND ARCHIVES CANADA

At a retirement dinner in Montreal on January 25, 1922, Haultain outlined his idea to a captive audience of seven past presidents of the Engineering Institute of Canada, including John Maurice Roger Fairbairn, chief engineer for the Canadian Pacific Railway. Haultain hoped to develop an oath committing graduate engineers to high standards and uniting all engineers as members of a proud profession, mindful of the safety of the public entrusted to them. The men formed a committee to consider the idea and decided that an engineering initiation ceremony was in order.[1]

Cranberry Portage/Flin Flon cairn. HARRY FALCONER MCLEAN COLLECTION, ACCESSION 1981-064. PA 212868, LIBRARY AND ARCHIVES CANADA

Rudyard Kipling's 1907 poem "The Sons of Martha" was an anthem to the engineering profession. After its publication, the British Laureate enjoyed an enthusiastic following among Canadian engineers, including the seven past presidents of the Engineering Institute of Canada. Who better to compose the ceremony, they thought, than Kipling? He understood

Grand Falls cairn. HARRY FALCONER MCLEAN COLLECTION, ACCESSION 1981-064. PA 212869, LIBRARY AND ARCHIVES CANADA

the societal responsibilities of engineers and could express them eloquently. Haultain, at the urging of Fairbairn, wrote to Kipling on October 18, 1923, hoping to convince him to compose the ceremony.

Kipling was immediately enthusiastic about the idea.[2] He envisaged the ritual as senior engineers welcoming new graduates into the profession, as distinguished from the ceremonial granting of degrees by the school: "The larger part of the working would be, naturally, obligating graduates in Engineering immediately after they had taken their Degrees, or before they embarked on their career."[3]

Guysborough cairn. COURTESY OF COLIN CHURCHER

The inaugural ritual was held in Toronto. Kipling wrote to Fairbairn on June 3, 1925, stating that the "ritual may really become useful in time."[4] The ritual included the placing of an iron ring on the little finger of the working hand, to be worn permanently.[5] Kipling acknowledged receipt of a sample iron ring, sent by Haultain, that had been made in the occupational therapy program of a Toronto veterans' hospital.[6] Haultain suggested to

Wolfe's Cove cairn. COURTESY OF BILL LINLEY

Kipling that future rings could be further refined, but Kipling was adamant that the design should remain untouched: "...one should never allow any deviations to be made except under the gravest necessity, and the rougher the Ring the better. It is not half as rough as the life ahead of most of the boys."[7]

Kipling and his wife, Carrie, arrived in Montreal in June 1930. Mrs. Kipling had been seriously ill, hospitalized in Bermuda for three months. The stopover in Montreal was intended to break the journey from Bermuda to England.[8]

The Montreal *Gazette* reported that "Hotel officials have had four strenuous days keeping autograph hunters from interrupting the privacy desired by the poet, whose telephone was kept busy by persistent callers."[9] Harry McLean joined Fairbairn to meet with Kipling at the Ritz-Carlton Hotel on June 5th to discuss the ritual.[10] Kipling wrote out several copies of the poem "The Sons of Martha" for McLean to give to his employees.[11] Kipling returned to England on board the *Duchess of Bedford* on June 6th.[12]

Fairbairn, recalling McLean's enthusiasm for Kipling's engineering ritual, visited him years later in Merrickville to secure a donation for the Corporation of the Seven Wardens, the custodian and administrator of the ritual, to ensure its survival. McLean contributed fifteen thousand dollars to the fund.[13]

Anne McLaren and Lois Bradley posing in front of Moosonee cairn with an unidentified boy. Harry Falconer McLean Collection, Accession 1981-064. PA 212870, Library and Archives Canada

Abitibi cairn. Photograph: Wilfred Watson

Hawk Lake cairn, left, and Washburn, North Dakota, cairn. COURTESY OF COLIN CHURCHER AND THE CITY OF WASHBURN, RESPECTIVELY.

McLean also erected monuments with "The Sons of Martha" as their theme. As a tribute to his workers, he erected cairns at his major construction sites and at both rock quarries. Some were built of concrete, others of stone. A large bronze plaque on the front was engraved with the words "In loving memory of those who worked and died here," followed by the first two verses of "The Sons of Martha." The remainder of the poem was divided among three smaller plaques, one affixed to each of the other sides of the cairn.

McLean built a total of nine cairns, at the following sites: Deeks Quarry (in the township of North Grenville, Ontario), 1925; Hawk Lake, Ontario, 1946; Flin Flon, Manitoba, 1929; New Town, Nova Scotia (Guysborough Railway), 1929; Wolfe's Cove, Quebec, 1931; Grand Falls, New Brunswick, 1929; Moosonee, Ontario (T&NO Railway), 1932; Abitibi Canyon, Ontario, 1932.[13] The ninth cairn is located in the City Park at Washburn, North Dakota, and McLean intended to dedicate it to "King John" Satterlund, an old friend of his father and of the McLean family. The Washburn cairn was erected in August 1952.[14]

All of the cairns still exist but are in various states of repair. Some local governments or engineering societies have made efforts to restore and preserve the cairns, having recognized their unique value as artifacts.

A Message to Garcia

By Elbert Hubbard

IN ALL THIS Cuban business there is one man stands out on the horizon of my memory like Mars at perihelion. When war broke out between Spain & the United States, it was very necessary to communicate quickly with the leader of the Insurgents. Garcia was somewhere in the mountain vastness of Cuba– no one knew where. No mail nor telegraph message could reach him. The President must secure his cooperation, and quickly.

What to do!

Some one said to the President, "There's a fellow by the name of Rowan will find Garcia for you, if anybody can."

Rowan was sent for and given a letter to be delivered to Garcia. How "the fellow by the name of Rowan" took the letter, sealed it up in an oil-skin pouch, strapped it over his heart, in four days landed by night off the coast of Cuba from an open boat, disappeared into the jungle, & in three weeks came out on the other side of the Island, having traversed a hostile country on foot, and delivered his letter to Garcia, are things I have no special desire now to tell in detail.

The point I wish to make is this: McKinley gave Rowan a letter to be delivered to Garcia; Rowan took the letter and did not ask, "Where is he at?" By the Eternal! There is a man whose form should be cast in deathless bronze and the statue placed in every college of the land. It is not book-learning young men need, nor instruction about this and that, but a stiffening of the vertebrae which will cause them to be loyal to a trust, to act promptly, concentrate their energies: do the thing– "Carry a message to Garcia!"

General Garcia is dead now, but there are other Garcias.

No man, who has endeavored to carry out an enterprise where many hands were needed, but has been well nigh appalled at times by the imbecility of the average man– the inability or unwillingness to concentrate on a thing and do it. Slip-shod assistance, foolish inattention, dowdy indifference, & half-hearted work seem the rule; and no man succeeds, unless by hook or crook, or threat, he forces or bribes other men to assist him; or mayhap, God in His goodness performs a miracle, & sends him an Angel of Light for an assistant. You, reader, put this matter to a test: You are sitting now in your office– six clerks are within call.

Summon any one and make this request: "Please look in the encyclopedia and make a brief memorandum for me concerning the life of Correggio."

Will the clerk quietly say, "Yes, sir," and go do the task?

On your life, he will not. He will look at you out of a fishy eye and ask one or more of the following questions:

Who was he?

Which encyclopedia?

Where is the encyclopedia?

Was I hired for that?

Don't you mean Bismarck?

What's the matter with Charlie doing it?

Is he dead?

Is there any hurry?

Shan't I bring you the book and let you look it up yourself?

What do you want to know for?

And I will lay you ten to one that after you have answered the questions, and explained how to find the information, and why you want it, the clerk will go off and get one of the other clerks to help him try to find Garcia– and then come back and tell you there is no such man. Of course I may lose my bet, but according to the Law of Average, I will not.

Now if you are wise you will not bother to explain to your "assistant" that Correggio is indexed under the C's, not in the K's, but you will smile sweetly and say, "Never mind," and go look it up yourself.

And this incapacity for independent action, this moral stupidity, this infirmity of the will, this unwillingness to cheerfully catch hold and lift, are the things that put pure Socialism so far into the future. If men will not act for themselves, what will they do when the benefit of their effort is for all? A first-mate with knotted club seems necessary; and the dread of getting "the bounce" Saturday night, holds many a worker to his place.

Advertise for a stenographer, and nine out of ten who apply, can neither spell nor punctuate– and do not think it necessary to.

Can such a one write a letter to Garcia?

"You see that bookkeeper," said the foreman to me in a large factory.

"Yes, what about him?"

"Well he's a fine accountant, but if I'd send him up town on an errand, he might accomplish the errand all right, and on the other hand, might stop at four saloons on the way, and when he got to Main Street, would forget what he had been sent for."

Can such a man be entrusted to carry a message to Garcia?

We have recently been hearing much maudlin sympathy expressed for the "downtrodden denizen of the sweat-shop" and the "homeless wanderer searching for honest employment," & with it all often go many hard words for the men in power.

Nothing is said about the employer who grows old before his time in a vain attempt to get frowsy ne'er-do-wells to do intelligent work; and his long patient striving with "help" that does nothing but loaf when his back is turned. In every store and factory there is a constant weeding-out process going on. The employer is constantly sending away "help" that have shown their incapacity to further the interests of the business, and others are being taken on. No matter how good times are, this sorting continues, only if times are hard and work is scarce, the sorting is done finer– but out and forever out, the incompetent and unworthy go.

It is the survival of the fittest. Self-interest prompts every employer to keep the best– those who can carry a message to Garcia.

I know one man of really brilliant parts who has not the ability to manage a business of his own, and yet who is absolutely worthless to any one else, because he carries with him constantly the insane suspicion that his employer is oppressing, or intending to oppress him. He cannot give orders; and he will not receive them. Should a message be given him to take to Garcia, his answer would probably be, "Take it yourself."

Tonight this man walks the streets looking for work, the wind whistling through his threadbare coat. No one who knows him dare employ him, for he is a regular fire-brand of discontent. He is impervious to reason, and the only thing that can impress him is the toe of a thick-soled No. 9 boot.

Of course I know that one so morally deformed is no less to be pitied than a physical cripple; but in our pitying, let us drop a tear, too, for the men who are striving to carry on a great enterprise, whose working hours are not limited by the whistle, and whose hair is fast turning white through the struggle to hold in line dowdy indifference, slip-shod imbecility, and the heartless ingratitude, which, but for their enterprise, would be both hungry & homeless.

Have I put the matter too strongly? Possibly I have; but when all the world has gone a-slumming I wish to speak a word of sympathy for the man who succeeds– the man who, against great odds has directed the efforts of others, and having succeeded, finds there's nothing in it: nothing but bare board and clothes.

I have carried a dinner pail & worked for day's wages, and I have also been an employer of labor, and I know there is something to be said on both sides. There is no excellence, per se, in poverty; rags are no recommendation; & all employers are not rapacious and high-handed, any more than all poor men are virtuous.

My heart goes out to the man who does his work when the "boss" is away, as well as when he is at home. And the man who, when given a letter for Garcia, quietly take[s] the missive, without asking any idiotic questions, and with no lurking intention of chucking it into the nearest sewer, or of doing aught else but deliver it, never gets "laid off," nor has to go on a strike for higher wages. Civilization is one long anxious search for just such individuals. Anything such a man asks shall be granted; his kind is so rare that no employer can afford to let him go. He is wanted in every city, town and village– in every office, shop, store and factory. The world cries out for such: he is needed, & needed badly– the man who can carry a message to Garcia.

On the Trail of
"Big Pants" Harry F. McLean

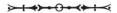

TO GET A better idea of how McLean lived, worked and played, I embarked on several research trips. My first stop was his last: Montreal, Quebec. As my friend Lindsay was attending an early-spring conference in Montreal, I seized the opportunity to go necropolis-hopping in the big metropolis. Arriving in the late afternoon, we walked around the unexpectedly muggy city until our hands were swollen to the size of baseball gloves. After dining at a Mexican restaurant where water was scarce but sangria was not, we retired for the night.

Early the next morning I left my snoozing pal and summoned a taxi. My destination: two gigantic cemeteries. McLean's first wife, Irene, is buried in Mount Royal Cemetery, and Harry and his second wife, Reta, are buried right next door, in Notre-Dame-des-Neiges Cemetery. My driver was Parisian, with an accent like Inspector Clouseau from the *Pink Panther* movies. Upon hearing my unusual destination, he raised a bushy eyebrow and left it suspended until I explained why I was going there. Then he relaxed, becoming more animated with each passing kilometre. He told me he had come to Canada thirty years before and asked me if I had ever heard the name "Rothschild." I asked, "Why? Are you one?" "Non, non, non," he tittered. He told me he had been a waiter in Paris and had served members of that family many times. He sped around a corner to catch the tail end of the yellow light, making a gleeful French exclamation as I clung to the door handle.

We were driving for an awfully long time. I suspected that Mr. Rothschild Impersonator didn't know where he was going. In response to my impatient sighs, he confessed. Based on no knowledge of Montreal whatsoever, I directed him to Mount Royal Cemetery. Pulling my belongings out of his trunk, he gave me a photocopy of a newspaper clipping – something to do with him, France and World War II. He then pointed to a bag in his trunk and said something about the Japanese trying to steal his soup. It was too early in the morning to make out what he was saying, so I nodded politely and backed away.

I felt like a ghoul being in a graveyard at that hour. Slightly hung over and without coffee or makeup, I was certain that I looked like one too. Time constraints had forced me to take along my luggage and laptop computer to the cemetery, and I pulled them behind me on a squeaky cart. I stopped at the "You are here" map to locate Irene's grave.

Mount Royal is a Protestant cemetery located in Outremont ("the other side of the mountain") adjacent to the Catholic Notre-Dame-des-Neiges Cemetery. Section I is the top left section of Mount Royal Cemetery and is one of the older sections – there were no flowers placed at any of the monuments; any relatives of the people buried there were likely long since deceased themselves. I was starting to get frustrated in my search efforts when I spotted Irene's headstone. It read simply "McLean" – no reference to her date of birth, date of death, nothing. Given the little information I'd been able to find about her, this practically blank tombstone was perfectly reasonable. I took some pictures and headed for Notre-Dame-des-Neiges.

Irene McLean's gravestone, Mount Royal Cemetery, Montreal. Photograph by the author

A high iron fence separates the two cemeteries, and

menacing spikes at the top serve as an effective deterrent for anyone thinking about jumping it. Although I had read that there was a break in the fence somewhere, this proved difficult to find. Eventually I located a narrow opening near the graves of some soldiers. Sending laptop and luggage through first, I performed excruciating body contortions, relieved that I didn't have to risk impaling myself on the sharp spikes.

I found myself in Section M and, using my superior detective skills, deduced that I must therefore be close to Section L. However, the alphabetical coding system at Notre-Dame-des-Neiges is not what one might expect. Right next to Section M is Section U, hence my difficulty in locating Section L. After hours of searching, I was no closer to cracking the code – having regrettably left my secret decoder ring at home. The sky was getting darker and I considered my options in the event of a downpour. The trees were barely green and would provide no protection from the rain. I spotted some mausoleums and figured I might hole up in one of them. After wandering around for more than three hours, I can confirm that Notre-Dame-des-Neiges is one of the largest cemeteries in North America, boasting more than a million permanent residents.

On this unexpectedly lengthy journey I spotted the tombstone of one of the more notable residents: Pierre Laporte, who was murdered by the Front de Libération du Québec in 1970. By then I was too tired and crabby to think about anything but the blisters forming on my feet. I decided to gather my wits and find a live person to ask for directions – no small feat considering my whereabouts. I found a gravedigger and asked him where the elusive Section L was. He didn't know either, as he relied on landmarks to find his way around. He directed me to the administration office, where I grabbed a map.

I figured that with a map in hand I would have no trouble cracking the code, but the logic was no more discernible. Even though I found Section L on the map, I had problems locating the actual grave. Wearily giddy, I laughed at the thought that if I didn't find it soon there would be little point in leaving. I could ask a gravedigger to throw some dirt over me and be content with the opportunity to lie down. After reflecting on having actually laughed out loud, alone, in a graveyard, I contemplated giving up altogether.

Harry and Reta McLean's gravestone, Notre-Dame-des-Neiges Cemetery, Montreal.
PHOTOGRAPH BY THE AUTHOR

Then I spotted it – L-376 – a mere fifty kilometres or so from where I had started. I limped towards it, cursing myself for not wearing sensible shoes. I expected the McLean headstone to be elaborate and grandiose but it is ordinary and modest. Both Harry and Reta are buried there, along with a relative of Reta's (likely her sister) whose name is engraved on the back of the stone. I was told that Reta's brother, Bill, was a detective with the Montreal police but I was unable to find the graves of any other relatives. I took photographs of the headstone at every conceivable angle, like a fashion photographer.

I walked out of the cemetery, dodging the gravediggers' trucks that sped along the narrow pathways, and was retrieved by a less vivacious taxi driver than my first. After my near fatal trip to the graveyard, I proceeded to the McGill University archives hoping to find some record of McLean's first wife, Irene, who reportedly worked as a nurse at the Royal Victoria Hospital in Montreal. I looked through books and papers for hours without success. I asked if it was possible to obtain medical reports, thinking I might be able to get my hands on McLean's hospital records from his bout of pneumonia after the Halifax Explosion, but without luck. I returned home to Merrickville and started planning my next research trip.

>-+-♦>-•-O-•-<♦-+-<

One month later, combining business with pleasure, I went to New York City for a weekend getaway with my husband. We managed to do some research at the New York City Municipal Archives. Having done a little investigating on the Internet beforehand, I knew that District Attorney Frank Hogan's file on the Delaware Aqueduct extortionists, Fay and Bove, was available for viewing. This time we hit the research jackpot, finding a scathing letter written by Hogan about McLean and plenty of other related materials, as well as a letter signed by J. Edgar Hoover. We spent a pocketful of dimes at the photocopier and continued our tour of the Big Apple.

The Delaware Aqueduct has since sprung several leaks and has been losing water at an alarming rate for over a decade. It is uncertain whether the section built by Seaboard Construction is the culprit. As the aqueduct cannot be drained, a parallel aqueduct is being built beside it and is expected to be completed by 2020. The cost will likely exceed $6 billion.

>-+-♦>-•-O-•-<♦-+-<

In July 2002 I travelled with my daughters, Sabina, ten, and Emily, seven, to Cochrane in northern Ontario to ride the Polar Bear Express – in the midst of a sweltering heat wave. On the train from Smiths Falls to Toronto three boisterous, unescorted preteen girls sat across the aisle from us. Hours passed without a hint of silence. The shrill laughter from the trio pierced our skulls and we longed for the sanctuary and relative peace of Union Station. When we arrived in Toronto we quickly divested ourselves of our noisy neighbours and went in search of some lunch. Under the shadow of the CN Tower we ordered hamburgers, which, despite looking edible, actually tasted like Styrofoam. After lunch we discovered an oasis amidst the oppressive heat – one small air-conditioned room in Union Station. I learned a valuable lesson about travelling with two kids: pack everything in one suitcase. I got stuck in a narrow stairwell with several suitcases, battling throngs of zombie-like commuters while simultaneously directing the girls to the train.

In 1946 the name of the Temiskaming and Northern Ontario Railway was changed to the Ontario Northland Railway, for two reasons: it was thought the name of the railway should be identified with the whole of the province of Ontario; and the Texas and New Orleans Railroad used the same abbreviation, and boxcars owned by the Ontario railway were being commandeered by the Texan railroad; worse still, the Ontario railway frequently was charged rental fees and invoiced for debts incurred by the other.

We happily boarded the Ontario Northland train and settled in for the long ride north. People who are travelling in threesomes or foursomes get seated first, in seats facing each other. I sat with Sabina, and Emily shared her seat with a person who was spilling into it. A group of three sat across the aisle, engaged in incomprehensible conversation. It was déjà vu. Their sentences generally ended with chortling laughter and the volume increased steadily as the evening wore on. By two in the morning the buoyant chatter was making us quite restless. The seats, meanwhile, were not designed for twelve-hour journeys. While Emily was comfortably settled into her neighbour's ample body folds, Sabina and I were like writhing pretzels. We eventually gave up on the idea of sleep and just listened enviously as Emily snored away.

We arrived in Cochrane around five in the morning. The Station Hotel in Cochrane is fairly new and is clean and well kept. Our panoramic view was of the parking lot, some shops and the railway museum, aptly housed in old railway cars. Although I was still reeling from sleep deprivation, I had made arrangements to rent a car and drive to Abitibi Canyon. Our car rental agent showed up at the hotel with a Grand Am along with the world's longest map, the scale of which must have been actual size. As he extended the map, Sabina took one look and said, "We're never going to get there."

Driving out of Cochrane, the girls fell asleep immediately. I had to chew my tongue to stay awake. Although the pine trees were sparse and spindly, the land was pristine and beautiful. The seventy-four-kilometre road into Abitibi Canyon from Smooth Rock Falls is paved for the benefit of the Ontario Power Corporation, which now operates the Canyon. When we arrived at Abitibi we were greeted by swarms of horseflies the size of golf balls. I thought, I've driven all the way here and now I can't even get out of the car. Mustering every ounce of courage, I told the half-awake girls to stay put. I flung myself out of the car, discovering that the mammoth flies were attracted by the engine exhaust and once I was away from the car they posed no problem. I spotted the well-maintained Sons of Martha cairn and pulled out my camera.

A woman with two girls photographing a slab of concrete in the middle of nowhere does generate some curiosity. Although my visit was not prearranged, the hydro workers were friendly and helpful. They were also aware of the history of the facility – most had seen McLean's Abitibi Canyon construction film. Before long I was introduced to the person in charge, Paul Schaeffer, who graciously provided us with our own tour guide, Bob Arnott.

Sons of Martha cairn at Abitibi Canyon, July 2002. PHOTOGRAPH BY THE AUTHOR

The view from the dam was breathtaking. Unfortunately the elevator to the lower level was out of order. Because of concern for our safety, and particularly to avoid making the girls descend three hundred steps on foot, we were piled into a shiny new truck and driven down a side road near the river to see the power house and dam. Most of the work done by Dominion Construction is still functional and surprisingly little has been replaced since the 1930s. The men marvel at how well the company's work has held up, particularly the concrete work, the riveting and the wood in the tunnels.

We toured the staff buildings, both old and new, talking with people along the way. One man had lived at Abitibi Canyon as a young boy and thought it a wonderful place to grow up. He said that when the Canyon kids transferred to regular high school they were ahead of the pack because of the individual attention they had received. The colony was closed in the early 1980s, mainly because of the cost of running

Abitibi Canyon power house. PHOTOGRAPH BY THE AUTHOR

the facility, but the people who lived there over the years still get together for reunions.

We drove back, dropped off the car and dragged ourselves to the railway museum for a ten-minute tour. One rail car is dedicated to the memory of Tim Horton, the hockey player (Toronto Maple Leafs) and doughnut entrepreneur, who was a native of Cochrane. By then I was partially delirious and convinced the girls to retire to our hotel for the night.

We boarded the Polar Bear Express first thing the next morning. The line from Cochrane to Moosonee was built by Dominion Construction, as was the Moose River Bridge. Looking out of the window at the terrain below, I imagined the difficulties that must have been encountered by the men who built the railway – the muskeg, boot-sucking black mud, extreme temperatures, flies, isolation. I imagined the milquetoast

The graves of workers killed at Abitibi. Photographs by Paul Schaeffer

gentlemen at my day job attempting to build this railway, dismissed the thought with a snort and concluded that men back then were made of tougher stuff.

The train ride to Moosonee takes about four hours. There's a small park near the Moosonee train station where the Sons of Martha plaques are mounted, but close examination would have to wait. We were whisked into old school buses for a whirlwind tour of Moosonee. We chugged past the hardware store and the liquor store and then stopped on the shores of the Moose River. Following a spectacular dismount by Emily down the slippery steps of the bus, we travelled by boat to Moose Factory for yet another tour aboard a clunky bus. We peered out the fogged-up windows at the oldest wooden church in Ontario, but the highlight of the tour was stopping at a tepee to eat raisin-studded bannock cooked over an open fire. After shopping for souvenirs offered by the women's auxiliary, we returned to Moosonee and reboarded the Polar Bear Express.

On the way out of town I noticed, out of the corner of my eye, a cairn suspiciously like the one at Abitibi but without plaques. Then I remembered reading, in a letter to Charlie Hyson, that the plaques had

Emily and Sabina Charland in front of Sons of Martha plaques at Moosonee, July 2002. Photograph by the author

been removed from the cairn because no one ever saw them there. Unfortunately I was unable to snap any pictures of that curiosity.

We arrived in Cochrane late in the evening and prepared for the long journey home the next day.

⊱─┤⊶⊙⊷├─⊰

In September 2002 my friend Wendell "Dell" Bower accompanied me to North Dakota. With the heightened vigilance after September 11, 2001, the airport security people were searching every fourth person. Even though the two passengers I was sandwiched between looked like an assassin and a drug lord, they were free to board the plane and I was searched – twice. The landing in Minneapolis was precluded by bad weather, so we flew around Iowa for a while. Remarkably, when we arrived in Minneapolis our luggage was sitting there waiting for us. We took that as a good omen and proceeded to pick up our rental car.

It isn't easy to find an address at night in an unfamiliar city, particularly one the size of St. Paul/Minneapolis. The main problem was that the people giving us directions were from places other than St. Paul/ Minneapolis. We drove around hoping for the best, eventually arriving at the hotel. It was in the middle of a business park with no obvious signage. By then it was very late, so we reluctantly gave up on the idea of going for a beer.

The next morning we drove to the Oakland Cemetery in St. Paul, located near the state capitol buildings, to see the McLean family plot. The same nonsensical numbering system used at Notre-Dame-des-Neiges Cemetery was in place here. I asked an old, red-nosed gent who looked as if he had forty ounces too many and forty winks too few if he knew anything about the numbering system. He had no idea, but asked the insightful question "Are you here looking for a grave?" We found the grave marker by using the same technique we had used for finding the hotel – driving in random circles. Although there are six people buried in the McLean family plot, there were only five grave markers. Harry's older brother, William, was the marker-less one.

We found our way out of St. Paul and onto the Interstate to our next destination – Fargo, North Dakota, and the Institute of Regional Studies, part of North Dakota University.

Western Minnesota and eastern North Dakota consist largely of farmland and vast fields of sunflowers. In Fargo the franchises are rampant. There's a K-mart, a Wal-Mart and every other mart you might care to think of. Fargo has a population of ninety thousand. It has fifteen taco restaurants. That's one taco restaurant for every six

McLean family plot in Oakland Cemetery, St. Paul, Minnesota. PHOTOGRAPH BY THE AUTHOR

thousand people. There were no souvenir shops, but we would have no problem finding tires, a tractor, a trailer or a tractor-trailer. There's a huge trailer park in West Fargo. I used to think it was a strange coincidence that tornadoes always seem to hit trailer parks in the United States. I now realize it's because there are so many trailer parks in the United States.

Fargo has some lovely old homes on tree-lined streets with the branches arching gracefully inward. There are signs of the pioneer town that Fargo once was, but for the most part the city has been modernized. Judging by the traffic flow, West Fargo is the destination of choice. Dell and I ate at the Speedway Restaurant surrounded by photographs of the stars of NASCAR. A steak "so rare a vet could bring it back to life" seemed a mighty fine idea.

The Institute of Regional Studies in Fargo is located in a strip mall. I drove by it a couple of times before I clued in. Our research there was successful, with the help of friendly and accommodating staff. We found plenty of genealogical information written by Hazel Falconer, a relative of McLean's. Next on the agenda was a visit to McLean's hometown of Bismarck, a four-hour drive from Fargo.

Upon arriving in Bismarck we went to the state capitol to photograph *The Pioneer Family* statue. It is truly awe-inspiring and remains the focal point of the grounds. Dr. Eugene Fairbanks, son of the sculptor, Avard Fairbanks, told me that a similar statue today would cost two hundred and fifty or three hundred thousand. McLean's money was well spent.

Fort Abraham Lincoln State Park was our other destination that day. Once home to Lieutenant Colonel George Armstrong Custer, his wife, Elizabeth, and the 7th Cavalry, Fort Abraham Lincoln was at one time a sprawling complex of seventy-eight buildings. When the fort was abandoned some fifteen years after the Battle of the Little Big Horn, local residents helped themselves to the building materials to construct their own farms and homes. In the past several years some buildings have been reconstructed: the commissary storehouse, a granary, barracks, and George and Elizabeth Custer's home. The replica captures the essence of the fort down to the last detail, including many articles owned

Reproduction of the Custer home, Mandan, North Dakota. PHOTOGRAPH BY THE AUTHOR

by the Custers. Tour guides dressed as soldiers offer the visitor a choice: modern speech, or the type of speech that would have been used by soldiers of the time. We chose the latter, and the tour was wonderfully entertaining.

We spent many hours at the Archives of the State Historical Society of North Dakota examining old editions of the *Bismarck Tribune* on microfilm. We located all of the McLean obituaries except that of Harry's little brother, James Garfield McLean. And Dell found some photographs of Harry and his family, nine in all.

We congratulated ourselves on our success and headed back to St. Paul to tour the James J. Hill House, home of the builder of the Great Northern Railway. "House" is an understatement. The five-storey mansion is decorated in mahogany and oak throughout, and is gloomy in places due to the lack of sunlight. The floor plan measures thirty-six thousand square feet, including a two-storey art gallery with a pipe organ. Technically advanced for its time, the mansion boasts central heating, gas and electric lighting, and a security and communications system.

Home of James J. Hill, St. Paul, Minnesota. PHOTOGRAPH BY THE AUTHOR

The house is now a museum, operated by the Minnesota Historical Society.

Though many people had made comparisons between Hill and McLean, I found no evidence of a relationship between the two.

The U.S. phase of my research was as complete as it was going to be, I decided, and we headed back to Canada where I started preparations for another research trip.

I visited the Archives of Ontario in Toronto to view the papers of Richard Hearn and Frederick Ker. Hearn went on to become chairman of Ontario Hydro (in 1955). He was a visionary, like McLean, and was an early proponent of the CANDU nuclear program as well as Atomic Energy of Canada Limited. In 1974 he was made a member of the Order of Canada. Hearn died in his ninety-seventh year. Ker became editor and publisher of the Hamilton *Spectator* and president of Canadian Press. He died at the age of ninety-two. Both of these collections provided some useful information for the book.

I have often wondered what would have become of McLean's companies had he had sons to inherit the business. Many of the companies that McLean dealt with still exist today: Perini is a huge corporation with annual revenues approaching $2 billion. The S. A. Healy Company was bought in 1982 by Impregilo S.p.A. of Milan but still operates in the United States under the Healy name, with revenues even greater than those of Perini. Joseph McNally's companies will continue to be a force to be reckoned with into the future: McNally International is Canada's leading tunnel contractor. H. G. Acres Company became Acres International, was bought out by Hatch Limited of Toronto in 2004 and now operates as Hatch Acres.

>–·–◂▸–·–O–·–◂▸–·–◂

Guysborough cairn. PHOTOGRAPH BY THE AUTHOR

On a blustery day in October 2002 I flew to Halifax. This time I didn't have a lovely research assistant. I chose Route 7 out of Halifax because it seemed to be the most scenic route to my destination. The road hugs the Atlantic shoreline and touches many uniquely named towns along the way. I was tempted to stop for the Fireman's Dinner

Monument at Pictou, Nova Scotia. PHOTOGRAPH BY THE AUTHOR

at Mushaboom but had other commitments. I read some road signs about the Scarecrows at Ecum Secum but was too scared to stop.

I was headed for Aspen, where, I had been told, I would find the Guysborough cairn. First I stopped at a post office for directions. The postmaster told me to go to Denver first. I told her that this was sounding altogether too much like Colorado, but she assured me I would find what I was looking for in New Town. Except that there is no New Town per se. If I hadn't glanced up into the woods I would have missed the cairn altogether. I snapped the requisite ten pictures and continued on.

If McLean and the men who worked on the Guysborough Railway were alive today, they might be happy to know that the abandoned rail line forms part of the Trans Canada Trail. The Guysborough Nature Trail runs some twenty-six kilometres between Country Harbour Cross Roads and Guysborough and is used for recreational activities such as hiking, cycling and cross-country skiing.

As I was ahead of schedule, I decided that I would travel first to Pictou to see the Second Construction Battalion memorial. One of the first buildings off the highway at Pictou is that of the Royal Canadian Legion. I assumed that if anyone would know where the monument was, it was the Legion. Sure enough, I was escorted from the bar by a burly woman and invited to follow her pick-up truck. I snapped pictures of the monument, stopped at Tim Hortons for a self-congratulatory coffee and took to the road. I was off to Sydney to try to locate some remnants of Point Edward Naval Base/HMCS *Protector*.

I passed road signs for towns like Whycocomagh and Wagmatcook and arrived in Sydney at half-past five. I set about searching for my hotel. None of my maps had an embedded street map of Sydney, so I had only my keen intuition to rely on. Since I had landed in a new part of town and my hotel was described as "old," I kept driving until I found a part of town that seemed old – and there was the hotel.

I brought in my luggage and asked about a restaurant. Hands down, without a doubt, I was told, the restaurant at Casino Nova Scotia was the best value for the dollar. I'm not a casino person and do not intend to become one. But despite my vow to never set foot in a casino – ever – I was on my way to one. I strolled out of the hotel, ventured across to the casino and made my way down the stairs, through the flashing lights and all of those "lucky" people about to "strike it rich."

Casinos are bizarre places. As you enter, there is a barrage of light and an unrelenting, infernal high-pitched wail from the slot machines. The perky, ample-breasted redhead behind the desk showed me to a table right away, even though other people were waiting. That's one benefit of dining alone. I ate an insipid, limp salad simply for sustenance. Politely declining the offer of dessert, I opted instead for a walk along the waterfront.

Although the gusty sea air was wonderfully cathartic, I found few remnants of the base and decided to cut my investigation short, given my time constraints.

When I opened the door to my hotel room that night there was a musty odour that I associated with the antique furniture. Then later, when I turned back the sheets, I saw several hairs from different heads on the pillowcase. Peeking under the blankets, I found nothing crawling. When I got into bed and pulled up the sheets it was like being in a gym bag surrounded by mouldy running shoes and sweaty clothes that someone had urinated on three weeks before. Although the room was chilly and damp, I had to keep the blankets well south of my nose lest I retch uncontrollably.

Meanwhile, gale-force winds were raging outside, making the exhaust vent in the bathroom rattle loudly. The only way to stop the noise was to turn on the fan, which sounded like an outboard motor. I tried to reach the fan while perched on top of the toilet, having come up with the half-baked scheme of shoving a facecloth in there to muffle the sound, but I was at least a foot shy of the target. Stuffing my ears with toilet paper, I got back into bed. If not for the need to breathe, I would have plugged my nose with tissue as well. Between the noise and the smell, sleep was not going to come easily.

I lay there considering my options. The owner of the hotel was close to her expiry date. Her crotchety little dog had growled as it hid under the furniture downstairs, and would likely attack me if I requested a room change. Briefly I considered sleeping in the car, but thought better of it – the old "I paid money for this, so I'm staying" way of thinking. I consoled myself by plotting my way out of the building, deciding to be rebellious and take the fire escape the next day even though I had been ordered by the owner not to do so. I tried not to think about what might crawl up my leg during the night.

The next morning my escape went according to plan. I headed out at twenty past five, Digby bound, my stomach lurching from the smell embedded in my nostrils. After reaching mainland Nova Scotia at about half-past six, I stopped for a coffee and buttery bagel at Tim Hortons. There are a lot of Tim Hortons in Ontario, but there seemed to be one on every corner there. I couldn't find a variety store, but at least I wouldn't be without a doughnut.

My drive to Digby took about six hours. I stopped at the first seafood restaurant I could find in Digby, resolving to eat seafood chowder, because if there's a place to eat seafood, it must be there. I didn't realize how much I was enjoying my meal until the waiter asked, "How are you making out with the chowder?" I decided to slow down and not lick my lips so much.

While on a side trip to a gift shop, I discovered to my dismay that the ferry from Digby to Saint John did not leave until four-thirty in the afternoon. Having done all that I needed to do, there was little point in my staying around all day. I probably would get sick on the ferry anyway, not being an old sea dog. I headed towards Deep Brook and my next stop, the Cornwallis Military Museum.

Douglas Moore kindly agreed to give me an off-season tour of the museum, which is housed in one of the old churches on the base. The museum is run by a dedicated group of volunteers without the benefit of government funding.

Cornwallis, Nova Scotia. PHOTOGRAPH BY THE AUTHOR

Most of the exhibits, which range from uniforms and guns to Nazi armbands and flags with swastikas, have been donated by former military people. Hanging on the wall is a life raft that was found with a German sailor clinging to it. Also on display are a photograph taken at the time of the rescue and a photograph of the sailor in his naval uniform. Apparently he was taken as a prisoner of war but was contacted after many years and developed a friendship with people in Canada. As I listened to Douglas Moore speak, I was struck by the thought that that there might be a million stories under that roof. Of all the places I visited during my research, that museum was the most impressive – a place where I would be more than happy to see my tax dollars go.

That night I stayed in the picturesque town of Annapolis Royal. I settled into my room, checked the pillows for hair, bugs and other unsavoury items, and, satisfied that there were none, drifted off. My blissful rest was short-lived, however. The bowl of chowder proved to be my undoing. I was sick most of the night and considered waiting until four-thirty the next afternoon for the ferry to Saint John. After some reflection on my tendency to get seasick and the fact that I was already nauseous, I opted for the Pepto Bismol drive. At eight o'clock, feeling marginally better, I gathered my things together and said goodbye to my hosts. This is when I discovered that my hosts were sadists – they discussed food in minute detail, knowing full well that I had been sick all night. I extricated myself and found the nearest gas station/ convenience store, filling the car with gas and myself with thick, mint-pink chalky fluid.

It took eight hours to drive from Digby to Grand Falls. The New Brunswick town has a dramatic setting. It sits atop a high rocky ridge with a gorge running through it. I went to the power station but unfortunately they weren't giving tours. I found the hotel merely by locating the highest hill – the name of the hotel (Hill-Top) being a dead giveaway.

Intake at Grand Falls, New Brunswick. Photograph by the author

Grand Falls cairn. PHOTOGRAPH BY THE AUTHOR

I had written to the Grand Falls Historical Society and had been introduced to Patrick McCooey, former president of the Society and a lifelong resident of Grand Falls. McCooey's father had worked at the power plant and remembered Harry McLean well. We had traded letters and phone calls and it was wonderful to finally meet him. We spent hours talking about local history, the hydro project and life in general. McCooey had prepared a file of articles about McLean and the hydro project, and he had lots of photographs of the construction, taken in the 1920s, some of which he let me borrow in order to make slides.

Grand Falls is an interesting place and has attracted its share of unique people. A man by the name of Van Morrell walked on a tightrope across the gorge in 1904. His balancing pole is displayed in the museum. Another person who lived in Grand Falls was *The Great Impostor,* Fred Demara, played by Tony Curtis in the movie version of the book about his life. McCooey remembered that he found Demara intimidating and that his mother immediately sensed something insincere about the man. (One of the identities that Demara stole was that of Dr. Joseph Cyr, who took over Dr. Berton Puddington's hospital.) Another famous person with Grand Falls in his history is Ron Turcotte, the jockey who rode Secretariat to glory and the man for whom the town's bridge is named. The boots that Turcotte wore while riding Secretariat are on display in the museum (he must be the size of a leprechaun). The main bridge has collapsed four times since 1858; the last replacement dates from the 1970s.

We took a walking tour of Grand Falls, down the main street and over to the local lovers lane and on to the location of the Grand Falls Sons of Martha cairn. Although the original cairn is still there, it is no longer accessible. As we strolled, McCooey spoke about growing up in Grand Falls – crawling around areas of the gorge (his nephew actually scaled the area underneath the bridge), eating green apples by the ton and getting chased by derelicts in the park.

We walked to the graveyard where Jack Puddington's parents are buried and back towards the museum where we said our goodbyes.

After a fitful sleep I drove back to Halifax, arriving there in a little over six hours. I went directly to the archives to finish my research. There I found a biographical file on McLean submitted by Charlie Hyson. Then I went to the Maritime Museum to view the Halifax Explosion picture collection. I found photographs of the hotel where McLean reportedly stayed but no additional proof, to back up the evidence I had already gathered, that he had been there during the explosion.

In February 2004 I visited the Thomas Fisher Rare Book Library at the University of Toronto to view Sir Frederick Banting's war diaries. It was one of those rare occasions during my research when I found what I was looking for the minute I sat down. Reading Banting's diaries and personal correspondence was a pleasurable and interesting experience. He seemed very down to earth, with worries and concerns like everyone else. He longed to be back in his quiet laboratory again doing the research he loved. I empathized with Banting's yearning for the time to do the things he really wanted to do.

Deeks Quarry cairn in Ontario. PHOTOGRAPH BY
THE AUTHOR

Finally, in October 2004, I had an opportunity to be a tourist in my own village and visit McLean's house. The current owner, Rose Fader, and her daughter, Dianne Mason, kindly allowed us to tour the house. Maureen Lunam of the Flin Flon Archives had sent a request for information about McLean to the village office. The query found its way to me and e-mails flew wildly back and forth between Manitoba and Ontario. Maureen, her husband, Duncan, and their daughter, Karen Ann, along with Fred Miller, a researcher who helped guide the Flin Flon Archives with respect to cairn-related queries, and his wife, Anne Marie Bazinet-Miller, had come to Merrickville for a visit. Everyone was thrilled to have a chance to view this incredible house.

We took this opportunity to show the Flin Flon people our Sons of Martha cairn at Deeks Quarry, which, unfortunately, is in ruins. Deeks has not been an operating quarry since the Depression. Every building was torn down and all of the locomotives sold or scrapped. The only evidence of a once-viable business is what is left of the cairn. The area is desolate and for generations has served as a makeshift dump – discarded objects ranging from automobile seats to oil tanks are strewn from one end of the property to the other. Upon close examination one can still find blast holes and the cold storage pit where food was kept temporarily. Deeks Quarry is located off Highway 43 between Kemptville and Merrickville on an unopened section of the Scotch Line Road.

Canyon Ferry Mansion, once the home of A. B. Cook, Townsend, Montana.
<small>PHOTOGRAPH BY THE AUTHOR</small>

My last research venture involving airplanes was a trip to North Townsend, Montana, in December 2004 to visit the mansion of McLean's mentor, Andrew Braid Cook, and the Montana Historical Society in Helena, where sixty-five boxes awaited me. I had a feeling that by finding out more about Cook I would gain more insight into McLean. As with many other places I've visited while doing research for this book, my initial viewing of the mansion was on the Internet. Cook's summer home is now called Canyon Ferry Mansion, a bed and breakfast, wedding resort and antique shop. I e-mailed the owners with my standard request for information and a blurb about the book, and received a pleasant note in return followed by an invitation to visit Montana.

Sandy Rose, who owns the Mansion with her husband, Steve, offered me free accommodation in exchange for swapping information with her. It was an offer I couldn't pass up. Quite out of the blue, I found myself making travel arrangements for a trip that was only eighteen days away. Anyone who knows me can attest to the fact that this is highly unusual:

I plan everything months or years in advance. Sandy and Steve are talented people, masters of everything, including cooking – they are both wonderful chefs. Sandy is an event planner; Steve owns a construction company specializing in reconstruction of old homes such as the Mansion. As a side business, Sandy sells tassels of every shape and variety. One of the attractions at the Mansion is Chop-Chop, a wonderful Shar-Pei full of personality. Sandy and Steve treat their Canyon Ferry Mansion guests like royalty. I would have quite happily moved in with them.

Sandy took a day out of her busy schedule and drove me to the headquarters of the Montana Historical Society in Helena. We found such a wealth of information and photographs there that I had to return the next day for another marathon of photocopying and note-taking.

At the Mansion I stayed in the Governor's Room, which was the bedroom of Franklin (Hervey) Cook, A. B. Cook's stepson. Hervey restored the home but became increasingly reclusive with age. During a robbery attempt he was murdered just outside the building. Sandy told me that there are ghosts in the house – seven distinct phantom personalities in fact. I'm not one to believe in such things, but it's funny how stories can stay in the back of your mind. Just as I was about to leave the Mansion the door to the attic suddenly flew open and slammed against the wall. I thought I was going to become a ghost myself!

>-+◆>-○-<◆+-<

During a visit to the National Archives of Canada (since renamed Library and Archives Canada), my lovely new research assistant, Melinda Harwood, and I took a side trip to W. L. Mackenzie King's residence, Laurier House, which King bequeathed to the country as a museum. Once home to Sir Wilfrid Laurier, the house is maintained by Parks Canada. King's statuette featuring Pat Number One is on show, and the cougar skin that Pat loved is displayed in front of the library fireplace. It struck me that the cougar may well have lived at McLean's zoo before its demise. The house reflects mainly the King era, with a few rooms containing items that belonged to the Lauriers. King spent several years renovating the house, covering many of the walls with white oak panels carved in Scotland. Paintings, sculptures and precious antiques abound – evidence of gifts to the prime minister from all over the world. We found King's séance room particularly interesting, even though it is now taken   up by a heating and air-conditioning unit.

>–·–◊–·–○–·–◊–·–<

In September 2005 Dell and I hit the road for the last time. On this occasion the trip was local, down Highway 43 to the town of Alexandria and the Land Registry Office, then to Lancaster, where the farmhouse of McLean's great-grandfather, William Falkner, still stands. It is now MacPine Farm's Bed & Breakfast, located just off Highway 401 at the Lancaster exit on the South Service Road, and is owned by Guelda and Robert MacRae. I was directed to drive through a cornfield from the MacPine Farm to the Old Cemetery by the Lake, located on the shores of the St. Lawrence River. William Falkner and a few of his relatives are buried here – William, a Justice of the Peace, was credited with naming the town of Lancaster. A plaque in a corner of the graveyard marks Falkner's Settlement.

FALKNERS SETTLEMENT
1784 - 1984

In 1784, at or near this site, the United Empire Loyalists landed and founded this settlement which was named in honour of William Falkner, J.P., the representative in the area of Sir John Johnson. Many of these settlers are buried in this cemetery. This plaque is also placed here in memory of John & James Dunlop & their descendants.

The Lancaster Township Bicentennial Committee.
June 23rd 1984

My "official" research had ended as it had begun, in a graveyard. To mark the end of a successful venture, we stopped in Morrisburg at the Sober Pub and Restaurant, a place that probably would not have been Harry's first choice for a refreshment break.

>–·–◊–·–○–·–◊–·–<

Finally, everything was checked off the long "to do" list that I had drawn up ten years before. I resigned myself to the fact that I would be unable to go to all of Harry McLean's locations, find every shred of material written about him or learn what he did every minute of every day. I'll eventually visit Wolfe's Cove, Flin Flon, Hawk Lake and Washburn, just to say that I've seen all of the cairns. I hope to some day visit McLean's more exotic destinations like Katima Mulilo on the Zambezi River or Rome and Paris with their epicurean delights, and maybe even drop in for a visit with the Pope. But as the saying goes, "One can never read all the books in the world, nor travel all its roads." The time had come to finish the book.

Notes

The following abbreviations are used in the notes:

ABC = Andrew Braid Cook
ANS = Archives of Nova Scotia
AO = Archives of Ontario
GFHS = Grand Falls Historical Society
HFM = Harry Falconer McLean
IRS = Institute for Regional Studies, North Dakota State University Libraries
LAC = Library and Archives Canada
MANY = Municipal Archives of New York
MHS = Montana Historical Society
MUA = McGill University Archives
SHSND = State Historical Society of North Dakota
TFRBL = Thomas Fisher Rare Book Library, University of Toronto
WLMK = William Lyon Mackenzie King

Prologue: On Being a Character

1. William O. Grenalds, "Frontier Buster," *American Magazine,* May 1932, 52.
2. Walter Turner, "Bountiful Harry McLean," Montreal *Standard* (1943?), 11.
3. WLMK Diary, July 29, 1947. Available at www.collectionscanada.ca. Diaries of Prime Minister William Lyon Mackenzie King, MG26-J13, LAC.
4. John Curless "Jack" Puddington, interview by author (tape recording, Ottawa, Ont., Sept. 26, 1997).
5. Leslie Roberts, "A Pair of Aces, Frontier Style," *Canadian Magazine,* June 1932, 7.
6. Harry McLean, quoted by John MacLean, " 'Mr. X' He Threw Away $50,000 but Now Is a Lonely Man," *Toronto Telegram,* July 12, 1956, 12.
7. Frederick Griffin, "Men against the Moose," *Toronto Star Weekly,* Jan. 24, 1932, 1.
8. Frederick I. Ker, interview by Charles Hyson (tape recording, Toronto, Ont., Oct. 12, 1973). LAC, HFM Coll.
9. Roberts, "A Pair of Aces, Frontier Style."

10. Harry McLean, quoted in "Pioneer Railroad Contractor Delights in Battling Nature," Toronto *Mail and Empire,* Mar. 18, 1930.
11. Sir Frederick Banting, War Diary, Oct. 14, 1939. TFRBL, University of Toronto.
12. WLMK Diary, Sept. 19, 1944.
13. Harry McLean, quoted by MacLean, " 'Mr. X' He Threw Away $50,000."
14. WLMK Diary, Sept. 4, 1942.
15. Russell Owen, "M'Lean's Art of Giving," *New York Times Magazine,* Apr. 9, 1944.
16. Turner, "Bountiful Harry McLean."
17. Puddington interview.
18. Grenalds, "Frontier Buster."
19. Ibid.
20. Joseph Justin McNally, interview by author (tape recording, Grimsby, Ont., Apr. 20, 2001).
21. Grenalds, "Frontier Buster."
22. Leonard H. Newman, *Harry Falconer McLean 1883–1961* (Merrickville, Ont.: n.p., n.d.).
23. Turner, "Bountiful Harry McLean."
24. Leslie Roberts, "Frontier Buster," Montreal *Standard,* May 1934, 16.
25. Turner, "Bountiful Harry McLean."
26. WLMK Diary, July 29, 1947.
27. Harry McLean, quoted in Puddington interview.
28. Turner, "Bountiful Harry McLean."
29. Harry McLean, quoted in Turner, "Bountiful Harry McLean."
30. Note written by Joseph McNally on the back of a portrait of Harry McLean.
31. Roberts, "Frontier Buster," 17.
32. Harry McLean, quoted by Nicholas Morant in draft version of article published in *CP Rail News,* Jan. 20, 1981, 6.

Introduction

1. [Ian MacKenzie?], "Canadian Railway Troops: Initial Movements – Organization in England." Ian Mackenzie Papers, MG 27, Series III B5, Vol. 1, File 2. LAC 8.
2. Harry McLean, quoted in Frederick Griffin, "Men against the Moose," *Toronto Star Weekly,* Jan. 24, 1932.
3. Shirley McLean (Switzer) Goodman, e-mail to author, Aug. 5, 2005.
4. John MacLean, "Dangled Waiter from 17th Floor," *Toronto Telegram,* July 12, 1956.
5. Paul McNally and C. E. Hyson, "H. F. McLean and the Sons of Martha Cairns," *Engineering Journal,* July–Aug. 1977, 29.
6. Ralph Hyman, as seen on *Close-Up,* CBC Toronto Kine Collection. CBC #11687, T/C May 30/62, Item #15 #072, 16mm B/W Comp. Eng., LAC.
7. MacLean, "Dangled Waiter from 17th Floor."
8. Pat Floyd, as seen on *Close-Up,* CBC Toronto Kine Collection. CBC #11687, T/C May 30/62, Item #15 #072, 16mm B/W Comp. Eng. LAC.

Chapter One: The Frontier Busters

1. W. A. Bell, quoted in Grenville M. Dodge, *How We Built the Union Pacific Railway* (Readex Microprint, 1966), 31.

2. Mary Louise Falconer (McLean), "A Biographical Sketch" (July 8, 1922), in Steven R. Day, *A Journey into the History of Canada and the United States: A Book about Falkner, MacLean, Smith, Day and Krieg* (Mukilteo, Wash.: Privately published by Steven R. Day, 2000), 92.

3. Shirley A. Leckie, *Elizabeth Bacon Custer and the Making of a Myth* (Norman, Okla., and London: University of Oklahoma Press, 1993), 153.

4. Falconer (McLean), "Biographical Sketch," in Day, *A Journey*, 92.

5. James was born circa 1798 in Lancaster, Ontario; Day, *A Journey*, 4. William Falkner was a United Empire Loyalist. He lost two thousand acres of land after fleeing the United States in June 1778. He became a Justice of the Peace and settled on the sixteen hundred acres granted to him for his service to the British government. Day, *A Journey*, 1–5.

6. James Falkner and Jane McLellan were married in Hawkesbury on January 27, 1842, before the Reverend James McNally of the Methodist Episcopal Church. Archives of Ontario microfilm MS 248, Reel 3, transcribed at homepages.rootsweb.com/~maryc/ottawadist.htm

7. Abstract Index, Township of Lochiel, Lot S½ Concession 8, Land Registry Office, Alexandria, Ontario; Day, *A Journey*, 8–9.

8. Barry B. Combs, *Westward to Promontory: Building the Union Pacific across the Plains and Mountains* (New York: Garland, 1969), 63; "Billy Falconer Is Pioneers' Pioneer: Is Student of Past," *Bismarck Tribune*, Golden Jubilee Edition, Aug. 15, 1939, 6.

9. Hazel L. Falconer, "Norman and Flora McLennan Falkner (Falconer)," in Beth Hughes Bauman and Dorothy J. Jackman, *Burleigh County: Prairie Trails to Hi-ways* (Bismarck, N.D.: Bismarck–Mandan Genealogical and Historical Society, 1978), 329.

10. Laramie was later described by the acerbic journalist and railroad historian Lucius Morris Beebe as a "suburb of Hell."

11. 1870 Wyoming Census. Information provided by Steven Day.

12. Falconer, "Norman and Flora," in Bauman and Jackman, 329. The Falkners were in Red Desert, Wyoming, as the Union Pacific and the Central Pacific joined at Promontory, Utah, on May 10, 1869. A good map of the Union Pacific's progress can be found at www.uprr.com/aboutup/maps/graphics/goldspik.gif

13. It is difficult to pinpoint when, where and why the family changed the spelling of their name from Falkner to Falconer. The First Methodist Church in Brainerd recorded John McLean's marriage to Helen Falconer on September 4, 1873 (www.rootsweb.com/~mncwcghs/mfm1873.htm). One can assume that the name change took place somewhere between Wyoming and Minnesota. Steven Day points out that the family believed they were related to royalty. There are indications that they may have changed their name to appear more closely related to William Falconer, the Earl of Kintyre, in the hope of inheriting some of his estate; Day, *A Journey*, 95.

14. Falconer, "Norman and Flora," in Bauman and Jackman, 329.

15. Falconer (McLean), "Biographical Sketch," in Day, *A Journey*, 92.

16. Biographical Note, Jay Cooke Papers, University of Delaware Library, Special Collections (http://www.lib.udel.edu/ud/spec/findaids/cooke.htm).

17. Leckie, *Elizabeth Bacon Custer*, 154.

18. *Treaty of Fort Laramie*, 1868. To this day, ownership of the Black Hills remains the subject of a legal dispute between the U.S. government and the Sioux.

19. North Dakota State Department, *History of Fort Abraham Lincoln* (http://www.ndparks.com/Parks/Lincoln/History.htm).

20. Hazel L. Falconer, "John McLean Family," in Bauman and Jackman, *Burleigh County: Prairie Trails to Hi-ways*, 333. John attended Prince of Wales College in Prince Edward Island and

taught school for a year: "John A. M'Lean, Pioneer, Dies in Boston," *Bismarck Tribune,* Aug. 2, 1916, 1.

21. Bismarck was originally named Edwinton in honour of Edwin L. Johnson, chief engineer of the Northern Pacific Railroad. On July 17, 1873, Edwinton was renamed Bismarck in honour of the "Iron Chancellor," Prince Baron Otto Von Bismarck of Germany, in hopes that the name would attract German investment to the town and the railroad; George F. Bird and Edwin J. Taylor Jr., *History of the City of Bismarck, North Dakota: The First 100 Years 1872–1972* (Bismarck, N.D.: Bismarck Centennial Association, 1972), 11, 25.

22. "Billy Falconer Is Pioneers' Pioneer," *Bismarck Tribune,* Aug. 15, 1939, 6; Clement Lounsberry, "Founder of Tribune Tells Story of Brave Old Days in Bismarck," *Bismarck Tribune,* July 7, 1928, 3.

23. Bird and Taylor, *History of the City of Bismarck, North Dakota,* 76.

24. Earl C. Leslie, "First Methodist Church, Brainerd, Minnesota, Marriages 1873–1889" (http://www.rootsweb.com/~mncwcghs/mfm1873.htm).

25. Article by William A. Falconer in the *Bismarck Capital,* May 13, 1932, reprinted in Day, *A Journey,* 34.

26. The new city directory was released in September 1879. The finished product revealed some vital statistics for the city, as follows: male adults – 1,024; bakers – 4; dentist – 1; doctors – 4; lawyers – 9; general merchandise – 6; mechanics – 96; ministers – 4; saloons – 24; taxidermist – 1; *Bismarck Tribune,* Sept. 19, 1879 (Vol. 7, no. 17), 1.

27. Bird and Taylor, *History of the City of Bismarck, North Dakota,* 19.

28. William A. Falconer, *Early History of Burleigh County* (n.p., n.d.). IRS.

29. Mary L. McLean, "Reminiscences of Frontier Life," read at meeting of Current Event Club, held at the residence of Mrs. Frank Grambs, 32 Broadway, Bismarck, North Dakota, in Oct. 1907. Copy of document provided to the author by Steven Day.

30. William A. Falconer, *Early Experience of W. A. Falconer: Pioneer Resident of Bismarck, Dakota Territory* (n.p., n.d.). IRS.

31. Leckie, *Elizabeth Bacon Custer,* 162.

32. Colonel Clement A. Lounsberry, *Early History of North Dakota* (Ch. 21: Politics in Indian Affairs) (Duluth, Minn.: F. H. Lounsberry, 1913), 313–314.

33. *Bismarck Tribune,* June 17, 1874, from Herbert Krause and Gary D. Olson, *Prelude to Glory: A Newspaper Accounting of Custer's 1874 Expedition to the Black Hills* (Sioux Falls, S.D.: Brevet Press, 1974), 11.

34. *Treaty of Fort Laramie,* 1868.

35. For instance, cf. *Chicago Daily Inter-ocean,* Aug. 28, 1874, 1, in Krause and Olson, *Prelude to Glory,* 1.

36. Krause and Olson, *Prelude to Glory,* 3–4.

37. Elizabeth B. Custer, *Boots and Saddles or, Life in Dakota with General Custer,* Vol. 17 in Western Frontier Library series (Norman, Okla., and London: University of Oklahoma Press, 1961), 200.

38. Richard Slotkin, *The Fatal Environment: The Myth of the Frontier in the Age of Industrialization, 1800–1890* (New York: Atheneum, 1985), 418–419, quoted in Leckie, *Elizabeth Bacon Custer,* 169.

39. Falconer, *Early Experience of W. A. Falconer.*

40. Falconer (McLean), "Biographical Sketch," in Day, *A Journey,* 93.

41. Falconer, *Early Experience of W. A. Falconer.*

42. Mary L. McLean, "Reminiscences of Frontier Life."

43. Bird and Taylor, *History of the City of Bismarck,* 77–78.

44. Mary L. McLean, "Reminiscences of Frontier Life."

45. Obituary, *Bismarck Tribune,* Nov. 4, 1874.

46. Cemetery Records, Oakland Cemetery, St. Paul, Minnesota, re: Lot No. 3, Block No. 17 – John A. McLean owner.

47. Day, *A Journey,* 33.

48. Falconer, *Early History of Burleigh County.* In the middle of William A. Falconer's description of the murder and the subsequent deaths of the sheriff and his associate was the hair-raising description of an attempt to recover the bodies. It was a digression and did not fit well in the text of the chapter; however, I could not leave it out of the book altogether. The description made my skin crawl:

> Finally a French man by the name of Joe Laundre, a tinner by trade, who was working in the hardware store of H. F. Douglas, decided he would do something to recover the bodies. Laundre made a large oblong box of heavy tin; the box was about eight feet long and three feet square. He put a window in the front and a door in the rear; there were four heavy iron rings fastened to the corners of the box and an air tube connected so as to give air into the box. When all was ready, Joe loaded the box into a sleigh and a large crowd of men went along to the scene of the drowning.
>
> Arriving at the air hole the box was unloaded and placed on the ice; then Laundre called for volunteers – someone who would crawl into the box and be let down into the water. Laundre's diving bell did not appeal to the spectators and they were reluctant to take a chance with their lives. Finally, L. N. Griffin, as brave a man as ever migrated to the West, said "I will go in." Griff, as he was commonly called, crawled into the tin box and the box was pushed into the water and down under the ice. Strong inch ropes were fastened to each upper corner of the box and two men held each rope. The eight men holding the ropes let the box drift down the river over fifty feet under the ice. Laundre would call out "Griff, can you see anything?" But the trouble was that Laundre's contraption would not sink to the bottom of the river; it kept close to the underside of the ice all [the] time and while in the box Mr. Griffin could not see a thing. The box was hauled out and Mr. Griffin appeared none the worse for his experience. But poor Joe Laundre – the boys made lots of fun of him and his diving bell.

49. Ibid.

50. Elwyn B. Robinson, *The Themes of North Dakota History,* revision of address delivered by Elwyn B. Robinson at the University of North Dakota (http://www.library.und.edu/Collections/Robinson/themes.html).

51. Ed Henderson, "A Monstrous Wrong," *Bismarck Daily Tribune,* Mar. 7, 1901, 8.

52. "The City Election: The People's Ticket the Winning One," *Bismarck Tribune,* Apr.7, 1875,4.

53. John A. McLean Inaugural Address, *Bismarck Weekly Tribune,* Apr. 14, 1875.

54. John A. McLean, "An Ordinance Concerning Dogs," *Bismarck Tribune,* May 5, 1875.

55. Falconer, *Early Experience of W. A. Falconer.*

56. "The Townsite Contest," *Bismarck Tribune,* Nov. 4, 1874.

57. Bird and Taylor, *History of the City of Bismarck,* 13.

58. "The Townsite Contest."

59. John A. McLean Inaugural Address.

60. "The Townsite Contest."

61. "Mayor McLean," *Bismarck Tribune,* Nov. 26, 1877.

62. "John A. M'Lean, Pioneer, Dies in Boston."
63. "The Decision," *Bismarck Tribune,* Nov. 27, 1875.
64. Bird and Taylor, *History of the City of Bismarck,* 23.
65. "A Mammoth Establishment," *Bismarck Tribune,* Oct. 27, 1875.
66. Ward Renwick, "William C. (A.) Falconer Biography," Historical Data Project, Liberty Memorial Building, Bismarck, North Dakota.
67. Ibid.
68. Falconer, *Early History of Burleigh County.*

Chapter Two: Those Stirring Times

1. W. A. Falconer, *Early History of Burleigh County* (n.p., n.d.). IRS.
2. "The Question of Arms," *Bismarck Tribune,* Oct. 27 (Vol. 3, no. 16), 1875.
3. Day, *A Journey,* 35.
4. McLean, "Reminiscences of Frontier Life."
5. Lounsberry, "Founder of Tribune Tells Story," 3. The gold sample is in the possession of McLean's niece, Hazel L. Falconer: Hazel L. Falconer, "John McLean Family," in Bauman and Jackman, *Burleigh County,* 333.
6. William A. Falconer, *Bismarck Tribune,* May 13, 1932, quoted in Day, *A Journey,* 36.
7. Bird and Taylor, *History of the City of Bismarck, North Dakota,* 27.
8. William A. Falconer, *Bismarck Tribune,* May 13, 1932, quoted in Day, *A Journey,* 34–35.
9. Leckie, *Elizabeth Bacon Custer,* 175; Derek Batten, *Custer and the Battle of the Little Big Horn* (http://www.bbc.co.uk/history/war/custer_battle_02.shtml).
10. Lounsberry, "Founder of Tribune Tells Story," *Bismarck Tribune,* July 7, 1928, 3; "John A. M'Lean, Pioneer, Dies in Boston."
11. "Chamber of Commerce: They Adopt Resolutions to Work for the Bismarck Route," *Bismarck Weekly Tribune,* Feb. 9, 1876, 1.
12. Ibid.
13. Lounsberry, "Founder of Tribune Tells Story," 3.
14. Frank E. Vyzralek, Archivist, State Historical Society of North Dakota, letter to C. E. Hyson, dated June 24, 1974, quoting Lounsberry, *Early History of North Dakota.*
15. Leckie, *Elizabeth Bacon Custer,* 169.
16. Lounsberry, "Founder of Tribune Tells Story," 3.
17. Ibid.; Leckie, *Elizabeth Bacon Custer,* 177–178; Custer, *Boots and Saddles,* 210.
18. Lounsberry, "Founder of Tribune Tells Story," 3; Custer, *Boots and Saddles,* 210–211.
19. Custer, *Boots and Saddles,* 211.
20. Ibid., 212.
21. Ibid.
22. Ibid. Whether it was because her corset was too tight or she had a flair for the dramatic, Elizabeth Custer fainted a lot. When the General came home, she would rush outside and faint just in time for him to catch her.
23. Lounsberry, "Founder of Tribune Tells Story," 3; Custer, *Boots and Saddles,* 213.
24. Leckie, *Elizabeth Bacon Custer,* 178–180.
25. McLean's case: *John A. McLean v. The United States.* United States Court of Claims, 17 Ct. Cl. 83; 1881.
26. "Mrs. Mary McLean, Bismarck Pioneer, Dead: Widow of City's First Mayor, Friend of Custer, Dies from Illness," *Bismarck Tribune,* Oct. 14, 1928.

27. "Bismarck Bade Farewell to Custer 53 Years Ago," *Bismarck Tribune,* May 17, 1929, 1.

28. Undated Elizabeth Custer interview, *Monroe Evening News,* Apr. 7, 1933, quoted in Leckie, *Elizabeth Bacon Custer,* 182.

29. Leckie, *Elizabeth Bacon Custer,* 191. Note on the breaking news of the Battle of the Little Big Horn: At page 190 in her book *Elizabeth Bacon Custer and the Making of a Myth,* Shirley Leckie writes that before the news of the battle was officially announced by the military, an Indian scout named Horn Toad told the horrific story to the military wives, but it was dismissed as a rumour. Horn Toad said, "Custer killed. Whole command killed…Speckled Cock, Indian scout, just come. Rode pony many miles. Pony tired. Indian tired. Say Custer shoot himself – at end. Say all dead." Just like in the old movies.

30. Colonel Lounsberry wrote that the story of Custer's last battle "is a part of the history of Dakota…because of those slain, every one of whom had friends or acquaintances at Bismarck. Some had wives or children there, others near and dear ones. All had friends, and friendship seemed closer then, when Bismarck was a frontier city."

31. "Mayor McLean," *Bismarck Tribune,* Nov. 26, 1877.

32. *Bismarck Tribune,* Feb. 21, 1878; Feb. 21, 1880; Apr. 16, 1880; May 28, 1880.

33. "Articles of Association: Bismarck, Ft. Lincoln and Black Hills Railroad Company," *Bismarck Tribune,* Nov. 28, 1877; "The Railroad Meeting," *Bismarck Tribune,* Apr. 14, 1882.

34. "The Republican Convention," *Bismarck Tribune,* Sept. 1, 1882.

35. "The Stark Farm," *Bismarck Tribune,* Chamber of Commerce Edition, Jan. 27, 1882. John McLean's partner, Robert Macnider, and his family suffered a terrible loss. On March 19, 1878, his wife, Eliza, gave birth to twins. On April 16, 1880, the *Tribune* reported that Robert Macnider's twin daughter Anna had died on March 27, 1880. The cause of death was thought to be "brain fever" due to a fall several weeks before.

36. "Close of a Successful Business," *Bismarck Tribune,* Oct. 6, 1882.

37. "Mortgage Sale," *Bismarck Weekly Tribune,* Nov. 3, 1882, 6.; "A Peck of Trouble," *Bismarck Weekly Tribune,* n.d., 2; McLean's case.

38. Falconer (McLean), "Biographical Sketch," in Day, *A Journey,* 92.

39. "Purely Personal," *Bismarck Tribune,* Dec. 31, 1880.

40. Falconer (McLean), "Biographical Sketch," in Day, *A Journey,* 93.

41. Day, *A Journey,* 41.

42. Cemetery Records, Oakland Cemetery, St. Paul, Minnesota, re: Lot No. 3, Block No. 17 – John A. McLean owner.

43. 1885 Dakota Territory Census; Day, *A Journey,* 41.

44. Mary L. McLean (Falconer), "Harry McLean," July 8, 1922, in Day, *A Journey,* 41.

45. "Business Meeting," *Bismarck Tribune,* Jan. 27, 1882. The first major fire in Bismarck started at the Arcade Saloon on March 15, 1877; nine buildings were destroyed. By December 1879 fire protection was the hot topic in Bismarck. John McLean was appointed to a committee to look into providing adequate fire protection for the city.

46. "Welcome to McLean County," North Dakota GenWeb Project.

47. Bird and Taylor, *History of the City of Bismarck,* 97.

48. The directors were given a one-year deadline and $50,000 to construct a brick or stone prison large enough to house one hundred twenty-five prisoners. Forty acres of land within one mile of the city was required for the project and area landowners were invited to submit bids to sell their property. After the completion of the prison, anyone convicted north of the forty-sixth parallel would be sent there to serve their sentence. *Bismarck Weekly Tribune,* June 22, 1883.

49. "Astounding Figures," *Bismarck Weekly Tribune* (abt. June 1883), 2.

50. "The Capital City," *Bismarck Weekly Tribune,* June 29, 1883, 8.

51. 1885 Dakota Territory Census; information was gathered two years earlier.

52. "A Capitol Railroad Job," North Dakota Supreme Court History, at www.court.state.nd

53. Ibid.

54. "Fibs, Facts and Fancies: The Story of a Family," *Bismarck Tribune,* July 9, 1938, 4.

55. "The Place to Live," *Bismarck Daily Tribune,* Sept. 5, 1883, 16.

56. "Married" (Miss Emma Bentley to Wm. A. Falconer), *Bismarck Weekly Tribune,* Aug. 31, 1883, 5.

57. Burleigh County Book of Remembrances at "Generation No. 3, 7. Jane McLellan." Day, *A Journey,* 143.

58. Falconer (McLean), "Biographical Sketch," in Day, *A Journey,* 93.

59. Day, *A Journey,* 125.

60. *Bismarck Daily Tribune,* Sept. 5, 1893, 3. Mattie eventually ran the photography studio herself after John White went insane. He spent at least twenty-two years in the New Westminster Asylum: epe.lac-bac.gc.ca/100/200/300/david_mattison/camera_workers/2001-09/cw1-w-names.html

61. North and South Dakota were admitted as states on November 2, 1889.

62. Crazy Horse was bayoneted in the back by a military guard on September 5, 1877. Sitting Bull was killed at Wounded Knee on December 15, 1890. Gall died in 1894.

63. *History of Fort Abraham Lincoln: The Military Years* (Bismarck: North Dakota Parks and Recreation Department, 2003). © 2003 ndparks.com/parks/Lincoln/history.htm

64. Bird and Taylor, *History of the City of Bismarck,* 103.

65. Clarice Belk, "H. F. McLean, '02, Builder of Railroads," in *The William Moore School: In the Service of the Youth of Bismarck for Fifty Years: 1883–1933* (Bismarck, N.D.: n.p., 1933), 12. IRS.

66. "Canada's Greatest Railroad Builder Spent His Boyhood in Bismarck," *Bismarck Tribune,* Mar. 12, 1931.

67. Falconer, *Early Experience of W. A. Falconer.*

Chapter Three: The Spoilers

1. *Bismarck Tribune,* Mar. 27, 1880.

2. *Bismarck Weekly Tribune,* Oct. 27, 1882.

3. Geo. W. Bowles, *Bismarck Weekly Tribune,* Sept. 5, 1899.

4. *Bismarck Tribune,* Jan. 24, 1878.

5. Ibid., Aug. 22, 1884. Kalamazoo is the world's leading grower of celery!

6. HFM to William McLean, Nov. 28, 1898. William John McLean Papers, 1898–1933, SHSND.

7. Ibid.

8. "M'Lean Funeral Will Be Tuesday," *Bismarck Tribune,* Feb. 10, 1960.

9. William J. McLean to the Editor, *Bismarck Daily Tribune,* July 5, 1898; "Soldier Boys Trip," *Bismarck Daily Tribune,* July 20, 1898, 3.

10. Ibid.

11. Ibid.

12. The *Maine* sank on February 15, 1898. "The World of 1898: The Spanish-American War." Hispanic Division, Library of Congress: loc.gov/rr/hispanic/1898/intro.html.

13. William J. McLean to the Editor, 3.

14. "The World of 1898: The Spanish-American War."
15. M. H. Jewell of the *Bismarck Tribune* to the President of the Military Examining Board, Presidio, San Francisco, Sept. 29, 1900. William John McLean Papers, 1898–1933, SHSND.
16. "Elizabeth Robins at Cape Nome," *Seattle Post Intelligencer,* Aug. 19, 1900, edited by Joanne E. Gates, referencing *The National Cyclopedia of American Biography* (New York: James White & Company, 1945), 92–95 (www.jsu.edu).
17. Noyes, No. 701 Circuit Court of Appeals, Ninth Circuit, 121 F. 209; 1902 U.S. App. Jan. 6, 1902.
18. Ibid.
19. "A Monstrous Wrong," *Bismarck Daily Tribune,* Mar. 8, 1901.
20. Alexander McKenzie, 180 U.S. 536, Supreme Court of the United States.
21. "A Monstrous Wrong."
22. "M'Kenzie Pardoned by M'Kinley," *Bismarck Tribune,* May 25, 1901.
23. Noyes, No. 701 Circuit Court of Appeals, Ninth Circuit, 121 F. 209; 1902 U.S. App. Jan. 6, 1902.
24. Rex Beach, *The Spoilers* (New York: A. L. Burt, 1905), 307.
25. McLean (Falconer), "Harry McLean," in Day, *A Journey,* 41.
26. "Native Son's Work on Monstrous Dam Shown Here in Film," *Bismarck Tribune,* May 25, 1933.
27. "The City," *Bismarck Daily Tribune,* Mar. 17, 1902.
28. *The William Moore School: In the Service of the Youth of Bismarck for Fifty Years: 1883–1933* (Bismarck, N.D.: n.p., 1933), 22. IRS.
29. Charles Switzer, Untitled Paper on Harry McLean and Dominion Construction (unpublished, handwritten), Nov. 1972. HFM fonds, LAC, Vol 1, File 1-10, MS, 1–2. MG 30, B 131.
30. Guide to the A. B. Cook papers, Biographical Note, Northwest Digital Archives, at nwda-db.wsulibs.wsu.edu.
31. Clarice Belk, "H. F. McLean, '02, Builder of Railroads."
32. Prairie Public Television/North Dakota Public Radio, "Dakota Business College," *Dakota Datebook,* Feb. 11, 2004, at www.prairiepublic.org.
33. McLean (Falconer), "Harry McLean," in Day, *A Journey*, 41.
34. Switzer, Untitled Paper on Harry McLean and Dominion Construction, 1.
35. Ibid.
36. Victor Lauriston, *Romantic Kent* (Chatham, Ont.: Shepherd Printing, 1952), at Deeks Genealogy jhowell.com.
37. Switzer, Untitled Paper on Harry McLean and Dominion Construction, 1.
38. Leslie Roberts, "A Pair of Aces, Frontier Style."
39. Affidavit of ABC and Louis Nelson re: *Thomas Burke v. Cook and Hinds Railroad Contractors,* 1906, ABC Collection, Coll. 280, Bx/Fd. No. 47/8 MHS.
40. "People Who Come and Go," *Bismarck Daily Tribune,* Nov. 18, 1906.
41. 1906 Marriages, Peel County, Ontario, MS 932 # 15748-06, Archives of Ontario transcribed at http://homepages.rootsweb.com~/peel06.htm.
42. Switzer, Untitled Paper on Harry McLean and Dominion Construction.
43. "Harry McLean Makes Good," *Bismarck Daily Tribune,* Aug. 18, 1910 (reprinting an article from the *"St. John's Daily Telegraph"* – likely the *Saint John Daily Telegraph*).
44. Ibid.
45. Ibid.
46. Sandy Rose, "Arsenic, Herefords and Old Lace: The Mystery and Majesty with the Legends and Tragedies of the Renowned Montana A. B. Cook Family," unpublished, undated paper available at Canyon Ferry Mansion, North Townsend, Montana.
47. ABC to HFM, May 19, 1909. A. B. Cook Papers, Coll. 280, Bx/Fd No. 57/11, MHS.

48. Ker interview.
49. Frederick I. Ker to C. E. Hyson. HFM Collection. LAC., MG 30 Vol. 2.
50. Ker interview.
51. Ibid.
52. Rev. Donald R. Sutherland to the author, Jan. 27, 2005.
53. Ker interview; Switzer, Untitled Paper on Harry McLean and Dominion Construction.
54. Switzer, Untitled Paper on Harry McLean and Dominion Construction.
55. "M'Lean Funeral Will Be Tuesday," *Bismarck Tribune,* Feb. 10, 1960; [C. E. Hyson] Paper, "Dominion Construction Corporation Limited," Nov. 22, 1973. TS, 2. MG 30 B 131 Vol. 2, File 2-2 Dominion Const (LAC).
56. [C. E. Hyson] Paper, "Dominion Construction Corporation Limited," Nov. 22, 1973, 1. TS, MG 30 B 131 Vol. 2, File 2-2 Dominion Const (LAC).
57. Various Dominion Construction employees claim that McLean met Kipling and saw him read his poem "The Sons of Martha." I was unable to confirm any direct correspondence between Kipling and McLean. However, from discussions with Karen Smith, Librarian at Dalhousie University, and with Dr. Thomas Pinney, I have determined it is quite likely that McLean saw Kipling during the latter's tour of Canada in 1907. Charles Switzer reported that McLean and Kipling met at a Halifax hotel and spent an evening together; however, Kipling scholars advise that Kipling never set foot in Halifax and that he saw the foggy city only from the rail of a ship. It is a great story, but, unless they were mistaken about the venue, that, I'm afraid, is all it is.
58. George M. Deeks to ABC. A. B. Cook Papers, Coll. 280, Bx/Fd No. 57/10, MHS.
59. Memorandum of Agreement, George S. Deeks and ABC. ABC Papers, Coll. 280, Bx/Fd No. 57/10, MHS.
60. *Cook v. Deeks,* [1915] O.J. No. 163, Mar. 2, 1915.
61. Ibid.
62. "Bismarck Boy Makes Good," *Bismarck Daily Tribune,* Apr. 15, 1912. In the early morning hours of April 15, 1912, the *Titanic* sank.
63. "Bismarck Youth Died at Toronto," *Bismarck Weekly Tribune,* Nov. 1, 1912.
64. Walter McLean to ABC, Jan. 9, 1910. A. B. Cook Papers, Coll. 280, Bx/Fd No. 57/10, MHS.
65. [C. E. Hyson] Paper, "Dominion Construction Corporation Limited," 2.
66. Ker interview.
67. Ibid.
68. Ibid.
69. Articles of Incorporation, Cook Construction Co., July 31, 1912. ABC Papers, Coll. 280, Bx/Fd No. 47/17, MHS; Affidavit of ABC regarding customs seizure, June 6, 1914. ABC Papers, Coll. 280, Bx/Fd No. 47/9, MHS.
70. Walter McLean to ABC, July 18, 1912. ABC Papers, Coll. 280, Bx/Fd No. 12/23, MHS.
71. "Bismarck Youth Died at Toronto."
72. "Attended Her Son's Funeral," *Bismarck Weekly Tribune,* Nov. 8, 1912.
73. "Society Notes," *Bismarck Daily Tribune,* Jan. 13, 1913.
74. "City News: Mary McLean Returned," *Bismarck Daily Tribune,* May 10, 1913.
75. Affidavit of ABC regarding customs seizure, June 6, 1914.
76. Ker interview.
77. *Cook v. Hinds,* 44 D.L.R. 586, Ontario Supreme Court, Mar. 1, 1918.
78. ABC to the National Bank of Montana, July 19, 1913. ABC Papers, Coll. 280, Bx/Fd No. 47/21, MHS; 1913, City of Montreal, Direction of Public Works, Specification of the

Works to be done for the Enlargement of the Aqueduct in accordance with the By-Law No. ( ). ABC Papers, Coll. 280, Bx/Fd No. 47/28, MHS.

79. ABC to Mr. Geo. Prince, Chairman Board of Directors, Merchants National Bank, St. Paul., July 19, 1913. ABC Papers, Coll. 280, Bx/Fd No. 47/21, MHS.

80. W. J. Boland to ABC, Oct. 4, 1913. ABC Papers, Coll. 280, Bx/Fd No. 47/3, MHS.

81. Ker interview; Statement of Claim, *The City of Montreal v. The Cook Construction Company, et al.,* Dec. 17, 1915. ABC Papers, Coll. 280, Bx/Fd No. 47/28, MHS.

82. Ker interview.

83. Statement of Claim, *Montreal v. Cook Construction.*

84. Ker interview; ABC Papers, Coll. 280, Bx/Fd No. 47/18, MHS.

85. Pierre Taschereau, "Development of the Halifax Railway Cut (1912–1918)," extract from "South End Railway Cutting: Report No. 2 of the Area Studies Groups," *Halifax Field Naturalists News,* no. 27 (Spring) 1982, at www.halifax.ca/greenway/interpretation/railway_cut_history.htm.

86. Customs Department, Notice of Seizure, Feb. 20, 1914. ABC Papers, Coll. 280, Bx/Fd No. 47/9, MHS.

87. O. W. Memsen to G. Roys, Bucyrus Co., Apr. 23, 1914. ABC Papers, Coll. 280, Bx/Fd No. 47/21, MHS; HFM to ABC, June 13, 1914. ABC Papers, Coll. 280, Bx/Fd No. 47/23, MHS.

88. Vladimir Dedijer, "European Crisis, July–August 1914, Sarajevo," in *History of the 20th Century,* Vol. 16 (n.p., n.d.), 437.

Chapter Four: Triumph and Disaster

1. [Ian MacKenzie?], "Canadian Railway Troops: Initial Movements – Organization in England," ch. 2, 9. Ian Mackenzie Papers. LAC.

2. [MacKenzie?], "Canadian Railway Troops," 2–3; "Railways and the War," in *The Times History and Encyclopedia of the War,* Vol. 6, part 70 (ch. C) (London: Sampson Low, Marston, 1916), 170–171.

3. Fred F. Angus, "The Canadian Railway Troops in World War I: 'Lest We Forget'," *Canadian Rail,* no. 437 (Nov.–Dec. 1993), 192.

4. Ibid.; [MacKenzie?], "Canadian Railway Troops," 8–9.

5. Ibid.

6. [MacKenzie?], "Canadian Railway Troops," 11.

7. Angus, "The Canadian Railway Troops," 192.

8. Ibid., 192; Peter Wilson, ed., *Canadian Railway Troops during World War I: 1st Battalion Canadian Overseas Railway Construction Corps November 1917–April 1918* (Campbellford, Ont.: Wilson's Publishing, 1995).

9. Ibid.

10. "Corps Advance Agent," Montreal *Gazette,* Apr. 1, 1915. ABC Papers, Coll. 280, Bx/Fd No. 46/10, MHS.

11. Switzer, Untitled Paper on Harry McLean and Dominion Construction.

12. HFM, Diary, Africa, Nov. 8, 1951. HFM Papers. MG 27 III C 18, Vol. 22. LAC; HFM to ABC, Mar. 31, 1915. ABC Papers, Coll. 280, Bx/Fd No. 46/10, MHS.

13. Angus, "The Canadian Railway Troops," 192.

14. Switzer, Untitled Paper on Harry McLean and Dominion Construction. "Biography with Battalion Orders appointing HFM Honorary Lt. Col of No. 2 Construction Battalion," Mar. 14, 1917. HFM Papers. MG 30, B 131, Vol. 1. LAC.

15. MacLean, " 'Mr. X' He Threw Away $50,000."

16. HFM to ABC, Apr. 12, 1915. ABC Papers, Coll. 280, Bx/Fd No. 46/10, MHS. The *Lapland* was on the scene after the sinking of the *Titanic,* picking up passengers.

17. A few weeks later, on May 7, 1915, German submarines sank the *Lusitania* off the coast of Ireland; 1,198 people died, including 360 Canadians and Elbert Hubbard, author of *A Message to Garcia* (http://www.firstworldwar.com/features/lusitania.htm).

18. Passenger record, Apr. 24, 1915 (ellisisland.org).

19. [C. E. Hyson], "Dominion Construction Corporation Limited," Nov. 22, 1973. TS, HFM Coll. MG 30 B131, Vol. 2, File 2-2 Dominion Construction, LAC.

20. HFM to ABC, May 9, 1915. ABC Papers, Coll. 280, Bx/Fd No. 46/10, MHS.

21. HFM to ABC, undated. ABC Papers, Coll. 280, Bx/Fd No. 46/10, MHS.

22. Ibid.

23. HFM to ABC, May 28, 1915. ABC Papers, Coll. 280, Bx/Fd No. 46/10, MHS.

24. Ibid.

25. HFM to ABC, June 8, 1915. ABC Papers, Coll. 280, Bx/Fd No. 46/10, MHS.

26. "Former Publisher of *Spectator* Dies," Hamilton *Spectator,* Sept. 26, 1977.

27. Charles Switzer, Attestation Papers, Mar. 13, 1915, Canadian Over-Seas Expeditionary Force. LAC.

28. ABC to HFM, June 10, 1915. ABC Papers, Coll. 280, Bx/Fd No. 46/10, MHS.

29. Angus, "The Canadian Railway Troops," 193.

30. Application, The Honorable Orlando T. Daniels, Attorney General for the Province of Nova Scotia on the relation of G. Fred Peareon and Cook Construction Company, Limited, and Wheaton Brothers, Aug. 3, 1915. ABC Papers, Coll. 280, Bx/Fd No. 47/21, MHS.

31. HFM to ABC, Aug. 5, 1915. ABC Papers, Coll. 280, Bx/Fd No. 46/10, MHS.

32. Ibid., Aug. 13, 1915.

33. Ibid.

34. "Carlos Warfield Died in 59th Year," Montreal *Gazette,* Feb. 19, 1923.

35. Carlos Warfield to ABC, Sept. 17, 1915. ABC Papers, Coll. 280, Bx/Fd No. 18/34, MHS.

36. Ibid., Nov. 6, 1915. ABC Papers, Coll. 280, Bx/Fd No. 18/34, MHS.

37. "Funeral Services Monday," *Bismarck Daily Tribune,* Dec. 12, 1915.

38. "Judge Falconer Passes Away," *Bismarck Daily Tribune,* Dec. 21, 1915.

39. Statement of Claim, *The City of Montreal v. The Cook Construction Company, et al.,* Dec. 17, 1915. ABC Papers, Coll. 280, Bx/Fd No. 47/28, MHS.

40. Ibid.

41. "City News," *Bismarck Daily Tribune,* Feb. 2, 1916.

42. "Biography with Battalion Orders," Mar. 14, 1917. HFM Papers, MG 30, B 131, Vol. 1. LAC.

43. Dr. Leonard Newman, handwritten notes on McLean correspondence, undated, private collection, Lenore Newman, Merrickville, Ont.

44. Calvin W. Ruck, *The Black Battalion 1916–1920: Canada's Best Kept Military Secret* (Halifax: Nimbus, 1987), 14.

45. Ibid., ch. 1–2.

46. Major, Officer i/c, Railway Troop Services, Canadians to Lt. Col. the Hon. A. McDonnell, Mar. 28, 1917, Reinforcements (No. 2 Const. Co/"Coloured," C.W.R.O. 718, RG 9, Col 4464, LAC.

47. Ibid.

48. Newman, handwritten notes. Mrs. Reta McLean gave Dr. Newman many notes and letters to copy, as he was writing a biography of Harry McLean for the Historical Society in Ottawa. These notes and letters were passed along to another person intending to write a book on McLean (not this author). The book was never written and the notes and letters were never returned, but Dr. Newman's handwritten notes remain and proved to be a good source of material.

49. Ruck, *The Black Battalion,* 14.

50. Ibid., ch. 1–2. The singer Anne Murray's grandfather, Daniel, was a well-liked officer of No. 2 Construction Battalion; see the film *Honour Before Glory,* by Anthony Sherwood (Toronto: Anthony Sherwood Productions, 2001).

51. [MacKenzie?], "Canadian Railway Troops," 12.

52. Ibid., 15; Angus, "The Canadian Railway Troops," 196.

53. "Death Near in Shipwreck on the Missouri," *Bismarck Daily Tribune,* June 20, 1916.

54. Cemetery Records, Oakland Cemetery, St. Paul, Minnesota re: Lot No. 3, Block No. 17 – John A. McLean owner.

55. "M'Lean Funeral at St. Paul," *Bismarck Daily Tribune,* Aug. 6, 1916; "Mayor Lucas at M'Lean Funeral," *Bismarck Daily Tribune,* Aug. 8, 1916.

56. "M'Lean Funeral at St. Paul."

57. Patrick Watson, *The Canadians: Biographies of a Nation.* Part 13: *Sam Hughes: The Enigma* (Toronto: McArthur, 2000), 257–276.

58. Newman, handwritten notes.

59. "Mrs. H. F. McLean Dies of Burns," Toronto *Globe,* July 11, 1942.

60. Ship's manifest, Apr. 4, 1917, at ellisisland.org.

61. Irene McLean to Mr. and Mrs. A. B. Cook, Sept. 6, 1917. ABC Papers, Coll. 280, Bx/Fd No. 46/13, MHS.

62. Lt. Col. Daniel Hugh Sutherland to HFM, Feb. 17, 1917. Private collection, Reverend Donald Sutherland, River John, N.S.

63. "Biography with Battalion Orders," Mar. 14, 1917. HFM Papers. MG 30, B 131, Vol. 1. LAC.

64. Newman, handwritten notes.

65. Ruck, *The Black Battalion,* 20.

66. Ibid., 20–21.

67. [MacKenzie?], "Canadian Railway Troops," 81.

68. Ibid., 99–100.

69. HFM to ABC, July 4, 1917. ABC Papers, Coll. 280, Bx/Fd No. 46/13, MHS.

70. Ibid., Aug. 17, 1917 (two letters).

71. McLean (Falconer), "Harry McLean," in Day, *A Journey,* 42.

72. Janet F. Kitz, *Shattered City: The Halifax Explosion and the Road to Recovery* (Halifax: Nimbus, 1989), 25–26.

73. "Society," *Bismarck Evening Tribune,* Dec. 7, 1917.

74. Turner, "Bountiful Harry McLean."

75. Leslie Roberts, "Harry Falconer McLean" (n.p., n.d.).

76. Kitz, *Shattered City,* 72–73.

77. Taschereau, "Development of the Halifax Railway Cut (1912–1918)."

78. Sir Robert Borden to HFM, Dec. 12, 1917. #46553 Microfilm, Prime Minister's Correspondence, LAC.

79. Turner, "Bountiful Harry McLean."

80. "To New York," *Bismarck Evening Tribune,* Mar. 30, 1918.
81. Turner, "Bountiful Harry McLean."
82. *Citizens Association vs. City of Montreal and Cook Construction,* Dec. 10, 1917. Frederick I. Ker Collection, Archives of Ontario, Ref. F1198.
83. Cook Construction to Citizens Association, Dec. 20, 1917. Frederick I. Ker Collection, Archives of Ontario, Ref. F1198.
84. Frederick I. Ker, handwritten note on list of members of the Citizens Association (n.d.). Frederick I. Ker Collection, Archives of Ontario, Ref. F1198.
85. Corporal Hugh Gray to HFM, Nov. 9, 1917. HFM Papers. MG 30, B 131, Vol. 1. LAC; Corporal Hugh Gray to HFM, Jan. 10, 1918. HFM Papers. MG 30, B 131, Vol. 1. LAC. Gray's attestation papers show that he had two tattoos: on the left forearm a heart and arrow with the initials AL, and on the right forearm a heart and arrow with the initials BT. His wife's name was Euphemia.
86. Commonwealth War Graves Commission, "In Memory of H Gray, Corporal 1039055" (http://yard.ccta.gov.uk).
87. *Cook v. Hinds,* [1918] O.J. No. 89, Mar. 1, 1918.
88. *Cook v. Deeks,* [1916] D.L.R. 1, Feb. 23, 1916.
89. *Cook v. Hinds,* 44 D.L.R. 586, Mar. 1, 1918.
90. Settlement, Nov. 28, 1918. ABC Coll 280, Bx/Fd No. 57/11, MHS.
91. [Hyson], "Dominion Construction Corporation Limited," 1A.
92. "Charming Event of the Week Is the Reception Given by Mrs. Mary M'Lean," *Bismarck Daily Tribune,* Apr. 25, 1919.
93. "City News," *Bismarck Daily Tribune,* Apr. 25, 1919.
94. HFM to ABC, July 1, 1919. ABC Papers, Coll. 280, Bx/Fd No. 46/12, MHS.
95. Frederick Ker, autobiographical note, 1915–1921, OA. Frederick I. Ker Papers.
96. Frederick Ker to ABC, Aug. 29, 1919. F1198, Box 1, File :1.2, K001, F.I.K. Correspondence, 1915–1920 [Part B], OA.
97. "Former Publisher of *Spectator* Dies," Hamilton *Spectator,* Sept. 26, 1977.
98. Ker, autobiographical note.

Chapter Five: The Gear Engages

1. Rudyard Kipling, "The Sons of Martha," 1907. In Rudyard Kipling, *Twenty Poems* (London: Methuen, 1918).
2. Harold Bolton, interview by author (tape recording, Merrickville, Ont., Oct. 11, 1997).
3. Alexander McKenzie to ABC, Sept. 8, 1919. ABC Papers, MHS, Coll. 280, Bx/Fd. No. 12/17.
4. Switzer, Untitled Paper on Harry McLean and Dominion Construction. A marshalling yard is a multiple-track facility where trains are assembled and disassembled according to destination. A hump yard is much the same but has an incline at one end so that, after being moved by the engine, the disassembled trains can roll, using their own momentum, to separate tracks.
5. Charles Hyson, Reminiscences. HFM Collection, MG 30 B 131, Tape 7, LAC; George Richardson, "H. F. McLean: Part II, Quarries at Merrickville and Hawk Lake" (unpublished paper), HFM Coll, MG 30 B131 Vol. I, LAC, 30.
6. Richardson, "H. F. McLean," 31.

7. C. E. Hyson, "Deeks Quarry, 1919–1920" (n.p., n.d.). HFM Coll, MG 30 B131 Vol. II, LAC.
8. Harold Bolton, W. J. Evans and Edison Hanlan, "Deeks," in G. Jean Newans, *All Around the Township* (Oxford Mills, Ont.: n.p. [cerlox bound], 1984), 28.
9. Robert V. V. Nicholls, "Harry Falconer McLean, Engineer-Contractor Extraordinary" (abstract), in *Proceedings of the 1995 Annual Conference of the Canadian Society for Civil Engineering, June 1–3, 1995* (Ottawa: Canadian Society for Civil Engineering, 1995), 327.
10. Switzer, Untitled Paper on Harry McLean and Dominion Constructon; Hyson, "Deeks Quarry," 1.
11. Hyson "Deeks Quarry," 1.
12. Richardson, "H. F. McLean," 31–33.
13. Hyson, "Deeks Quarry," 1–3.
14. McNally interview; Puddington interview.
15. HFM to ABC, June 22, 1921. ABC Papers, MHS, Coll. 280, Bx/Fd. No. 46/12.
16. Ibid., Sept. 22, 1920.
17. ABC to HFM, July 11, 1921. ABC Papers, MHS, Coll. 280, Bx/Fd. No. 46/12.
18. HFM to ABC, June 22, 1921. ABC Papers, MHS, Coll. 280, Bx/Fd. No. 46/12.
19. ABC to HFM, Apr. 11, 1922. ABC Papers, MHS, Coll. 280, Bx/Fd. No. 46/12.
20. HFM to ABC, Dec. 1, 1921. ABC Papers, MHS, Coll. 280, Bx/Fd. No. 46/12.
21. Ibid., May 13, 1922.
22. Ibid., Apr. 18, 1922.
23. William Henry, *Merrickville Village: A Walking Tour* (Merrickville, Ont.: Parks Canada and Merrickville and District Historical Society, 1985), 1.
24. Larry Turner, *Merrickville: Jewel on the Rideau* (Ottawa: Petherwin Heritage, 1995), 117.
25. Henry, *Merrickville Village,* 12.
26. The MacLean name can be traced back to two clans: the Duarts and the Lochbuies. Harry McLean traced his roots to the Duart clan. Day, *A Journey,* 17, 20. Kinlochaline Castle was granted to the MacLeans of Duart in 1319 by the Lord of the Isles.
27. "Great Throng Pays Tribune to Alex. M'Kenzie, Pioneer Builder of City and Territory," *Bismarck Tribune,* June 26, 1922.
28. "Alexander McKenzie," *Bismarck Tribune,* June 28, 1922.
29. "Pioneer Efforts of Alex M'Kenzie for Bismarck Recounted by Friends," *Bismarck Tribune,* June 23, 1922.
30. Bird and Taylor, *History of the City of Bismarck, North Dakota,* 32.
31. "Alexander McKenzie," *Bismarck Tribune,* June 28, 1922.
32. "Portraits of M'Kenzie's Children by Secret Marriage Revealed Only When Will Was Read at St. Paul Following His Sudden Death," *Bismarck Tribune,* Sept. 13, 1922.
33. HFM to ABC, Nov. 9, 1922. ABC Papers, MHS, Coll. 280, Bx/Fd. No. 46/12.
34. ABC to HFM, Dec. 20, 1922.. ABC Papers, MHS, Coll. 280, Bx/Fd. No. 46/12.
35. Ibid.
36. HFM to ABC, Dec. 27, 1922. ABC Papers, MHS, Coll. 280, Bx/Fd. No. 46/12.
37. ABC to Charles B. Foster, Assistant Passenger Traffic Manager, CPR, July 13, 1922. ABC Papers, MHS, Coll. 280, Bx/Fd. No. 47/2.
38. Ibid., Jan. 24, 1923. ABC Papers, MHS, Coll. 280, Bx/Fd. No. 46/3. Victory Bonds, otherwise known as Dominion of Canada War Loans, were promoted by the Dominion government to finance the war effort.
39. W. A. MacFarlane, Manager, The Canadian Bank of Commerce, Crescent and St. Catherine Branch, Montreal to HFM, Jan. 25, 1923. ABC Papers, MHS, Coll. 280, Bx/Fd. No. 46/3.

40. ABC to George B. Flannery, Dec. 29, 1923. ABC Papers, MHS, Coll. 280, Bx/Fd. No. 8/14.

41. "Carlos Warfield Died in 59th Year," Montreal *Gazette,* Feb. 19, 1923. Warfield was buried in Prescott, Ontario.

42. Switzer, "Untitled Paper on Harry McLean." Mary McLean spent the summer of 1923 in Merrickville with Harry and Irene: "Social and Personal," *Bismarck Tribune,* July 2, 1923.

43. "Touring the Canal Zone," *Bismarck Tribune,* Mar. 17, 1924.

44. Passenger record, Mar. 23, 1924 (ellisisland.org).

45. Robert J. Surtees, *The Northern Connection: Ontario Northland since 1902* (North York, Ont.: Captus, 1992), 109–111.

46. Ibid., 109; quoting Official Statement Handed Out by Chairman, T&NO Railway, Mr. George W. Lee, Apr. 13, 1923. ONA, B-93(a) Rouyn Extension.

47. Albert Tucker, *Steam into Wilderness* (Toronto: Fitzhenry & Whiteside, 1978), 48.

48. Surtees, *The Northern Connection,* 111.

49. Catherine Stephenson, "Robert Bell and Family," in Newans, *All Around the Township,* 11.

50. Tucker, *Steam into Wilderness,* 98.

51. [C. E. Hyson] Chronology, HFM Coll, MG 30, B-131, Vol I, File 1-20; Surtees, *The Northern Connection,* 111.

52. Surtees, *The Northern Connection,* 115–118.

53. Ibid., 118.

54. Ibid., 119; Tucker, *Steam into Wilderness,* 85.

55. Surtees, *The Northern Connection,* 120–121.

56. Ibid., 125.

57. Tucker, *Steam into Wilderness,* 86.

58. Bolton, Evans and Hanlan, "Deeks," 28; Earl Sears, "Plant Operations at Deeks," in Newans, *All Around the Township,* 29.

59. Ibid.

60. Sears, "Plant Operations at Deeks," 30.

61. Ibid.; Bolton, Evans and Hanlan, "Deeks," 28.

62. Sears, "Plant Operations at Deeks," 30.

63. Bolton, Evans and Hanlan, "Deeks," 29.

64. Ibid., 28.

65. Joseph Kelso, interview by author (tape recording, Oxford Mills, Ont., May 31, 1997).

66. Bolton interview.

67. Ibid.

Chapter Six: Against Great Odds

1. Puddington interview. John Curless "Jack" Puddington was the son of Dr. Berton Puddington and a former Grand Falls resident.

2. Ron Levesque, "Grand Falls Hydro Station: A Monument to Man's Creative Genius," *Victoria County Record,* Jan. 14, 1987, 1; Anita Lagacé, *How Grand Falls Grew* (Saint John, N.B.: n.p., 1945), 70–73.

3. Levesque, "Grand Falls Hydro Station," 2.

4. A. C. D. Blanchard, "Power Development at Grand Falls, N.B.," *Canadian Engineer,* Vol. 53, no. 22 (Nov. 29), 1927, 562.

5. C. E. Hyson, "Sons of Martha Monuments" (n.p., n.d.), 2. HFM Collection, MG 30 B 131, Vol. 1, LAC.

6. Arthur McLaren, interview by C. E. Hyson (tape recording, Niagara Falls, Ont., Dec. 31, 1972). HFM Collection, MG 30 B 131, LAC.

7. Margaret Marceau in collaboration with Patrick McCooey, *Grand Falls Yesterdays: A History of Grand Falls* (Grand Falls, N.B.: Grand Falls Historical Society, 1991/Merritt Press, 2001), 204; Hyson reminiscences, Tape 7.

8. Hyson reminiscences, Tape 7.

9. "Will Return Thursday," *Bismarck Tribune,* July 21, 1926.

10. Marceau with McCooey, *Grand Falls Yesterdays,* 203.

11. Puddington interview.

12. Ibid.

13. Ibid.

14. See Appendix 3.

15. Puddington interview.

16. Blanchard, "Power Development," 559–560.

17. Marceau with McCooey, *Grand Falls Yesterdays,* 204.

18. Blanchard, "Power Development," 560.

19. Ibid., 561.

20. Ibid., 560.

21. Webster's dictionary defines a cofferdam as "a watertight temporary structure enclosing part of a body of water to enable it to be pumped dry for construction purposes, etc."

22. A. C. D. Blanchard, "Construction Methods on Grand Falls, N.B., Hydro-Electric Development: Rapid Progress Made Possible by Harmonizing Working Schedule," *Contract Record and Engineering Review,* Nov. 23, 1927, 1187.

23. Blanchard, "Power Development," 559.

24. Blanchard "Construction Methods," 1189; Hyson reminiscences, Tape 7.

25. Blanchard, "Construction Methods," 1190.

26. Marceau with McCooey, *Grand Falls Yesterdays,* 123.

27. Puddington interview.

28. Hyson interview.

29. Blanchard, "Power Development," 599.

30. Blanchard, "Construction Methods," 1190.

31. Marceau with McCooey, *Grand Falls Yesterdays,* 204–205.

32. Puddington interview.

33. Blanchard, "Power Development," 561.

34. Puddington interview.

35. Ibid.

36. Ibid.

37. "Tunney/Dempsey 1927 Fight Announcement" (genetunney.org). Tunney won the fight by decision.

38. Puddington interview.

39. "Social and Personal," *Bismarck Tribune,* Nov. 10, 1927.

40. Blanchard, "Construction Methods," 1190.

41. Marceau with McCooey, *Grand Falls Yesterdays,* 205.

42. Hyson reminiscences, Tape 7.

43. Marceau with McCooey, *Grand Falls Yesterdays,* 123.

44. H. G. Acres, "The Maritimes' Largest Project," *Electrical News,* June 15, 1927, 82; Blanchard, "Construction Methods," 1192.

45. Acres, "The Maritimes' Largest Project," 81.

46. Ibid.
47. Ibid., 82.
48. Ibid., 81.
49. Puddington interview.
50. "Little Red God," in Robert Fotheringham, ed., *Songs of Men* (New York: Houghton Mifflin/Cambridge, Mass.: Riverside Press, 1918).

Chapter Seven: The Baloney Road

1. J. E. Preston-Muddock, *The Sunless City* (London: F. V. White, 1905), quoted in *Sci-Fi Lives!! In Northern Canada!!* City of Flin Flon, Manitoba, promotional pamphlet (n.p., n.d.).
2. Valerie Hedman, Loretta Yauck and Joyce Henderson, *Flin Flon* (Flin Flon, Man.: Flin Flon Historical Society, 1974), 4.
3. Preston-Muddock, *The Sunless City,* quoted in *Sci-Fi Lives!! In Northern Canada!!*
4. Ibid.
5. Hedman, Yauck and Henderson, *Flin Flon,* 11.
6. Ibid., 12.
7. Ibid.
8. Ibid., 12–20.
9. Ibid., 8–9.
10. Ibid., 37.
11. "Gertrude Vanderbilt Whitney" (biography.ms). H. P. Whitney also enjoyed his thoroughbred racehorses. The contest for the Triple Crown in 1927 ended with the Whitney horses Whiskery winning the Kentucky Derby and Bostonian the Preakness. Another stable owned Chance Shot, winner of the Belmont Stakes. So Whitney settled for winning two out of three of thoroughbred racing's top jewels that year.
12. Hedman, Yauck and Henderson, *Flin Flon,* 38, 52.
13. "Lines Reaching Further North," *Canadian National Railways Magazine,* Apr. 1928, 37.
14. "Agreement Reached with Provincial Government and the Whitney Interests," *The Pas Herald and Mining News,* Nov. 18, 1927; research notes, M. Lunam.
15. *The Operation of a Railway to the Flin Flon Mines Act,* RSM 1990, c. 133.
16. "Lines Reaching Further North," 37.
17. "Flin Flon Option Definitely Taken Up," *The Pas Herald and Mining News,* Dec. 2, 1927; research notes, M. Lunam.
18. Hon. Frank Oliver, ex-commissioner, Board of Railway Commissioners, "Manitoba Northern Railway Construction to Flinflon Mine," *Canadian Railway and Marine World,* Nov. 1928, 637.
19. Jack Paterson, "Steel's March to Flin Flon," *Maclean's,* Oct. 15, 1929, 9.
20. Switzer, Untitled Paper on Harry McLean and Dominion Construction.
21 Robert Ayre, "New Line to Tap Mineral Wealth," *Canadian National Railway Magazine,* Dec. 1928, 11; Paul McNally and C. E. Hyson, "H. F. McLean and the Sons of Martha Cairns," *Engineering Journal,* July–Aug. 1977, 29; Bird and Taylor, *History of the City of Bismarck, North Dakota,* 62–63.
22. "Work Commenced on Flin Flon Railway," *The Pas Herald and Mining News,* Dec. 16, 1927; research notes, M. Lunam.
23. Oliver, "Manitoba Northern Railway Construction," 637.
24. *The Operation of a Railway to the Flin Flon Mines Act.* RSM 1990, c. 133.
25. Ibid.
26. *The Operation of a Railway to the Flin Flon Mines Act.*

27. (Lt. Colonel) Kenneth Alan Ramsay, Service Records, World War I RG 150, Acc.# 92-93/166 Box 8084, LAC; Geoffrey W. Taylor, *The Railway Contractors: The Story of John W. Stewart, His Enterprises and Associates* (Victoria: Morriss Publishing, 1988), 108. Colonel Kenneth Alan Ramsay is not to be confused with Colonel Colin Worthington Pope Ramsey, who was Commander of the CORCC and partner, briefly, of Sam Deeks and Dominion Construction.

28. Charles Switzer, Service Records, World War I RG 150, Acc. # 92-93/166, Vol 9469, LAC.

29. Jack B. Humphrey, interview by C. E. Hyson (tape recording, Leaside, Ont., n.d.). LAC.

30. McNally interview.

31. Oliver, "Manitoba Northern Railway Construction," 637.

32. "Work Commenced on Flin Flon Railway."

33. McNally interview.

34. "Work Commenced on Flin Flon Railway."

35. Paterson, "Steel's March to Flin Flon," 9.

36. Ibid., 10.

37. "Harry M'Lean, Bismarck Son, Lauded as Railroad Builder," *Bismarck Tribune,* July 6, 1929, quoting Arthur Hunt Chute, "Canada's Golden North," *World's Work,* July 1929.

38. Ibid.

39. Paterson, "Steel's March to Flin Flon," 10.

40. "Harry M'Lean, Bismarck Son."

41. Paterson, "Steel's March to Flin Flon," 10.

42. Ibid.

43. "Rushing Work on Flin Flon Railway," *The Pas Herald and Mining News,* Jan. 6, 1928; research notes, M. Lunam.

44. Not aliens but men with no experience of this nature.

45. "Local News," *The Pas Herald and Mining News,* Jan. 6, 1928; research notes, M. Lunam.

46. "Railway Construction Being Rushed," *The Pas Herald and Mining News,* Jan. 27, 1928; research notes, M. Lunam.

47. "Mandy Mine to Resume Operations: Flin Flon Line to Be Extended to Cold Lake," *The Pas Herald and Mining News,* Feb. 24, 1928; research notes, M. Lunam.

48. Humphrey interview.

49. "C. E. Knudson Tells Rotarians of Travels," *Bismarck Tribune,* Feb. 2, 1928; "H. F. McLean Tells Lions of Boyhood Days Spent Here," *Bismarck Tribune,* Feb. 7, 1928.

50. "Social and Personal," *Bismarck Tribune,* Feb. 11, 1928.

51. Oliver, "Manitoba Northern Railway Construction to Flinflon Mine."

52. Paterson, "Steel's March to Flin Flon," 10.

53. "Good Progress on Flin Flon Railway," *The Pas Herald and Mining News,* Apr. 20, 1928; research notes, M. Lunam.

54. "New Town at Cranberry Portage," *The Pas Herald and Mining News,* Apr. 27, 1928; research notes, M. Lunam.

55. Ibid.

56. "Lines Reaching Further North," 7.

57. Paterson, "Steel's March to Flin Flon," 10.

58. Ibid.

59. Ibid.

60. Ibid.

61. "Getting Results Sourdough Bay: A Few Facts about Flin Flon," *The Pas Herald and Mining News,* Aug. 17, 1928; research notes, M. Lunam.

62. Oliver, "Manitoba Northern Railway Construction to Flinflon Mine," 637.

63. "Hudson Bay Line and Flin Flon to Be Ready Early," *The Pas Herald and Mining News,* Sept. 21, 1928; research notes, M. Lunam.

64. McNally and Hyson, "H. F. McLean and the Sons of Martha Cairns," 30; Hedman, Yauck and Henderson, *Flin Flon,* 65.

65. McNally and Hyson, "H. F. McLean and the Sons of Martha Cairns."

66. Humphrey interview.

67. Grenalds, "Frontier Buster," 100.

68. "Social and Personal," *Bismarck Tribune,* Aug. 4, 1928.

69. Ibid., Aug. 24, 1928.

70. "Premier Bracken Drives Golden Spike in New Northern Manitoba Railway," *The Pas Herald and Mining News,* Sept. 1928; research notes, M. Lunam.

71. Ibid.

72. Ibid.; Ayre, "New Line to Tap Mineral Wealth," 48.

73. Ibid.

74. Ayre, "New Line to tap Mineral Wealth," 48.

75. Ibid.

76. Mary McLean to Christine "Criss" Gilbert, Sept. 25, 1928, in Day, *A Journey,* 96.

77. Day, *A Journey,* 95.

78. Mary McLean, in Day, *A Journey,* 96.

79. Levesque, "Grand Falls Hydro Station," 1.

80. Marceau with McCooey, *Grand Falls Yesterdays,* 123.

81. "Mrs. Mary McLean, Bismarck Pioneer, Dead: Widow of City's First Mayor, Friend of Custer, Dies from Illness," *Bismarck Tribune,* Oct. 14, 1928; "Mrs. Mary McLean Is Buried in St. Paul, *Bismarck Tribune,* Oct. 17, 1928.

82. "Helena Bank Sues Clark and Butte Free Press for Libelous Charges," *Helena Daily Independent,* Oct. 28, 1928.

83. Ibid.

84. Ibid.

85. Rose, "Arsenic, Herefords and Old Lace," 10. The date of A. B. Cook's death was Saturday, November 24, 1928.

86. "National Bank of Montana Rests Its Case in Libel Suit," *Helena Daily Independent,* Feb. 16, 1930.

87. "A. B. Cook Laid in His Eternal Rest," *Helena Daily Independent,* Nov. 29, 1928.

88. Humphrey interview.

89. McNally and Hyson, "H. F. McLean and the Sons of Martha Cairns," 30; Grant MacEwan, *The Battle for the Bay* (Saskatoon: Western Producer, 1975), 181.

90. Ruth Patterson and Jack Patterson, *Cranberry Portage* (Toronto: McClelland & Stewart, 1970). Some townspeople escaped the flames by going out onto the lake in their boats, while others tried to save their belongings by flinging them into their wells.

91. Humphrey interview.

92. Flin Flon Geology, Historical Overview, at arcmetals.ca.

93. Ayre, "A New Line to Tap Mineral Wealth," 48.

Chapter Eight: The End of the Line

1. J. C. Tory, *Legislative and Other Addresses* (Ottawa: Mortimer, 1932), 117.

2. Ibid., 63.

3. Ibid., 64–68.

4. Bruce MacDonald, *The Guysborough Railway: 1897–1939* (Antigonish, N.S.: Inukshuk Trading Company, 1973), 17–18.

5. Ibid., 18–19.

6. Tory, *Legislative and Other Addresses,* 118.

7. MacDonald, *The Guysborough Railway,* 31.

8. Ibid., 34, quoting from Debates, House of Commons, Session 1925, Vol. V, 4249.

9. MacDonald, *The Guysborough Railway,* 34.

10. J. L. Granatstein, *W. L. Mackenzie King* (Markham, Ont.: Fitzhenry & Whiteside, 2002), 20.

11. Ibid., 22, 23.

12. MacDonald, *The Guysborough Railway,* 37.

13. Ibid., 38, quoted from *Eastern Chronicle,* June 4, 1929.

14. Ibid., 39. McLean's uncle William A. Falconer and his wife, Emma, visited Merrickville in September 1929: "Social and Personal," *Bismarck Tribune,* Sept. 21, 1929.

15. MacDonald, *The Guysborough Railway,* 39, quoting *Eastern Chronicle,* Oct. 18, 1929.

16. Ibid., 40.

17. C. E. Hyson, "Guysborough Railway, Can. Nat. Rly" (n.p.), July 3, 1973. HFM Coll. MG30 B 131, Vol. I, LAC.

18. MacDonald, *The Guysborough Railway,* 40–41, quoting *Eastern Chronicle,* Nov. 22, 1929.

19. Ibid., 41–42.

20. Grenalds, "Frontier Buster," 100.

21. Ibid.

22. MacDonald, *The Guysborough Railway,* 43.

23. Ibid.

24. Ibid.

25. McLaren interview.

26. MacDonald, *The Guysborough Railway,* 44–45.

27. Richard L. Hearn, interview by C. E. Hyson and Joseph and Paul McNally (tape recording, Queenston, Ont., Dec. 6, 1973). HFM Coll, LAC.

28. Granatstein, *W. L. Mackenzie King,* 25–27.

29. "Canadian National Railways Construction, Betterments, Etc.," June 1931, 364; MacDonald, *The Guysborough Railway,* 47.

30. "Canadian National Railways Construction, Betterments, Etc.," 364.

31. MacDonald, *The Guysborough Railway,* 45.

32. "Canadian National Railways Construction, Betterments, Etc.," 364.

33. MacDonald, *The Guysborough Railway,* 50, quoting J. R. Kirk, Liberal Member for Antigonish-Guysborough, quoting, in turn, *Eastern Chronicle* in Debates, House of Commons, Session 1939, Vol. II, 1405.

34. McLaren interview.

35. Gordon Turner, *Empress of Britain: Canadian Pacific's Greatest Ship* (Toronto: Stoddart/Erin, Ont.: Boston Mills Press, 1992), 9–10.

36. Ibid., 15.

37. Ibid., 17.

38. Ibid., 27.

39. Ibid., 9.

40. Lt. Col. D. Hillman, "Wolfe's Cove Branch Line and Tunnel, Canadian Pacific Railway," *Canadian Railway and Marine World,* July 1931, 423; "Canadian Pacific Drives Mile Tunnel to

Reach New Ship," *Railway Age,* June 27, 1931, 1228. HFM Coll., MG 30, Series B-131-2, Vol. II, LAC.

41. Turner, *Empress of Britain,* 9–10.
42. "Methods of Driving One Mile Railway Tunnel under City of Quebec: Canadian Pacific Railway Co. Building Connection to New Wolfe's Cove Landing," *Contract Record and Engineering Review,* Mar. 25, 1931. HFM Collection, MG 30, LAC.
43. Hillman, "Wolfe's Cove Branch Line and Tunnel," 425.
44. Ibid.
45. Hyson reminiscences.
46. "Wolfe's Cove Terminal Tunnel, Quebec: Provides New Route between Point Near C.P.R. Palais Station and New Deepwater Docks," *Canadian Engineer,* Aug. 18, 1931, 10. HFM Collection, MG30, LAC.
47. Hyson interview.
48. "Methods of Driving," 352.
49. Hillman, "Wolfe's Cove Branch Line and Tunnel," 425–426; "Canadian Pacific Drives Mile Tunnel," 1231.
50. "Methods of Driving," 354.
51. "Canadian Pacific's Wolfe's Cove Tunnel, Quebec City," translated by Denis Fortier from Administrative Committee Records, Report 901 [1930], Quebec City Archives.
52. "Canadian Pacific Drives Mile Tunnel," 1228–1230.
53. Ibid., 1230.
54. "Methods of Driving," 353.
55. "Canadian Pacific Drives Mile Tunnel," 1230–1231.
56. Colin Churcher, "Significant Dates in Railway History" (railways.incanada.net/candate/candate.htm).
57. Turner, *Empress of Britain,* 51.
58. Ibid.
59. Ibid., 53.

Chapter Nine: Men Against the Moose

1. *1922 Annual Report, Temiskaming & Northern Ontario Railway,* quoted in Tucker, *Steam into Wilderness,* 93.
2. Armand Racine, *Temiskaming and Northern Ontario Railway Inquiry,* Aug. 8, 1934 (Toronto: T. E. Bowman, Printer to the King's Most Excellent Majesty, 1935), 9.
3. Ibid., 6.
4. Ibid.
5. Surtees, *The Northern Connection,* 64.
6. Ibid., 63; Tucker, *Steam into Wilderness,* 12.
7. Tucker, *Steam into Wilderness,* 17; Surtees, *The Northern Connection,* 25–26, 31–34.
8. Racine, *T&NO Inquiry,* 5, 7–8.
9. Tucker, *Steam into Wilderness,* 88.
10. Ibid., 90.
11. Ibid., 92.
12. Surtees, *The Northern Connection,* 164.
13. Ibid., 164–165.
14. Ibid., 164, quoting Lee to Drury, Aug. 22, 1922. OA, RG3, Drury Papers, Box 128.

15. Ibid., 167, quoting Lee to Clement, Feb. 7, 1923. Ontario Northland Archives, B-2557, James Bay Extension, Main File.
16. Ibid., 164.
17. Racine, *T&NO Inquiry,* 9.
18. Surtees, *The Northern Connection,* 169.
19. Tucker, *Steam into Wilderness,* 95–96; Surtees, *The Northern Connection,* 170.
20. Tucker, *Steam into Wilderness,* 98; Surtees, *The Northern Connection,* 170.
21. Surtees, *The Northern Connection,* 171.
22. Ibid.
23. Ibid.
24. Ibid., 172; "Temiskaming and Northern Ontario Railway Extension to James Bay Opened," *Canadian Railway and Marine World,* Aug. 1932, 399.
25. Racine, *T&NO Inquiry,* 11.
26. Tucker, *Steam into Wilderness,* 98.
27. Racine, *T&NO Inquiry,* 11.
28. Paul Montgomery, "Reclaiming a Lost Empire," *Canadian Magazine,* Sept. 1931, 17, 36.
29. "On to James Bay," Toronto *Globe,* Aug. 21, 1930.
30. Paul Montgomery, "Ontario's Newest North: The Real Reasons for the Extension of the T&NO Railway to the Shores of James Bay," *Saturday Night* (magazine), n.d.
31. F. D. L. Smith, "Temiskaming and Northern Ontario Railway Extension to James Bay," *Canadian Railway and Marine World,* Aug. 1930, 496.
32. Ibid.
33. Ibid.
34. Frederick Griffin, "Men against the Moose," *Toronto Star Weekly,* Jan. 24, 1932.
35. Ibid.
36. Ibid.
37. McLean used old railway cars for several purposes; many employees lived in them temporarily.
38. Nicholas Morant, "The Sons of Martha Cairns," *CP Rail News,* Vol. 12, no. 5 (Apr. 14), 1982, 6.
39. MacLean, "Dangled Waiter from 17th Floor."
40. "Pioneer Railroad Contractor Delights in Battling Nature," Toronto *Globe,* Mar. 18, 1930.
41. Roberts, "A Pair of Aces, Frontier Style," 7.
42. "Capital City-Bound Flyer Forced Down," *Bismarck Tribune,* Jan. 14, 1930.
43. Griffin, "Men against the Moose."
44. Roberts, "A Pair of Aces, Frontier Style."
45. Griffin, "Men against the Moose"; Tucker, *Steam into Wilderness,* 98.
46. Griffin, "Men against the Moose."
47. Ibid.
48. "Temiskaming and Northern Ontario Railway Extension to James Bay Opened," 399.
49. Racine, *T&NO Inquiry,* 111.
50. Ibid., 10.
51. Ibid., 12.
52. Tucker, *Steam into Wilderness,* 99.
53. Racine, *T&NO Inquiry,* 12.
54. "Business Men on Trip through the North of Ontario," *North Bay Nugget,* July 1931. Harold Ferguson, Premier of Ontario, Reels, OA.
55. Ibid.
56. G. Lee to G. S. Henry, Sept. 2, 1931. G. S. Henry, Premier of Ontario, Correspondence, OA, MS 1746.
57. Racine, *T&NO Inquiry,* 12.

58. G. Lee to G. S. Henry, Sept. 23, 1931. G. S. Henry, Premier of Ontario, Correspondence, OA, MS 1746.

59. Ibid., Lee quoting letter from Colonel Geo. P. Murphy, President, Ottawa Transportation Company, Sept. 15, 1931.

60. G. Lee to G. S. Henry, Sept. 22, 1931, quoting T. A. Beament letter. G. S. Henry, Premier of Ontario, Correspondence, OA, MS 1746.

61. G. Lee to G. S. Henry, Sept. 22, 1931, quoting Dr. J. D. Courtenay letter. G. S. Henry, Premier of Ontario, Correspondence, OA, MS 1746.

62. Tucker, *Steam into Wilderness*, 99; Surtees, *The Northern Connection,* 174.

63. Ibid.

64. "List of Guests to be invited – Official Opening James Bay Extension – July 15, 1932." G. S. Henry, Premier of Ontario, Correspondence, OA, MS 1746.

65. Tucker, *Steam into Wilderness,* 99.

Chapter Ten: Powerful White Horses

1. *"H. F. McLean Presents Abitibi Canyon." A Talking Picture Produced by Photo-Sound Corporation for Dominion Construction Corporation Limited.* Tentative Story to Accompany Abitibi Canyon Picture, 2. R. L. Hearn Coll., MU 8651, OA.

2. Grenalds, "Frontier Buster," 52.

3. Neil McKenty, *Mitch Hepburn* (Toronto: McClelland & Stewart, 1967), 40–45; Tucker, *Steam into Wilderness,* 107. Three of the four power companies operated in Quebec.

4. Richard L. Hearn to Glen Rowlandson, Oct. 3, 1978. HFM Coll. MG 30 B 131 Vol. 2, LAC.

5. Ibid.; Hyson reminiscences.

6. McNally and Hyson, "H. F. McLean and the Sons of Martha Cairns," 32; Hyson reminiscences; McLaren interview.

7. Hyson reminiscences, Tape 5; C. E. Hyson, "Abitibi Canyon Power Development," handwritten paper (n.p., n.d.). HFM Coll. MG 30, B 131, Vol. 2, File 2–23, 1.

8. Hyson reminiscences, Tape 5.

9. Ibid.

10. Ibid. McLean commissioned a motion picture that depicted each phase of the work: excavation of the rock, concrete work, tunnelling, and erection of the power house, the town and the various facilities. The entire construction process was documented on 16mm film. The motion picture was to be used as a marketing tool.

11. Hyson reminiscences, Tape 5; "Conquering Long Winters at Abitibi Dam" (n.p.), Apr. 16, 1936. TS, R. L. Hearn Papers, MU 8636, OA.

12. Hyson, "Abitibi Canyon Power Development."

13. Hyson reminiscences, Tape 5.

14. Ibid.

15. "Conquering Long Winters at Abitibi Dam."

16. Hyson, "Abitibi Canyon Power Development," 4.

17. Hyson reminiscences, Tape 5.

18. Ibid.

19. "Townsite, Camp, Food & Housing Studies" (n.p., n.d.). R. L. Hearn Papers, AO, MU 8656; "Summary of Camps, Dwellings, Stores, Etc., and Plant Structures," Dec 31, 1930. HFM Coll. MG 30 B 131 Vol. 2, File 2-24, LAC.

20. Hyson, "Abitibi Canyon Power Development"; Hyson reminiscences.
21. Hyson, "Abitibi Canyon Power Development."
22. Hyson reminiscences, Tape 5.
23. Ibid. Abitibi's Shay can be seen on the museum grounds in Iroquois Falls. It had been purchased used through a Chicago equipment broker.
24. "Analysis of General Payroll," Apr. 5, 1932. R. L. Hearn Papers, MU 8636 OA; Hyson reminiscences, Tape 5.
25. Hyson reminiscences, Tape 5.
26. McLaren interview.
27. Hyson reminiscences, Tape 5.
28. Ibid.
29. Ibid.
30. McNally and Hyson, "H. F. McLean and the Sons of Martha Cairns," 32.
31. "Conquering Long Winters at Abitibi Dam."
32. Ibid.
33. Ibid.
34. Hyson reminiscences, Tape 5.
35. Gordon Mitchell interview by C. E. Hyson (tape recording, Toronto, Ont., Jan. 1973). HFM Coll. LAC.
36. Hyson reminiscences, Tape 5.
37. Roberts, "A Pair of Aces, Frontier Style."
38. Grenalds, "Frontier Buster," 52.
39. Ibid.
40. Hyson reminiscences, Tape 5.
41. "Conquering Long Winters at Abitibi Dam."
42. Ibid.
43. Hearn interview.
44. McLaren interview. McLean himself returned home that summer to see friends and family visiting from Bismarck, notably Mr. and Mrs. J. B. Belk and their daughters, Clarice and Emily: "Society News," *Bismarck Tribune,* July 17, 1931.
45. Hyson reminiscences, Tape 5.
46. Ibid.
47. J. R. Montague, Hydraulic Department, and G. H. Bradshaw, Electrical Engineering Department, H.E.P.C. of Ont., Oct. 1933, *The Bulletin* (published by the Hydro-Electric Power Commission of Ontario), Vol. 20, no. 10, 354.
48. "Conquering Long Winters at Abitibi Dam."
49. Scotty Watson to HFM, Dec, 1931. R. L. Hearn Papers, MU 8656, OA.
50. Ibid.
51. Hyson reminiscences, Tape 5.
52. Watson to HFM, Dec. 1931.
53. Hyson reminiscences, Tape 5; Hyson "Abitibi Canyon Power Development." Hyson said that Wharram resembled Colonel Sanders of Kentucky Fried Chicken fame.
54. Ibid.
55. Ibid.
56. Hyson reminiscences, Tape 6.
57. Ibid.
58. Ibid.; McNally and Hyson, 32; "Conquering Long Winters at Abitibi Dam."

Chapter Eleven: A New Broom Sweeps Clean

1. Hyson reminiscences, Tape 6.
2. HFM to Stewart Lyon, Esq., Chairman, Hydro-Electric Power Commission of Ontario, Aug. 17, 1934. R. L. Hearn Papers, MU 8651, File: Dominion Construction Co., Misc, OA.
3. McKenty, *Mitch Hepburn*, 43.
4. Ibid., 44–45.
5. HFM to Stewart Lyon; J. Homer Black to Stewart Lyon, Esq., Chairman, Hydro-Electric Power Commission of Ontario, Aug. 17, 1934. R. L. Hearn Papers, MU 8651, File: Dominion Construction Co., Misc, OA.
6. Ibid.; McNally interview.
7. [C. E. Hyson] Chronology, HFM Coll, MG 30, B-131, Vol I, File 1-20.
8. HFM to Stewart Lyon; J. Homer Black to Stewart Lyon.
9. McKenty, *Mitch Hepburn*, 44.
10. "Memorandum Re: Settlement of Claim of Dominion Construction Corporation," May 31, 1937. RG3 268 File Dominion Construction Corps. Ltd. Hepburn Papers, ONA.
11. Switzer, Untitled Paper on Harry McLean and Dominion Construction; Hyson reminiscences, Tape 5.
12. "Judicial Sale of the Property, Assets and Undertaking of Ontario Power Service Corporation Limited" (n.p., n.d.).
13. McKenty, *Mitch Hepburn*, 45.
14. Mitchell interview.
15. McKenty, *Mitch Hepburn*, 45.
16. "Native Son's Work on Monstrous Dam Shown Here in Film," *Bismarck Tribune*, May 25, 1933.
17. "Lieut-Governor Would Not Sign $500,000 Order" [*Toronto Star*], n.d.
18. Ibid.; "Memorandum Re: Settlement of Claim of Dominion Construction Corporation," May 31, 1937. RG3 268 File Dominion Construction Corps. Ltd., Hepburn Papers, ONA.
19. McKenty, *Mitch Hepburn*, 56.
20. Ibid., 61, 62; Tucker, *Steam into Wilderness*, 106.
21. Tucker, *Steam into Wilderness*, 107.
22. Ibid., 112.
23. Racine, *T&NO Inquiry*.
24. Tucker, *Steam into Wilderness*, 109.
25. L. G. McNeice, Engineer, Orillia Water, Light and Power Commission, Orillia, Ont., "Workman's Falls Power Development on Gull River, Near Minden, Ont." *Canadian Engineer*, Oct. 1, 1935, 5–8; McLaren interview.
26. Hyson reminiscences, Tape 5.
27. Ibid.
28. Racine, *T&NO Inquiry*, 7–8.
29. Ibid., 8–9.
30. Ibid., 10.
31. W. B. Russel, Manager and Engineer, Construction and Engineering Company Ltd., to Harold J. Kirby, M.P.P., Sept. 20, 1934. RG3 231 File: RG3 Hepburn Gen. Correspondence, Private, 1934.
32. Racine, *T&NO Inquiry*, 10.
33. Ibid., 12.
34. Ibid.

35. Ibid., 15.
36. Ibid., 15–16.
37. Ibid., 15.
38. Ibid., 17.
39. Ibid., 23.
40. Ibid.
41. McKenty, *Mitch Hepburn,* 62.
42. Ibid.
43. Ibid., 65.
44. Ibid., 65–66.
45. "Lieut-Governor Would Not Sign $500,000 Order."
46. Ibid.
47. Ibid.
48. "Memorandum Re: Settlement of Claim of Dominion Construction Corporation."
49. "Trick Question, Is Charge," *Toronto Star,* n.d.
50. "Society and Clubs," *Bismarck Tribune,* July 5, 1936.
51. Ibid., July 11, 1936.
52. Ibid., July 13, 1936.
53. Hyson reminiscences, Tape 6.
54. Murray Cooke. Reminiscences (tape recording, Kenora, Ont., n.d.). HFM Coll. LAC; Richardson, "H. F. McLean: Part II, Quarries at Merrickville and Hawk Lake."
55. Hyson, "Deeks Quarry."
56. Cooke reminiscences.
57. Ibid.
58. Hyson, "Deeks Quarry."
59. Cooke reminiscences.
60. Ibid.
61. Ibid.; Richardson, "H. F. McLean: Part II, Quarries at Merrickville and Hawk Lake."
62. Cooke reminiscences.
63. Ibid.
64. Ibid.
65. HFM to R. L. Hearn, Dec. 25, 1936. R. L. Hearn Papers, MU 8656, Hearn, R. Correspondence, 1936, OA.
66. Dominion Construction Corporation Limited, "Experience of Harry F. McLean," June 1950, Merrickville. HFM Coll., MG 30, B 131, Vol. 1, File 1-22, LAC.
67. McNally interview.
68. Ibid.

Chapter Twelve: Ruthless, Grasping Thieves

1. Barry Cunningham with Mike Pearl, *Mr. District Attorney* (New York: Mason/Charter, 1977), 102.
2. Switzer, Untitled Paper on Harry McLean and Dominion Construction; Diane Galusha, *Liquid Assets: A History of New York City's Water System* (Fleischmanns, N.Y.: Purple Mountain Press, 1999), 179.

3. Whitman Knapp (Argued By), "Respondent's Brief," People of the State of New York against Joseph S. Fay and James Bove, District Attorney's File, Fay and Bove, MANY, 2.

4. Ibid.

5. Galusha, *Liquid Assets*, ch. 20: "Assessing the Damage."

6. Knapp, "Respondent's Brief," 2.

7. Switzer, Untitled Paper on Harry McLean and Dominion Construction.

8. Ibid.; Hyson reminiscences, Tape 6.

9. "John Paris Bickell," *The Canadian Encyclopedia*, 2nd ed. (Edmonton: Hurtig, 1988), Vol. 1, A-Edu, 212; *Maloof v. J. P. Bickell and Co.* (1919), 59 S.C.R. 429; *J. P. Bickell & Company v. Cutten* [1926] S.C.R. 340; *Barthelmes v. Bickell* (1921), 62 S.C.R. 599.

10. John Brooks, *Once in Golconda: A True Drama of Wall Street 1920–1938* (New York: Harper & Row, 1969), 122.

11. Ibid.

12. Ibid.

13. McNally interview.

14. Knapp, "Respondent's Brief."

15. Vincent G. Terenzio, Chief Engineer, The City of New York, Board of Water Supply, to Col. Shuldham H. Hill, Dec. 4, 1972. Personal Collection, Dr. Leonard Newman Papers.

16. Hyson reminiscences.

17. Terenzio to Hill, Dec. 4, 1972; Knapp, "Respondent's Brief," 18.

18. McNally interview.

19. Knapp, "Respondent's Brief," 18.

20. Ibid.

21. Ibid.

22. Ibid., 18–19.

23. Ibid., 19.

24. McNally interview.

25. John Hutchinson, *The Imperfect Union: A History of Corruption in American Trade Unions* (New York: E. P. Dutton, 1972), 45–46.

26. Westbrook Pegler, "Fair Enough: Case of Joe Fay, Brutal Racketeer, Had All the Earmarks of a Fix," *Berkshire Evening Page* (Pittsfield, Mass.), Dec. 15, 1942.

27. Cunningham with Pearl, *Mr. District Attorney*, 101–102; Hutchinson, *The Imperfect Union*, 45–47.

28. Knapp, "Respondent's Brief," 26.

29. Ibid., 4.

30. McNally interview.

31. Pegler, "Fair Enough," *Dixon* (Illinois) *Evening Telegraph*, Mar. 23, 1945.

32. Ibid., Apr. 24, 1945.

33. Cunningham with Pearl, *Mr. District Attorney*, 102.

34. "A Mystery of Labor Politics: Who Murdered the Sandhog Leader?" *Life*, Vol. 2, no. 10 (Mar. 8), 1937, 9–11.

35. Ibid.

36. Hutchinson, *The Imperfect Union*, 46.

37. Ibid.

38. "Sandhogs Leader in Strike Is Slain at Home in Jersey," *New York Times*, Feb. (n.d.), 1937; "A Mystery of Labor Politics," 11.

39. "Labor Chiefs Fay and Bove Indicted for Extortion on Aqueduct Project," *Troy* (New York) *Record*, May 20, 1943.

40. Redwood's murder remains unsolved.

41. Hyson reminiscences, Tape 6.

42. McKenty, *Mitch Hepburn*, 163. The celebration came just weeks after Hepburn, Bickell and Smith's plane went astray briefly as bad weather grounded their flight en route to Juneau, Alaska.

43. Ibid.

44. McNally interview.

45. Switzer, Untitled Paper on Harry McLean and Dominion Construction.

46. Hyson reminiscences, Tape 6.

47. Hyson, "Sons of Martha Monuments."

48. "Plan to Fly Around the World," Montreal *Gazette*, May 22, 1939.

49. "Toronto City Centre Airport: A History" (http://www.torontoport.com/airport_history.asp).

50. Shirley M. Goodman, daughter of Charles Switzer, e-mail to author, Aug. 7, 2005.

51. Cooke reminiscences.

52. Ibid.

53. A. J. P. Taylor, "The Outbreak of War," in *History of the 20th Century*, Vol. 4 (London: BPC Publishing, n.d.), ch. 60, 1655.

54. Charles M. Clark, Chief Engineer, Board of Water Supply, City of New York Engineering Bureau, To Whom It May Concern, re: Contract 323, Delaware Aqueduct, Sept. 23, 1940. HFM Coll, MG 30 B 131, Vol. I, File 1-22, Experience of Harry F. McLean.

55. Hyson reminiscences, Tape 6.

56. Westbrook Pegler, "More Tickets Than Plates," *Times Recorder*, Oct. 12, 1962.

57. Ibid.

58. [Leslie Roberts], "Men o' War, No. 7: The McLean" (n.d., n.p.).

59. Galusha, *Liquid Assets*, 182.

60. [Roberts], "Men o' War."

61. McNally interview. Joseph McNally recalled, "He got the job up and running and then his partners decided he was spending too much money. They didn't need him. So they ganged up on him and put the run on him."

62. Merrickville resident Arthur Heroux recalled that McLean hired bodyguards around that time.

63. "Memorandum on the Fay-Bove Case," July 23, 1947, Office of the District Attorney, MANY, 1.

64. Ibid.

65. Cunningham with Pearl, *Mr. District Attorney*, 100.

66. "Memorandum on the Fay-Bove Case," 3.

67. Ibid.

68. Hutchinson, *The Imperfect Union*, 47.

69. "Memorandum on the Fay-Bove Case," 3.

70. McNally interview.

71. "Memorandum on the Fay-Bove Case," 3.

72. Ibid.

73. Ibid.

74. Cunningham with Pearl, *Mr. District Attorney*, 103.

75. Westbrook Pegler, "Fair Enough" © 1935 by King Features Syndicate, *Dixon* (Illinois) *Evening Telegraph,* Mar. 23, 1945.

76. Galusha, *Liquid Assets*, 182.

77. Chum was Jimmy Therrien's brother. During his last working years, Chum worked for J. J. McNally.

78. McNally interview.

79. Grand Jury Indictment, The People of the State of New York against Joseph S. Fay and James Bove, Court of General Sessions, County of New York (n.d.).

80. Cunningham with Pearl, *Mr. District Attorney*, 101.

81. Mr. Glynn to Mr. Hogan, Memorandum Re: Fay-Bove Jury, Feb. 9, 1945, MANY.

82. "Memorandum on the Fay-Bove Case," 2.

83. Knapp, "Respondent's Brief," 28.

84. Ibid., 29.

85. Hutchinson, *The Imperfect Union*, 47.

86. "Bove and Fay Get 8½-Year Terms; Worse Than Gunmen, Hogan Says," *New York Times*, Apr. 6, 1945.

87. Frank S. Hogan to Mr. Emile Paturel, Exporter of Canned, Smoked, Fresh and Salt Water Fish – Shell Fish, Mar. 30, 1945. Fay-Bove Case File, District Attorney's Office, MANY.

88. Ibid.

89. "Bove and Fay Get 8½-Year Terms."

90. Westbrook Pegler, "As Pegler Sees It" "© 1947 by King Features Syndicate, Inc. *Dixon* (Illinois) *Evening Telegraph,* 17 Feb. 1947.

91. "Bove and Fay Get 8½-Year Terms."

92. Ibid.

93. "District Attorney's Office, County of New York, Memorandum of Sentence," Apr. 5, 1945. Fay-Bove File, District Attorney's Office, MANY.

94. Frank S. Hogan to Honorable William H. Munson, Sept. 5, 1947. Fay Bove File, District Attorney's Office, MANY. Judge Munson sent Hogan a stack of letters of support for Fay from his loyal lackeys. Compliments of a sickly sweet nature abounded: "...we know of no finer, more decent and upright man in this or any other city...Mr. Fay is that rarity among all men, a true and instinctive gentleman who has treated us with the greatest consideration and respect at all times..." Hogan responded to Munson, "Thank you for sending me the letter from the faithful friends of the felonious Fay. Will nobody say a kind word for Bove?" Pegler paid tribute to Fay as well: "Joe has always shown a correct respect for the hoodlums' code. He is vicious, a thief, a brutal thug and a brawling drunkard but he has his pride as well as his price." Westbrook Pegler, "Fair Enough" © 1935 by King Features Syndicate, *Dixon* (Illinois) *Evening Telegraph*, Mar. 23, 1945.

95. "Bove and Fay Get 8½-Year Terms."

96. Ibid.

97. "Memorandum on the Fay-Bove Case," 4.

98. Hutchinson, *The Imperfect Union*, 47.

99. Cunningham with Pearl, *Mr. District Attorney*, 102. Being an inmate was no more than an inconvenience to Fay. He managed to maintain his network of thugs while behind bars, his power only mildly diminished. A steady stream of people, including some high-level politicians, made the trip to Ossining, New York, during his incarceration to ask for favours. Arthur H. Wicks, Acting Lieutenant Governor of New York, sought Fay's assistance in straightening out jurisdictional disputes in his district on large construction projects, fearing that they would be delayed. In explaining his actions after being caught in the act, Wicks said that he recognized that there was another level of government run by labour leaders: "It is impossible for any competent representative in government to be unconscious or unmindful of the organized interests of this other government." He claimed to loathe

the fact that Fay was still clearly in charge of the union while in prison: "Labor chose to continue to respect his opinions while he was in jail – it was labor's decision to make, not mine. He was not my representative, but the one to whom I went for the sake of those I represented." The visits to Fay eventually cost Wicks his job, as his resignation was demanded by Governor Thomas E. Dewey. David Lawrence, "Labor Thugs Have Headlock on Democrats," *Salisbury* (Maryland) *Times*, Oct. 23, 1953; *Gettysburg* (Pennsylvania) *Times*, Jan. 20, 1958.

Chapter Thirteen: Stand To Tiger Moth

1. About the chapter title: This four-word telegram was sent by McLean to Prime Minister Mackenzie King. I thought it rather cryptic and for the longest time had no idea what it meant, being aware only that the Tiger Moth was a plane. Finally, an Internet search turned up "Stand-To" at First World War.com (http://www.firstworldwar.com/atoz/standto.htm). Stand-To is short for Stand-to-Arms, which was part of a soldier's daily routine. In the morning and evening the soldiers would have to stand ready, with their rifles loaded, as a precaution because most attacks occurred at dawn or dusk. But I still do not know the meaning of the obscure phrase "stand to Tiger Moth." Another telegram to King still causes me to lose sleep. It reads: "Your Sagatarius [sic] Part Man Part Horse/Always Clean Minded/Ruled by Jupiter Knowing Intelligently His Bow and Arrow/Target Practice Gives Great Confidence/Harry McLean can Coincide." Dec, 16, 1944. Edith Wakeman Hughes, Hollywood, California, to WLMK. WLMK Personal Papers, MG 26, Series J3, Vol. 93, File 2, McLean, Harry, LAC.
2. McNally interview.
3. Leslie Roberts, *C. D.: The Life and Times of Clarence Decatur Howe* (Toronto: Clarke, Irwin, 1957), 84–89.
4. Ibid.
5. Ibid., 86–87.
6. John R. Leslie, "Summary Record and History of Allied War Supplies Corporation," July 26, 1945, Chapter II, 2. RG 61, Vol. I. File T5 155 A43 8th, LAC.
7. Ibid., 1.
8. W. G. Mitchell, "Summary Record of Project No. 2/17: Explosives and Propellants Plant, De Salaberry Island, P.Q." Allied War Supplies Corporation, Montreal, Jan. 2, 1941. Section I, 2. RG 61, Vol. I, File T5 155 A 43, LAC.
9. "Our History," DuPont Canada (www.dupont.ca).
10. Mitchell, "Summary Record of Project," Section I, 2. Propellants are the explosives used to thrust projectiles from guns or to launch torpedoes.
11. Ibid. Canada was not alone with its expedited building plans – Adolf Hitler had ordered the construction of the concentration camp at Auschwitz approximately one month earlier.
12. Ibid., Section 1, 3.
13. Leslie, "Summary Record and History," ch. 1, 1.
14. Mitchell, "Summary Record of Project," Section 1, 2–4.
15. Ibid., Section 4, 2.
16. Ibid., Section 4, 4.
17. Ibid., Section 1, 2–3.
18. McNally interview.
19. "C. D. Howe," Juno Beach Centre: www.junobeach.org.

20. Roberts, *C. D.: The Life and Times of Clarence Decatur Howe,* 89.
21. Mitchell, "Summary Record of Project," Section 4, 3.
22. McNally interview.
23. Hyson reminiscences, Tape 6.
24. Mitchell, "Summary Record of Project," Section 4, 5.
25. Ibid.; Hyson reminiscences, Tape 6.
26. McNally interview.
27. Ibid.
28. Turner, *Empress of Britain,* ch. 24, 25.
29. Mitchell, "Summary Record of Project," Section 4, 5.
30. McNally interview.
31. Mitchell, "Summary Record of Project," Section 4, 6.
32. Roberts, *C. D.: The Life and Times of Clarence Decatur Howe,* ch. 2, 24.
33. Ibid., ch. 7, 85.
34. Hyson reminiscences, Tape 6.
35. *Agreement between His Majesty the King and Dominion Construction Corporation Limited to Construct the Point Edward Naval Base at Sydney, Nova Scotia,* Nov. 6, 1941, 3–4. RG 28, Vol. 462, File 30-2-47, LAC.
36. Hyson reminiscences, Tape 6.
37. *Agreement,* 8.
38. Hearn interview.
39. McNally interview.
40. *Agreement,* 2.
41. Ibid., Appendix: Labour Conditions, Nov. 20, 1941.
42. McNally interview.
43. Hyson reminiscences, Tape 6.
44. John MacLean, " 'Mr. X' from Water Boy to 'Top Builder'," *Toronto Telegram,* July 13, 1956.
45. McNally interview.
46. Charles Switzer to HFM, Mar. 4, 1942. R. L. Hearn Papers, MU 8656, Correspondence, 1942, OA.
47. Michael L. Hadley, *U-boats against Canada: German Submarines in Canadian Waters* (Montreal and Kingston: McGill-Queen's University Press, 1985), 112.
48. Stephen Kimber, *Sailors, Slackers and Blind Pigs: Halifax at War* (Toronto: Doubleday, 2002), 116.
49. McNally interview.
50. Ibid.
51. Ibid.
52. Mary Cummings, "Adaptive Reuse in Three Acts," at hamptonsview.com.
53. *Investigator's Report. Death of Irene McLean,* Office of the Fire Marshal, Parliament Buildings, Toronto, July 10, 1942. Case Number 10039. Office of the Fire Marshal, RG 33-30, OA.
54. Ibid.
55. WLMK to HFM, July 9, 1942. WLMK Personal Papers, MG 26, Series J3, Vol. 93, File 2, McLean, Harry, LAC.
56. "Mrs. H. F. McLean Dies of Burns," Toronto *Globe,* July 11, 1942.
57. Mike Murphy, *My Kind of People* (Westport, Ont.: Butternut Press, 1987), 116.
58. Joseph McNally, note on back of Point Edward blueprint.
59. Rev. Donald R. Sutherland to Charland, Jan. 27, 2005.
60. McNally interview.

61. Ibid.
62. Ibid.
63. Joseph McNally notes to Cornwallis photographs.
64. McNally interview.
65. Puddington interview.
66. Amendment No. 5, July 15, 1943, to *Agreement between His Majesty the King and Dominion Construction Corporation Limited to Construct the Point Edward Naval Base at Sydney, Nova Scotia,* Nov. 6, 1941, 3-4. RG 28, Vol. 462, File 30-2-47, LAC.
67. The History of HMCS/CFB Cornwallis, Cornwallis Military Museum (wvcn.ns.ca/~cmm/CornwallisHistory.htm).
68. McNally interview.
69. Ibid.

Chapter Fourteen: Forward and Onward

1. Avard Fairbanks, inscription on base of *The Pioneer Family* statue.
2. "John Harvey Kellogg," Battle Creek Historical Society at geocities.com/Athens/oracle/9840/Kellogg.html; David Ricardo Williams, *Mayor Gerry: The Remarkable Gerald Grattan McGeer* (Vancouver and Toronto: Douglas & McIntyre, 1986), 11–13, 37.
3. A reference to the injections of "double chloride of gold" administered by some Midwestern institutions in the late 1800s as a cure for alcoholism.
4. "John Harvey Kellogg," Battle Creek Historical Society.
5. Williams, *Mayor Gerry,* 234.
6. Ibid., 245.
7. Francis Breidenbach, "Master of Bronze," *North Dakota Horizons,* Vol. 14, no. 4 (Fall), 1984, 4. While visiting with his cousin Lulu in Seattle, Fairbanks showed her photographs of *Lincoln the Frontiersman.* Lulu suggested he show the photographs to Gerry McGeer (life member of the unofficial Abraham Lincoln fan club in Canada, comprising McGeer, King and McLean). An appointment was arranged and McGeer was duly impressed. McGeer commissioned Fairbanks to sculpt a bust of himself to be displayed at Vancouver City Hall. Source: Eugene Fairbanks (son of Avard Fairbanks) to author, private correspondence, Nov. 19, 2001.
8. Breidenbach, "Master of Bronze," 4.
9. Eugene F. Fairbanks, *A Sculptor's Testimony in Bronze and Stone: Sacred Sculpture of Avard T. Fairbanks* (Salt Lake City: Publisher's Press, 1972), 1–5.
10. "Artists Inspiration," *Bismarck Tribune,* Apr. 15, 1948.
11. Breidenbach, "Master of Bronze," 4.
12. Eugene Fairbanks to author, private correspondence, Nov. 19, 2001; Breidenbach, "Master of Bronze," 4.
13. Ibid.
14. Ibid.
15. In his letter to me (Nov. 19 , 2001), Fairbanks recalled that "the statue wasn't entirely upright; it listed to starboard (or maybe it was to port)."
16. Fairbanks to author, private correspondence, Nov. 19, 2001; Breidenbach, "Master of Bronze," 5.

17. "Presentation of the Statue of a Pioneer Family to the State of North Dakota, 20 Sept 1947," in Russell Reid, ed., *North Dakota History* (State Historical Society of North Dakota), Vol. 14, no. 4 (Oct.), 1947, 243.
18. Williams, *Mayor Gerry,* 291.
19. "Presentation of the Statue," 275.
20. Ibid., 273.
21. Ibid., 274.
22. Ibid., 278.
23. Ibid., 283–284.
24. "Dedicate 'Pioneer Family' Monument," *Bismarck Capital*, Vol. 26, no. 1 (Sept. 23), 1947.
25. Ibid.
26. Ibid.
27. Fairbanks to author, private correspondence, Nov. 19, 2001.
28. "Presentation of the Statue," 285.

Chapter Fifteen: A Perfect Fool

1. WLMK Diary, Apr. 27, 1942, 345 (king.collectionscanada.ca), LAC.
2. WJT to WLMK, Memorandum to the Prime Minister, Dec. 18, 1944. WLMK Personal Papers, MG 26, Series J3, Vol. 93, File 2, McLean, Harry, LAC.
3. WLMK Diary, Sept. 4, 1942, 741.
4. Ibid.
5. Ibid., Jan. 29, 1943, 85.
6. Ibid.
7. WLMK to HFM, May 3, 1943, Office of the Prime Minister. WLMK Papers, Microfilm, LAC.
8. Ibid.
9. Ibid.
10. WLMK Diary, May 14, 1943, 5.
11. Ibid., July 7,1943, 1. After the death of little Pat (No. 1), McLean sent King some Easter flowers with a card reading "Forget-me-not – Harry." King noted in his diary: "I often notice truths come to one thro' these simple seemingly foolish minds – I think the meaning of the message was a relation to little Pat – forget me not– he was saying having reference to his years of endurance – to our last struggle together."
12. Ibid., Oct. 11, 1943, 900.
13. Ibid., Oct. 12, 1943, 904; the second Pat was kindly posing as a stand-in for the first (and preferred) Pat.
14. Ibid., Oct. 13, 1943, 910.
15. Ibid., Oct. 15, 1943, 914.
16. Ibid.
17. Ibid., 915.
18. Ibid.
19. Ibid., Oct. 16, 1943, 918.
20. Ibid., 919.
21. Ibid., 921.
22. Ibid.
23. Ibid.

24. Williams, *Mayor Gerry,* 256–257.

25. "Quebec Court Fines Mr. X," Toronto *Globe,* July 5, 1944.

26. HFM to WLMK, July 18, 1944, Telegram. WLMK Personal Papers, MG 26, Series J3, Vol. 93, File 2, McLean, Harry, LAC.

27. WLMK Diary, Aug. 7, 1944, 733.

28. Ibid.

29. G. G. McGeer, "Part of Address at Complimentary Dinner to the Rt. Hon. W. L. Mackenzie King, P.C., M.P., Prime Minister of Canada, The Portrait Bust"; provided to author by Eugene Fairbanks, son of Avard Fairbanks, on Nov. 19, 2001.

30. Williams, *Mayor Gerry,* 257. Williams writes, "One would have thought from McGeer's encomium that he was John the Baptist introducing the Messiah at a service-club banquet."

31. McGeer, "Part of Address."

32. WLMK Diary, Aug. 7, 1944, 733.

33. Ibid., 735. King observed months later that McGeer and Mackenzie "use poor Harry McLean to help their end." WLMK Diary, Nov. 24, 1944, 1235.

34. WLMK Diary, Jan. 23, 1944, 60. King disliked many of McLean's friends and associates, particularly Hepburn, Bickell and Smith. The power and notoriety of Bickell and Smith are evident in the fact that they were agenda items at a meeting between President Roosevelt and Prime Minister King on August 18, 1938. Among the topics to be discussed, such as the King and Queen, Hitler, and Hepburn's behaviour, King noted: "Ben Smith: worse speculator in New York.: Bickell: mining speculator in Canada." Then on July 16, 1940, he noted: "I see Jack Bickell is going to England to join that group. He belongs to the worst money and gambling gang in Canada. They are the people who have been interested in the air business from the start." On August 12, 1941, King wrote "…Hepburn too has been advertising his intention to go to England to assist Bickell in London. I thought most Liberals in the country will be glad to have him, like Bennett, out of Canadian politics altogether. It would be the best thing that could happen and would give him an honourable exit…" And two days later, on August 14th: "I was immensely amused in hearing over the radio that Hepburn, after announcing that he was going to help Bickell in the Air Ministry, had been forced to say, after leaving the Cabinet meeting, that he did not know what he was going to do as Bickell had left the Air Ministry and his whereabouts as at present were unknown. These are the men to whom are being entrusted the destiny of a country at a time of war!"

35. Stalin was not there. He did not want to leave his command post.

36. WLMK Diary, Sept. 19, 1944, 873.

37. Ibid.

38. Ibid.

39. Ibid., 874.

40. Ibid.

41. Ibid.

42. Ibid., 874–875.

43. Ibid. Aside from the ongoing relationship with a long-dead mother and three dogs named Pat, the "King of Quirk" had an obsession with the hands on a clock. His diary reveals continual references to the time of day. Upon completion of a task, King would check the clock: if the two hands were together or in a straight line, this was taken to be a good omen.

44. "Minutes of Meeting of the Directors of the Dominion Construction Corporation Limited," Oct. 12, 1944. RG 95, Vol. 599, Dominion Construction Co., LAC.

45. Turner, *Merrickville: Jewel on the Rideau,* 103–104.

46. Paragraph written by Colin Churcher.

47. Ibid.

48. Bolton interview.
49. Ibid.
50. Hyson reminiscences; Charles Switzer to HFM, Nov. 9, 1944. HFM Coll., MG 30, B 131, Vol. 2, Hawk Lake Quarry, ON – Grenville Crushed Rock Co. (1944–49), LAC.
51. Ibid.
52. Ibid.
53. Ibid.
54. Robichaud Frères Ltd. [New Brunswick Fish and Seafood Dealers] to WLMK, Nov. 9, 1944. WLMK Personal Papers, MG 26, Series J3, Vol. 93, File 2, McLean, Harry, LAC.
55. Roberts, *C. D.: The Life and Times of Clarence Decatur Howe*, 130–32.
56. Hyson reminiscences; Charles Switzer to HFM, Nov. 9 1944. HFM Coll., MG 30, B 131, Vol. 2, Hawk Lake Quarry, ON – Grenville Crushed Rock Co. (1944-49), LAC.

Chapter Sixteen: The Mysterious Mr. X

1. John MacLean, "Money Gone – No Regrets," *Toronto Telegram,* July 13, 1956.
2. "Merrickville McLean Is Master Magician in Matter of Money," *Ottawa Citizen,* Nov. 17, 1943.
3. "Generous Mr. X Is Identified as H. F. McLean," Toronto *Globe,* Nov. 9, 1943.
4. Turner, "Bountiful Harry McLean," 11.
5. "Generous Mr. X."
6. Puddington interview.
7. Val Andrews, *Goodnight Mr. Dante* (London: Goodliffe, 1978). The two Harrys, McLean and Dante, had a few other things in common. They were born in the same year, and although Dante was born in Copenhagen, Denmark, both men grew up in the American Midwest, Dante in St. Paul and McLean in Bismarck. And they shared a fondness for liquor.
8. " 'Mr. X' Scatters $3,300 in Second Pre-Yule Visit to Christie St. Hospital" (n.p.), Nov. 17, 1943.
9. Ibid.; Turner, "Bountiful Harry McLean."
10. Puddington interview.
11. "Customs Officials Given to Show Girls by 'Mr. X'," Toronto *Globe,* Dec. 1 1943; "Girl Gets Her Mink Coat; One of Six Pays $1000 Duty at Border," *New York Times,* Dec. 24, 1943.
12. "It Was Also Raining Money in Windsor Yesterday," *New York Times,* Mar. 30, 1944.
13. "Mr. X. Financially Cut Off: 'Look Out for Me Again'," *Toronto Star,* Mar. 30, 1944.
14. "Philanthropy with Flourish," *Zanesville* (Ohio) *Signal,* Apr. 4, 1944.
15. "Mr. X. Financially Cut Off."
16. Ibid.
17. "M'Lean Cheques Are Uncashed," Toronto *Globe,* Apr. 3, 1944.
18. "A Suggestion for Mr. X," Toronto *Globe,* Apr. 19, 1944.
19. "Philanthropy with Flourish."
20. "Mr X's Generosity Inspires Great Flood of Fan Mail," Toronto *Globe,* Dec. 6, 1943.
21. MacLean, "Money Gone – No Regrets." One letter from a "crackpot" McLean kept, likely because it was the most extreme of the lot. Written by a thirty-six-year-old transient living in San Francisco, the fourteen-page letter outlined in excruciating detail the writer's every imaginable want and need. Citing ill health, the woman began by asking for "enough money to get a good long rest in an electric heated cabin with a private tub and bath" and naming

Yosemite National Park as the venue of choice. She itemized her immediate requirements, which included $25 reading glasses, one hat, one dress, one coat, two one-hundred-percent wool petticoats, twelve cakes of good soap, a pair of Florsheim shoes for $14.50 and ten nails to fix the loose slats in her bed.

The self-proclaimed "Deaconness" said she owed money to various religious organizations: $13 to the Salvation Army, $4 to the Methodist Church and $20.40 (dues for two years) to the First Baptist Church of Los Angeles. She was indebted to many doctors she had consulted for advice on the numerous health concerns that prevented her from being gainfully employed. Among the woman's list of ailments was a "big double tumor" – the direct result of an attempt on her life by her ex-husband, sinus trouble, and shooting pain in her thighs and knees – neuritis, arthritis or rheumatism. She pinpointed March 18, 1942, as the very date that her "early change of life" began and described an acute vitamin deficiency that caused her eyes to water – both of which conditions required medication.

She claimed to be malnourished for ninety-eight percent of her life.

She also claimed to be a highly moral person ("a virgin, Honest God's truth"), engaging in no illicit activity such as dancing, bingo, movies or risqué books. As further evidence of her chaste character, she proclaimed that she possessed "*no* abbreviated undies, *no* abbreviated evening gown or abbreviated swimsuit." Upon her arrival in San Francisco, she had gone to forty-one hotels before finding a room, ultimately having to settle for a room with spotted wallpaper at the Grand Pacific Rooming House. On average, she slept only three hours a night due to "100 noises" from drunken men of all nationalities loitering outside her door or setting fires in the hallway. Teetering on the brink of a nervous breakdown, she could no longer tolerate the squalor of her life and appealed to McLean for relief. Hearing nothing, she wrote again:

Dear Friend – I forgot to tell you that I have a clear record and that I pawned my 3 small diamond rings in the Remedial Loan Co. Mission Station 5th San Francisco in Sept. for $57 because I was hungry. Of course the interest is growing! I have to eat less because I registered this letter *but* it is the only way I know that you will get it safely – You can verify my record – Personnel Manager U.S. Govt McClellan Field – Sacramento California – Honorable Discharge failed to pass trial period due to ill health.

Whether McLean sent the woman any money is unknown. Anna Schmidt to HFM, Dec. 1, 1943. HFM Coll., MG 30 B 131 Vol. I, File 1-13, LAC.

22. Eugene Fairbanks to author, private correspondence, Nov. 19, 2001.

23. Joan Finnigan, "Where It's Christmas Every Day!" Ottawa *Journal,* n.d.; "Address of Dr. L. H. Newman to the Merrickville and District Historical Society on the Subject of Harry McLean," Oct. 26, 1972; Fred Inglis, "Home of Millionaire 'Harry' McLean," *Ottawa Citizen,* n.d.

24. "Native of Bismarck, Harry F. M'Lean, Rail Builder, Dies," *Bismarck Tribune,* May 25, 1961.

25. "Address of Dr. L. H. Newman."

26. "Smithsonian Institution Patron Certificate," issued to H. F. McLean; "The King George V Silver Jubilee Cancer Fund for Canada," issued to "Colonel H. F. McLean for his generous contribution"; "Certificate of Appreciation to Harry F. McLean," issued by the Canadian Legion of the British Empire Service League. MG 30, B 131, Vol. 1, File 1-15. The results of two of McLean's donations endure today; see Appendices 1 and 2.

27. Morant, "The Sons of Martha Cairns," 6.

28. *Therrien v. Dominion Construction Corp. Ltd. et al.; Therrien v. Grenville Crushed Rock Co. Ltd. et al.* [1944] 4 D.L.R. 400 Ontario High Court, Barlow, J. Sept. 20, 1944.

29. Ibid.

30. Ibid.

31. Ibid.

32. Handwritten note by F. I. Ker on letter from James A. Therrien to Cook Construction Co. Ltd., May 7, 1915. F. I. Ker Papers, OA.

33. McNally interview.

34. "Generous 'Mr. X' Again Showers Cash on Troops," Toronto *Globe,* Aug. 9, 1945.

35. "Mr. X. Is in Town Again, with Orchids This Time," Toronto *Globe,* Feb. 8, 1946.

Chapter Seventeen: Power-Drunk Political Tin Gods

1. HFM to WLMK, Dec. 28, 1945. WLMK Personal Papers, MG 26, Series J3, Vol. 93, File 2, McLean, Harry, LAC.

2. McNally interview.

3. Ibid.

4. Roberts, *C. D.: The Life and Times of Clarence Decatur Howe,* 151.

5. McNally interview.

6. Ibid.

7. Switzer, Untitled Paper on Harry McLean and Dominion Construction.

8. Richard I. Frears, *Frears Annotated Income War Tax Act and Excess Profits Tax Act 1947* (Toronto: Canadian Law List Publishing, 1947), 1.

9. McNally interview.

10. Ibid.

11. "Annual Christmas Tree" (n.p.), 1944.

12. Joan Finnigan, "Where It's Christmas Every Day," Ottawa *Journal,* n.d.

13. Murphy, *My Kind of People,* 115.

14. Wendell "Dell" Bower, e-mail to author, May 15, 2005.

15. Bolton interview.

16. C. E. Hyson to HFM, Sept. 6, 1945. HFM Papers, LAC.

17. "Books-Authors," *New York Times,* Mar. 23, 1945. McLean read Bishop's *Winged Peace* three times. Bishop had to phone his publisher, Viking, to alert them to the large order.

18. OSW to Mr. Turnbull, "Office of the Prime Minister Memorandum," Apr. 16, 1945. WLMK Correspondence – Microfilm, 346879.

19. Granatstein, *The Canadians. W. L. Mackenzie King,* 58.

20. Murphy, *My Kind of People,* 113–114.

21. HFM to The Hon. Mr. J. S. Ilsley, Minister of Finance, Oct. 17, 1945. WLMK Personal Papers, MG 26, Series J3, Vol. 93, File 2, McLean, Harry, LAC.

22. HFM to WLMK, Dec. 28, 1945. WLMK Personal Papers, MG 26, Series J3, Vol. 93, File 2, McLean, Harry, LAC; "A History of the Canadian Dollar, Canada under Exchange Controls, The War Years (1939–45)" (justiceplus.org/thedollar/htm).

23. Department of National Revenue Taxation Division, to HFM, Dec. 8, 1945. WLMK Personal Papers, MG 26, Series J3, Vol. 93, File 2, McLean, Harry, LAC.

24. HFM to W. S. Mackenzie, Esq. Officer in Charge of Legal Processes, Department of National Revenue, Dec. 28, 1945. WLMK Personal Papers, MG 26, Series J3, Vol. 93, File 2, McLean, Harry, LAC.

25. HFM to W(S) Mackenzie, Officer in Charge of Legal Processes, Department of National Revenue, Dec. 21, 1945. WLMK Personal Papers, MG 26, Series J3, Vol. 93, File 2, McLean, Harry, LAC.

26. Ibid.

27. HFM to WLMK, Dec. 28, 1945. WLMK Personal Papers, MG 26, Series J3, Vol. 93, File 2, McLean, Harry, LAC.

28. Ibid., [abt. 1947].

29. [L. B. Abbott] H. F. McLean Limited to D. S. Kirby, Apr. 4, 1950. H. F. McLean Limited, RG 95, Vol. 783, LAC.

30. HFM to WLMK, Dec. 28, 1945. WLMK Personal Papers, MG 26, Series J3, Vol. 93, File 2, McLean, Harry, LAC.

31. Ker interview.

32. Thomas H. Turner, "In Merrickville They 'Go to the Dogs' Every Day. Village Sports Flourish, Thanks to Mr. 'X'," *Evening Citizen* (Ottawa), Jan. 29, 1947.

33. Finnigan, "Where It's Christmas Every Day."

34. "Address of Dr. L. H. Newman."

35. Kelso interview.

36. Lenore Newman, daughter of Dr. L. H. Newman, discussion with author.

37. McNally interview.

38. Arthur Heroux, discussion with author.

39. Bolton interview.

40. Kelso interview.

41. Ibid.

42. MacLean, "Mr. X' He Threw Away $50,000."

43. "Merrickville on the Rideau: A Good Place to Live: McLean Estate" (n.d., n.p.).

44. Kelso interview.

45. "Merrickville on the Rideau: A Good Place to Live: McLean Estate."

46. Bolton interview.

47. Kelso interview.

48. Frank Finnigan Sr., interview by Joan Mackenzie (Finnigan), Jan. 1978. A1 2003-05-0093 (46:50 min) ISN 154526, LAC; Joan Finnigan, *Giants of Canada's Ottawa Valley* (Burnstown, Ont.: The General Store Publishing, 1981), 117.

49. Ibid.

50. Frank Finnigan Jr., interview by Joan Mackenzie (Finnigan), Jan. 1978. A1 2003-05-0092 (58:47 min) ISN 154480, LAC.

51. Lenore Newman, discussion with author.

52. Frank Finnigan Jr. interview

53. McNally interview.

Chapter Eighteen: The Evening of Our Lives

1. William Shakespeare, Seven Ages of Man, from *As You Like It,* Act II, Sc. 7.

2. Hyson reminiscences, Tape 5; HFM to WLMK, 1947. WLMK Personal Papers, MG 26, Series J3, Vol. 93, File 2, McLean, Harry, LAC; Hyson interview. He spent the time fishing and the only work he engaged in was to direct C. E. Hyson to build another Sons of Martha cairn at the side of the tracks. Shortly thereafter, the plant was sold and dismantled.

3. WLMK Diary, July 29, 1947, 685.

4. Ibid.

5. Ibid.

6. Ibid.

7. Ibid., Dec. 10, 1935, 7.

8. Ibid., Aug. 21, 1947, 818.

9. Ibid., Oct. 8, 1949, 91/94.

10. HFM to WLMK, Dec. 23, 1947. WLMK Personal Papers, MG 26, Series J3, Vol. 93, File 2, McLean, Harry, LAC.

11. WLMK Diary, Dec. 23, 1947, 1234.

12. HFM to WLMK, Jan. 22, 1948. WLMK Personal Papers, MG 26, Series J3, Vol. 93, File 2, McLean, Harry, LAC.

13. Ibid., Dec. 31, 1947.

14. Ian Mackenzie, Minister of Veterans Affairs, to WLMK. WLMK Papers, Microfilm, Jan. 17, 1948, 401078, LAC.

15. J. L. Granatstein and Norman Hillmer, *Prime Ministers: Ranking Canada's Leaders* (Toronto: HarperCollins, 1999), 100.

16. HFM to WLMK, Jan. 22, 1948.

17. WLMK to HFM, Feb. 17, 1945. HFM Coll. MG 30 B 131, Vol. I, Correspondence, General, LAC.

18. HFM to WLMK, Feb. 19, 1948. WLMK Personal Papers, MG 26, Series J3, Vol. 93, File 2, McLean, Harry, LAC.

19. William A. Falconer, Biography, 1859–1943. Papers Mss 228, IRS.

20. "Burleigh Pioneer Dies Here Monday," *Bismarck Tribune,* June 22, 1948.

21. "Son of Bismarck's First Mayor Dies in California," *Bismarck Tribune,* Sept. 13, 1948. Clarence McLean was not interred in the family plot in St. Paul.

22. McLean paid $6,000 for the property. Deed of Sale, Province of Quebec, District and County of Bonaventure, July 26, 1949. Part of Lot 614 on the east of the Little Cascapedia River. This lot now forms Camp Brûlé, a fishing lodge of which McLean was a member; see campbrule.com.

23. Puddington interview. The platinum king whom Puddington referred to was the millionaire Charles Engelhard, president of the Engelhard Minerals and Chemicals Co. of Newark, New Jersey. Engelhard had many world-famous guests at his fishing camp, including Ian Fleming, author of the James Bond series. Engelhard was Fleming's inspiration for the character Goldfinger.

24. On August 12, 1946, black mine workers went on strike to address the wage inequity between black and white miners. The miners had tried, but failed, to discuss a wage increase with the mine magnates. Not surprisingly, no one with wealth was in a hurry to end the policy of cheap labour and the pleas for more money were ignored. Typically, white workers made twelve times more than their black counterparts. Jan Christian Smuts, the South African prime minister, sent in the police to force the miners back to work. The violence went on for five days, and in the end the workers gained nothing. Charles Engelhard sat on the Board of Directors of the Witwatersrand Native Labour Association and Native Recruiting Agency.

25. HFM to WLMK, Nov. 12, 1949. WLMK Personal Papers, MG 26, Series J3, Vol. 93, File 2, McLean, Harry, LAC.

26. Ibid. I wonder if this is a true translation of what the Natives said and if the actual names were less than complimentary. I have been unable to determine what language they spoke.

27. Ibid.

28. Ibid.
29. Ibid.
30. McLean Home Movie, *The Ashwin Hunt, South Rhodesia,* 1950. VI 2003 05 0023 – 20 Min., HFM Coll, LAC.
31. HFM to WLMK, Nov. 12, 1949.
32. WLMK Diary, Dec. 17, 1949, n.p.
33. HFM to Hon. Jean François Pouliot, M.P. Temiscouata, Quebec, May 3, 1952, enclosing Africa Diary of HFM, Nov. 8, 1951. MG 27 III C18, Vol. 22, TS, LAC. McLean flew to Bismarck in his seven-passenger plane in May 1951: "Visitor," *Bismarck Tribune,* May 18, 1951.
34. Shirley M. Goodman, daughter of Charles Switzer, e-mail to author, Aug. 7, 2005.
35. HFM to Hon. Jean François Pouliot.
36. Ibid.
37. Ibid.
38. "Croydon Air Crash Takes 12 Lives; 3 Nuns and a Family of 4 Victims," *New York Times,* Jan. 25, 1947.
39. Accident description, Jan. 25, 1947. Douglas C-47A-85-DL, Spencer Airways, VP-YFD. A Web site devoted to ghost sightings in the United Kingdom, aviation-safety.net, reports that the three nuns on board with Ted Spencer continue to haunt the Roundshaw Estate neighbourhood in Croydon (http://www.mystical-www.co.uk/ghost/zsee.htm).
40. HFM Africa Diary, 1951.
41. Ibid.
42. Ibid.
43. Ibid.
44. Ibid.
45. Ibid.
46. Ibid.
47. Murphy, *My Kind of People,* 110.
48. HFM to Charles Switzer, Aug. 19, 1953. J. J. McNally private papers. The petition to surrender the charter of Dominion Construction Corporation Limited was signed in Merrickville by McLean and Switzer on August 11, 1954, some five years after Switzer had made inquiries as to how to proceed to cease operations.
49. Ibid.
50. Cooke reminiscences.
51. William B. Falconer to Erling Ralfsrud, Apr. 23, 1954. Erling Ralfsrud Papers, HFM file, IRS.
52. William was eighty-five when he died. His body was sent to the family burial grounds in St. Paul. Cemetery Records, Oakland Cemetery, St. Paul, Minnesota re: Lot No. 3, Block No. 17 – John A. McLean owner.
53. MacLean, " 'Mr. X' He Threw Away $50,000."
54. Ibid.
55. Ibid.
56. Ibid.

Epilogue: A Good Life

1. MacLean, "'Mr. X' He Threw Away $50,000."
2. Puddington interview.

3. Roberts, "On Being a Character."
4. "Native of Bismarck, Harry F. M'Lean, Rail Builder, Dies," *Bismarck Tribune,* May 25, 1961.
5. As told to author by Betty Weedmark, Merrickville. Betty's husband, Fred, was one of the men who were called upon.
6. See Postscript.
7. "Mr. X's Estate Set at $108,058; $75.62 in Cash," Toronto *Globe,* July 26, 1961.
8. Morant, "The Sons of Martha Cairns," 6.

Appendix 1: The Franks Flying Suit

1. Banting War Diaries, Oct. 15, 1939. Official Stenographers Note Book, Box 32A, TFRBL.
2. Andrew Duffy, "Canada's Anti-gravity Suit," *Ottawa Citizen,* Nov. 11, 2001.
3. Ibid.
4. Ian Montagnes, "The Franks Flying Suit," *Varsity Magazine* (University of Toronto), n.d., 20.
5. Ibid., 90.
6. Duffy, "Canada's Anti-gravity Suit."
7. Banting War Diaries, Oct. 10, 1939. Sir Frederick wrote an interesting little note about the prime minister: "King is a public enemy & a public nuisance, a senile, bigoted, egotistical vote getting-politician who baths in Virginia when a young active leader is required in Ottawa."
8. Ibid., Oct. 14, 1939; Montagnes, "The Franks Flying Suit," 92.
9. Ibid. Rose Fader, who with her husband bought McLean's house after his death, told me that during one night of marathon telephone calling to people all over the world, the harried operator told McLean, "Go to bed, Harry!"
10. Ibid.
11. Ibid.
12. Montagnes, "The Franks Flying Suit," 92.
13. Ibid., 94.
14. Banting War Diaries, Oct. 30, 1939.
15. Ibid., Nov. 8, 1939.
16. Montagnes, "The Franks Flying Suit," 90.
17. Ibid.
18. Duffy, "Canada's Anti-gravity Suit."
19. War Technical and Scientific Development Committee Minutes, Sept. 20, 1940. Part of Chalmers Jack Mackenzie fonds – MG 30, B 22, Vol. 2, R1686-0-4-E, LAC.
20. Ibid.
21. Montagnes, "The Franks Flying Suit," 96.
22. Duffy, "Canada's Anti-gravity Suit."
23. War Technical and Scientific Development Committee Minutes, Feb. 25, 1941. Part of Chalmers Jack Mackenzie fonds – MG 30, B 22, Vol. 2, R1686-0-4-E, LAC.

Appendix 2: The Iron Ring Ceremony and the Sons of Martha Cairns

1. Nicholas Morant, "Kipling's Verses Adorn Mystery Cairn: Calling of an Engineer Based on Biblical Tale," *CP Rail News,* Vol. 12, no. 4 (17 Mar.), 1982.
2. Ibid.
3. Rudyard Kipling to H. E. T. Haultain, Nov. 9, 1923. Provided to author by Thomas Pinney.
4. Rudyard Kipling to H. E. T. Haultain, June 3, 1925. Provided to author by Thomas Pinney.
5. "Engineer's Heart Was in Our Mines," *Toronto Star,* Apr. 8, 1978.
6. Notes by Thomas Pinney about the correspondence from Kipling to Haultain, Sept. 1994, 46; June 1995, 40.
7. Rudyard Kipling to H. E. T. Haultain, July 6, 1930. Provided to author by Thomas Pinney.
8. Karen Smith, Kipling Librarian at Dalhousie University, to Greg Gatenby, Artistic Director, Harbourfront, Toronto, July 15, 1991; provided to author by Karen Smith.
9. "Kipling's Message to His Own Craft," Montreal *Gazette,* June 7, 1930.
10. Discussions with the Kipling scholars suggest that the visit to Montreal is the most likely occasion for the meeting between McLean and Kipling. The existence of the handwritten poems indicates that such a meeting occurred, as do the statements from McLean's employees, such as Charles Switzer.
11. The daughter of R. A. Ross, an engineer, has in her possession one of the handwritten "Sons of Martha" poems that Kipling gave to McLean.
12. Rudyard Kipling to H. E. T. Haultain, July 6, 1930; provided to author by Thomas Pinney; Pinney, notes to letter from Kipling to Haultain, Nov. 9, 1923; Switzer, Untitled Paper on Harry McLean and Dominion Construction.
13. [C. E. Hyson], "Sons of Martha Monuments" (n.p., n.d.), handwritten. HFM Coll, MG 30, B 131, Vol. 1, File 1-21, LAC.
14. "Monument to Pioneers Erected at Washburn," *Bismarck Tribune,* Aug. 20, 1952; Tom Isern, "Plains Folk: Sons of Martha," *North Dakota State University News* (NDSU Agriculture Communication), Nov. 28, 2002.

Bibliography

The following abbreviations are used in the bibliography:

ANS = Archives of Nova Scotia
AO = Archives of Ontario
GFHS = Grand Falls Historical Society
IRS = Institute for Regional Studies, North Dakota State University Libraries
LAC = Library and Archives of Canada
MANY = Municipal Archives of New York
MHS = Montana Historical Society
MUA = McGill University Archives
SHSND = State Historical Society of North Dakota
TFRBL = Thomas Fisher Rare Book Library, University of Toronto

Archival Collections

Allied War Supplies Corporation sous fonds, LAC.

Banting, Sir Frederick Grant. War Diaries – Aviation Medicine & Other Wartime Research. TFRBL.

Biographical Sketches of the Falconer Family. IRS, North Dakota State University Libraries, Fargo, North Dakota.

Borden, Robert Laird (1854–1937) Prime Ministers Fonds, LAC.

Canadian Expeditionary Force sous fonds, LAC.

Cook, Andrew Braid. Papers. Coll. No. 280 MHS, Helena, Montana.

Department of National Defence fonds (HCMS Cornwallis, Point Edward Naval Base) LAC.

Department of Transport fonds, LAC.

Government of Canada Files (Munitions and Supply, Canadian National Railways), LAC.

Hearn, Richard L. Papers. AO, Toronto, Ontario.

Hepburn, Mitchell. Papers. AO, Toronto, Ontario.

Hogan, Frank. Fay-Bove File. MANY, New York, New York.

Howe, C.D. fonds, LAC.

Ker, Frederick I. Papers. AO, Toronto, Ontario.

King, William Lyon Mackenzie. Diary. LAC online, Ottawa, Ontario.

King, William Lyon Mackenzie. Papers. LAC, Ottawa, Ontario.

Latchford, Francis Robert. Collection, LAC.

Mackenzie, Ian. Papers. LAC, Ottawa, Ontario.

McLean, Harry Falconer Fonds, LAC, Ottawa, Ontario.

McLean, William J. Service Records. SHSND, Bismarck, North Dakota.

Merrilees, Andrew Audubon fonds, LAC.

Rolfsrud, Erling Nicholai. Papers. IRS, North Dakota State University Libraries, Fargo, North Dakota.

Interviews

Bolton, Harold. Interview by author. Tape recording. Merrickville, Ont., Oct. 11, 1997.

Cooke, Murray. Reminiscences. Tape recording. Kenora, Ont., n.d. Harry Falconer McLean Collection, LAC.

Hanlan, Edison. Interview by Charles Hyson. Tape recording. Toronto, May 15, 1973. Harry Falconer McLean Collection, LAC.

Hearn, Richard L. Interview by Charles Hyson and Joseph and Paul McNally. Tape recording. Queenston, Ont., Dec. 6, 1973. Harry Falconer McLean Collection, LAC.

Heroux, Arthur. Interview by author. Handwritten notes. Merrickville, Ont., Oct. 8, 1997.

Humphrey, Jack B. Interview by Charles Hyson. Tape recording. Leaside, Ont., n.d. LAC.

Hyson, Charles. Reminiscences. Tape recording. Etobicoke, Ont., n.d. Harry Falconer McLean Collection, LAC.

Kelso, Joseph. Interview by author. Tape recording. Oxford Mills, Ont., May 31, 1997.

Ker, Frederick I. Interview by Charles Hyson. Tape recording. Toronto, Oct. 12, 1973. Harry Falconer McLean Collection, LAC.

Leeder, Ted. Interview by author. Tape recording. Charleston Lake, Ont., Oct. 12, 1997.

McLaren, Arthur. Interview by Charles Hyson. Tape recording. Niagara Falls, Ont., Dec. 31, 1972. Harry Falconer McLean Collection, LAC.

McNally, Joseph J. Interview by author. Tape recording. Grimsby, Ont., Apr. 20, 2001.

Mitchell, Gordon. Interview by Charles Hyson. Tape recording. Toronto, Jan. 1973. Harry Falconer McLean Collection, LAC.

Puddington, Jack. Interview by author. Tape recording. Ottawa, Sept. 26, 1997.

Richardson, W. George. Self-interview. Tape recording. Kingston, Ont., Aug. 17, 1978. Harry Falconer McLean Collection, LAC.

Outside Interviews

Finnigan, Frank Sr., interviewed by Joan Mackenzie (Finnigan), Jan. 1978. A1 2003-05-0093 (46:50 min) ISN 154526. LAC.

Finnigan, Frank Jr., interviewed by Joan Mackenzie (Finnigan), Jan. 1978. A1 2003-05-0092 (58:47 min) ISN 154480. LAC.

Films

Abitibi Canyon: The Story of the Conquest of a River. Harry Falconer McLean Collection, LAC ISN 33246.

The Ashwin Hunt: South Rhodesia. Harry Falconer McLean Collection, LAC. 1950 V1 2003 05 0023.

Close-Up. CBC Toronto Kine Collection. CBC #11687 T/C May 30/1962.

Durban Sea Shore: Home Movie. Harry Falconer McLean Collection, LAC. V1 2003 05 0023.

McKenna, Brian. *War at Sea: U-boats in the St. Lawrence*. Montreal: National Film Board of Canada, 1995.

Parker, Alan. *The Road to Wellville*. Culver City: Parker, Alan; Bernstein, Armyan, and Colesberry, Robert F., 2002.

Sherwood, Anthony. *Honour Before Glory*. Toronto: Anthony Sherwood Productions, 2001.

Public Documents

Office of the Fire Marshal, Parliament Buildings, Toronto. *Investigator's Report. Death of Irene McLean,* July 10, 1942.

Racine, Armand. *Temiskaming and Northern Ontario Railway Inquiry,* Aug. 8, 1934. Toronto: T. E. Bowman, Printer to the King's Most Excellent Majesty, 1935.

Reported Court Cases

Alexander McKenzie, 180 U.S. 536, Supreme Court of the United States.

Barthelmes v. Bickell (1921), 62 S.C.R. 599.

Cook v. Deeks, [1915] O.J. No. 163, 2 Mar. 1915.

Cook v. Deeks, [1916] D.L.R. 1, 23 Feb. 1916.

Cook v. Hinds, 44 D.L.R. 586, Ontario Supreme Court, 1 Mar. 1918.

Fay v. New York 332 U.S. 784.

Fay v. New York 329 U.S. 697.

Fay v. New York 332 U.S. 261.

John A. McLean v. The United States, United States Court of Claims, 17 Ct. Cl. 83; 1881.

Joseph S. Fay v. Commissioner, James Bove v. Commissioner 12 T.C.M. (CCH) 14.

J. P. Bickell & Company v. Cutten [1926] S.C.R. 340.

Maloof v. J. P. Bickell and Co. (1919), 59 S.C.R. 429.

Noyes, No. 701 Circuit Court of Appeals, Ninth Circuit, 121 F. 209; 1902 U.S. App. 6 Jan. 1902.

People v. Fay et al. 43 N.Y.S. 2d 826.

People v. Fay et al. 54 N.Y.S. 2d 541.

People v. Fay 268 A.D. 135.

People ex rel. Bove v. McDonnell 128 N.Y.S. 2d 643.

Phelan v. Famous Players Canadian Corp. [1939] O.J. No. 291.

Therrien v. Dominion Construction Corp. Ltd. et al. [1944] 4 D.L.R. 400.

Legislation

Frears, Richard I. *Frears Annotated Income Tax War Act and Excess Profits Tax Act 1940.* Toronto: Canadian Law List Publishing, 1947.

The Operation of a Railway to the Flin Flon Mines Act, RSM 1990 c. 133.

Treaty of Fort Laramie, 1868.

Books

Andrews, Val. *Goodnight Mr. Dante.* London: Goodliffe, 1978.

Ball, Norman R., ed. *Building Canada: A History of Public Works.* Toronto: University of Toronto Press, 1988.

Bauman, Beth Hughes, and Dorothy J. Jackman. *Burleigh County: Prairie Trails to Hi-Ways.* Bismarck, N.D.: Bismarck-Mandan Genealogical and Historical Society, 1978.

Beach, Rex. *The Spoilers.* New York: A. L. Burt, 1905.

Beschloss, Michael. *The Conquerors: Roosevelt, Truman and the Destruction of Hitler's Germany 1941–1945.* New York: Simon & Schuster, 2002.

Bird, George F., and Edwin J. Taylor Jr. *History of the City of Bismarck, North Dakota: The First 100 Years 1872–1972.* Bismarck, N.D.: Bismarck Centennial Association, 1972.

Brooks, John. *Once in Golconda: A True Drama of Wall Street 1920–1938.* New York: Harper & Row, 1969.

Combs, Barry B. *Westward to Promontory: Building the Union Pacific across the Plains and Mountains.* New York: Garland, 1969.

Cunningham, Barry, with Mike Pearl. *Mr. District Attorney.* New York: Mason/Charter, 1977.

Custer, Elizabeth B. *Boots and Saddles or, Life in Dakota with General Custer.* Volume 17 in Western Frontier Library series. Norman, Okla., and London: University of Oklahoma Press, 1885/ 1961.

Day, Steven R. *A Journey into the History of Canada and the United States: A Book about Falkner, MacLean, Smith, Day and Krieg*. Mukilteo, Washington: Privately published by Steven R. Day, 2000.

Dodge, Grenville M. *How We Built the Union Pacific Railway and Other Railway Papers and Addresses*. Washington: Government Printing Office, 1910/Readex Microprint Corporation, 1966.

Essex, James W. *Victory in the St. Lawrence*. Erin, Ont.: Boston Mills Press, 2004.

Fairbanks, Eugene F. *A Sculptor's Testimony in Bronze and Stone: Sacred Sculpture of Avard T. Fairbanks*. Salt Lake City: Publisher's Press, 1972.

Finnigan, Joan. *Giants of Canada's Ottawa Valley*. Burnstown, Ont.: General Store Publishing, 1981.

Finnigan, Joan. *Legacies, Legends and Lies*. Toronto: Deneau, 1985.

Fotheringham, Robert, ed. *Songs of Men*. New York: Houghton Mifflin/Cambridge: Riverside Press, 1918.

Galusha, Diane. *Liquid Assets: A History of New York City's Water System*. Fleischmanns, N.Y.: Purple Mountain Press, 1999.

Granatstein, J. L. *The Canadians. W. L. Mackenzie King*. Markham, Ont.: Fitzhenry & Whiteside, 2002.

Granatstein, J. L., and Norman Hillmer. *Prime Ministers: Ranking Canada's Leaders*. Toronto: HarperCollins, 1999.

Hadley, Michael L. *U-boats against Canada: German Submarines in Canadian Waters*. Montreal and Kingston: McGill-Queen's University Press, 1985.

Hedman, Valerie, Loretta Yauck and Joyce Henderson. *Flin Flon*. Flin Flon, Man.: Flin Flon Historical Society, 1974.

Hutchinson, John. *The Imperfect Union: A History of Corruption in American Trade Unions*. New York: E. P. Dutton, 1972.

Kimber, Stephen. *Sailors, Slackers and Blind Pigs: Halifax at War*. Toronto: Doubleday, 2002.

Kipling, Rudyard. *Something of Myself for My Friends Known and Unknown*. New York: Doubleday, Doran, 1937.

Kitz, Janet F. *Shattered City: The Halifax Explosion and the Road to Recovery*. Halifax: Nimbus, 1989.

Krause, Herbert, and Gary D. Olson. *Prelude to Glory: A Newspaper Accounting of Custer's 1874 Expedition to the Black Hills*. Sioux Falls, S.D.: Brevet Press, 1974.

Lagacé, Anita. *How Grand Falls Grew*. Saint John, N.B.: n.p., 1945.

Lauriston, Victor. *Romantic Kent*. Chatham, Ont.: Shepherd Printing, 1952.

Leckie, Shirley A. *Elizabeth Bacon Custer and the Making of a Myth*. Norman, Okla., and London: University of Oklahoma Press, 1993.

Lounsberry, Colonel Clement A. *Early History of North Dakota* (Chapter 21: Politics in Indian Affairs). Duluth, Minn.: F. H. Lounsberry, 1913.

MacDonald, Bruce. *The Guysborough Railway: 1897–1939*. Antigonish, N.S.: Inukshuk Trading Company, 1973.

MacEwan, Grant. *The Battle for the Bay*. Saskatoon: Western Producer, 1975.

Marceau, Margaret, in collaboration with Patrick McCooey. *Grand Falls Yesterdays: A History of Grand Falls.* Grand Falls, N.B.: Grand Falls Historical Society, 1991/Merritt Press, 2001.

Maxtone-Graham, John. *The Only Way to Cross.* New York: Collier, 1972.

McKenty, Neil. *Mitch Hepburn.* Toronto: McClelland & Stewart, 1967.

Murphy, Mike. *My Kind of People.* Westport, Ont.: Butternut Press, 1987.

Newans, G. Jean. *All Around the Township.* Oxford Mills, Ont.: n.p. (cerlox bound), 1984.

Newman, Leonard H. *Harry Falconer McLean 1883–1961.* Merrickville, Ont.: n.p., n.d.

Patterson, Ruth, and Jack Patterson. *Cranberry Portage.* Toronto: McClelland & Stewart, 1970.

Preston-Muddock, J. E. *The Sunless City.* London: F. V. White, 1905.

Ray, Joel. *We Remember Dante.* Jackson, Miss.: Northpointe Publishing, 1992.

Roberts, Leslie. *C. D.: The Life and Times of Clarence Decatur Howe.* Toronto: Clarke, Irwin, 1957.

Rolfsrud, Erling Nicolai. *Extraordinary North Dakotans.* Alexandria, Minn.: Lantern Books, n.d.

Rolfsrud, Erling Nicolai. *Notable North Dakotans.* Farwell, N.D.: Lantern Books, 1987.

Ruck, Calvin W. *The Black Battalion 1916–1920: Canada's Best Kept Military Secret.* Halifax: Nimbus, 1987.

Shakespeare, William. Seven Ages of Man, from *As You Like It,* Act II, Sc. 7. Le Gallienne, Richard. *The World's Best Poetry* (Volume 7). Philadelphia: John D. Morris and Company, 1904.

Slotkin, Richard. *The Fatal Environment: The Myth of the Frontier in the Age of Industrialization, 1800–1900.* New York: Atheneum, 1985.

Stacey, C. P. *A Very Double Life: The Private World of Mackenzie King.* Toronto: Macmillan, 1976.

Surtees, Robert J. *The Northern Connection: Ontario Northland since 1902.* North York, Ont.: Captus, 1992.

Taylor, Geoffrey W. *The Railway Contractors: The Story of John W. Stewart, His Enterprises and Associates.* Victoria: Morriss Publishing, 1988.

Tory, J. C. *Legislative and Other Addresses.* Ottawa: Mortimer, 1932.

Tucker, Albert. *Steam into Wilderness.* Toronto: Fitzhenry & Whiteside, 1978.

Turner, Gordon. *Empress of Britain: Canadian Pacific's Greatest Ship.* Toronto: Stoddart/Erin, Ont.: Boston Mills Press, 1992.

Turner, Larry. *Merrickville: Jewel on the Rideau.* Ottawa: Petherwin Heritage, 1995.

Watson, Patrick. *The Canadians: Biographies of a Nation.* Toronto: McArthur, 2000.

Williams, David Ricardo. *Mayor Gerry: The Remarkable Gerald Grattan McGeer.* Vancouver and Toronto: Douglas & McIntyre, 1986.

Wilson, Peter, ed. *Canadian Railway Troops during World War I: 1st Battalion Canadian Overseas Railway Construction Corps November 1917–April 1918.* Campbellford, Ont.: Wilson's Publishing, 1995.

Articles and Book Chapters

Acres, H. G. "The Maritime's Largest Project." *Electrical News,* June 1929.

Angus, Fred F. "The Canadian Railway Troops in World War I: 'Lest We Forget'." *Canadian Rail,* no. 437 (Nov.–Dec.), 1993.

Ayre, Robert. "New Line to Tap Mineral Wealth." *Canadian National Railway Magazine,* Dec. 1928.

Belk, Clarice. "H. F. McLean '02, Builder of Railroads." In *The William Moore School: In the Service of the Youth of Bismarck for Fifty Years: 1883–1933* (Bismarck, N.D.: n.p., 1933).

Blanchard, A. C. D. "Construction Methods on Grand Falls, N.B., Hydro-Electric Development: Rapid Progress Made Possible by Harmonizing Working Schedule." *Contract Record and Engineering Review,* Nov. 23, 1927.

Blanchard, A. C. D. "Power Development at Grand Falls, N.B." *Canadian Engineer,* Vol. 53, no. 22 (Nov. 29), 1927.

Breidenbach, Francis. "Master of Bronze." *North Dakota Horizons,* Vol. 14. no. 4 (Fall), 1984.

"Canadian National Railways Construction, Betterments, Etc." (n.p.), June 1931.

"Canyon Townsite to Close." *Hydroscope,* May 1980.

Dedijer, Vladimir. "European Crisis, July–August 1914, Sarajevo." *History of the 20th Century,* Vol. 16. (n.p., n.d.).

"Deputy Treasurer Falconer." *North Dakota Magazine,* Vol. 3, no. 3 (Feb.), 1909.

"Dominion Construction Limited: Harry McLean Has Handled Some of Canada's Toughest Jobs." Contractors and Their Achievements No. 3. *Engineering and Contract Record,* Nov. 19, 1941.

Farrell, Ted. "Richard Hearn Looks Back over 90 Years." *Hydroscope,* May 1980.

Grenalds, William O. "Frontier Buster." *American Magazine,* May 1932.

Hillman, Lt. Col. D. "Wolfe's Cove Branch Line and Tunnel, Canadian Pacific Railway." *Canadian Railway and Marine World,* July 1931.

Legget, Robert F. "A Contractor Who Erects Cairns in Honor of Those with Whom He Worked." *Canadian Consulting Engineer,* Aug. 1976.

"Lines Reaching Further North." *Canadian National Railways Magazine,* Apr. 1928.

McNally, Paul, and C. E. Hyson. "H. F. McLean and the Sons of Martha Cairns." *Engineering Journal,* July–Aug. 1977.

McNeice, L. G. "Workman's Falls Power Development on Gull River, Near Minden, Ont." *Canadian Engineer,* Oct. 1935.

"Methods of Driving One Mile Railway Tunnel under City of Quebec: Canadian Pacific Railway Co. Building Connection to New Wolfe's Cove Landing." *Contract Record and Engineering Review,* Mar. 25, 1931.

Montagnes, Ian. "The Franks Flying Suit." *Varsity Graduate* (University of Toronto), n.d.

Montague, J. R., and G. H. Bradshaw. "The Hydro-electric Development at Abitibi Canyon." *Electrical News and Engineering,* Dec. 1, 1933.

Montgomery, Paul. "Ontario's Newest North: The Real Reasons for the Extension of the T&NO Railway to the Shores of James Bay." *Saturday Night Magazine*, n.d.

Montgomery, Paul. "Reclaiming a Lost Empire." *Canadian Magazine*, Sept. 1931.

"A Mystery of Labor Politics: Who Murdered the Sandhog Leader?" *Life*, Vol. 2, no. 10 (Mar.), 1937.

Nicholls, Robert V. V. "Harry Falconer McLean, Engineer-Contractor Extraordinary." Abstract. In *Proceedings of the 1995 Annual Conference of the Canadian Society for Civil Engineering, June 1– 3, 1995*. Ottawa: Canadian Society for Civil Engineering, 1995.

"Notable Maritime Power Development Now Operating." *Contract Record and Engineering Review*, Oct. 1928.

Oliver, Frank. "Manitoba Northern Railway Construction to Flin Flon Mine." *Canadian Railway and Marine World*, Nov. 1928.

Owen, Russell. "McLean's Art of Giving." *New York Times Magazine*, Apr. 9, 1944.

Paterson, Jack. "Steel's March to Flin Flon." *Maclean's*, Oct. 15, 1929.

"Railways and the War." In *The Times History and Encyclopedia of the War*, Vol. 6, part 70 (ch. C). London: Sampson Low, Marston, 1916.

Reid, Russell, ed. "Presentation of the Statue of a Pioneer Family to the State of North Dakota." *North Dakota History*, Vol. 14, no. 4 (Oct.), 1947.

Roberts, Leslie. "Frontier Buster." Montreal *Standard*, May 1934.

Roberts, Leslie. "Men o' War, No. 7: The McLean." n.p., n.d.

Roberts, Leslie. "On Being a Character." Montreal [?] *Standard*, n.d.

Roberts, Leslie. "A Pair of Aces, Frontier Style." *Canadian Magazine*, June 1932.

"Space-Age Achievements." *Varsity Graduate* (University of Toronto), n.d.

Taschereau, Pierre. "Development of the Halifax Railway Cut (1912–1918)." Extract from "South End Railway Cutting: Report No. 2 of the Area Studies Groups." *Halifax Field Naturalists News*, no. 27 (Spring), 1982.

Taylor, A .J. P. "The Outbreak of War." In *History of the 20th Century*, Vol. 4 (ch. 60). London: BPC Publishing, n.d.

Taylor, Linda. "Frontier Buster's Memory Lives On." *Hydroscope*, Oct. 1982.

"Temiskaming and Northern Ontario Railway Extension to James Bay Opened." *Canadian Railway and Marine World*, Aug. 1932.

"Wolfe's Cove Terminal Tunnel, Quebec: Provides New Route between Point Near C.P.R. Palais Station and New Deepwater Docks." *Canadian Engineer*, Aug. 18, 1931.

Unpublished Papers

Falconer, William A. "Early Experience of W. A. Falconer. Pioneer Resident of Bismarck, Dakota Territory" (n.p., n.d.). IRS.

Falconer, William A. "Early History of Burleigh County" (n.p, n.d.). IRS.

McLean, Mary L. "Reminiscences of Pioneer Life." Read at meeting of Current Event Club, Bismarck, North Dakota, Oct. 1907.

Newman, Dr. L. H. "Address of Dr. L. H. Newman to the Merrickville and District Historical Society on the Subject of 'Harry McLean'," Oct. 26, 1972.

Newman, Dr. L. H. "Harry Falconer McLean" (n.p., n.d.).

Roberts, Leslie. "Harry Falconer McLean" (n.p., n.d.).

Rose, Sandy. "Arsenic, Herefords and Old Lace: The Mystery and Majesty with the Legends and Tragedies of the Renowned Montana A. B. Cook Family," n.d., available at Canyon Ferry Mansion, North Townsend, Montana.

Newspapers

Berkshire Evening Page (Pittsfield, Massachusetts), Dec. 1942.

Bismarck Capital, May 1932; Nov. 1943; Sept. 1947.

Bismarck Daily Tribune, May 1874; Mar. 1901; Apr. 1912; Jan., May 1913.

Bismarck Tribune, June, Nov. 1874; Apr., May, Oct., Nov. 1875; Feb. 1876; Nov. 1877; Jan., Feb. 1878; Sept. 1879; Feb., Mar., Apr., May, Dec. 1880; Jan., Apr., Oct., Nov. 1882; June, Aug., Sept. 1883; Aug. 1884; Sept. 1893; July 1898; May 1901; Mar. 1902; Nov. 1906; Aug. 1910; Dec. 1915; Feb., June, Aug. 1916; Apr. 1919; June, Sept. 1922; July 1923; Mar. 1924; July 1926; Nov. 1927; Feb., July, Aug., Oct. 1928; May, July, Sept. 1929; Jan. 1930; Mar., July 1931; May 1932; Apr., May 1933; July 1936; July 1938; Aug. 1939; June, Sept. 1948; May 1951; Aug. 1952; Feb. 1960; May 1961.

Bismarck Weekly Tribune, Apr. 1874; Apr. 1875; Feb. 1876; Oct. 1882; Nov. 1912.

Canadian Weekly (n.d.).

Chicago Daily Inter-Ocean, Aug. 1874.

CP Rail News, Jan. 1981; Apr. 1982.

Dixon (Illinois) *Evening Telegraph,* Mar. 1945; Feb. 1947.

Gettysburg (Pennsylvania) *Times,* Jan. 1958.

Grand Falls (New Brunswick) *Cataract,* Apr. 1977.

Hamilton *Spectator,* Sept. 1977.

Helena Daily Independent, Oct., Nov. 1928; Feb. 1930.

Montreal *Gazette,* Apr. 1915; Feb. 1923; June 1930; May 1939; Mar. 1944; May 1961.

Montreal *Standard,* 1943.

New York Times, Feb. 1937; Mar.–Apr. 1944; Mar.–Apr. 1945; Jan. 1947; May 1961.

North Bay Nugget, July 1931.

Ottawa Citizen, Nov. 1943; Jan. 1947; Nov. 2001.

Ottawa *Evening Citizen,* Jan. 1947.

Salisbury (Maryland) *Times,* Oct. 1953.

The Pas (Manitoba) *Herald and Mining News,* Nov., Dec. 1927; Jan., Feb., Apr., Aug., Sept. 1928.

Times Recorder, Oct. 1962.

Toronto *Evening Telegram,* May 1935.

Toronto *Globe,* Mar., Aug. 1930; Apr. 1935; July 1942; Nov.–Dec. 1943; Mar.–Apr., July 1944; Aug. 1945; Feb. 1946; July 1961.

Toronto *Globe and Mail,* July 1961.

Toronto *Mail and Empire,* Mar. 1930.

Toronto Star, Mar. 1944; Apr. 1978.

Toronto Star Weekly, Jan. 1932.

Toronto Telegram, July 1956.

Troy (New York) *Record,* May 1943.

Victoria County Record, Jan. 1987.

Windsor Star, Mar. 1944; Jan. 1984.

Zanesville (Ohio) *Signal,* Apr. 1944.

Acknowledgements

>─┼─◄►─●─◄►┼─◄

ALTHOUGH WRITTEN IN isolation, this book could not have come to be without the contributions of many.

I am eternally grateful to a group of men who took the time to record their memories of their years working with Harry McLean. A monumental research effort spearheaded by Joseph McNally and Charles Hyson in the late 1970s and early 1980s captured the voices of Richard Hearn, Frederick Ker, Arthur McLaren, Gordon Mitchell, Edison Hanlan, Jack Humphrey, Murray Cooke and Charles Hyson. Charles Switzer left a handwritten account of his experiences. The recordings and research of Charles Hyson are the foundation for this book. I had the opportunity to meet Joseph McNally, the last survivor of McLean's men, who shared his recollections of working with McLean. McNally had the best memory of anyone I have ever met and was invaluable to my research. He died on February 4, 2003, and I deeply regret that he never saw the book he so very heavily influenced. I thank John Hutton and Patrick McNally of McNally Construction for their kind assistance.

I was fortunate to have an opportunity to interview the son of Berton Puddington of Grand Falls, John Curless "Jack" Puddington, who was introduced to me by Debbie Bonfield. Puddington told me about the well-read, caring and generous side of Harry McLean. He passed away in April 2000. Another Grand Falls resident, Patrick McCooey, treated me to a tour of the town and its museum and gave me photographs of the Grand Falls construction project. Reverend Donald Sutherland and his daughter, Mary Beth Sutherland, of River John, Nova Scotia (son and granddaughter of Lieutenant Colonel Daniel Sutherland), provided me with photographs and information. Others who graciously shared their firsthand knowledge of Harry McLean include Shirley McLean Goodman (daughter of Charles Switzer), Ken Edwards, Ted Leeder, and Merrickville residents Harold Bolton, Bill Clark, Arthur Heroux, Jack Jessup, Joe and Mary Kelso, Lenore Newman, John Sawarna, Wayne Trusty and Betty Weedmark.

Numerous scholars and specialists gave generously of their time. Karen Smith, Dalhousie University Librarian, Special Collections, went above and beyond the call of duty. Dr. Thomas Pinney, Kipling expert and author of many books on the subject, provided me with background material on Kipling's connection to the Iron Ring Ceremony. Janet F. Kitz, author of *Shattered City: The Halifax Explosion and the Road to Recovery,* kindly redirected my queries about the Halifax Explosion. Neil McKenty allowed me to reproduce a photograph from his book *Mitch Hepburn.* Diane Galusha, author of *Liquid Assets: A History of New York's Water System,* offered research suggestions. Tom Isern provided friendly assistance in connection with the Washburn cairn.

I am grateful to helpful staff members at Library and Archives Canada, the Ontario Archives, the Maritime Museum of the Atlantic, the Nova Scotia Archives, the McGill University Archives, the Institute for Regional Studies in Fargo, and the historical societies of North Dakota and Montana. I am particularly indebted to Lory Morrow, Photograph Archives Supervisor of the Montana Historical Society, and Sharon Silengo, Photograph Archivist for the State Historical Society of North Dakota.

Douglas Moore kindly opened the Cornwallis Naval Museum during the off-season to give me a personal tour. Paul Schaefer and Bob Arnott of Ontario Power Generation at Abitibi were also gracious hosts to unannounced visitors. Eugene Fairbanks (son of Avard Fairbanks), introduced to me by his nephew, provided details and amusing stories about *The Pioneer Family* statue.

Many other people went the extra mile as well. I am indebted to Lee Jacobs for information on Dante the Magician; Jane Keskar of the Kipling Society for her guidance; Ludo Wurfbain, big game hunter extraordinaire at Safari Press, for his cool name; the staff of the Oakland

Cemetery for their assistance; Linda Carman of Bismarck for sending me John McLean's obituary; John Caron for giving me a photograph of the Dakota Business College; Sandy and Steve Rose of Canyon Ferry Mansion in Montana for their warm hospitality; Bob Kennell of the Canadian Pacific Archives; Maureen Lunam of Flin Flon for the generous gift of her own photographs and painstaking research; Diane Mason and Rose Fader for allowing me to tour Harry McLean's house on more than one occasion; Murray Gross and Ida Van Lindt of the Manhattan district attorney's office for photographs of Frank Hogan; Roger Hyman, son of Ralph Hyman, for permission to publish excerpts from the *Close-Up* transcript; Colin Fairn for permission to use the Cornwallis photographs of his father, Herbert S. Fairn; an anonymous photographer in Washburn County, North Dakota, for a photograph of the cairn there; Leonora A. Gidlund, Director of the New York City Archives, for wonderful mugshots of Fay and Bove; Betty Davenport of Davenport's Magic in London for the Dante photographs; and countless others who, over the years, took the time to answer my e-mails and letters.

Many of Harry McLean's relatives have had a keen sense of their own history and have laboured diligently to preserve it. Steven Day of Mukilteo, Washington, is one of several present-day Falconer family historians. It is because of Day's efforts in preserving the family history in his own book, and kindly permitting me to include quotations by Mary McLean and Will Falconer, that these voices from the past could be heard in Harry's story. Ken Pettitt and Janice Hensel of California, also McLean relatives, provided me with photographs.

I am indebted to a group of men, handpicked for their various areas of expertise, who reviewed the manuscript and offered invaluable suggestions: the railway historian Colin Churcher, the engineer and member of the National History Committee of the Canadian Society for Civil Engineering, Ken Mackenzie, and Bruce MacDonald, author of *The Guysborough Railway,* and his father, H. Joseph MacDonald.

I cannot even begin to thank the dedicated members of the Ottawa Railway History Circle, who provided a wealth of information and insight. I am especially grateful to Colin Churcher for all of his assistance with the captions for the locomotive photographs and his annotation of the

Deeks Quarry photograph, David Knowles for his advice and Bill Linley for the photograph of the Wolfe's Cove cairn. Colin's Web site (www.railways.incanada.net) is an unparalleled source of railway material.

I am especially grateful to the Canadian Society of Civil Engineering, particularly its National History Committee and member Ken Mackenzie. The Committee's interest in the project and its generous monetary support are truly appreciated.

My mother-in-law, Rhena Charland, generously contributed airline points for my Toronto/Nova Scotia/New Brunswick research trip. Jack and Ann Murphy of Etobicoke provided hospitality during that trip, and my brother-in-law, Shawn Charland, kindly acted as my airport chauffeur at four in the morning.

I owe a special debt of gratitude to my friend Wendell "Dell" Bower, who actively supported my efforts over the years and never appeared bored discussing my writing progress over wings and beer. He was the perfect travel companion on the research jaunt to St. Paul, Fargo and Bismarck. Dell intuitively knew that the less said the better at certain crucial moments, such as when a rock hit the window of the rental car I was driving, leaving a crack, or when I almost lost hope of ever finding the entrance to the Minneapolis airport. We accomplished much while staying in mediocre hotels and surviving on a diet of execrable franchise food in alien surroundings.

I am grateful to my meticulous editor, Jane Broderick, and my talented graphic designer, Janet Watson. I also appreciate the technical assistance with photographs provided by Melinda Harwood and Trevor Sweeney. For his steadfast support, my deepest thanks to Ricardo Rodas.

Thanks to my wonderful daughters, Sabina and Emily, for their patience as well as their humorous and sometimes earth-shattering interjections. Finally, I am indebted to my husband, Brent, for quietly being there and providing me with a steady supply of life-sustaining elixirs during this long endeavour.

Index